# A Global Approach to National Policy

Written under the auspices of the Center of International Studies,
Princeton University

# A Global Approach
# to National Policy

Richard A. Falk

Harvard University Press
Cambridge, Massachusetts, and London, England
1975

Printed in the United States of America
Library of Congress Catalog Card Number ~~72-2817~~ 75- 326242
ISBN 0-674-35445-1

*for*

Georges Abi-Saab
Johan Galtung
Gennadi Gerassimov
Horacio Godoy
Rajni Kothari
Gustavo Lagos
Paul Lin
Ali Mazrui
Saul Mendlovitz
Yoshikazu Sakamoto
Nathan Shamuyarira
Carl von Weizäcker   —

*friends who have shared
the vision of a just and
peaceful world
    as colleagues in the
World Order Models Project*

# Acknowledgments

My colleagues in the World Order Models Project have in recent years been my best teachers; hence, the dedication.

I owe a great deal to the consummate editorial skill of Janet Lowenthal, my research associate at Princeton, and Virginia LaPlante, my editor at Harvard University Press.

A few others have exerted a sufficiently distinct influence to warrant mention: Eqbal Ahmad, Fouad Ajami, Richard Barnet, Leonard Boudin, Gidon Gottlieb, Robert Jay Lifton, William Irwin Thompson, Beverly Woodward, my wife, Florence, and our children, Noah and Dimitri.

My work during this period has been made more efficient and pleasant because I have been part of the Center of International Studies at Princeton. I am especially grateful to Cyril Black, its Director and a valued collaborator, and to Jane G. McDowall, its presiding administrative presence. I want to thank also the gifted Center secretarial staff, especially June Carr and Dorothy Dey, who typed the final version during Princeton's hottest months.

It is also my pleasure to acknowledge the permission of the following journals and publishers, thereby enabling me to use here previously published material: *The Year Book of World Affairs, Yale Law Journal, Foreign Policy Magazine, Bulletin of Peace Proposals, Columbia Journal of Transnational Law, Contact Magazine,* Stevens & Son, Dunellen Press, University of North Carolina Press, Princeton University Press, Macmillan Publishing Company, and George Braziller.

# Contents

# FIGURES

# A Global Approach to National Policy

# Introduction

There is a need for nations to reconsider the basis of their participation in world politics. This need to reconsider seems particularly acute for the United States, because of its size, the global spread of its involvements, its reformist tradition in foreign policy, and its recently-felt sense of failure and dependence, which has shaken the confidence of its older people and withered the hopes of many of its young. One dimension of such a reconsideration, though admittedly only one, lies in re-examining issues of national policy from a global perspective, that is, a perspective as liberated as possible from the interests, biases, and habitual attitudes of any particular place or nation in the world. To be globalist in outlook these days also means to be futurist: it is virtually impossible to appraise what is already happening without at the same time making judgments about what is likely to happen decades hence and disclosing preferences about what ought to happen.

Thus, a globalist outlook requires a series of intellectual developments at odds with the mainstream approaches to international relations and foreign policy. This kind of reorientation of perspective is beginning to gain wider support under the rubric of "world order" or its academic designation, "world order studies." With increasing frequency we hear statesmen from many countries invoke the rhetoric and imagery of world order to express their growing conviction that ways must be devised for organizing the political life of the planet as a whole—both for the sake of their individual societies and for the benefit of mankind in general. This conviction is often presented as the necessary foundation for a new approach to international relations, but it is usually accompanied by the sober appreciation that failure to bring about a new, more integrated world order will lead to decay and chaos, possibly even to catastrophe. But while leaders of powerful nations talk in these terms, partly expressing their own awareness and partly sensing the concerns of their citizens, it is not yet evident that their talk corresponds to any real disposition or capacity to match their words with deeds. Nor is it clear that such spokesmen are purposefully re-directing their energies toward the awesome preliminary task of envisioning the broad contours of such a new world order system. Most of the political work of global reform still remains to be done.

Even to define world order is a difficult task. It is a broad term often used in vague and loose ways, sometimes employed inconsistently and sometimes for purely rhetorical effect. There is a great need to establish definitive boundaries of world order that command widespread assent among academic specialists and policy-makers, but I do not think a new perspective on global political issues has developed far enough for this to happen yet. The most that can be expected at this time is for serious observers to present reasonably clear conceptions of their own.

I use the term world order to mean the aggregation of norms, procedures, and institutions that give shape and structure to international society at a particular time. However, the term in no way implies that a given system of world order is benevolent in the sense of promoting peace and justice, or any other set of normative political goals, at the planetary level. World order is an analytic concept, although world order analysis usually centers upon normative issues such as the extent to which preferred norms are followed and chosen values are realized in particular international settings.

My primary purpose in this volume is to examine critically both the existing system of world order, in which the logic of state sovereignty continues to be the prevailing mode of political organization, and the American embodiment of this logic, that is, the international posture which American policy-makers have evolved over the past decade as the basis for United States participation in the present world order system. As my major criteria for appraising both national policy and the status of world order at any given time, I have taken the four central values adopted by the scholars from various parts of the world who collaborated in the World Order Models Project: the minimization of violence; the maximization of social and economic welfare; the maximization of social and political justice; and the maximization of ecological balance.[1] On the basis of these criteria, the essays in this volume are highly critical not only of existing patterns of American statecraft but also of statecraft in general.

Such criticism is a necessary precondition for fashioning a more constructive and positive view of national policy and global reform, but it is hardly enough by itself. We must then turn our attention from what is wrong, to what can we do about it and how we shall proceed. Such constructive undertakings require visions of alternative preferred systems of world order, as well as specifications for transition tactics and strategies capable of taking us from here to there.[2]

At the global level the central political challenge of our time involves the capacities of the state system to cope with the major problems confronting humankind. We have taken the state system for granted for so long that alternatives to it strike us as "utopian." Yet the problems posed by proliferating nuclear capabilities, poverty and hunger, environmental decay and resource depletion, population pressure and multiple infringements on human dignity, strike an increasing number of informed observers as unmanageable, given the organization of the world into about 150 sovereign states, each jealous of its own prerogatives. The difficulties can reduce us to adopting a posture either of utopian hope (yearning for what is needed but unattainable) or of realistic despair (perceiving that what can be achieved is woefully insufficient even to safeguard the rather miserable status quo).

Our cultural mood is in fact caught between these attitudinal poles. Both are immobilizing. Utopians are romantics, unable to gain the leverage needed to carry out their projects within the political realm. Realists have no projects to carry out that are commensurate with the problems which beset the human species and the planet earth. This book is part of a wider effort to find a middle way, one that transcends the constraints of realism, but accepts the centrality of a political imperative to devise a peaceful transition to a new system of world order.

To clarify this middle way requires more than intellectual effort. It requires above all a willingness to listen as well as to speak. Global solutions cannot emerge from one point in time or space. Their emergence requires the crisscrossing of energies and wills from all the major cultures and ideologies active in world affairs. They also require a better fusion of feeling, thought, and action than has been customary in past efforts to promote global reform. The goals need to be embodied in daily activities of individuals in all social roles so as to manifest an elemental seriousness and sincerity. The most brutal power-broker can entertain utopian dreams, provided they are kept at a safe remove from present policy.

A ridiculous and tragic spectacle is that of governments who, having met to deal with problems of poverty, population pressure, and pollution, end by celebrating the unassailability of their sovereign prerogatives. Yet this is precisely what has happened at many heralded world conferences, such as the one on the human environment at Stockholm in 1972, on world population at Bucharest in 1974, or on the oceans at Caracas in 1974. Speaker after speaker laments the gathering storm, only to conclude with an assurance that whatever else may be contemplated, there will be no intrusion on the discretion of the state. Yet we should not be surprised, for these delegates are sent as spokesmen for individual sovereign governments who have a vested interest in avoiding sovereignty-cutting solutions. If a delegate failed to uphold that interest, he would be recalled and discredited, with a resulting loss of even a nominal appreciation of the need for global solutions.

Thus, let us not be so naive as to expect the Mafia to do away with organized crime. The state system is tied to war-making and to territorial notions of economic, social, and political well-being. This territorial logic is highly competitive and has been compatible with food surpluses in country $X$ and famine in country $Y$. Or has it?

India's explosion of a nuclear device in Rajasthan in May 1974 may be the most important signal of distress yet sounded in this decade. Experts agree that as many as twenty-four countries could have a nuclear weapons capability within the next ten years. Apparently there are already 100,000 or more scientists and engineers who possess the know-how to assemble a bomb of Hiroshima magnitude. President Nixon, seeking favor in the Middle East during a visit in 1974, dispensed nuclear reactors as emperors of old gave gilded bird cages or polished ivories to foreign potentates. In a world of misery and injustice, we can expect recourse to the politics of desperation or—and this may be no better over time—to extreme forms of repression to prevent such movements of radical opposition from making any headway.

Such trends are already manifest. There is a rise of terrorism, on the one hand, and an increase in brutal styles of government, on the other. Past wars have often been started by leaders who knowingly risked unfavorable odds to overcome an unfavorable political and economic situation. A generation ago both Germany and Japan felt justified in launching high-risk "wars of aggression" as an alternative to national degradation. In a world of acute poverty and nuclear weapons, decent people might well tremble as they contemplate future recourses to "Hitler solutions" or "Pearl Harbor strategies." The historical handwriting on the wall is unmistakable. Hence, the quest for a middle way between the twin futilities of utopianism and realism. This volume is one expression of that quest.

It may be helpful to offer some brief remarks about the plan of the book as a whole. My purpose in Part One is to provide an orientation for themes to be pursued in more depth later. I consider the challenge confronting the present system of world order and emphasize its deficiencies. Although the possibilities of response are briefly considered, my main purpose is to offer a diagnosis and to consider some ethical preferences relevant to that response. With regard to both critique and solution, my outlook is geared to no dogma. Rather, I am committed to an open search for a more peaceful and just basis for organizing world society in a manner that is mindful of present ecological well-being as well as of future life prospects.

International law bears directly, but ambiguously, on the interface between national policy and the quality of world order. In essence, law plays a dual role within the state system, serving either as a cover for destructive and indecent behavior or as a restraint on the worst tendencies of the state system. This distinction must be sharpened in connection with the role of law and lawyers in state bureaucracies. The task is especially important in the United States, where the rule of law is taken so seriously except on matters international. It was as predictable as it is revealing that Richard Nixon's foreign transgressions of law were completely excluded from the impeachment consensus that finally drove him from the presidency. The search for a visionary nonutopianism entails the discovery of ways to make the rule of law apply to *all* of our public policy and not just to our relations within national boundaries. Besides, the path from Vietnam led straight to Watergate. Even political figures associated with the pre-Nixon period are beginning to acknowledge this link. For instance, Arthur Schlesinger, Jr., in writing on the American presidency, argues that "[t]he constitutional Presidency—as events so apparently disparate as the Indochina War and the Watergate affair showed—has become the imperial Presidency and threatens to be the revolutionary Presidency." And further: "the imperial Presidency received its decisive impetus, I believe, from foreign policy; above all, from the capture by the Presidency of the most vital of national decisions, the decision to go to war."[3] The United States, as a great democracy with a strong legalist faith, is in a position to help make international law an active force for stability and justice in world affairs, a force needed not only to prevent the worst possibilities from occurring in the state system but also to help build the confidence and innovate the means to accomplish a peaceful transition to a more desirable system of world order.

There are reasons enough to shake us out of our nuclear complacency. The persisting dangers of holocaust and the enormous waste of resources and human energies are obvious. More subtle, perhaps, is the corrosive effect over time of the mass hostageship of civilian populations caught up in a security system that depends on "deterrence." India's explosion of a nuclear device underscores the fact that efforts by established nuclear powers to post a sign "Proliferation Stops Here" are as ineffectual as they are misguided. What is needed above all is a shared interpretation of our planetary plight, of the need for mutuality and reciprocity, as well as for common norms of behavior for all parts of the world. The nuclear issue may be the prime testing-ground of such a philosophy. Just as China and France refused to curtail their nuclear tests to satisfy Soviet-American demands for ending atmospheric testing, so India and others are not willing to renounce their nuclear options while some nations retain and even perfect theirs. I therefore discuss a proposal to initiate the process of denuclearization in world society by securing the agreement of all nuclear powers to a commitment never to be the first to use nuclear weapons. There are difficulties, but no practical objection of sufficient merit to offset the many symbolic and behavioral advantages of such a step; yet the "realists" who crowd the corridors of power are united in their refusal even to consider this or similar proposals, despite the new rhetoric of global concern. And this brand of realism seems likely to prevail for a long time, perhaps for so long that the issue becomes "academic" in the worst sense—namely, until after the feared catastrophe has occurred.

From these more general considerations of the use of national or state power in the nuclear age, I shift in Part Two to a series of critiques of American policy in Vietnam. These critiques of national policy attempt to apply standards and make judgments that have applicability far beyond the case of Vietnam. Indeed, their overall objective is to show not only the inadequacy of American policy, given the present system of world order, but also the inadequacy of this system of world order itself, which possesses no reliable means to interpret or implement restraints on national uses of military power, especially if strong states seek forcibly to impose their will on weak states.

The American involvement in Indochina has provided the major testing-ground for thinking about world order during the last decade. The issues posed by the Vietnam debate touch on all facets of what it means for this country to try to achieve peace and justice for others and for the world as a whole. Of course, there were honest differences of opinion over facts and over what was at stake. It was possible to regard the whole conflict as a rerun of Munich. Indeed, both superpowers were faced with appeasement controversies mounted from opposite political perspectives. The Soviet Union and even China were attacked for their failure to safeguard a small socialist ally from the fury of American "aggression," at the same time that United States leaders were convinced that North Vietnam was the stalking horse for China, which was in turn the stalking horse for Soviet "aggression." These geopolitical controversies had tragic consequences for the Indochinese peoples, prime low-technology victims of high-technology warfare, subjected to the most brutal, sustained, and intensive warfare of modern history. This tragedy persists despite Henry Kissinger's receipt of a

Nobel Peace Prize for negotiating the Paris Agreement of 1973. Vietnamese casualty figures since January 1973 are only marginally different from those of earlier years.[4]

Part Two mounts an argument against counterinsurgency policies and tactics on the basis of moral, legal, and political considerations. The argument is ultimately linked to the more general case for global reform. In my view, the most fundamental wrong of American intervention in Indochina was the refusal to abide by the dynamics of national self-determination. These dynamics would have led to political independence for the three Indochinese countries and social transformations of a drastic kind, probably resembling the outcome in China. The economies of the resulting societies would have been built around egalitarian, if austere, principles. Hardship and coercion would undoubtedly accompany such transformations, but the efforts, especially from outside the area, to stem such a populist tide are accompanied by even more severe hardship and coercion.

These chapters focus primarily on the issue of state crime in a time of war. The Nuremberg judgment rendered after World War II was based on the view that individuals, whatever their station in society, must heed the claim of universal norms even in defiance of the legal mandates of their own government. This conclusion, embodied in the Nuremberg Principles (Appendix 1) raises questions about subsequent events. Should such norms have been brought to bear against United States leaders in the Indochina War, not so much to punish their transgressions as to discredit their policies? Should the undertakings of antiwar activists such as Daniel Ellsberg and Karl Armstrong have been viewed in an altered legal light because these citizens reasonably regarded themselves as acting to stop the commission of war crimes? These questions are not simple to dispose of, even if they are posed in abstract terms. Admittedly it is dangerous to create precedents that vindicate taking domestic law into one's own hands. Yet the dangers of giving government officials an unregulated monopoly right to engage in lawless behavior needs also to be appraised. How do we introduce notions of legal and moral accountability of government officials into an interdependent world? Opposition to state crime, whether it be genocide in Uganda or torture of political prisoners in scores of other countries, is a crucial element of any honorable movement for global reform. It is to the credit of the American system that these questions could be posed at all; in most countries this kind of discussion would not have been tolerated. But taking note of this openness is almost irrelevant if nothing is done about the problem; *substance* is far more important. The unfulfilled promises made at Nuremberg and Tokyo by the victors of World War II—promises that were repeated by the world community as a whole in formal acts at the United Nations—cry out still for implementation, even if only through the processes of self-restraint.

Part Three returns to more general issues of world order. It represents an effort to consider central structural problems involving the role of the United Nations and the character of superpower diplomacy, from the perspective of the kind of global policy that can be expected given the realities of the highly unequal distribution of power among nations and the competitive logic of state sovereignty.

One trouble with earlier global reformist efforts was a tendency to substitute sentiment for understanding. A precondition of change is a correct interpretation of what needs to be changed, as well as an explanation of why and how to do so and a realization of the formidable obstacles.

The United Nations is one fruitful context for inquiry, partly because its status in the world is ambiguous. If governments lived up to the charter that they solemnly proclaimed in 1945, the prospects for global reform would be brighter and the need far less urgent. The United Nations as a political actor in the world is both an instrument of statecraft at its geopolitical worst and an idealistic alternative to such statecraft. As such, the United Nations is at once an arena for statist maneuvering and for developing the sort of integrated global community that is needed. To recognize either role without the other is to diminish the reality of the United Nations. I offer a framework of analysis that keeps the distinction in focus without losing sight of either component.

The same kind of effort is used to reach beyond the myth of state equality. This myth has relevance to issues of formal status, but it is largely ignored in zones of superpower control, which typically consist of a single dominant state actor and a larger number of dependent state actors within an area where the dominant state has strong strategic interests. Such hegemonial patterns are extreme forms of departure from the juridical premise of state equality. Many lesser variations are part of the yin of political inequality that does daily combat with the yang of juridical equality. Understanding these geopolitical processes is connected with grasping the character of "stability" in the state system, namely, that prudent diplomacy is grounded on a bedrock of mutual tolerance among superpowers. In concrete terms, a superpower does not seriously challenge a rival's transgression on sovereignty if the affront occurs within the rival's domain of geopolitical primacy: it is simply too dangerous to mount opposition in a world of nuclear capability.

Part Four offers some ideas about a more constructive direction of effort for global reform. It tries to bind together in a single statement an attitude toward national policy and proposals for reforming the current system of world order that provides the setting for national policy. I adopt a posture that is globalist, futurist, and value-laden, in hopes of eliciting support, at least to the minimal extent of encouraging others to make alternative proposals of their own.

Perhaps our greatest need at present is to form a viable vision for the future, a vision that does not create false expectations, but nevertheless provides the foundation for hope, without which political activity becomes psychologically impossible. This vision must connect what exists with what is preferred, must help to build a consensus on what needs to be done, and must have distinct formulations reflecting the diversities of place and circumstance.

As matters now stand, we are losing ground with respect to every vital dimension of world order: the war system, poverty, human rights, and ecological decay. George Wald's assessment of the situation is bleak—delivered, appropriately enough, at the Twentieth World Conference Against Atomic and Hydrogen Bombs in 1974: "Human life is now threatened as never before, not, by one but by many perils, each in itself capable of destroying us, but all interrelated, and all coming together. I am one of those scientists who does not see how to bring the human race much past the year 2000. And if we perish, as seems more and more possible, in a nuclear holocaust, that will be the end not for us but for much of the rest of life on the earth." [5] This stark prospect has guided my own search for a viable vision.

Later in the same address Wald observed, "It is too late for declarations, for popular appeals, here or anywhere. All that matters now is political power." But in my view, and most tragically, it is too early for political power. We are not ready. The consciousness of what is needed is not yet dispersed widely enough. The relation of forces remains unfavorable to any direct attempt to challenge the preeminence of the state system. The hopes for global reform are certain to be dashed unless the political basis for power is created. Hence, despite the urgencies of the situation, it remains necessary to hold back yet awhile.

Part Four considers how to think and what to do about the future of world order. Elements of a nonutopian vision are set forth that draw their inspiration from several sources: the nonterritorial central guidance of medieval Europe; the checks and balances of constitutional order; ideas about man and nature long prevalent in the Orient; notions of human solidarity manifest in the main cultural traditions of the past; concepts of peace and justice in the political and moral traditions of nonviolence, humanism, and socialism; and a distrust of government found in such diverse sources as philosophical anarchism and populist politics. In the end, I share George Wald's sense that only one saving prospect exists: "Unless the people of this world can come together to take control of their lives, to wrest political power from those of its present masters who are pushing it toward destruction, then we are lost—we, our children and their children."

# Part One: The Framework

# 1 | The State System under Siege

Ever since the mutual destructiveness of World War I sank into the political imagination, sensitive observers of the international scene have questioned the adequacy and durability of the state system as the basis of world order. World War II, especially in its dramatic ending at Hiroshima and Nagasaki, deepened this process of questioning. With the advent of atomic weapons, the fulcrum of concern moved from the desirability of eliminating warfare from the political life of organized society, to the alleged necessity to do so. The prospect of World War III became a vision of global catastrophe that was widely believed to threaten human survival, or at least the survival of high technology civilization.

But so far the danger has not materialized. Indeed, influential strategic planners in the West argue that the development of nuclear weaponry on a mutual basis is the best possible deterrent to World War III. Approaches as dissimilar as those of the civilian strategist Herman Kahn and of Mao Tse-tung agree that nuclear warfare is something of "a paper tiger," at least with respect to ultimate issues of survival. Gradually, even those segments of public opinion initially appalled by the danger of nuclear warfare have become adjusted to living beneath a protective nuclear umbrella. Debate has shifted to whether Mutual Assured Destruction (MAD) is "MAD" because there is too much weaponry or too little. For example, there are those who, like the former science adviser to President Eisenhower, Herbert York, urge a negotiated minimum deterrent capability to avoid surplus or overkill weaponry, while others, such as strategic analysts Donald Brennan or Fred Iklé, believe that greater attention should be given to defending populations from nuclear attack. The mind of man seems MAD indeed, unable to decide whether it is better to reduce the risk of nuclear war altogether but accept greater damage should it occur, or to concentrate instead on limiting damage in the event of nuclear war and thereby risking greater likelihood of warfare. Leading defense planners cannot even agree on whether our security and destiny as a nation are better upheld by ending the arms race or by accelerating it.[1]

India's nuclear explosion on May 18, 1974, followed by Richard Nixon's promise of nuclear reactors to several major Middle East leaders, has aroused new fears associated with the proliferation of nuclear weaponry. These fears appear at a time of massive poverty in many parts of Asia, Africa, and Latin America, of world food shortages, and of increasing recourse to terrorist tactics by frustrated political groups. Already, according to atomic scientist Edward Teller, there are at least one hundred thousand people in the world with the skills needed to assemble a bomb. Given these world conditions, one does not need a warped imagination to envisage an escalation of terror tactics and a crossing of the nuclear threshold by practitioners of the politics of desperation.

In this setting, it is difficult not to be discouraged about the future of world order, even if world order is conceived in minimal rather than optimal terms.[2] The war system poses challenges that must be answered by governments of soverign states, especially by the richest and most powerful of these states. In a global setting of distrust and gross inequality it is difficult to negotiate restraining arrangements. Major governments are accustomed to correlating national security with military strength, both internally and externally. Within the two superpowers, mounting pressures have sustained the defense sector of the economy, and it is virtually impossible to enlist a national consensus for more than marginal arms control steps back from the nuclear brink. Increasingly, the perspective of disarmament has been replaced by the notion of "arms control," which tries to stabilize the nuclear balance and to place fiscal constraints on the arms race, but which makes no pretense of reversing the arms race or dismantling the war system. Despite the dangers of nuclear war and the associated problems of nuclear proliferation, there is still no political mandate for curtailing the free play of the war system in world affairs.

In the aftermath of World Wars I and II, however, the outcry of anguished peoples generated experiments in international organization. Both the League of Nations and the United Nations were given the historic mission of eliminating war from international relations—but not the means by which to accomplish that mission. These international organizations were instruments of statecraft, not alternatives to it. The main actors in the war system were in no way disposed to shackle their capacity for using force whenever it served their view of national purpose. In essence, the League and the United Nations have been dominated by prowar forces in world affairs; antiwar elements have been successfully excluded from influence. Such an observation is not intended to deny the positive role of the United Nations, but only to place it in realistic perspective. The Charter of the United Nations does include an antiwar claim on behalf of the peoples of the world and tips the balance of normative opinion against war-minded factions and governments. Furthermore, the existence of the United Nations provides a continuous forum for communication among adversary governments; it encourages the formation of mutually beneficial compromises to avoid, contain, or end warfare; and it provides stalemated belligerents with the potential for third-party mediation in the context of small-scale but destructive conflicts, as in Cyprus.

In addition to the unabated dangers of war, a new set of global challenges has emerged in connection with the world's ecological overload. Although the severity of these challenges and the capacity of cooperating governments to meet them is in dispute, the reality of the ecological agenda is not.[3] The problem encompasses several interlinked issues: population pressure, pollution of the oceans and atmosphere, risks of catastrophic accident, depletion of critical resources, and food shortages. Governments have acknowledged the importance of these issues in official rhetoric; the United Nations has amid considerable fanfare sponsored a series of consciousness-raising conferences; and various nongovernmental groups have actively publicized existing problems and the prospect of worse to come. The essence of the ecological challenge is captured in the phrase "global interdependence." The problem for world order is whether the state system has the capacity to manage this global interdependence well enough to maintain minimum world order. Contradictory tendencies are evident.

On the optimistic side, realization of global interdependence has penetrated the centers of influence in most parts of the world. However, in the environmental arena, unlike the military arena, there is no way to proceed rationally without negotiating a whole new set of rules of the game and backing them up with effective regulatory capacities. There is no ecological equivalent to military deterrence in which an exchange of threats discourages recourse to war by national leaders. Some means of international cooperation—what might be called a central guidance capability—must be evolved, or the world as a whole will gradually suffer the consequences of ecological decay. No form of ecological self-help is sufficient, even in the sense that nuclear deterrence might be argued to be sufficient. A general understanding of these requirements for minimum world order is beginning to take shape, inducing a genuine search for bargains in global cooperation among diversely situated governments, and building public and community expectations that significant chunks of sovereignty must be ceded for the sake of national well-being.

However, there have been some negative developments as well. Powerful governments of second-order geopolitical status seem prepared to risk ecological collapse in order to achieve superpower status for themselves. Perhaps most notable in this regard is Brazil's proclaimed intention to double its population of one hundred million by the year 2000 because it has noticed that states which matter the most in geopolitics today have populations of two hundred million or more. The official American response to the rising costs and increasing instability of foreign energy supplies has been to make a noncredible commitment to national self-sufficiency by the early 1980s, a program known as Project Independence. However, in view of the fact that realistic prospects are for increased, not diminished, dependence on energy imports, the official posture can only be interpreted as a disturbingly nostalgic way of seeking to vindicate statist notions of autonomy in a period of interdependence. Equally disconcerting is the evident interest of numerous governments in keeping open the nuclear option and the even clearer intention of the nuclear powers to sustain the nuclear component of their position of geopolitical preeminence. Without reciprocity, there is no way this side of catastrophe to denuclearize international politics, and denuclearization is a *sine qua non* for effective international cooperation on the main ecological issues. Furthermore, the international conferences designed to cope with ecological concerns have produced a torrent of rhetoric, but little by way of significant action.

The 1974 Caracas Conference on the Law of the Sea provides a milestone test of the state system's capacity to strike bargains or reach agreements that uphold minimum world order. However, as shown by the struggle to save the great whale, merely to strike the bargain is not enough; its implementation must be secured as well. The question is therefore whether the state system has the capacity, even if the majority of its governments have the will, to strike effective implementing bargains.

In my view the patterning of relations in global politics is moving toward some form of integration. It is uncertain how quickly this movement will proceed or which values and interests will predominate, but the realities of transition beyond the state system seem almost irresistible, whether one adopts the outlook of the multinational corporate board room or of the anguished humanist.[4] Underlying this transition process is the contradiction between the statist and the ecological imperatives.

## *Statist Imperatives*

Ever since 1648 at the Peace of Westphalia, the world system has been dominated by territorially organized sovereign states.[5] These states are very dissimilar in size, orientation, capability, and background. The quality of world order at any particular historical time has depended primarily on the pattern of voluntary and coercive relations among governments representing states. It continues to do so, despite the nominal existence of a more centralized network of political institutions in the form of the United Nations. The present system of world order, despite the rise of transnational economics and politics and the multiplication of specialized international activities of a functional sort, remains dominated by large state actors. The patterns of statecraft have been shifting significantly as a result of increasing economic interdependence and the decreasing utility of military power, but not in fundamental structural respects that bear on the compatibility between statist logic and the achievement of ecological balance.[6]

Some shifts in the international setting have altered statecraft during the last three decades: a realization by principal governments that general war would entail mutually destructive consequences of awesome magnitude; an extension of the scope of participation and an increase in the number of active participants in intergovernmental relations, producing a cumulative tendency toward the globalization of world politics; a realization that changes in the relative power of states depend primarily on industrial development and technological prowess rather than on territorial conquest; a recognition that domestic and international politics are increasingly interlinked; an appreciation of the need to stabilize expectations at the frontiers of human development by achieving quasi-universal voluntary arrangements that satisfy the perceived interests of quite different kinds of states, as well as the need to reach agreements among governments in such areas as the exploitation of ocean minerals or the nonproliferation of weapons of mass destruction, both of which needs require that trade-offs be embodied in the agreement so that governments can find a *quid pro quo*[7]; and an appreciation of the growing complexity and interrelatedness of international life which, together with the accelerating mobility of people, things, and ideas, generates a need for common standards and procedures of coordination, which in turn seem increasingly likely to result in the growth of international institutions.

These tendencies in world relationships are consistent with the evolution of the state system. The nuclear dimension introduces a pervasive element of caution into international relations that reduces the prospect of a drift into world war. Such caution combines with the complexity and interdependence in the economic area to produce a more collaborative and moderate system, in which negotiation tends to displace confrontation as a style of interaction, at least among actors with the capacity to inflict system-wide as distinct from regional destruction. The same tendency has been evident in the evolution of the bargaining styles of labor and management in domestic life. In pre-ecological times, the challenge of nature was thought to involve only the discovery of more effective modes of exploitation; but by now we are discovering that the very effectiveness of these modes creates deeper problems than it solves. As yet, the focus of governmental planning and action everywhere lags behind the emerging appreciation that the primary crisis for world order concerns the dynamics of ecological disequilibrium.[8] The following seven statist imperatives are clearly at odds with any effort that seeks to restore ecological equilibrium by planned, human effort.

The first virtually universal statist imperative is the quest for maximum rates of economic growth. Almost every government, regardless of economic, technological, or ideological variables, is trying to increase its Gross National Product as rapidly as possible. Such goals are understandable for poor and weak countries, less so for rich and strong ones. The effect of GNP-maximizing strategies is to increase the annual drain on world resources as well as the problems and hazards of waste disposal. The competitive dynamics of productive relations means that cost-cutting pressures make it difficult to restrain the exploitation of scarce resources or to pay the costs of protecting the environment from further deterioration. In the United States, labor leaders have joined with industrial managers to fight against environmental concerns. Harry Bridges, head of the International Longshoremen's and Warehousemen's Union, called the ecology movement "obviously anti-worker" and "a product of the ruling class." Or as J. William Hawn, speaking on behalf of the National Association of Manufacturers, put his opposition to proposed antipollution legislation: "Given finite resources, as a society we must balance our desire for a high-quality physical environment with our standard of living. Undermining this balancing process by adopting a national program of effluent reduction based on 'best praticable technology' and 'best available control measures' will divert resources urgently needed to solve other problems in our society, such as poverty, unemployment, housing and transportation. While this diversion may improve the physical environment, it may concurrently degrade the quality of life—the total environment."[9] Third World spokesmen have taken the same position within the international context. In essence, the priorities of maintaining and raising income levels for the poor, whether a class or a region of the world, take precedence over any pressure for adjustment to ecological realities.

The second statist imperative is the fact that the fulfillment of the national destiny depends on frustating the goals of rival governments. Whether the crux of interstate competition involves territory, influence, or raw materials, the forces of competition, backed by naked military power, achieve unequal allocations.[10] In turn, this inequality needs to be justified and protected. Without a centralized apparatus, there is a tendency for competition to degenerate into warlike conduct, the ultimate allocational energy in human affairs. Therefore, the war system underlies the logic of interstate rivalry, and governments often calculate national interest on an assumption of the normalcy of war. Because of the rapid pace of innovation and the ultrasophistication of military technology, expenditures of resources in the war system are increased. These tendencies are accentuated by the globalization of world politics and the impact of competitive logic on arms sales.[11]

Another statist imperative is the low deference to world community values and procedures. The world system remains a self-help regime. Each government regards itself as autonomous and participates in the world system to maximize its national goals. Alliances are mutually advantageous contracts to preserve a status quo against an ambitious rival. There is little tradition of deference to a general assessment of planetary needs. Statist imperatives, then, lead to generally destructive results whenever the welfare of the community is not protected by the combined and cumulative effects of policies adopted by individual governments. In ecological terms, individual governments define their goals in terms of maximizing output, strength, and even population. The largest is the best. Such dynamics of growth tend toward chaos in a finite universe, but the adverse effects are perceived and experienced only at the point at which excess capacity begins to disappear and a condition of scarcity starts to emerge.[12]

As matters now stand, there is no autonomous actor in the world who can identify and clarify world interests. The United Nations reflects primarily the collectivity of individual state interests. Only symbolic figures like the Secretary-General and the Pope can formulate world interests, although the former is constrained by the practical politics of being elected by governments to function in an intergovernmental setting, and the latter is hampered by a religious heritage that is weighted down with roles and doctrines inimical to ecological equilibrium. The dominance of the state is partly expressed by filling the field of political action so completely that other kinds of political actors seem insignificant by comparison.

Still another characteristic of statism is the weakness of the values of external empathy. The organization of the state involves mainly the satisfaction of interests of the ruling groups. External calamity or hardship is not often regarded as a sufficient basis for domestic sacrifice. If strong bonds of transnational identity exist, such as that of the many American Jews who identify their personal destiny with the fate of Israel, then the government of one country may make substantial contributions to the welfare of others. But in general the role of foreign aid as a form of world philanthropy is suspect, partly because it involves nominal help and partly because it involves characteristic statist pressure to influence societies. The foreign aid specialist of today in the Third World bears a resemblance to the missionary of earlier periods, both being agents of the dominant states who make a mixture of positive and negative contributions to the target societies.

What seems clear, however, is that substantial empathy, whatever the limited extent to which it reaches diverse groups within the national domain, normally stops at the territorial boundaries. As a result, there is no realistic hope that equalizing pressures can be generated within the existing statist framework of global relationships, and without such equalizing pressures there is no prospect for a peaceful transition toward ecological equilibrium. Strengthening the values of empathy would also create the normative basis for genuine community sentiments and institutions, which could in turn generate an alternative set of imperatives for governing.

A fifth statist imperative is that family size is exempt from government relations. Governments regulate a wide range of private relationships. Homosexuality is often treated as a crime, and sexual relations outside of marriage are discouraged if not actually proscribed. But all governments seem reluctant to regulate family size, even indirectly by a system of economic rewards and punishments. This reluctance has something to do with the sanctity of the family and with the awkwardness of governmental interference on such intimate levels of interaction. But the failure to bring the net reproduction rate of national populations to a condition of unity or below will greatly aggravate the tasks of achieving ecological equilibrium. Here, too, some kind of uniform and reciprocal pattern of regulation seems essential to correct the impression that governments are using population policy as a lever for competitive purposes.

Leaders in many states, including those with high rates of unemployment and general conditions of poverty, associate population growth with national potency. In some instances, such as Brazil, this notion is coupled with an explicit correlation between population size and national security or geopolitical ambition. Romanian officials have said privately that a threefold increase in population would give the country protection against future Soviet ambitions, whereas Thai leaders, also for security reasons, set population increase on a par with economic growth as a national goal. In some countries that are already over-crowed the rate of economic expansion has created prospects of a labor shortage, which in Japan recently stimulated the government to en-courage its citizens to have more children. The Japanese case illustrates the fantastic primacy accorded the dynamics of economic growth, but even so the solution could have been to acquire additional labor from abroad rather than to breed it at home.

In the statist system, moreover, emigration and immigration flows are nationally determined for national advantage. Governments control the flow of people across international frontiers. Increased mobility could induce equalizing tendencies by the impact of market force; that is, labor shortages would be filled by unemployed manpower, high-wage societies would attract low-wage labor, and so on. But the domestic pressures are such that governments respond mainly to con-cerns about national living standards or ethnic exclusivity. This is part of a larger governmental disposition to shape policy in accordance with domestic priorities, especially in view of the declining value of territorial expansion. The effect of these policies is to accentuate in-equalities. The phenomenon of the "brain drain," for example, has induced migrations of skilled individuals from places of greatest need to those of greatest opportunity, namely, the richest societies.

A seventh and last statist imperative is that governmental policy-making is dominated by the assessment of short-term payoffs. In general, governments seek to satisfy immediate desires. This is partic-ularly true where governments are elected every few years. However, these desires are generally inconsistent with safeguarding the interests of future generations. Maximization postulates are related to periods of one to twenty-five years, but almost everywhere the "dilemma of in-sufficient resources" induces short-run strategies that seek to satisfy immediate interests at the expense of future generations. Governments are staffed by individuals whose outer horizon of relevance is often bounded by their own lives, or at most by the lives of their children and grandchildren.[13] Even more constraining, perhaps, are the political horizons of relevance that limit the effective reach of policy to periods between one and five years; it matters not whether political accountability is to the electorate by way of an election, as in the United States, or to a central committee by way of continuing confidence, as in the USSR. The notion that man's use of the earth is a sacred trust for future generations has been lost in industrial societies, although it had a prominent place in many preindustrial patterns of thought and action.

This time perspective is accompanied by a highly materialistic and sensate cultural drift in which the performance of government is related closely to the provision of material goods to its citizenry. Such criteria prevail even in affluent societies where the needs of the influential portions of the population have been amply satisfied. The ethos of the counterculture is both a challenge to the social and political order built around values stressing secular materialism, and a commitment to create a new order based on values of love for people and things.

This pattern of statist imperatives, constituted by growth, competition, maximization, self-help, absence of empathy, autonomy of reproductive dynamics, controlled mobility, and short-term goals, suggests that the path to ecological equilibrium barely exists within the present structure of interstate rivalry. Governments do not have the disposition to exercise ecological self-restraint, for the calculus of present and prospective national interests does not accord with the minimal requirements of a peaceful transition to ecological equilibrium. Neither do governments have the disposition to equalize transnational and intergenerational life-prospects in such a way as to facilitate the normative adjustments that must accompany a transition to ecological equilibrium.

## Ecological Imperatives

The analysis so far suggests, first, the deepening dangers on a planetary scale being caused by the dynamics of growth, especially as evidenced in the interplay of rising resource requirements, population size, and GNP, and second, the incompatibility between statist imperatives and a planned transition to ecological equilibrium. "Ecological equilibrium" refers to a condition of stability in the relations between human activity and the nonhuman natural environment. Stability does not suggest a static relationship, but one in which life prospects in subsequent years are not impaired as a result of a deteriorating ecological balance between man and nature. There could conceivably be some form of unplanned or traumatic transition to an equilibrium model, but probably only after a period of widespread suffering and chaos, which would lead to either a reign of terror or enforced primitivism.

Such an apocalyptic outcome seems inevitable unless rectifying tendencies emerge in the years ahead and lead to new thinking about equilibrium, especially in the highly industrialized parts of the world.

The crucial question is whether the statist imperatives that underlie the organization of political relations on a world scale can be reoriented, or whether the state as such can be displaced as the central unit or organization on a world scale. The answer depends largely on the course of dominant political consciousness in the principal centers of state power. A convergent realization of common danger would greatly enhance the prospects for common solutions. These solutions must depend for effectiveness on genuine correlations between the locus of power and the locus of authority. As we have seen with regard to issues of peace and security, because premature centralizations of authority do not significantly alter behavioral patterns even though they may alter rhetorical patterns, they tend to widen the gap between the rhetoric of world order and the realities of statecraft.[14]

The prospects for the transformation of statist imperatives by a transition to an equilibrium model are poor without the pressure that might be supplied by a global catastrophe. The altered technology of war has not transformed statist imperatives, except in marginal respects. Decentralized military decision-making and national military establishments continue to prevail; collective security is neither universal nor norm-based, but is alliance-based. There is no realistic prewar prospect for drastic disarmament or denuclearization. "Prewar" refers here to the period leading up to a possible third world war, and especially to the attitudes toward global reform taken by the leaders of the two superpowers. War continues to function on the periphery of the world system to resolve bitter disputes and to effect radical internal changes in policy and personnel.[15] That is, from the perspective of the question of war or peace, there is no ground for optimism about the transformation of statist imperatives. The most optimistic reading of the situation is moderation of goals, prudence in the choice of means, and a slow loss of confidence in the utility of large-scale violence as a technique for promoting national aspirations. But such changes are not structural in the sense of redistributing the base of power and authority or redefining the logic of interstate relations.

The ecological crisis, however, poses a more profound threat to traditional statist imperatives. It is too early to tell what to expect by way of government response. A diagnosis of the significance of ecological considerations from the standpoint of world order is only beginning to be made in terms relevant for statecraft. The impact of these dire ecological diagnoses depends on a variety of virtually unpredictable factors, including the attitude of principal leaders and the shape of domestic public opinion. Much depends on whether the storm warnings of ecological danger are coherently and correctly interpreted as part of an overall ecological imbalance and on whether a tolerable path to equilibrium can be traced with sufficient vividness and equity. If the storm warnings are reinforced by ecological minidisasters, then the learning process may be greatly accelerated. A great deal also depends on whether progressive social tendencies prevail or are repulsed within principal domestic societies. In the short run there may be a competition between dollars for poverty programs and for the environment, but over the next decade or so the basic ideology of progressive forces will crystallize around the need to combine economic equity with ecological equilibrium, and around the ethical coherence of an approach that supplements a search for justice among men with a search for harmony between man and nature.

The initial impact of the ecological agenda is to strengthen the co-operative tendencies of international relations. Universal cooperation has been generally successful in the past only where states have common interests, as with postal service or the protection of ambassadors. The ecological area, however, with greatly differing views of cause and cure, and in circumstances of intense perceived diversity, does not lend itself easily to a voluntarist solution by way of international contract. Issues of equity are bound up so closely with the transition to equilibrium that the prospects for far-reaching agreements seem remote so long as governments serve national populations. Although specific environmental hazards may be dealt with co-operatively, the need to organize as rapidly and humanely as possible a shift from growth dynamics to equilibrium dynamics constitutes the larger ecological crisis. Environmental decay and specific disasters are symptoms of this underlying disorder.

The most successful experiments in international cooperation have involved wartime alliances. In these settings common dangers associated with an external enemy are perceived and a common approach by way of military effort is agreed upon among governments. Some commentators, while avoiding the alliance rhetoric based on an analogy to a military threat, have urged that the large industrial states form a cooperative approach in response to environmental deterioration.[16] Here again the diagnosis tends to be based on cooperative efforts to control pollution without accepting the need to reach the underlying dynamics of competition and growth. As soon as the ecological model based on a desirable balance of man and nature is accepted, it becomes clear that a response of planetary scope is entailed. It makes no international sense (although it may make temporary domestic sense) for a few countries to shift away from economic and demographic growth, if others do not; the problems will not be overcome, and the renunciations entailed by the transition of some states will appear worthless. The war analogy applied to the ecological hazard does not seem successful because no "victory" can be had without the eventual participation of all, although it is logically coherent to begin with the leading industrial states.[17] Given the absence of an "enemy," the prospects for rich-state cooperation seem uncertain, even if the governing elites perceive the ecological danger in enlightened and convergent terms.

Statist imperatives arise from competitive pressures and the primacy of domestic goals.[18] These imperatives are not likely to change in fundamental respects so long as the notion of national autonomy persists as a justification for inequality. So long as major governments feel pressure from deprivation of various sorts, the dynamics of organization for growth seem assured. Given the degree of poverty, unemployment, urban blight, and population expansion expected over the next several decades, very few governments, if any, will feel secure enough to forgo immediate improvements of material conditions out of deference to an ecological diagnosis.

Statist imperatives thus seem unlikely to be transformed in accordance with the requirements of a planned transition to an ecological model of world order. Such a model presupposes a central guidance capability to define the world interest and to secure equity as well as equilibrium. In a preindustrial condition of mild disequilibrium, such as the slow exhaustion of resources or crowding of land spaces, no central guidance is required because the maintenance of ecological equilibrium is assured by automatic checks of limited and general reversible impact, such as disease, famine, and war. But the scale of modern technology and the diffuseness of causal impact mean that the entire ecosphere is in jeopardy, perhaps irreversibly so. The depletion of the earth's ozone shield, the spread of DDT in the sea or carbon dioxide in the air, are indicative of characteristic modern processes of cumulative effects remote in time and place from the initial impact of cause.

During the period of transition to an equilibrium model, it will be necessary to increase capabilities for coordinating policy and behavior on a global scale. To avoid associations with domestic patterns of governance, I refer to these capabilities as the machinery of central guidance, or simply as central guidance. The most telling concerns relate to feasibility: will it be possible to establish an adequate central guidance system, given the prevailing attitudes of statesmen? Under what conditions might this become possible? What can be done to help create such conditions? There are three main avenues for reaching an equilibrium: traumatic transition, imperial transition, and contractual transition. As far as the first is concerned, the difficulties of predicting the occasion and circumstances make speculation worthless. It seems clear that the rigidity of the state system would be lessened by a major ecological breakdown. But how major? Under what terms of recovery and survival? The distinctive context of the catastrophe would be so influential in shaping the transition process that it is not possible to consider the post-catastrophe path toward equilibrium, except to note that the occurrence of a catastrophe of sufficient magnitude might alter the prospects for transition in a most dramatic way. As matters now stand, some form of traumatic transition is both the most probable and the least desirable of the three main paths.[19]

As for the second path to equilibrium, imperial transition, this seems unlikely to evolve in view of the relative stability of deterrence. Of course, the pursuit of a design for world conquest, possibily even out of a sense of ecological desperation, might combine elements of catastrophic transition with the notion of a state entity expanding its scope of effective authority to embrace the entire world. Perhaps a technological or strategic breakthrough will occur in the near future. Suppose that conquest and pacification can be achieved by drugs and electronic surveillance, administered on a massive basis with high levels of surprise. Again, the context of imperial transition seems so exotic, given present realities, as to defy any useful conjecture.

Emphasis should properly be placed on the prospects and character of the third path to equilibrium, contractual transition. The nature of the contract and the parties to it need to be kept flexible. The least likely mode of contractual transition would seem to involve an inter-governmental compact to establish a world government. Here, too, as in the first and second cases, the context of transition would be so dis-tinctive as to make present speculation about its attributes appear foolish. However, in the third instance, it is possible to design specific strategies aimed at education, mobilization of support, and trans-formation of power structures. We remain, at present, locked in a condition of general ignorance. The ecological imperative needs to be specified in positive as well as negative terms, in light of the human yearnings for unity, wholeness, and harmony. The diagnosis has to make plain the interconnection between ecological equilibrium and economic equity. Movements have to arise that challenge the viability of the state system and develop links across boundaries. A world party based on these ideals will have to emerge, in which the platform is drafted and redrafted in many parts of the world. Members of this party may have to be revolutionaries, for it may not be possible to gain orderly access to government control. The seizure of power in leading states by those who are convinced that the survival and welfare of the part (their state, race, or region) depends on the guidance of the whole (the world) may begin to happen. The intervention to displace leaders still committed to eco-suicide may be the last awesome death struggle to occur within the state system, insinuating elements of catastrophic and imperial transition into the search for a contractual basis for transition to an ecological mode.

The longer this process of organization for contractual transition is deferred, the more painful and drastic will be the transition and the less contractual it is likely to be. It would obviously be easier to achieve a recycling economy for resources at a world population of 1 billion, rather than 5, 15, or 25 billion. However, the longer the period of transition, the more likely that a consensus as to means and ends will underlie the contractual basis of central guidance. If reformist tactics succeed during the next two decades, then by the year 2000 ecological radicals may be in control or contending for control of several prominent states. "Ecological equilibrium" in one country is a virtual contradiction in terms; therefore, the missionary phase following the acquisition of power will be turbulent in terms of revolution and counterrevolution.

Such a view of contractual transition stresses the prospect of illegal and extraconstitutional actions; it does not, however, involve a necessary reliance, especially in the latter stages of world transformation, on large-scale violence. Notions of "coexistence" may re-emerge in the decades ahead to stave off catastrophe. Gandhian tactics or new variants involving nonviolent confrontation and disruption may be effective, especially in the event that economic growth patterns are perceived as leading quickly to collective doom. The role and orientation of multinational corporate entities may be of critical importance in shaping the pace and character of adjustment. At this point, these economic units are the only world actors with both a vision of a new world order and some instruments of power and influence to put their vision into competition with statist logic. To date, corporate visions of a market as big as the planet have been based on an expansive growth ethic and have not considered, even in a speculative fashion, a planetary market without the distortions of national boundaries and responsive to the ecological imperative. A coalition of the burgeoning forces of multinational enterprise and of ecological awareness might be in a position to mount a truly effective assault on the continued capacity of the state system to hold in its grip the political imagination of the human race.

In conclusion, planetary problems arise in part from an overload of the system. This overload makes for a serious situation, which the momentum of pressures will steadily worsen. Of critical significance in this crisis is the incompatibility between statist imperatives and the pursuit of a model of ecological equilibrium.

From a perspective of world order, it does not seem plausible to anticipate the transformation of statist imperatives in ecologically beneficial directions. The ecological model of equilibrium depends on bringing into being a new centralized structure that can manage the affairs of the planet on a unified basis. A contractual transition to centralization would combine normative and ecological considerations, presupposing that stability involves perceived equity as well as aggregate cutbacks in the direction of zero population growth and zero economic growth. Any realistic reliance on a contractual transition must combine an educational effort at enlightenment with an ideology of political action, which will probably have to evolve appropriate revolutionary tactics so as to acquire, possibly to seize, power from regressive forces associated with statism, growth dynamics, and short-term interests in profits and power.

# 2 | Law, Lawyers, and the Conduct of American Foreign Relations

The role of law in international affairs has been a subject of frequent debate between legalists and antilegalists. The legalists argue that world peace depends on enlarging the scope and range of legal rules, the growth of habitual respect for law, and the creation of international institutions capable of interpreting and enforcing the law.[1] The antilegalists argue that in a world of independent sovereign states the expectations of the legalists are naive and misleading, and that the best prospects for peace depend upon maintaining a balance between the capabilities and commitments of antagonistic countries and ideologies. This balance must be grounded in a diplomatic equilibrium in which no state has any rational prospect of achieving significant expansion by conquest. As the world changes, the legalists, by and large, would alter and reform the legal rules, whereas the antilegalists would concentrate on making political readjustments to preserve the balance.[2] The assumed dichotomy between law and politics poses three key problems: lawyers as foreign policy planners; adherence to law and the conduct of foreign policy; and law and the future of world order. The debate should focus instead on an intermediate position that makes a more precise and realistic estimate of the contributions, limitations, and potentialities of law and lawyers to the foreign policy-making process of the United States.

The polarity of the opposing positions was clearly visible at a 1963 meeting attended by Dean Acheson, former secretary of state, and Abram Chayes, then legal adviser to the secretary of state. Acheson, in terms as unqualified as any used in recent years by a person of high stature, dismissed the importance of law in matters of high sovereign concern. He argued that international law is of no significance in the resolution of important issues of foreign policy: "I must conclude that the propriety of the Cuban quarantine is not a legal issue. The power, position, and prestige of the United States had been challenged by another state; and law simply does not deal with such questions of ultimate power—power that comes close to the sources of sovereignty."[3] Chayes, in contrast, commended the role that law had played in moderating and shaping the execution of the decision to interdict the placement of Soviet missiles on Cuban territory.[4] Acheson was himself an eminent international lawyer, who had returned to the practice of law after leaving the government in 1952. To counter his argument, it is not difficult to show that many governmental decisions on matters of war and peace are shaped in beneficial ways by a sophisticated handling of international law.[5] Moreover, there are many practical drawbacks to a position that encourages all governments to insist on the legitimacy of sovereign prerogative on occasions of their own choosing.

But the antilegalist position has been disputed too mechanically and without sufficient consideration of the way in which legal arguments can be and in fact have been used. In the 1960s a series of controversial American foreign policy undertakings drew heavily on legal rhetoric and argumentation for their defense, especially in response to domestic critics. For instance, Leonard D. Meeker, as legal adviser to the State Department, went to considerable lengths to demonstrate a legal basis for the American military occupation of the Dominican Republic in April 1965. Meeker suggested that his approach to international law "would properly be described as practical idealism." In his thinking, "fundamentalist views on the nature of international legal obligations are not very useful as a means to achieving practical and just solutions of difficult political, economic, and social problems." Meeker went on to say that "it does not seem to me that law and other human institutions should be treated as abstract imperatives which must be followed for the sake of obeisance to some supernatural power or for the sake of some supposed symmetry that is enjoined upon the human race by external forces. Rather, it seems to me that law and other institutions of society should be seen as deliberate and hopefully rational efforts to order the lives of human communities—from small to great—in such a way as to permit realization by all members of a community of the full range of whatever creative powers they may possess."[6]

The cosmic vision expressed by these sentiments is widely shared but arouses suspicion when used to validate what appears to most impartial observers as a blatant violation of one of the basic norms of modern international law: the prohibition of unilateral recourse to force except in a situation of self-defense. However one might interpret the Dominican turbulence at the time of the American military involvement, it was not a situation in which the United States could purport to be acting in collective self-defense, that is, to protect the Dominican Republic against external attack.[7] Rather, the intervention in Dominican affairs bears an obvious, if odious, resemblance to the Soviet intervention in

Czechoslovakia in August 1968. The strength of the comparison is heightened by the reliance of both principal governments on a regional or collective endorsement to veil the unilateral nature of their military interference with the domestic politics of a foreign country.[8] Certainly the Soviet claim to maintain the integrity of governments within the socialist community, when it is used to justify suppressing Czech domestic developments that appear to be merely antithetical to Soviet interests, has a hollowness comparable to the State Department's "practical idealism."

This excursion into the dark domains of interventionalist diplomacy adds a dimension to the debate between the legalists and the antilegalists. The antilegalists are entitled to complain when a government dresses rationalizations of policy in legal language. In such circumstances, law functions less as a fig leaf than as a transparent garment. Consequently, there is a strong impulse to strip away the legalistic pretension: better to see policy as naked power than to disguise the choice by enshrouding it in a gauzy film of legalism. Such a call for directness, perhaps one element of Acheson's remarks, is evident in more recent comments on the role of law and lawyers in the making of foreign policy.

Henry Kissinger, formerly influential as assistant to President Nixon on National Security Affairs, and now as secretary of state, has often inveighed against what he regards as the detrimental effects of legalism on the formulation of American foreign policy. In an article on settling the Vietnam War, Kissinger argued that the United States government's legalistic tendencies inhibited the commencement of negotiations with the North Vietnamese. He suggested that ours is "a government which equates commitments with legally enforceable obligations," and that our preoccupation with this equation prevented us from even discerning North Vietnamese signals indicating a willingness to take satisfactory action in exchange for a bombing halt, provided that such action did not have to be based on a formal commitment. Contending that "the legalistic phrasing" of Washington's demands "obscured their real merit," Kissinger was arguing, in effect, that the language of law was inappropriate to the setting and had an undesirable impact on diplomacy.[9] By repeating this point several times, Kissinger made clear how strongly he felt that a policy-maker may, by talking like a lawyer, fail both to perceive and to resolve "the real issues."

This point of view is even more pronounced in a general essay on foreign policy that Kissinger wrote just before taking office. Kissinger contended that "we have historically shied away" from inquiring "into the essence of our national interest and into the premises of our foreign policy" because we insist on casting our political interests in the form of legal responsibilities; "It is part of American folklore that, while other nations have interests, we have responsibilities; while other nations are concerned with equilibrium, we are concerned with the legal require-ments of peace." Kissinger's rejection of law was particularly signifi-cant because he reoriented his entire analysis of foreign policy in the direction of world order: "The greatest need of the contemporary inter-national system is an agreed concept of order." At the close of his essay he implied that unless we "ask the right questions"—that is, those that bear on our interests—"we will never be able to contribute to building a stable and creative world order."[10] It seems fair to suggest that Kissinger regards law and legal rhetoric as an encumbrance rather than a resource in the construction of a stronger system of world order.

Presumably in the background of this antilegalist analysis lies John Foster Dulles' frantic search as secretary of state for treaties of alliance in the 1950s, as if a treaty, however fragile its political basis, could give assurance of the ability and willingness of governments around the world to contain communism. In the foreground of Kissinger's approach lies the defense of the United States involvement in the Vietnam War by an appeal to treaty commitments and by a claim that a world legal order is thereby sustained.[11] The pseudo-legalist ideology of Dean Rusk and Walt Rostow is the product of nonlawyers, who have frequently been more guilty than lawyers of the rigid invocation of legal rules and of the rhetorical use of the language of law. In fact, Acheson is just one of many attorneys to have served in the State Department who are exemplary exponents of the pragmatic traditions of the common law, yet are themselves antilegalist in their philosophy. What is disturbing about the simpler statements of the antilegalist position is their double confusion: first, an inaccurate and simplistic presentation of the legal tradition; second, a false depiction of the relationship be-tween "a characteristic legalism"[12] and recent extravagances in American foreign policy. The comments of Kissinger, among others, suggest how important it is to enter the debate between legalists and antilegalists, and to examine particular aspects of the controversy in order to analyze more realistically and constructively the role that lawyers should properly have in the process of making foreign policy in the United States.[13]

## Lawyers As Foreign Policy Planners

Kissinger characterized "the sort of analysis at which [Americans] excel" in the conduct of foreign relations as "the pragmatic, legal dissection of individual cases." The same point was made more negatively by Zbigniew Brzezinski, a foreign policy specialist and former government adviser, who wrote: "Coming from a society traditionally suspicious of conceptual thought (where a "problem-solving" approach is held in esteem and concepts are denigrated as "intellectual cubbyholes"), shaped by a legal and pragmatic tradition that stresses the case method and the importance of precedents, the understandable conditioned reflex of the policy-maker is to universalize from the success of specific policies, formulated and applied in the 'pre-global' age of American foreign policy."[14] Kissinger and Brzezinski were associating the case method, which is the main emphasis of the lawyer's professional training, with an inductive and pragmatic approach to foreign policy. Brzezinski also emphasized this approach as the distinctive characteristic of the common law as a legal system. Both authors found this strain expressed in the dominant philosophical traditions of the United States, themselves continuations and outgrowths of British empiricism, which emphasize problem-solving and pragmatic criteria of judgment. This kind of inductive orientation toward government policy-making contrasts with the more conceptual, deductive traditions associated with Continental jurisprudence and philosophy.[15] Each tradition has its distinctive strengths, weaknesses, biases, and predispositions, all of which have different impacts, depending on a country's particular historical setting.

What is more important, however, is that a particular legal style is derived from a wider tradition of thought prevailing within a particular society; it is a product of many influences and is not attributable in any illuminating way to a particular experience of vocational training in the law. Thus, it is not surprising that ideological predispositions might take precedence over the problem-solving mentality for both lawyers, such as Dulles, and nonlawyers, such as Rusk and Rostow, who are in the service of government. And whatever it is that is properly associated with the pragmatic approach of the common law is not at all identical with the legalistic patterns of justification invoked by some lawyers in the course of carrying out their governmental functions.

A parallel tradition of piety and self-sacrifice in foreign policy-making has its roots in the religious origins of the United States and can be seen clearly in the Puritan heritage. This religiosity seeks to disguise self-interested motives, aspires to act for the common good, and is interested in setting a moral example of unselfish sacrifice for those other governments which, according to this outlook, follow a much more self-centered course of action in foreign affairs.[16] The ideas underlying the doctrine of separation of church and state, together with the progressive secularization of American society, have stimulated a search for nonreligious modes of expression by those entrusted with the task of making and justifying American foreign policy. Law and lawyers have often fulfilled this social need, providing a kind of idealistic discourse that in part represents a genuine reformist tradition, and in part a hypocritical disguise for acquisitive behavior. Calvinism has contributed the zealously held notions of personal salvation and of a vigilant, omnipotent god; this combination has led to a confusion between what is beneficial for oneself and what benefits the general welfare. Socially, this confusion is compounded by the suggestively similar ideas of laissez-faire, the "invisible hand" of Adam Smith, and of Social Darwinsim, all of which are embodied in the American intellectual tradition. The world views of Woodrow Wilson after World War I exemplified these confusions: the idealistic groping for a grand design, conjoined to a search for American leadership and preeminence in world affairs.

The inductive particularism of the common law, therefore, is neither confined to law nor espoused by all American lawyers. The "case" approach reflects a broader kind of philosophical tradition associated with British empiricism and the whole struggle against Thomistic and Cartesian modes of thought and organization, modes that evolved out of Catholic dogma and Continental traditions of speculation.[17] Similarly, the legalism that is found in American diplomacy often represents displaced religious and moral sentiments which derive from the whole spiritual foundation of the Republic in colonial times. Legalism in formulation and approach is a way of maintaining the pristine integrity of a moral system in a pluralistic society; the emphatic piety remains resonant even when the rhetorical appeal has been shifted to more secular grounds. It seems no accident that Woodrow Wilson and John Foster Dulles, our two most eminent legalists, were both men of profound religious conviction who devoted themselves to careers in the vortex of secularism. The espousal of legalism appears to have little, if anything, directly to do with membership in the legal profession. Law may be a foil for suppressed religious concerns; equally, lawyers may be problem-solvers with neither the virtues nor the vices of statesmen of more grandiose vision.

## Adherence to Law and the Conduct of Foreign Policy

The value of a law-oriented foreign policy is obscured by the character of the legalist-antilegalist debate. The acceptance of a framework for legal restraint in the external relations of a country seems at least as much related to the promotion of national welfare as does adherence to law in domestic affairs. A discretionary basis for foreign policy in the nuclear age seems to increase the risks of self-destructive warfare. The scale of violence is now so large that we can no longer confidently entrust decisions affecting the interests and welfare of the world community to the particular policy appraisals made by small numbers of national executives.[18] The problems of the world—peace, welfare, dignity—increasingly presuppose some form of supranational control to protect the general interest. The prospects for building governmental structures at the world level remain poor, and so in the interest of preventing disastrous breakdowns, the restriction of national freedom of choice could function as one formidable source of restraint on the ruinous tendencies of our present international society. The norms of international law, impartially interpreted and applied, can exert meaningful pressure on the self-seeking proclivities of sovereign states. The real difficulty with Acheson's views about the conduct of diplomacy in a situation of crisis is a prudential one, namely, that to affirm the discretionary basis of foreign policy in the nuclear age is to invite eventual disaster. This point holds true even if, or perhaps especially if, the effective discretion to act is vested only in the governments of the major powers.

Kissinger has contended that our dedication to "principle" makes it hard for us to articulate a truly vital interest which we would defend against a challenge we thought was "legal." We deny that force is being used by the United States to uphold or enhance America's power and prestige, much less its wealth. American policy-makers normally rely on a selfless explanation for actions taken abroad. Thus, we tend to justify our foreign policy decisions by turning to principles of universal appeal, such as the need to resist "aggression." According to Kissinger, these patterns of generalized justification lead to an indefinite multiplication of commitments. He counsels, instead, a hard-headed appraisal of vital interests as a strategy for bringing our "commitments" into better correlation with our "interests" and "capabilities." In such a reorientation it may be necessary to undertake some "illegal" courses of action, and to refrain from joining many "legal" causes.[19]

Why is international law a better source of national self-restraint than the kind of interest calculus that Kissinger proposes? Clearly law has little to offer as a basis for guidance and restraint if it is manipulated in a self-serving and ex post facto fashion, or becomes assimilated into the tradition of formulating pious self-avowals in legal rhetoric.[20] At the same time, international law provides the potential basis for guiding the action of all governments within an agreed framework. It has relatively stable principles that are not easily altered by shifts in governmental conceptions of the national interest, or by miscalculations as to the intermeshing of definitions of national interests by adversary governments. By contrast, Kissinger's views seem overly dependent on the wisdom, prudence and benevolence of the particular governing group that has control at a particular time. In 1974 disclosures revealed that the CIA, with authorization from the highest policy-makers in the country, acted to "destabilize" the constitutionally elected government of Chile during the Allende years by engaging in a program of covert operations. These sorts of secret undertakings, in apparent violation of international law and shielded by secrecy from the normal processes of domestic scrutiny, illustrate vividly the consequences of liberating policy-makers from a restraining framework of accountability, which is the principal objective of international law guidelines.

Self-determination of rights and duties—a self-help system—is severely biased by self-serving interpretations of what is reasonable—interpretations that are marked by hostility, distrust, self-seeking, and wide cultural diversity. In this situation, the position and traditions of the United States make its adherence to international law especially important. The great power of the United States relative to every other country, including the Soviet Union, makes its acceptance of restraint particularly significant. Second, there is little incentive or likelihood that other principal states could take advantage of American adherence to international law. In the contemporary world, technological developments, much more than territorial expansion, hold the key to changes in relative power. As a result, the legal order presents neither obstacles nor temptations to the potential expansionist state. Third, the rules and expectations embodied in international law are sufficiently permissive to allow a government to take whatever action is needed to uphold its territorial integrity and political independence. Fourth, the United States needs to set certain examples of self-limitation in the interest of inducing reciprocal restraints by other states. Such reciprocity seems an essential part of any program designed to cope with the spread of weapons of mass destruction to more and more countries in the years ahead. Fifth, there is a genuine American tradition of respect for law and concern for justice that could play a part in seeking to strengthen the quality of world order. For all these reasons it is important to bring impartial legal perspectives to bear early in the formation of policy.

As in domestic law, it is both possible and necessary to distinguish between an ex parte manipulation of law, and its impartial and autonomous application. The present bureaucratic structure is ill-suited to serve the latter objective. The legal adviser to the secretary of state is a subordinate officer. His role is often couched in terms that require him to be an adversary litigator, with the government as his "client." While his advice on legal matters may be enlightened, and he may try hard to avoid violence, he is still a subordinate State Department official essentially advocating an adversary position within the government. This status and arrangement seem too haphazard, even though they may suffice for the routine affairs of international life that are rarely considered by the political officers of government.

The President needs to receive legal advice at the cabinet level from an attorney general for international affairs. The conception of official duty for this proposed post should stress the obligations of impartiality, the search for objective criteria of guidance, and the importance of participating at all stages in the formation and application of foreign policy. Such an attorney general should be assisted by official panels of experts on various dimensions of international life. These panels should have access to all governmental information and should be obliged to deliver expert opinions. The attorney general for international affairs should be regarded as a nonpolitical appointee, subject to removal from office only for cause. He should sit as an ex officio member of the National Security Council and command a budget sufficient to enable careful, rapid staff work on all legal questions.

## Law and the Future of World Order

Images of world order may be developed from both legal and nonlegal traditions of thought about international affairs. Unfortunately, the images drawn from traditions of legal thought have tended to be models of domestic legal systems generalized to apply to the whole of international society. These models are static; they tend to ignore the enormous difficulties of moving from the present decentralized structure of international society to a highly centralized one; and they appear artificial and unrealistic if offered as either a prediction of or a prescription for the future.

In contrast, the images of world order deriving from nonlegal traditions of thought tend to be models of interaction that are only marginally different from the existing structure of power and behavior in international society. Kissinger's notions about world order appear to be little more than an updating of Metternich's strategy for securing a stable and dynamic equilibrium in international society. The chief buttresses of the nonlegal model are alliances, an assessment of the correlation between capabilities and commitments, and a hierarchial ordering of interests vital to the country. The achievement of such world order depends on an acceptance of the international status quo for an indefinite period, or at least a perceived unwillingness on the part of all major governments to secure major gains through force of arms. The difficulty with this diplomatist image of world order is that it seems to accept decentralized procedures as adequate for maintaining minimum order and welfare in international society.

There is presently an intellectual vacuum that needs to be filled with more adequate images of world order. We need new images which are responsive to the history and traditions of a world of sovereign states, but responsive also to the emerging functional problems that cannot be handled, in many cases, by the national governments of even the most powerful states. The control of oceanic and atmospheric pollution, the regulation of weather modification and other uses of space, the beneficial use of data collection relevant to many phases of human existence, the regulation of the multinational corporation, problems of resource conservation and exploration, and the moderation of the effects of shifts in the supply of and demand for food, suggest the urgency of evolving functional bodies with a transnational center of authority and control. The maintenance of world order may depend on the design and acceptance of a scheme of overlapping, interlocking, and organizationally disparate functional institutions which ignore the confines of national boundaries and elude the control of national governments. Such a network may come to play an increasingly vital role, as problems of transnational armed violence are subordinated to the differential opportunities for and hazards of various strategies of technological exploitation. The deployment of fast-breeder nuclear reactors, capable of converting arid land into an agroindustrial complex, may become more significant than the deployment of missiles with nuclear warheads. Failures to take adequate precautions to prevent damage from radioactive waste may pose greater problems than the danger of war and surprise attack. The proposals for order and control should be responsive to the problems that are currently emerging from the international environment.

Moderate population projections predict a world population by the first decade of the twenty-first century that will be almost double what it is today.[21] This increase will be concentrated in the poorer parts of the world, which have no prospect of adequately feeding or caring for their populations. The problem is not only to prevent famine but also to secure health, education, housing, and a life of opportunity for most people in the world.[22] Population expansion vastly increases the difficulty of making reasonable progress along these other lines, and causes more than proportionate increases in garbage, pollution, and resource depletion. Increasing population densities also raise the propensity of social groups toward disease, riot, distress, and desperate politics. Such environments tend to encourage strategies of internal and external change that rely on violence.

Thus, like the Polish army of the thirties, supposedly buttressed by the balance of power and by impressive treaty systems, we are a knight errant facing the future in gallant ignorance, equipped with ideas whose time has passed. Nonlegal approaches to world order characteristically ignore the international dimension of the problems of pollution, population, and poverty. Legal approaches to world order ignore the problems of adapting to the new technological environment. Only in relation to nuclear war do we sufficiently understand the need for drastic change in our attitude toward world order.

There are several ways to start this process: the outline of a new kind of transnational functionalist world order should be put in explicit and coherent form; international lawyers should begin to include ecological, demographic, and technological developments within the province of their professional concerns; and the idea of a world order emphasizing the problems of war and peace should be rejected in favor of a broader concept that is equally concerned with the protection and promotion of dignity, safety, and security for individuals and groups.[23] Power and the mechanisms for restraining its use are no longer adequate foci of concern in our evermore interdependent and overcrowded world of shared danger and opportunity.

In conclusion, the debate on legalism can be redefined in terms that are more responsive to the international needs of the day.[24] Such an endeavor requires some clarification of what is truly characteristic and distinctive about the legal tradition, especially as it presents itself in our national setting. Only on this basis is it possible to assess the claims advanced for and against law in relation to the conduct of foreign policy. Above all, it is essential to distinguish between the intellectual traditions of an American lawyer and the ideological orientations of American statesmen, who may or may not be lawyers but who use legal rhetoric to express moral preferences that often spring from other and wider sources.

The rejection of legalism does not make the case for antilegalism. The argument for a common framework of restraint that has an objective standing independent of the judgment of government officials seems overwhelmingly persuasive in the nuclear age, when the margin of fatal miscalculation is so small and the prospect of mutually contradictory selection of facts and claims is so great. In such an atmosphere the search for objectivity deserves priority, and the techniques and vocation of the lawyer are admirably suited for the task, especially if the search is removed from governmental pressures by giving national legal advisers greater independence than they now enjoy. In the American context serious consideration should be given to the creation of a cabinet post of attorney general for international affairs. Such efforts at the national level should be accompanied by parallel and complementary efforts to create procedures for settling disputes on the international level, whether within specialized agencies, regional associations, or global institutions.

Both the traditional legalist and antilegalist notions of world order have been slow to adapt to a new set of international concerns that are becoming problems of the first magnitude. We must work for a system of world order which will not only diminish the probability of large-scale and sustained violence, but will also meet the threats that arise from overpopulation, pollution, technological innovation, and resource depletion. In other words, we need to redefine the task of global planning. That work should include a new, common effort by both legalists and nonlegalists. No single disciplinary perspective is adequate in either its analysis of the problems of world order or its design of strategies for their solution. The argument for interdisciplinary collaboration is both convincing and urgent, as is the case for forging a new synthetic concern for world order that engages specialists in many areas, including law, political science, economics, sociology, ecology, systems design, and the computer sciences.

The primary task is to keep the existing system under some degree of reasonable control during a period of transition to a more centralized system. The task is urgent. Cumulative and symbiotic developments in population growth, resource supply, pollution of oceans and space, and the technology of destruction suggest that only a few decades, at most, remain before the risks and costs of maintaining the existing system of world order will become unendurable.

# 3 | The Denuclearization of Global Politics

A persistent, if muted, theme in discussions of arms control and disarmament questions has been the status of nuclear weapons. The renunciation of nuclear weapons by governments can be made either in the form of a unilateral declaration of official policy or as an essential ingredient of an international convention. The Soviet Union and China have already made unilateral declarations of policy, and as recently as 1967 the Soviet Union, despite its conflict with China, proposed an international convention that embodies an absolute prohibition on initiating uses of nuclear weapons.[1]

The renunciation of the nuclear option, however, refers only to initiating use. A government retains possession of nuclear weapons, control over research and development of further weapons technology, and control over deployment. Most important of all, a government retains a residual option to retaliate with nuclear weapons against a prior use of nuclear weapons. This prior use may be a violation by another state of its own renunciation of the nuclear option or it could arise because nuclear weapons were never renounced. The renunciation of the nuclear option may be conditioned on reciprocity, but there is no reason why this should be so, and it has not been so conditioned in the Soviet and Chinese instances.

A renunciation of the nuclear option is not limited by time, place, or context. In this sense it is a categorical norm. At the same time this general renunciation can be associated with limited renunciations, such as the establishment of nuclear-free zones, or restricting the use of nuclear weapons to national territory or to targets outside populated areas.[2]

There are some reasons to favor making the categorical rule more absolute by denying the right of reprisal, research and development, or even possession, but such steps remain too far removed from current political attitudes to stand any chance of receiving serious appraisal. Hence, attention here will be limited to a renunciation of the nuclear option, that is, of the claimed right to initiate the use of nuclear weapons.

A great majority of the non-nuclear powers, as well as the Soviet Union and China, have advocated prohibitions on the use of nuclear weapons. The General Assembly in 1961, over the vigorous, if somewhat quiet, opposition of the United States government, passed by a vote of 55-20-26 Resolution 1653 (XVI), which declared that the use of nuclear weapons would violate the letter and spirit of the United Nations Charter and would constitute a crime against mankind.[3] Subsequent resolutions of the General Assembly have, by more one-sided votes, called upon governments to conclude an agreement prohibiting the use of nuclear weapons, and have invoked General Assembly Resolution 1653 as their authority.[4] The United States government has continued to oppose all formal and international efforts to withdraw legitimacy from nuclear weapons. Is there a persuasive basis for this opposition which flaunts the apparent sentiments of world public opinion on the status of nuclear weapons? Given the terrible consequences of recourse to nuclear weapons, it seems crucial to reconsider whether retaining a nuclear option serves the interests of the United States.[5]

## Legal Status of Nuclear Weapons

The present legal status of nuclear weapons remains in considerable doubt. More than two thirds of the United Nations voting membership regard the initiating use of nuclear weapons as both illegal and criminal. Yet most specialists continue to deny that the General Assembly possesses a law-creating capacity that binds dissenting sovereign states.[6] With respect to the status of nuclear weapons, the United States and the NATO group seem to be a dissenting minority important enough to block the creation of a new rule of prohibition by the United Nations either through a majority vote or a declaratory statement on the character of preexisting law. The General Assembly can merely declare the status of nuclear weapons and provide guidance for a government's proper interpretation of this status. As yet, however, dissenting governments seem to have no strong sense of obligation to respect the resolutions they have voted against, even if their dissenting votes were inadequate to block formal passage in accordance with United Nations voting rules.

However, it is possible to argue that the use of nuclear weapons, at least against populated areas, would be illegal under prior valid prohibitions upon weapons and tactics of indiscriminate destruction and lethal poison. Some international law experts have argued to this effect; others disagree, contending that nuclear weapons are a new development, not covered by earlier rules, and that the legality of their use depends on particular circumstances.[7] Thus, there is no clear consensus of experts about the status of these weapons.

Additional considerations serve to underline the basic condition of ambiguity. The United States has refrained from using or overtly threatening to use nuclear weapons during either the Korean War or the Vietnam War. Such conduct suggests the emergence of a subtle tradition of nonuse, at least under circumstances of limited war for limited ends. However, the official United States position insists on the right to initiate a nuclear response to what it regards as enemy aggression. Official service manuals conclude that nuclear weapons cannot be considered as prohibited weapons of war, in the absence of an explicit rule.[8]

The ambiguity in the legal status of nuclear weapons is reinforced by persistent international efforts to achieve an explicit rule of prohibition, either in the form of a series of declarations by nuclear powers or by a binding treaty rule. Such efforts would be largely superfluous if the legal status of these weapons was already clear to principal governments. Furthermore, the United States and the NATO group base a major portion of their military planning on their right and willingness to initiate a nuclear response to certain forms of non-nuclear provocation. Hence, it is impossible to infer any de facto prohibition upon a first use of nuclear weapons, and the desirability of some move in that direction remains an important and controversial arms control issue.

Any effort to control nuclear weapons must be based on two central premises. First, the issue of legal status is not presently resolved by U.N. action, attitudes of governments, or commentary by experts in international law. Second, the United States opposition to a rule of prohibition continues to be the critical obstacle to its emergence. An inquiry into the arguments and counterarguments with regard to the American position will reveal the grounds for changing the American position to one of support for either a declaratory statement or a treaty rule that prohibits an initiating, or first, use of nuclear weapons.

## Grounds for United States Opposition

In various official and semiofficial settings, the United States government has made clear its refusal to agree to any general ban on use of nuclear weapons. It is important ultimately to evaluate the cogency of this refusal, but first we need to understand its basis.

For a long time the principal reason that the United States, together with its NATO allies, has claimed the right to initiate the use of nuclear weapons has been to deter a possible Soviet attack on Western Europe. According to this position, conventional means of defense could not withstand a large-scale Soviet conventional attack, and therefore Soviet pressure on Western Europe could only be resisted through reliance on a threat of nuclear response. In fact, recent reports on NATO planning have disclosed decisions to deploy nuclear weapons near possible battle frontiers, so as to make clear that even a border-crossing probe by Soviet or Soviet-supported forces in Europe would almost inevitably provoke a nuclear response.[9]

The argument for relying on nuclear weapons rests on several propositions: that the Soviet Union would use military force to conquer or at least intimidate Western Europe, if it were not deterred from doing so by the prospect of a nuclear response; that Western Europe could not, or at any rate would not, develop a deterrent posture adequate to forswear reliance on nuclear weapons; that the United States is more concerned with the adequacy of European security than with any lessening of world tensions that might result from prohibiting the use of nuclear weapons; and that the effect of such a prohibition would be to stimulate the development of a credible European nuclear deterrent, rather than to remove nuclear weapons from a central role in defense planning. Thus, the prohibition would stimulate the proliferation of nuclear weapons—for instance, to West Germany—and hence would have an effect opposite from the one intended. There would be no reduction in the reliance on nuclear weapons, but only a shift away from American control over the decision to initiate their use.

America's far-flung security commitments can only be realistically met, another argument against a general nuclear ban proceeds, if "the nuclear option" is kept open. This position rests on a combination of military and political considerations. It has been clearly expressed by the strategist Bernard Brodie: "It is therefore quite possible that we could fight another war in the Far East as large as the Korean War, or even a repetition of that war, without using nuclear weapons—assuming the American people permitted the government to engage again in such a war . . . But surely it would be going about the job the *hard* way, especially since timely indication of readiness to use nuclear weapons is *bound* to have an enormous, and very likely a guaranteed deterrent power." Brodie added that "failure to use them under such circumstances would probably have repercussions for the future that would in the net be not to our liking."[10]

Despite the failure to use or even to threaten use of nuclear weapons throughout the Vietnam War, it seems correct to suppose that American military planners value the nuclear option as a residual possibility, to be exercised in non-European theaters of action only in exceptional circumstances. In essence, then, there seems to be a rather important belief that American superiority in nuclear weapons may be useful as a deterrent and as a response in unforeseen circumstances. This belief seems to be associated, in official American thinking, with the "stability" of relations between nuclear powers.

In opposition to the Soviet proposal for a treaty prohibition of the use of nuclear weapons, Adrian Fisher, then the United States representative in the First Committee of the General Assembly, said that "we must consider the role that the present nuclear forces play in the relatively stable strategic balance which now exists between the major nuclear powers in the world and the effect on that balance of an obligation not to use nuclear weapons under any circumstances." More to the point, Fisher argued that "the most effective way of minimizing the risk of nuclear war will be through the maintenance of mutual deterrence" and that "[a]s long as such a posture continues, an agreement not to use nuclear weapons, even in self-defense or in retaliation, would be, at worst deceptive—and therefore dangerous—and, at best, unrealistic." Underlying this position is the idea that world peace rests on deterrence and that deterrence extends beyond a nuclear surprise attack to include "aggression" by the adversary.[11]

The United States contends further that a prohibition on the use of nuclear weapons as a first-step measure "puts the cart before the horse, so to speak, or the plough in front of the ox." Fisher has explained that the "non-use proposal would not be a meaningful document unless something were also done about nuclear stockpiles" and that "the elimination of nuclear weapons from national arsenals could only be accomplished in the context of general and complete disarmament under effective international control."[12] In this view, the nuclear option needs to be maintained as a deterrent to major aggression until the virtual completion of the disarmament process.

Underlying this contention is the belief that the existence of nuclear weapons has maintained the peace during a period of tension and conflict in international history.[13] After World War II, the United States rested its security almost completely on its willingness and ability to use nuclear weapons if sufficiently provoked by communist action. This posture culminated in John Foster Dulles' formulation of a doctrine of "massive retaliation." Brodie wrote, "Even as late as the Quemoy crisis of 1958, few of our aircraft has bomb-racks suitable for carrying 'conventional' or non-nuclear bombs."[14] More recently, in connection with the *Pueblo* incident, the United States appeared to lack the capacity for an effective non-nuclear assertion of its military power. Reasons of fiscal economy have combined with a sense of technological advantage to stress the role of nuclear weapons in American military planning.

Under these circumstances, any step to curtail the use of nuclear weapons would appear to hurt the United States more than the Soviet Union, especially given the far-flung commitments the United States now has. As such, a prohibition on nuclear weapon use as a first-step measure could be viewed as inconsistent with the sixth principle of the Soviet-American official "Joint Statement of Agreed Principles for Disarmament Negotiations" of 1961, to the effect that "All measures of general and complete disarmament should be balanced so that at no stage of the implementation of the treaty could any State or group of States gain military advantage and that security is ensured equally for all." One specialist, Thomas B. Larson wrote that "the U.S.S.R. has always favored measures to 'blacken' nuclear weapons."[15] Such a curious contention takes for granted that Soviet initiatives with regard to prohibition are prompted by a desire to gain one-sided military advantages from making nuclear weapons illegitimate instruments of foreign policy.

A more moderate variant of this position is to view the issue of prohibition as one of bargaining significance. In other words, the United States should receive something from the Soviet Union and possibly China, in exchange for renouncing its right to initiate nuclear response. The exchange has never been spelled out by an American official, but it could involve political assurances as to objectives and zonal limitations on troop deployment. This view that a fair bargain should be struck arises from the belief that the United States would be giving up more than other governments by agreeing to the prohibition and that the issue is a suitable one for the normal bargaining characteristic of international diplomacy.

The use of atomic weapons in 1945 by the United States against Hiroshima and Nagasaki has a further subtle influence on the American attitude toward prohibition proposals. The United States has a defensive attitude toward the legitimacy of these weapons, because it has actually made a highly controversial use of nuclear weapons against heavily populated areas and because it is the only country ever to have used such weapons. For instance, in the *Shimoda* case, a Japanese district court decided, with the help of three separate expert opinions, that these attacks violated international law by their highly destructive and indiscriminate character.[16] But the United States government continues to defend its recourse to atomic weapons, partly by arguing that such weapons are legitimate weapons of war in the absence of a specific treaty prohibition.

In contrast, the Soviet Union harps on American use of atomic weapons as indicative of an unwillingness to limit the destructive capabilities at the disposal of the United States. The Soviet representative in the First Committee of the General Assembly, Lev Mendelevich, accounted for the United States attitude by observing that "the history of nuclear weapons started with the use of those weapons by the United States at Hiroshima and Nagasaki. That is probably what created a sort of complex about the use of nuclear weapons which prevents the United States from adopting a more constructive attitude towards proposals to prohibit the use of nuclear weapons."[17] There does seem to be American resistance toward taking a position on nuclear weapons that would cast a shadow across prior United States acts. However, such a shadow is already cast by the *Shimoda* decision, by General Assembly Resolution 1653 (XVI), and by world public opinion.

In addition, the United States has been traditionally reluctant to make sweeping commitments on nuclear use that might restrict choice in future international situations. In this respect, a prohibition on the use of nuclear weapons might have unfortunate applications that cannot be foreseen by a statement of general principal. The United States tends to favor a contextual approach to obligations of this sort, leaving officials free to adapt general rules to specific situations. American opposition to Soviet proposals for an agreed definition of aggression provides the other most obvious example of this distrust of general principle.

In addition, a prohibition of this sort can be taken more or less seriously by governments. When it comes to honoring a formal obligation, the United States tends to view itself as more scrupulous than the Soviet Union, and therefore as more likely to be subject to a greater restriction of its freedom of action, despite the formal equality of the burden. Private comment also emphasizes that a centralized and coercive society, such as the Soviet Union, has a greater capacity than the United States to maintain nuclear weapons research facilities at a high state of efficiency, in the event that nuclear weapons were shifted to the prohibited category.

Finally, there are a variety of uncertainties, perhaps irreducible, which are relied on to argue against a sweeping prohibition. First of all, there is the inherent difficulty in offering any precise description of "use" with regard to nuclear weapons. Are threats included? Are deployment patterns included? Are retaliatory uses confined in scope and scale to initiating uses? Second, there are difficulties inherent in the process of implementation. Does a government have to act as well as to give its formal assent? What happens to the rule of prohibition in the event of nonparticipation by some nuclear powers? These questions have been raised in a variety of ways during the course of formal debates on the status of nuclear weapons.

## Case Against the United States Position

The main refutations of the American arguments highlight the positive grounds for favoring a categorical form of nuclear weapons prohibition. First, United States security commitments in Europe and elsewhere vary according to country; but an established precedent based on the legitimacy of nuclear first use supports comparable claims in a variety of geographical settings. Europe's claim to defend itself with nuclear weapons against a non-nuclear attack seems like a far-reaching and generally undesirable precedent. Other states confronting serious challenges, such as Israel or South Africa, would be encouraged to assert comparable claims. In contrast, the establishment of a global prohibition on use of nuclear weapons, comparable to the prohibition on poison gas, would tend to discourage reliance on weapons of mass destruction by making such a claim illegitimate even in cases of self-defense.

Security interests extend and vary over time and space. To premise a nuclear option on a specific set of circumstances that happens to prevail in Europe at a particular historical moment, is not consistent with more general and long-range interests in avoiding the use of nuclear weapons during armed conflict. Besides, it is highly problematic that a substantial threat of Soviet attack on Western Europe now exists or is likely to exist in the foreseeable future. European capabilities are sufficient to meet Soviet probes and pressures without any reliance on a nuclear option; in fact, the renunciation of nuclear weapons as legitimate instruments of defense may lead to an overall reduction of European tensions and to increased East-West cooperation. In any event, the alleged danger of a massive attack by Soviet conventional armies does not seem to be either credible or significant enough to warrant a system-wide endorsement of the legitimacy of national defense policies based on the nuclear option.

Other American security interests, aside from those associated with the defense of homeland or with participation in United Nations operations, can also be met without relying on the nuclear option. In light of the Vietnam experience, these security interests are of doubtful validity, and their elimination might better serve the national interest than would their pursuit. But leaving aside this issue of policy, there seems to be no credible danger to major American interests in any part of the world that could not be dealt with at subnuclear levels of military violence.

An additional argument against the United States position is that world stability would be helped, not hindered, by the denuclearization of international relations. All states would be restored to a kind of prenuclear parity that is consistent with the overall objectives of nonproliferation. The nuclear powers, by forswearing the nuclear option, would help to eliminate the distinction between nuclear and non-nuclear powers, and would thereby remove one main incentive for the acquisition of nuclear weapons. As the deputy foreign minister of the Soviet Union, Vasily Kuznetsov, expressed the point in a United Nations debate on the Soviet proposal for a treaty prohibition, "if States undertook not to use nuclear weapons, this would decrease the threat of a nuclear war and would bring us closer to the possibilities of destroying nuclear weapons. The prohibition of the use of nuclear weapons would paralyze this weapon politically."[18] Even if there is no way to establish numerically the impact of a prohibition on the likelihood of nuclear war, there is some reason to believe that the impact of such a prohibition would be positive. Certainly this presumption underlies all legal efforts to prohibit behavior or instruments of conflict.

The discretion that individual governments presently retain over the use of nuclear weapons is also not persuasively explained as a way to deter aggression. For one thing, the perception of what constitutes aggression is very subjective and tends to be heavily biased in accordance with differing perspectives and interests.[19] Governments typically reach contradictory conclusions respecting the identity of the aggressor in a particular war. Because of this tendency to make biased judgments, it seems desirable not to entrust national governments with wide responsibilities to define and punish aggression. Given the awesome consequences of nuclear warfare, it seems especially desirable to limit as clearly and fully as possible a government's discretion to use these weapons.

The renunciation of the nuclear option would eliminate the temptation to develop doctrines of limited strategic use for nuclear weapons. These doctrines erode the underlying stability of deterrence by their tendency to normalize the recourse to nuclear weapons as an instrument of warfare and diplomacy.

In an even more central way, a commitment not to resort to the first use of nuclear weapons would facilitate negotiations on major arms control agreements. The present nuclear posture, based on extended deterrence rather than on minimum deterrence of a nuclear strike, requires ambiguity as to intentions, and the requirements for nuclear capabilities are thus expanded still further. The retention of a nuclear option for a variety of contingencies other than retaliation against a nuclear strike makes it very difficult to impose effective restraints on the acquisition of new weapons systems, or to impose ceilings on stockpiles. The outcome has been a continuous and expensive peacetime arms race and the accumulation of a huge "overkill" capability. It is overkill only in relation to a certain fixed mission. The weapons are all needed if each plausible mission and every conceivable theater of use is to be adequately supplied. Such contingency planning is what extended deterrence is all about.[20]

To renounce the right to use nuclear weapons first would also seem to have a variety of beneficial side effects. First of all, the nature of such a commitment would represent a dramatic effort to return the nuclear genie to its bottle and to defy the apostles of technological inevitability. This gesture would serve to educate and inform people about the reasons why the nuclear option is dangerous and otherwise undesirable.

Second, such an act of renunciation would probably, although not necessarily, lead to a slowing of the arms race, including inhibiting to some extent the deployment of ABM and MIRV weapons systems. Nuclear strategy would then tend to become unambiguously confined to problems of nuclear reprisal in response to a nuclear surprise attack. There is no question that governments would retain the nuclear reprisal option, should the prohibition on first use come into effect.

Third, the devaluation of the role of nuclear weapons would seem to encourage a substantial reduction of existing stockpiles, thereby further helping the cause of nonproliferation and of general disarmament. Only a small, highly dispersed, highly mobile second-strike capability would be achieved at a fraction of present costs, risks, and energies.

Fourth, a renunciation of nuclear weapons would tend to satisfy the repeated demands by non-nuclear states for "reciprocity" in arms control negotiations. As such, it could be expected to improve the overall atmosphere for reaching arms control agreements.

The tides of technological fortune change, and it is not to be assumed that the United States or any country will necessarily ever want to make use of the nuclear option. It therefore seems desirable to lessen the probability that any government will initiate nuclear war for any reason. The decision to use atomic weapons against Japanese cities at a time when the war was substantially won by the Allied side further suggests the ease with which a government might in the future justify its decision to resort to nuclear weapons.[21]

The renunciation of the nuclear option would help move the United States out beyond the shadow of Hiroshima and Nagasaki. Those atomic attacks, viewed as illegal by the only court that ever examined the question, have influenced the whole turn of the post-World War II world. A prohibition would look toward the future with a real determination to avoid a repetition of nuclear destruction.

To renounce the nuclear option would be a self-enforcing and unambiguous undertaking. Whether renunciation takes the form of a series of parallel national declarations of intent or of an international convention, it requires no elaborate bargaining.

In the course of international history, norms of prohibition have been proposed and developed for many weapons. As recently as November 25, 1969, President Nixon indicated his support for norms of prohibition applicable to chemical and biological weapons. He also recommended that the United States ratify the 1925 Geneva Protocol prohibiting the military use of poison gases and bacteriological weapons. Nixon's statement indicated a willingness by the United States to limit its research effort on biological weapons to defensive measures designed to moderate the effects of their use by others, and it solicited recommendations from the Department of Defense as to the proper way to destroy existing stockpiles of bacteriological weapons. The point is that a norm of prohibition—even without negotiation and enforcement—has been set "as an initiative toward peace." Nixon's statement went on to say that "by the examples we set today, we hope to contribute to an atmosphere of peace and understanding between nations and among men."[22]

The existence of a nuclear shield undoubtedly helped build a political basis for this action. Nevertheless, the same reasoning used to explain norms of renunciation in the bacteriological and chemical fields can be applied, and with far greater force, to nuclear weapons.

Finally, the formulation of this obligation in categorical rather than contextual form assures a certain clarity of standards. To allow national officials a limited option, based on claims that an initiating use of nuclear weapons is for defensive purposes or only against military targets or under circumstances of necessity, would reinforce traditions of a self-serving discretion that have already hampered every effort to bring law to bear on governments in the area of war and peace. Even a categorical prohibition on first use, which is largely self-defining in content, is of course vulnerable to violations. All rules of restraint seek to deter marginal violations by adding respect for enacted law as a consideration in decision-making and planning contexts. In relation to nuclear weapons, there already exists a weak tradition of nonuse, principally created by American unwillingness to use these weapons in

Korea and Vietnam; a rule of prohibition or a declaration of self-denial would merely serve to strengthen such a tradition.

There are also important domestic reasons associated with constitutional democracy that support a renunciation of the nuclear option. Because of the element of surprise, the initial use of nuclear weapons would almost always involve a presidential decision without benefit of congressional advice or authorization. A decision to respond with nuclear weapons after their prior use could be undertaken on the basis of broader participation by top officials, which would more closely fulfill expectations about "checks and balances" as an integral element in our form of constitutional democracy.[23]

Many difficult questions would arise if the United States government were to seriously consider shifting its position on the status of nuclear weapons. Would the United States be unable to uphold its vital interests in a less nuclear world? If nuclear weapons had not been developed, would the political map of the world look significantly different? There are no real answers to such questions. The assessment of comparative risk is largely based on a series of intuitive judgments that can never be conclusively proved by measurement or experience. We cannot know what would have happened had we made different judgments and policies in the past. Our choices are made in a setting of fundamental uncertainty. Because fundamental attitudes toward human experience are at stake, our choices can be guided only by overall interpretations of the lessons of history.

I am convinced that the renunciation of the nuclear option would serve national and world interests, principally by making nuclear war less likely to occur, by slowing the arms race, by inhibiting further proliferation of nuclear weapons, and by encouraging further steps toward positive disarmament. Beyond such expectations lies an awareness that a large-scale nuclear exchange will inevitably cause vast human and ecological damage to millions of innocent victims, many of whom may even oppose the government policy that provoked the nuclear attack, and will likely destroy or severely harm societies not even involved in the conflict. A weapon of such limitless destruction cannot reliably be entrusted to the greeds and fears of human beings.

Whatever can be done to remove this awesome power from human control seems, on balance, beneficial. A renunciation of the nuclear option thus seems to be a clear step back from the edge of catastrophe, especially at this moment of history.

At the very least, such a proposal warrants serious consideration by

American policy-makers. So far, a virtual consensus has prevailed within the American elite on the national benefits derived from retaining the nuclear option. This consensus can be explained only as a consequence of excluding from power those who view the long history of deterrence of the weak by the strong as largely a costly failure, even in the prenuclear years.

In conclusion, I would propose that the President recommend a joint resolution by Congress committing the United States to a renunciation of the nuclear option, and that the President then declare this renunciation to the world as official policy. It would also be beneficial to have a treaty rule confirm this renunciation. At minimum, it is time to initiate a high-level public inquiry into the status of nuclear weapons and its effects on national and world security. Both the President and the Congress should initiate studies of this issue and entrust the inquiry to civilians with no vested interest in nuclear technology. This kind of question should not be treated as a technical matter properly relegated to professional military planners. On the contrary, the role of nuclear weapons in our defense posture should become primarily a matter for political judgment and moral appraisal.

# Part Two: The Wider Lessons of Indochina

# 4 | Learning from Vietnam

Since 1950, five American Presidents have supported a series of policies designed to maintain a pro-West, anticommunist government in control of South Vietnam. The persistence of such policies exhibits remarkable continuity, given the enormous difficulties encountered in pursuing this objective. There have been many efforts to explain the origins and durability of the American commitment. None has proved entirely satisfactory. It seems clear that the impetus for the policy arose from at least three principal objectives: the containment of the world communist movement, the more specific containment of mainland China, and the containment of revolutionary nationalism. But such goals can be pursued in a variety of ways, and it remains unclear why over the years the United States was prepared to make such immense sacrifices in blood, treasure, and prestige in their pursuit.

One rationale offered was the recollection that policies of appeasement—in what might be called the "lesson of Munich"—had not prevented World War II. American policy-makers prominent during the buildup of a military commitment to defend the Saigon regime seemed to believe the idea that the international communist movement was monolithic and committed to world conquest; they therefore saw the choice as one between "standing up to aggression" or provoking World War III. The notion of "containment" or "holding the line" arose as a reaction to Stalinism but persisted into the 1960s, long after Stalin's death and despite hard evidence of a deep Sino-Soviet split. This notion was accompanied by an image of "falling dominoes": if South Vietnam should fall to communism, then Thailand, Cambodia, Laos, and the Malay Peninsula would also fall in inevitable succession. Therefore, although the stakes in Vietnam might appear small and remote if taken in isolation, it was argued that a large commitment was nevertheless justified because of these larger concerns—namely, the geopolitical stability of all of South Asia and the establishment as precedent of a significant prohibition against a communist aggressor.

Such reasoning is abstract and ideological and does not fit too well with the concrete facts of conflict in Asia, especially in Vietnam. When the United States made its original economic commitment to the French in 1950, the struggle for Indochina was a typical anticolonial war of independence of the sort that developed in Asia and Africa after World War II. True, the leadership of the Vietnamese independence movement had a communist background and might be suspected of bringing a liberated Indochina within the communist orbit of influence. But it was also true that the procolonial Vietnamese were politically isolated in their own country and were unlikely to govern effectively or humanely. As a result, the anticolonial movement in Vietnam developed into a broad united front effort that by the end of the first Indochina War in 1954 had attracted support from many noncommunist elements in the population. Ho Chi Minh had emerged as a national leader of extraordinary stature, commanding respect and allegiance from almost every segment of Vietnamese society.

In subsequent years the United States involvement has been shaped and facilitated by the Geneva Conference of 1974 that divided Vietnam into two zones. This division was initially provisional but with time assumed a certain permanence, as the zones of North and South Vietnam emerged as separate political entities. In this divided country setting the United States was compelled to rely on military means to perpetuate the geographical and ideological divisions embodied in the Geneva solution, and found itself drawn increasingly into a large-scale and prolonged counterinsurgency war. The American objective since 1954, despite incredible shifts in tactical stress, has remained surprisingly constant: to maintain an anticommunist government in South Vietnam and hence to assure the continuing division of Vietnam into two sovereign states.

When Nixon assumed the presidency, the tactics of American involvement came to emphasize the replacement of American by Vietnamese combat forces—the so-called "Vietnamization of the war" —reinforced by fantastic levels of air support. At the same time the zone of violence spread to Cambodia, and the American military involvement in Laos intensified. The Vietnam War remained unresolved until 1973, the negotiations in Paris being stalled on two issues: refusal by the American government to make a commitment to total withdrawal by a definite time, and the American unwillingness to accept a provisional government for South Vietnam that represented a fair coalition of contending forces.

The Paris Agreement of 1973 represented an immense step in the direction of satisfying these two preconditions for peace. However, the political side of the agreement has not been implemented. Although the United States has now disengaged itself from the combat level, the war

persists at high levels of intensity between well-armed Vietnamese anta-
gonists. American insistence on implementing the Paris bargain would
even today lead rapidly to peace in South Vietnam and to the
emergence of a government in Saigon that is neutralist in foreign policy
and reformist in domestic affairs, in other words, to an ideological
compromise between the goals of the United States and of the Provisional Revolutionary Government (PRG) of South Vietnam, which
was earlier known as the National Liberation Front (NLF). In addition,
the reunification of Vietnam would be put off for a number of years and
the longer-term future of South Vietnam would be allowed to reflect
internal forces of national self-determination. The balance of these
internal forces would and should lead during a period of several years
to the emergence of a pro-PRG government, but one that governs by
coalition politics and is quite autonomous in dealing with North
Vietnam.

With this background it seems possible to speculate about what
lessons American policy-makers should have learned from the long and
anguished experience of the Vietnam involvement. Future American
policy toward Asia is likely to be guided by whichever of several possibilities becomes the dominant interpretation of the Vietnamese
experience, although the combination of detente and a world economic
crisis may inhibit future American temptations to engage in Vietnam-
type conflicts whatever the Vietnam learning experience turns out to be.
Already much attention has been given in American intellectual circles
to the question "beyond Vietnam," and there are a variety of competing efforts to present the most influential statement of guidelines for
the future. An examination of this debate seems especially important,
as all of the positions being seriously considered carry forward into the
future our earlier mistakes of policy and perspective that prompted the
Vietnam involvment in the first place.

## Trustworthiness of the Official Debate

A major caveat must first be offered. Both the debate on "the lessons
of Vietnam" and my analysis of it proceed on the assumption that there
is a good faith connection between the persuasiveness of alternative
lines of public justification and the course of governmental policy.
Unfortunately, with respect to matters bearing on both interventionary
diplomacy and national security, I have become increasingly skeptical
about this connection.[1] In my judgment, the external debate may even
function as a mystification, obsuring the real bases of national policy;
that is, the explication of a rationale may serve to confuse and distract,

rather than to enlighten public opinion. Anyone who followed closely the evolving American official position on the deployment of an ABM system saw that the rationale was expendable, but the policy was not. The American involvement in the Vietnam War appears to have had the same quality.

This hypothesis is implausible without a fuller explanation of why the real bases of policy must remain obscure and therefore excluded, for the most part, from explicit mention. This is a complicated question, which can be only superficially discussed in this setting. It would appear that policy-makers are implementing a set of policies that contradict popularly held attitudes about why America uses military power in foreign affairs. These attitudes center around a self-righteous conception that whereas other governments have interests, the United States only has responsibilities.[2] As a result, it is an unwritten rule that no responsible defense or criticism of United States foreign policy positions takes account of self-interested economic motivations and pressures. Only radicals of the Right or Left, who are by definition outside the policy-making elite, give attention to issues of economic self-interest or, as the Left puts it, to the dynamics of economic imperialism.[3]

Similarly, it is not considered reasonable to attribute foreign policy positions to the pressures or momentum of domestic political forces. Yet in the Vietnam setting there is considerable evidence of a bureaucratic momentum that carried the policies forward independent of any rational assessment of their merit. The extent to which the government is itself an unwitting (and perhaps unknowing) captive of the military-industrial complex is part of the problem, one that is almost always excluded from "responsible" discussions of the future of American policy in Asia. The bureaucratization and militarization of American national security policy-planning efforts are treated like intellectual ghosts.

The influence of these economic and governmental forces on policy-making may well be decisive in the years ahead. If so, the dialectics of intellectual debate are misleading, as the outcome of the debate will depend on considerations other than degrees of evidence and persuasiveness. Indeed, the actual situation may be the reverse, namely, the argument that is finally appropriated may be the one which seems best calculated to uphold a preselected policy. Surely during the Kennedy-Johnson-Nixon period of Vietnam involvement, the official search was for a plausible defense of the interventionary policy rather than for an assessment of its plausibility. Thus, the various lines of explanation—such as to deter wars of national liberation, contain China, uphold the

SEATO commitment, avoid a bloodbath in South Vietnam, guarantee that no solution be imposed on South Vietnam, protect the honor of the United States, uphold the credibility of its commitments, and so on—were used, dropped, and revived with no particular qualms, so long as a particular rationale met the mounting criticisms directed at earlier justifications of the war and restored public confidence for a while. When the more recent rationale was in turn undermined, then it too would be superseded by new lines of justification, again calculated to maintain enough support to enable the leadership to carry on the policy.

Thus, the policy debate is a puppet show of sorts. To challenge it on its own grounds may dangerously tend to lend credence to the seriousness of the overall inquiry, by implying that evidence and reasoning are likely to shape future American policy in Asia. Nevertheless, it seems important to explicate the debate so as to demonstrate why the contending positions are inadequate, and to understand why a position heretofore excluded from serious attention provides a better guideline for future American policy in Asia.[4]

Several kinds of uncertainty could influence the course and explanation of American policy in Asia. These uncertainties may in the end make the present debate seem time-bound. First, the presentation of American foreign policy will depend heavily on the domestic and foreign stances of a number of key countries, especially Japan, China, the Soviet Union, and India. It is uncertain whether Japan will turn out to be a partner or a rival of the United States. There are already indications that Japan's continuing economic growth is beginning to hurt the American economy, and some respected analysts expect a revival of fierce economic competition and even trade wars between the United States and Japan. Similarly, the Soviet decision on whether or not to remain largely aloof from Asian politics is likely to influence United States choices in definite ways. Whether China remains preoccupied with domestic concerns, or reaches an enduring accord with either the Soviet Union or the United States, or both, or whether China pursues an avowedly expansionist foreign policy—all such factors are likely to shape the United States response. Finally, whether India is reasonably successful with a moderate government and remains nonaligned is likely to be important. These kinds of uncertainty are accentuated by their interactive character: China's response to Japan may influence the Soviet relationship to India, and so on. Also, these uncertainties and complications will be effected by what goes on in other regions of the world. A revolutionary surge in Latin America or Soviet pressure in Europe or the Middle East may lead to a total American withdrawal from Asia, especially if Japan assumes the American role as surety for the political status quo on the Asian rimland.

Even more important than these external contingencies are the uncertainties of the future course of domestic politics in the United States. It now appears that domestic social and economic forces are likely to determine the overall orientation of American government, including its foreign policy. In other words, imperialists, isolationists, or advocates of world order are likely to be swept into power by reference to issues of employment, inflation, crime control, and even pornography. The substance of foreign policy positions has little independent salience for the American voter at present. This situation may change, but probably not very soon, despite the salience of international economic issues.

It is even more difficult to assess the consequences for American foreign policy of the increasing significance of ecological strains. Serious forms of environmental decay, population pressure, and resource shortages are almost certain to emerge. But it is not clear whether this deepening ecological crisis will lead to more moderate forms of political competition, or will instead induce recourse to desperate political strategies by those governments under the greatest pressure from overpopulation, poverty, urban crowding, or mass unemployment. The recent upsurge of interest in environmental matters in the United States may lead in the years ahead to a lessening of national concern about maintaining influence in Asia and may even induce a partial reversion to isolationism, especially if the costs of maintaining clean air and clean water are mostly deducted from the defense budget rather than from the welfare budget.

Although their impact cannot now be anticipated in any useful way, these kinds of uncertainty with respect to foreign alignments, internal stresses, and ecological strains are of great potential significance. They underscore the speculative character of any assessment of American propensities to intervene militarily, and they may also make Americans more likely, even anxious, to revise their sense of the future.

## A Qualified Success

Despite these imponderables, in the concluding phases of American military involvement, three different interpretations dominated the debate over the consequences of the Vietnam conflict. According to the first position, which can be associated with the liberal internationalist who fully endorsed the cold war ideology, the war was a qualified success. This was the view taken by most professional military men and the American Right. They saw American involvement in Vietnam as a proper exercise of military power, but felt that the effort was compromised by presidential insistence on pursuing limited ends by limited means. They criticized Washington for seeking "settlement" rather than "victory," and joined the Left in condemning President Johnson for his failure to declare war on North Vietnam. They argued that the armed forces had to fight the war with one hand tied behind their backs, pointing as examples to the refusal to authorize unrestricted bombing of the dikes in North Vietnam, the early restrictions on targets in the Hanoi and Haiphong area, and the failure to impose a blockade on shipping to North Vietnam early in the war.

Even though victory was not pursued by all means at our disposal, this view does not regard the Vietnam War as a failure. In a characteristic statement, Colonel William C. Moore of Bolling Air Force Base, writing in the *Air University Review,* argued: "There is reason to believe that Ho Chi Minh would never have initiated action in Vietnam had he vaguely suspected that US determination would escalate the war to its current magnitude. There is also reason to believe that this lesson has not been lost on other would-be aggressors."[5] This interpretation of the lesson of Vietnam relied on two assumptions: first, that the Vietnam War was similar to the Korean War because in each case the United States shrank back from the complete execution of its mission, but did at least display its willingness to defend a noncommunist society against attack by a communist aggressor. Proponents of this view held that the Vietnam War was not a civil war but a war of conquest by one country against another; the NLF was a mere agent of Hanoi, whose role was to pretend that this was a civil war and thereby discourage any effective response in defense. Thus, they accepted fully the image of the war developed by Dean Rusk and Walt Rostow during the Johnson presidency. The implication for the future is that the United States should not be fooled into treating communist-led insurgencies any differently from outright communist aggression against a friendly state.

The second assumption behind Moore's assessment of the Vietnam War had an even greater implication for the future, because it perceived the Vietnam experience as a demonstration that deterrence works in the counterinsurgency setting as well as it has worked in the nuclear setting. In Moore's words, "This willingness to escalate is the key to deterring future aggressions at the lower end of the spectrum of war. This, I think, is why history will be kind to President Johnson and Secretary of State Rusk because if we continue to stand firm in Vietnam as they advocate, then the world will have made incalculable progress toward eliminating war as the curse of mankind."[6] Thus, the key to the future was America's willingness to escalate the conflict to high levels of destructivity—so high, in fact, that when confronted by such a prospect, no right-minded revolutionary would ever initiate a war. Those who supported this position were critical of Johnson's war diplomacy only insofar as it failed to carry the logic of escalation to even higher levels on the battlefield and at home.

This interpretation also claimed that the American decision to fight in Vietnam gained time for other anticommunist regimes in Asia to build up their capacities for internal security and national defense, assuming that the American effort in Vietnam created a shield that held back the flow of revolutionary forces across the continent of Asia. More extravagant exponents of this liberal internationalist line of interpretation even contended, on the most slender evidence, that the Indonesian generals would not have reacted so boldly and successfully to the communist bid for power in Djakarta in October 1965, had not the American presence in Vietnam stiffened their resolve.

Advocates of this position tended to admire the Dominican intervention of 1965, where massive force was used and results quickly achieved with little loss of life. The domestic furor over the Dominican intervention disappeared quickly, mainly as a consequence of the undertaking's "success" and brevity. Sophisticated adherents of this position also privately admired the Soviet intervention of August 1968 in Czechoslovakia for similar reasons. That model of overwhelming capability, rather than the slow escalation of capability as in Vietnam, is likely to influence the doctrine and future proposals of those who favor interventionary diplomacy.

## A Failure of Proportion

The second principal position taken in the debate over the Vietnam War, associated with the espousal of Machiavellian notions of state interest, adopted an increasingly critical stance toward the American involvement, regarding it as a failure of a sense of geopolitical proportion. This second view was widely held among moderate and influential Americans, especially among civilians of a less ideological and more geopolitical cast of mind. They felt that the Vietnam War had become a mistake, often isolating as the threshold of error President Johnson's decisions in 1965 to bomb North Vietnam and to introduce large numbers of American ground combat forces. This position also by and large rejected the notion that the war was caused by the aggression of one state against another, viewing it instead as an internal civil war with both sides receiving considerable outside support. A leading proponent of this position was Townsend Hoopes, who served in the Pentagon from January 1965 to February 1969, first as deputy assistant secretary of defense for international security affairs and then as undersecretary of the Air Force. Hoopes explained the failure of Vietnam as the result of a loss of a sense of proportion by the men at the top. He built a convincing insider's case that Johnson and his principal advisers were locked into a rigid and ideological view of the war, and hence were unable to moderate the objective to conform with the costs in blood, dollars, and domestic cohesion. Writing of the situation that prevailed in Washington late in 1967, just a few months before Johnson's withdrawal speech of March 31, 1968, Hoopes stated: "The incredible disparity between the outpouring of national blood and treasure and the intrinsic US interests at stake in Vietnam was by this time widely understood and deplored at levels just below the top of the government. But the President and the tight group of advisers around him gave no sign of having achieved a sense of proportion."[7]

This view of the lesson of Vietnam had no quarrel with the effort to defend Saigon or to defeat the NLF, but urged that the effort be abandoned if it could not be made to succeed within a reasonable time and at a reasonable cost. Many Kennedy officials who originally supported the United States role in Vietnam came later to hold similar views, concluding either that the war was weakening our ability to uphold more significant interests in Europe and the Middle East, or that the disproportionate costs resulting from the Vietnam War deprived the country of the energies and resources that were desperately needed to solve our own domestic problems.

Former Ambassador Edwin O. Reischauer, a respected figure among establishment groups, carried this kind of analysis to a more general level of interpretation:

> The "central lesson" of Vietnam—at least as the American public perceives it—is already quite obvious . . . the limited ability of the United States to control at a reasonable cost the course of events in a nationally-aroused less-developed nation . . . I believe that we are moving away from the application to Asia of the "balance of power" and "power vacuum" concepts of the cold war, and in the process we no doubt will greatly downgrade our strategic interest in most of the less-developed world.[8]

According to Reischauer, the means used in Vietnam were disproportionate to the end pursued, and in general, a country like the United States cannot effectively use its military power to control the outcome of Vietnam-type struggles.

David Mozingo, an Asian specialist, took this argument one step further, recognizing the need for a perspective on Asia that was suited to the special historical and political conditions prevailing there, a perspective that foresaw the end of a rigid policy of containment of China: "Since the Korean War . . . United States policy in Asia has been modeled after the containment doctrine so successfully applied in Europe after 1947 . . . Washington has seen the problem of Chinese power in Asia in much the same light as that posed by Soviet power in Europe and has behaved as if both threats could be contained by basically the same kind of responses." Mozingo argued that there were essential differences between Asia and Europe: "In Asia the containment doctrine has been applied in an area where a nation-state system is only beginning to emerge amidst unpredictable upheavals of a kind that characterized Europe three centuries earlier . . . The kinds of American technical and economic power that could help restore the historic vitality of the European systems would seem at best to have only partial relevance to the Asian situation."[9] Such a view of the Vietnam experience supported a policy shift in a non-military direction with respect to particular struggles for control in various Asian countries.

Among the lessons to be drawn from Vietnam, according to the school that called it a failure of proportion, was the futility—perhaps worse than futility—of aiding a foreign regime that lacked the capacity to govern its own society; in fact, certain types of intervention, if carried too far, can become counterproductive. Thus, the American failure in Vietnam was laid partly to ignorance about Vietnamese realities and partly to exaggerated confidence in the ability of massive military intervention to fulfill political objectives. This was essentially the view of Stanley Hoffmann, a respected academic critic of Washington's approach to Vietnam. Again, as with Hoopes, Hoffmann's concern was to delimit an effective foreign policy, imbued with a sense of proportion and an awareness of the inherent limits imposed on American capabilities. But like Moore's interpretation, his Machiavellian critique did not repudiate American objectives in Vietnam. According to Samuel Huntington, another influential advocate of this approach and the head of Hubert Humphrey's Vietnam task force during the 1968 presidential campaign, the main guideline for the future should be to keep Vietnam-type involvements "reasonable, limited, discreet, and covert."[10]

## A Qualified Failure of Tactics

The third main position taken in the debate over the Vietnam War was that it represented a qualified failure of tactics. This view combines a general approval of the outcome and effort, regarding the war as a qualified success, with a judgment that such results could have been achieved in more acceptable ways by an early adoption of the approach introduced in the final years of American combat involvement. This third interpretation was the one favored by President Nixon and important foreign advisers such as Henry Kissinger, William Rogers, and Melvin Laird. The Nixon Doctrine, announced at Guam on July 25, 1969, was an explicit effort to avoid repeating the mistakes of Vietnam, as these leaders understood them, without renouncing the basic mission of American policy. The Nixon Administration was critical of the Vietnam effort to the extent that it believed the same ends could have been achieved at less cost in American blood and treasure, and as a result, with less strain on American society. In his November 3, 1969, address to the nation on Vietnam, President Nixon explained the Nixon Doctrine as embodying "three principles as guidelines for future American policy toward Asia":

> First, the United States will keep all of its treaty commitments;
> Second, we shall provide a shield if a nuclear power threatens the freedom of a nation allied with us or of a nation whose survival we consider vital to our security;
> Third, in cases involving other types of aggression, we shall furnish military and economic assistance when requested in accordance with our treaty commitments. But we shall look to the nation directly threatened to assume the primary responsibility of providing the manpower for its defense.[11]

The "central thesis" of this doctrine, according to the President, was "that the United States will participate in the defense and development of allies and friends, but that America cannot—and will not—conceive *all* the plans, design *all* the programs, execute *all* the decisions and undertake *all* the defense of the free nations of the world. We will help where it makes a real difference and is considered in our interest."[12] Thus, the Nixon Doctrine backed a step away from the global absolutism of Johnsonian diplomacy. Instead, it advocated specific assessments of each potential interventionary situation in terms of its strategic importance to the United States, and of this country's ability to control the outcome.[13] It remains difficult, however, to extract concrete policy implications from Nixon's rhetorical statements regarding his doctrine, for example, that "The fostering of self-reliance is the new purpose and direction of American involvement in Asia."[14]

In practical terms this position remained ill-defined but seemed to fall midway between those of Moore and Hoopes: uphold all treaty commitments, give all allied regimes our help and advice, but get fully involved in a direct military way only when vital interests are at stake and when the military instrument can be used effectively, which means successfully, quickly, and without losing too many American lives. One expression of the Nixon Doctrine, Vietnamization, for several years left the main burden of ground combat to Saigon's armed forces, without any reduction in American logistic support from the air via B-52 strikes and long-distance artillery support. Ambassador Ellsworth Bunker was reported to have said that adopting Vietnamization as a policy involved only changing the color of the bodies. Another expression of the Nixon Doctrine was the escalation of American involvement in Laos prior to the Paris Agreement, increasing our covert role in training and financing government forces and engaging in saturation bombing of contested areas, thereby causing a new flow of Asian refugees while depriving the Pathet Lao of its population base.

These three positions defined the boundaries of the main political debate involving the relevance of the Vietnam experience for the future of American foreign policy. This debate has now lost some of its relevance because the combined effects of the pricing policy on oil supplies of the Organization of Petroleum Exporting Countries (OPEC) and of the related Arab-Israeli conflict have so overwhelmed the political imagination of the foreign policy establishment. Nevertheless, the interpretation of the Vietnam War lies just below the surface and is likely to have a bearing on the approach taken toward these new challenges directed at American interests. We may yet see a struggle for ascendancy, possibly worked out in relation to Middle East policy, between the more ideological advocates of a liberal internationalism on the one hand, and the neo-Nixonians on the other, those who contest only the means of interventionary diplomacy but fully accept the basic geopolitical mission implied by such tactics. Such a controversy over tactics for the future would ignore the claim that the Vietnam War successfully extended the deterrence doctrine to counterinsurgency situations. This view, associated above with the military judgment of Vietnam as a qualified success, might be revived if important revolutionary movements emerge in noncommunist countries and if the political forces behind George Wallace and Barry Goldwater gain greater influence as a "third force" in American politics.

The first position accepted "victory" as the proper goal of the American involvement in Vietnam and regarded the means used as appropriate to the end of defeating the insurgency in South Vietnam, whether that insurgency was viewed as a species of civil war or as an agency of North Vietnamese aggression. In contrast, the second position shifted away from victory as a goal, once it became evident that the means required for this goal were too costly in lives, dollars, and domestic support. This position moved instead toward advocating some kind of mutual withdrawal of foreign forces, in conjunction with an effort to reach a settlement by nonmilitary means. The third position specified its goal as establishing conditions of self-determination for South Vietnam and its present governing regime, a position that implied an outcome of the war that was close to total victory. However, there was some ambiguity as to whether the real goals were not more modest than the proclaimed goals. In any event, this position regarded the means used as having been unnecessarily costly, given the goals of the involvement. At least in theory, it accepted the desirability of a non-military outcome through a negotiated settlement of the war.

The first position seems to have interpreted Vietnam as a qualified success and to have favored, if anything, a less constrained military effort to defeat any future communist-led insurgencies that might erupt on the Asian mainland or elsewhere in the Third World. As with the strategic doctrine, the deterrence of insurgent challenges rests on possessing a credible capability and on indicating a willingness to respond with overwhelming military force to any relevant challenge.

The second position was much less tied to an overall doctrine, viewed the post-Kennedy phases of the Vietnam involvement as a clear mistake, and argued for a greater emphasis on nonmilitary responses to insurgent challenges. This position also sought to restrict overt intervention to situations in which its impact could be swift and effective. The position depends, therefore, on having a fairly secure regime in power in the country that is the scene of the struggle. It also emphasizes the need to keep a sense of proportion throughout such an involvement, either by explicitly limiting the magnitude of the commitment or by liquidating an unsuccessful commitment.

The third position was midway between the first two positions in tone and apparent emphasis. It developed a more globalist strategy, emphasizing that the United States had far-flung treaty relations with Asian countries, and urging that these commitments be honored for the sake of the overall preeminence of the United States in world affairs and the continuing need to resist communist pressures everywhere in the world. The merits of the particular case were thus tied to a global strategy, but an effort was made to shift more of the burden of response to the local government. But what does this mean in cases where the government cannot meet these burdens, as was surely the case in Vietnam all along? What happens when self-reliance fails? The prevailing response to this question may well determine the central line of American foreign policy in Asia throughout the coming decades. Both this position and the previous one look toward Japan as a more active partner in the development of a common Asian policy. President Nixon's decision to return Okinawa to Japan by 1972 arose out of this hope for sharing the geopolitical burdens of the region with Japan.

What was most surprising about these three positions was the extent to which they all accepted the premise that an American counter-revolutionary doctrine was applicable only in situations that appeared to be revolutionary. Where there was no formidable radical challenge on the domestic scene, as in India or Japan, the American preference was clearly for moderate democracy, the kind of political orientation that the United States imposed on Japan during the military occupation after World War II. However, where an Asian society was beset by struggle between a rightist incumbent regime and a leftist insurgent challenger, then American policy threw its support, sometimes strongly, to the counterrevolutionary side. As a result there was virtually no disposition to question the American decision to support the repressive and reactionary Saigon regime, provided that support could lead to victory at a reasonable cost. In fact, the four American Presidents from Eisenhower to Nixon were in agreement on the political wisdom of the decision to help Saigon prevail in its effort to create a strong anticommunist state in South Vietnam, even though this decision defied both the military results of the first Indochina War and the explicit provisions on the reunification of Vietnam embodied in the Geneva Accords of 1954. All three positions also shared an acceptance, although to varying degrees, of the basic postulates of the "domino theory." The second position was least inclined to endorse the image of falling dominoes; indeed, some of its adherents, such as the Asian political analyst Donald Zagoria, argued that the prospects for communism needed to be assessed on a country-by-country basis, because the success or failure of communism in Vietnam or Laos would not necessarily have much impact on the prospect for revolution in other Asian countries.

McGeorge Bundy, a belated convert to the second position after an earlier allegiance to a moderate form of the first position, gave up on the war because its burden was too great on American society. Nevertheless, he took pains to reaffirm the wisdom of the original undertaking: "I remind you also, if you stand on the other side, that my argument against escalation and against an indefinite continuation of our present course has been based not on moral outrage or political hostility to the objective, but rather on the simple and practical ground that escalation will not work and that a continuation of our present course is unacceptable."[15]

Arthur Schlesinger, Jr., has said: "The tragedy of Vietnam is the tragedy of the overextension and misapplication of valid principles. The original insights of collective security and liberal evangelism were generous and wise." Actually, adherents of the second position, while sharply dissenting from the Vietnam policies of both Johnson and Nixon, still maintained the spirit of an earlier statement by McGeorge Bundy, made at a time when he was rallying support for Johnson's air war against North Vietnam: "There are wild men in the wings, but on the main stage even the argument on Vietnam turns on tactics, not fundamentals."[16]

Unfortunately, all three positions affirmed the continuing wisdom of two American objectives in Asia. The first objective was to prevent Chinese expansion, if necessary by military means. The second was to prevent any anticommunist regime, however repressive, reactionary, or isolated from popular support, from being toppled by internal revolutionary forces, whether or not such forces were receiving outside help.

## The Excluded Fourth Position

There is another interpretation that has been largely excluded from the public dialogue on the war. It repudiates United States objectives in Vietnam on moral and political grounds. It holds, first, that there is no reason to believe that China has expansive military aims in Asia; second, that even if China were militarily expansive, it would still not be desirable or necessary for the United States to contain China by armed force; and third, that there is neither occasion nor justification for aiding repressive governments merely because they follow anticommunist policies. I favor this fourth position for several reasons. There is no evidence that China needed containing by an American military presence in Asia. Of course, small countries in the shadow of a dominant state tend to fall under the influence of that state whenever it is effectively governed. This process is almost universal and has deep historical roots in Asia. But there are important countervailing forces that qualify even this expectation.

First, China is preoccupied with its own domestic politics and with its principal foreign struggles against the Soviet Union and Formosa. Second, many of the countries surrounding China had struggled at great sacrifice to achieve independence, could count on Soviet support if Chinese pressure mounted, and treated their national search for domestic autonomy as more significant than common ideological sentiments. And third, China's foreign policy may often have been crude and ill-conceived, but it rarely exhibited any intention to rely on military force to expand its influence beyond its boundaries; its use of force against India, Tibet, and the Soviet Union was to support its claims to disputed territory, and its entry into the Korean War in 1950 seemed mainly motivated by a reasonable concern about danger to its industrial heartland.

The evidence thus suggests that the American effort to contain China in Asia was a determination to contend with a paper tiger. More significantly, the multifaceted conflicts in Asia and elsewhere in the Third World cannot be comprehended in abstract or ideological terms. Asia is undergoing a two-phase revolution that began as a struggle against colonialism and will continue for at least another decade. The first phase has been concerned with reacquiring national control over the apparatus of government by defeating foreign rule. This aspect of the struggle is now largely completed. In most parts of Asia the colonial system has finally collapsed and foreigners have been removed from power.

But in most Asian countries, including South Vietnam, the native groups allied with the colonial system have held onto political power, stifling social progress and economic reform. Thailand too, although never formally a colony, continues to be governed by a traditional elite that is ill-inclined to initiate the reforms vitally needed by the mass of its population. The residues of the colonial system include the more informal patterns of domination that result from large American donations of military equipment, foreign aid, covert "presence" (the CIA), and political and economic advice. Most governments in Asia today are composed of conservative forces that maintain their dominance with the aid of such donations and advice, usually at the expense of their own people. Therefore, the second, postindependence phase of the revolutionary struggle involves wresting political control from traditional ruling classes and instituting a mass-based program of land reform, education, public hygiene, social equality, radical consciousness, and economic development. In most of Asia, aside from India, the United States is allied with regimes that are trying to hold back this second surge of the revolutionary energy that has swept across the Third World to crush the colonial system.

The fourth position accepts this analysis of political conflict in Asia and seeks to adjust American policy accordingly. First of all, it seeks to proceed rapidly with an accommodation with China through a flexible compromise of outstanding issues, including the future of Formosa. What is implied here is the removal of the American military presence from the area, especially the withdrawal of the Seventh Fleet and the elimination of American military bases on Taiwan. Such a course would leave the outcome of the Chinese civil war, which has not yet been fully resolved, to the contending forces on both sides. It would encourage the possibility of negotiations between Peking and Taipei regarding the governance of Formosa, perhaps allowing for semi-autonomous status within the Chinese Peoples Republic, with guarantees of a measure of economic and political independence for the island.

An American accommodation with China would help the United States handle an increasingly competitive economic relationship with Japan and give Washington more bargaining power in relation to the Soviet Union. More importantly, accommodation with China could make it possible to proceed more rapidly with arms control and disarmament, to denuclearize world politics, and to resist pressures to proliferate weapons of mass destruction to additional countries.

The fourth position entails the total abandonment of America's counterrevolutionary foreign policy in Asia. This would mean renouncing all treaty relations with governments that are repressing their own populations and holding back the forces of self-determination. Clearly such a revision of policy would require the renunciation or at least the reinterpretation of American treaty obligations to promote the security of the regimes now governing South Vietnam, Cambodia, Laos, South Korea, Formosa, Thailand, and the Phillippines. The only commitment that should be reaffirmed is the United States obligation under the United Nations Charter to resist large-scale overt military attacks across internationally recognized boundaries. Civil strife is likely to eventually displace the current governments of several Asian countries. But to the extent that such conflict tends to reflect the true balance of political forces within these national societies, it would be in general beneficial for the welfare of the population and for the stability of the country and the region. At present, several regimes are being maintained in power only through a combination of domestic oppression and American support.

There seems virtually no prospect that this position will be adopted or even seriously considered unless major shifts occur within American political life. Only extraordinary domestic pressure, fueled perhaps by economic troubles at home and foreign policy setbacks abroad, is likely to produce a change of leadership and a change of world outlook in America.

Yet in historical retrospect, it is important to appreciate the fact that this position once came close to being our foreign policy. Its rejection by today's American leaders was not the inevitable outcome of America's Asia policy after World War II. Franklin D. Roosevelt was opposed to restoring the French colonial administration in Indochina at the end of the war. If Indochina had been allowed to become independent after the Japanese left, then Ho Chi Minh would clearly have emerged as the leader of a united Vietnam, and perhaps of a united Indochina. In his initial Proclamation of Independence of September 25, 1945, Ho Chi Minh explicitly referred to the French and American Revolutions as the main sources of inspiration for the Vietnamese struggle for national independence. The communist response to Ho in the West was not altogether enthusiastic: the Soviet Union withheld recognition from Ho Chi Minh's Republic of Vietnam; and in 1947, Maurice Thorez, the French communist leader who was then Vice-Premier of France, actually countersigned the order for French military action against the newly proclaimed Republic. As O. Edmund Clubb, an area expert, pointed out: "In 1945 and 1946 the Ho Chi Minh government looked mainly to the United States and Nationalist China for foreign political support."[17] In the period since World War II, anticolonialism would surely have been a better guideline for American foreign policy in Asia than anticommunism. And even now it makes better sense. Anticolonialism would work better because it accords more closely with historic trends in Asia and with the dynamics of national self-determination in most noncommunist Asian countries, and because it flows more naturally out of the United States' own heritage and proudest tradition. But the whole debate may well be irrelevant, or virtually so. Existing policy may merely represent the continuing potency of economic and bureaucratic pressures. If so, those who wield power and are sensitive to the parameters of acceptable variation are correct to ignore lines of argument that would have to be rejected. But also correct are those who say that no amount of working within the system can secure a humane and rational foreign policy for the United States if its basic orientation is set by those who would maintain an empire abroad for the benefit of its rulers at home. And indeed, those who stand outside the debate—the adherents of the fourth position—do in fact appear to be dissociated from any political base that might be used to gain lawful access to power in the near future. It is their dissociation from power, and not the poverty of their analysis, that explains the irrelevance of their plea for an end to empire and the diplomacy of counterrevolution. It is possible, of course, that economic pressures will so constrain America's foreign policy options in the near future as to lead this fourth position to prevail by default. Thus, America will not be in a position to respond militarily to revolutionary challenges directed at anticommunist governments, unless those challenges are directly perceived as bearing upon the overriding imperative of shoring up the Western position in a deteriorating world economic situation.

# 5 | Counterinsurgency Warfare in Vietnam and International Law

The methods and tactics used by the United States to conduct counterinsurgent warfare in Vietnam during the period 1962-1973 cannot be reconciled with customary law, nor with the treaty rules governing the conduct of international warfare. In fact, the methods and tactics of a large-scale counterinsurgent effort, especially if carried out with high-technology weaponry, necessarily violate these rules of law and amount to crimes under international law. As a result, this prima facie showing of criminality imposes primary responsibility on the civilian and military leaders who devised, approved, and carried out these war policies.

The traditional laws of war, however, did not contemplate the doctrinal interaction of an insurgent challenge and a counterinsurgent response. Neither did they foresee the tactical interaction of low-technology methods of warfare aimed at disguising military identity, and of high-technology methods aimed at preventing the immersion of guerrilla soldiers in the general population. These highly belligerent circumstances compel one of two conclusions: either the law must be virtually, or even totally, suspended under these new conditions, or a counterinsurgent war is ipso facto illegal if carried beyond certain bounds.

Paul Ramsey, a leading American theologian who has done significant writing on the just war doctrine under modern conditions, argued elaborately that the insurgents, by their prior choice of tactics—in particular, their selective terror against civilian officials and their refusal to separate themselves from the civilian population—bear full moral and legal responsibility for any indiscriminate counterinsurgent response. Therefore, according to Ramsey, it is permissible to attack as much of the civilian population as may be necessary in order to complete successfully the counterinsurgent mission.[1]

I cannot accept this analysis, for it seems to impose total responsibility on those who are in fact least able to select their methods and tactics of struggle.[2] The tactical options available to insurgents are particularly limited in many Third World countries, where the state

[75]

monopoly of force is frequently combined with the repression of political opposition. Furthermore, the technology gap inevitably produces very unequal destruction. According to the best information, most of the death and destruction in Vietnam can be attributed to the United States-Saigon military machine, which enjoyed an extraordinary edge in fire power, estimated as high as 450:1. The ratio of civilian casualties is estimated at 10:1.[3]

These figures account for the emphasis on counterinsurgent terrorism in recent war-crimes literature.[4] This concern with terrorism was aptly summarized by sociologist Philip Slater: "What most disturbs thoughtful Americans about Vietnam is the prevalence of genocidal patterns of thought."[5] These genocidal patterns of thought were exemplified by treating all Vietnamese as subhuman, referring to them as "Dinks" (an outlook among GI's generalized as "the Dink complex"), by the use of kill ratios as measures of military performance and progress, and by the evident belief of many American soldiers that even Vietnamese babies were "enemies" who would eventually grow up to serve the Viet Cong. In essence, then, the entire civilian population became the military enemy—either because of their sympathies, their activities, or their status as potential recruits, or even because they were physically indistinguishable from insurgent soldiers. The tendency to identify civilians as belligerents is particularly grotesque in counterinsurgent warfare, since antiguerrilla action is supposedly undertaken for the benefit and protection of the civilian population.

These issues were underscored by the political circumstances of South Vietnam in particular, but were generally relevant throughout Indochina. In the Vietnamese conflict, the major counterinsurgent capability and guidance came from sources external to the locus of the struggle for control. Central to this analysis is the conviction that the United States role as external actor was decisively different from that of North Vietnam as external actor. This distinction is sustained in Article 4 of the Paris Agreement of 1973, which obliges the United States to refrain from intervention in the affairs of South Vietnam, but does not in this context refer to North Vietnam. America's external status strengthened the genocidal tendencies of counterinsurgent warfare by weakening the bonds of empathy between the actors and their victims.

Vietnam provides just one example of intervention by the high-technology power seeking to help wage a distant counterinsurgent war. In all such cases, the external actor values its own lives far more than those of the government it "supports." The war, except for its domestic reverberations, becomes an abstraction for the external power. Consequently, that power prefers military methods and tactics which may cause indiscriminate damage to the enemy, but which help to minimize its own casualties. Because it is difficult to maintain a war effort when high casualties and financial outlays are prolonged and the war itself is unrelated to the defense of the national homeland, there are strong supplemental pressures either to maximize the covertness of the interventionary policies, or to use more expendable troops to carry out the counterinsurgent mission. [6]

Prior to American disengagement, President Nixon's policies of Vietnamization essentially returned the war to its early stages, when military policy-making was centered in Washington but the dying was largely reserved for the Vietnamese. Those tactics and methods that involved minimum American bloodshed, such as air strikes and long-range artillery, were maintained at high intensity despite insistent presidential proclamations about "winding down the war." [7] Indeed, to generalize from the first application of the Nixon Doctrine, Vietnamization may be the prototype for future American involvement in counterinsurgent warfare. Thus, the political lessons that we have apparently chosen to learn from the Vietnam War are: obtain combat soldiers from the regional combat theater; play a major role in training, equipping, and advising them; and supplement their efforts with heavy air support when necessary. [8]

Against this background, concerned Americans and international lawyers in particular must deal with two kinds of issues. To what extent can soldiers and leaders be held accountable for violations of international law? And to what extent can international law be made more responsive to the specific nature of large-scale counterinsurgent warfare?

When these broad legal issues are examined in relation to the Vietnam War and the Nuremberg trials, there emerge three kinds of basic and interdependent concerns regarding potential or hypothetical individual responsibility. First, under what conditions does an externally-based counterinsurgent effort amount to a "war of aggression" that consitutes a "crime against peace"? Second, under what conditions do the tactics and methods of counterinsurgent warfare amount to "war crimes"? And third, under what conditions do the tactics and methods of counterinsurgency amount to "crimes against humanity"? [9] In connection with the third concern, it is important to recognize that actions or persecutions are defined as "crimes against humanity" only if "carried on in execution of or in connection with any crime against peace or any war crime." For purposes of this discussion, it is assumed that at the time of the United States military involvement in Vietnam, Vietnamese civilians were protected persons under the definition of "crimes against humanity."

Four general principles of limitation underlie the specific legal norms with regard to war crimes. They are a prohibition on methods, tactics, and weapons calculated to inflict unnecessary suffering ("the principle of necessity"); a requirement that methods, tactics, and weapons generally discriminate between military and nonmilitary targets and between combatants and civilians ("the principle of discrimination"); a requirement that the military means used bear a proportional relationship to the military end pursued ("the principle of proportionality"); and an absolute prohibition on methods, tactics, and weapons that are inherently cruel in their effects and violate notions of humanity ("the principle of humanity").[10] In certain contexts, such as the treatment of prisoners of war, the sick, or the wounded, these principles are spelled out in detail by positive international law. But ambiguity pervades any operational test of the broader principles of necessity, discrimination, proportionality, and humanity. Does application of these principles therefore depend primarily on the good faith of field commanders and political leaders? And must "good faith" be demonstrated by some effort to assess collateral damage, to mitigate the suffering of civilians incident to the war, to punish flagrant violations of the rules of warfare, and to exercise reasonable diligence in negotiating a settlement?[11]

Various rationales could be used to deny the full protection of the laws of war to combatants in Vietnam. First, it could be argued that the Vietnam conflict was not an international one, even at the time of direct United States military participation, and was therefore subject only to the minimal protections of Article 3 of the 1949 Geneva Convention. However, this contention is unconvincing, in view of the fact that the combat theater generally embraced more than a single country, and each side considered its principal adversary to be the government of a "foreign" state.

A second rationale for disclaiming the applicability of the laws of war in Vietnam is that the overall protection of these laws does not extend to guerrillas, but only to those combatants who comply with the Geneva Convention requirements that soldiers be under the command of someone responsible for his subordinates, have a fixed, distinctive sign recognizable at a distance, carry arms openly, and conduct their operations in accordance with the laws and customs of war. Such requirements seem weighted heavily in favor of the constituted power of governments, infusing the laws of war with the statist bias of the overall system of world order.[12] Furthermore, even if the National Liberation Front guerrillas did not comply with these requirements, their failure to do so in no way should have diminished the duty of United States or Vietnamese military forces vis-a-vis civilian war victims.[13]

This background provides a foundation for examining some of the more controversial methods and tactics of counterinsurgency used in Vietnam, and for assessing the relationship of those methods and tactics to traditional legal concepts of limitation. I emphasize the methods and tactics that appear to violate most directly the general mandates of the law of war: discrimination, proportionality, necessity, and humanity.

The facts are not always clear regarding the character of the counterinsurgent methods and tactics employed in Vietnam, the relationship of those methods to overall military objectives, their impact on the civilian population, or their origins in policy-making procedures. It is also difficult to distinguish between authorized practices and goals, and unauthorized battlefield extensions. However, all these difficulties of investigation and appraisal tend to be exaggerated by those who are not disposed in any case to question the policies put into operation.

The United States government could and should have demonstrated its good faith in upholding the laws of war in Vietnam by undertaking three significant measures. First, it should have allowed a strong role for the function of policy review, whereby proposed methods and tactics could be assessed in light of the four underlying principles of the laws of war, as well as of more specific and substantive rules. Second, it should have maintained an oversight function to assess the military and non-military consequences of policies as implemented. And finally, it should have encouraged compliance by requiring military personnel to respect the limits contained in the laws of war, to report and investigate abuses, and to apprehend and punish those who exceeded authorized conduct on the battlefield.

But the counterinsurgent effort in Vietnam was bent on "drying up the sea," destroying the countryside's value as a sanctuary and political base. Thus, civilians were compelled either to come to the cities ("forced-draft urbanization") or to live under conditions of surveillance amounting to direct governmental control ("strategic hamlets" or refugee camps). Destroying the food supply ("crop-denial" program) and eliminating the protective cover of nature ("defoliation") were both significant facets of the overall counterinsurgent attempt to lay waste any area "liberated" by the insurgents. Because this tendency toward indiscriminate devastation prevailed during the period of active United States participation in the Vietnam War, it determines the appropriate context for evaluating the legal status of the counterinsurgency methods and tactics used during that war.[14]

## Air Warfare

In Vietnam the most characteristic method of large-scale counter-insurgent warfare was massive reliance on air power. This approach was chosen because the counterinsurgent, the United States, possessed a virtual monopoly on air power. Furthermore, continual air strikes, while highly destructive, could be maintained at little domestic political cost: they caused few American deaths.

The United States government generally claimed that its air power was used to disrupt insurgent supply lines and troop concentrations, and to provide close-in logistic support under combat conditions. But many observers alleged a far wider use, including the targeting of non-military objectives such as religious sites and medical facilities.[15] Vice President Spiro Agnew, appearing on national television, explicitly cited the destruction of National Liberation Front "hospital complexes" as one purpose of the 1970 invasion of Cambodia.[16]

In reality, rural Indochina had relatively few targets with direct military significance. Therefore, aside from interdiction bombing, counterinsurgent air power served primarily to clear the countryside of civilians. This broad use of American air power faithfully embodied the logic of the overall counterinsurgent military mission—to break the link between the insurgent armed forces and the general population. To help attain this objective, so-called "free-fire zones" were established, later renamed "specified strike zones" to neutralize adverse publicity.[17] In extensive areas of South Vietnam presumed to be under hostile control, everything that moved was made subject to slaughter from the air. Civilians, even animals, remained at their extreme peril and were treated as the "enemy."

There have been many eyewitness accounts of counterinsurgent air power in action. Congressman Paul McCloskey and Jacques Decornoy of *Le Monde* recorded the extensive bombing damage inflicted by American planes in Laos, where many villages in the northern part of the country were obliterated.[18] Fred Branfman, during his four years as a worker for International Voluntary Services, interviewed many people in Laotian refugee camps and reported that most civilian refugees were fleeing from their homes as a consequence of American air power.[19] Jonathan Schell, a *New Yorker* staff correspondent, and others showed that villages were bombed with the deliberate intention of "generating refugees." The bombardment led to terror and destruction of such magnitude that peasants were forced to abandon their ancestral homes.[20] It has been estimated that between one-fifth and one-half of the population in Laos, Cambodia, and South Vietnam became refugees at some point during the conflict.[21]

In Vietnam, the persistent attempt to separate the insurgents from the general populace led to a counterinsurgent air war that showed little discrimination among targets, no sense of proportion in relation to the desired military end, and precious little regard for the resultant human suffering. While it may be difficult to quantify the full impact of this policy, it is clear that the counterinsurgent air power used in Vietnam extended death and destruction to all sectors of a civilian population that was rarely consulted but seldom spared.

## Antipersonnel Weaponry

For its air attacks throughout Indochina, and especially in Vietnam, the United States relied heavily on massive use of so-called antipersonnel bombs. Although relatively harmless to property, these weapons could inflict the most severe damage on people and animals.[22] With their flesh-piercing pellets and fléchettes, they could maim, disfigure, and kill; delayed-action fuses were even timed to explode after people had left safe hiding places. Also used extensively were cluster bomb units, called CBU's, which sprayed pellets over an area as large as half a mile. These weapons created wounds that were difficult to treat under any circumstances, but especially so given Vietnam's primitive medical facilities.[23]

The use of such antipersonnel weaponry contravened the spirit of one of the earliest modern efforts to limit the conduct of war, the Declaration of St. Petersburg in 1868. This accord sought to outlaw particularly injurious bullets containing explosive, fulminating, or inflammable substances.

Why did American military planners deploy these weapons against civilian targets, knowing full well the inevitable horrendous results? Why were such weapons developed at all? The reason seems apparently to have been a desire to kill, wound, and terrorize as many people as possible with the smallest investment of American money and effort. Presumably, the concentrated use of antipersonnel weapons would influence the general population to sever its ties with the insurgents, and would also raise the kill totals that were used to measure progress in the war.

## Kill Ratios and Body Counts

Military casualty figures are important in any war, but with no fixed territories, often with no enemy armies in the usual sense, and few major battles, other measures of military success must be found to inhibit the tendency to make killing what the war is about. It is now well-known that the emphasis on indiscriminate *killing* of people was developed at the staff and command level as one of the major criteria of military progress during the period of heavy American involvement in ground combat, from 1965 to 1968. Body counts and kill ratios were measures that placed a premium on the sheer magnitude of death and highlighted the statistical comparison between "enemy" and "allied" dead. If these were the accepted indicators of "success," it was clearly in the interest of anti-Viet Cong forces to employ any tactics that increased the kill totals, as well as to catalogue all dead Vietnamese as Viet Cong (which was a natural tendency in any case, in view of the difficulty in telling civilians from combatants). By using body counts as a measure of efficiency, military commanders fostered lethal competition among military units of brigade or smaller size and further eroded inhibitions against killing civilians or attacking civilian target areas after minimum provocation. A single sniper bullet was deemed sufficient cause to obliterate an entire village. In addition, many sworn statements of veterans confirm what the *Duffy* case made clear: that body-count competition created a disposition to kill civilian prisoners, a policy approved by many field commanders.[24]

These measures of progress were logical outgrowths of the prevailing view of counterinsurgent struggle during the Vietnam War. If the people would not leave areas of suspected enemy strength, and if the enemy could not be isolated for discriminate destruction, then the only way left to destroy the insurgent force was to destroy indiscriminately all Vietnamese in the target area. The extraordinary ratio of civilian to military casualties in Vietnam emphasizes the extent to which such policies were inherently incompatible with, indeed antithetical to, the principles of discrimination and proportionality.

## Phoenix Program

During the last years before the Paris Agreement, the United States administered a program designed to destroy the political infrastructure of the NLF by rewarding the capture and assassination of "civilian" suspects. The Phoenix Program set monthly quotas for "elimination." In 1970, for instance, as Ivor Peterson wrote in the *New York Times*, the target was 1,800 "eliminations" a month; 22,341 individuals were killed, captured, or "rallied" to Saigon's side in 1970. Peterson noted that "it is impossible to know for sure" who the dead are. He went on, "They are supposed to be the enemy tax collectors, the political cadre and propaganda teams, the spies and the communications agents who make up the enemy underground. The Americans acknowledged that, inevitably, some of the dead were also in no way connected with the Viet Cong, but were merely the personal enemies of a province chief or some other influential official. Others, like many of the 'nurses,' were probably wives or children caught in the crossfire. As with other aspects of the counterinsurgent program in South Vietnam, much of the killing had little military impact."[25]

## Crop Destruction and Well Poisoning

The logic of counterinsurgency spawned unprecedented efforts to make the countryside as unlivable as possible—for the insurgents and, inevitably, for the population as a whole. The pressure of military logic generated devastating human consequences, through tactics like the massive use of lethal herbicides. Available figures are incomplete and sometimes controversial, but even "official sources agree that the diets of more than half a million civilians . . . [were] chemically destroyed [between the years] 1962-70."[26]

There is evidence to suggest that one widely-used herbicide, Agent Orange, not only caused genetic abnormalities in newborn babies but also produced high rates of miscarriage and stillborn births in heavily subjected areas. But even the knowledge of such possibilities did not prevent the continued use of Agent Orange until prominent American scientists engaged in a successful public demonstration. After official repudiation of Agent Orange, there were disturbing indications that American forces were using new chemicals, such as Agent Blue, with unknown effects on human beings, while leaving behind large quantities of Agent Orange for use by the South Vietnamese.[27]

To destroy food in an Asian country, where problems of widespread, chronic starvation and malnutrition already exist, is surely an extreme method of waging indiscriminate war, for soldiers, whether they be rural insurgents or traditional armies, are usually the last citizens affected by local food shortages. Consequently, the cruel suffering imposed by a program of crop denial must be borne almost exclusively by the noncombatant population.

To some extent, the outcry against herbicides merely led to new tactics designed to achieve the same results. Large earth-moving plows, called "Rome plows" because they were developed in Rome, Georgia, stripped vegetation from 750,000 acres of Vietnamese land as of 1971. They removed the topsoil in such a way that nothing can grow back, and the prospect of serious flooding was greatly increased. E. W. Pfeiffer, a zoologist, reported that "every day from dawn to dusk, between 100 and 150 huge plows . . . [were] making flat wastelands, while severely upsetting the environment."[28]

In a similar vein were the frequent efforts to poison or destroy wells in the Vietnamese countryside. This tactic, which violated the earliest Biblical injunctions, was routinely described in Lt. William Calley's account of his experiences that led to My Lai: "Our mission then was to blow up Vietnamese wells. Or try to. I think that a 500-pounder could do it, could anyhow make the water taste bad. But twenty tons of TNT would make the well deeper, that's all. Our colonel, though, had a thing about wells: a bag about wells, and he wasn't going to tell a lieutenant or listen to a lieutenant tell him, 'Sir, you can't destroy wells with TNT. A bulldozer, maybe . . .' "[29] This tactic, too, would naturally inflict its greatest damage on the very young, the very old, and the sick, because of priorities favoring allocation of scarce resources to insurgent soldiers.

## Atrocities and Torture

The dehumanization of a soldier confronted by brutal military directives has been painfully and abundantly documented. In view of the testimony of many returning Vietnam veterans, Col. Oran Henderson's comment that "every unit of brigade size has its My Lai hidden somewhere" does not seem fanciful. It is clear that the public condemnation of My Lai artificially isolated that massacre from the overall framework of the war.

The story of Lt. Col. Anthony Herbert sheds light on the pervasiveness of atrocities and on the military command's refusal to discourage them.[30] Herbert was virtually repudiated by the army for daring to report to his field commanders the atrocities that he witnessed. It is one thing to cover up atrocities; but it is quite another to indulge their commission, fail to prevent their occurrence, and explicitly encourage military personnel to subvert the conscientious application of the laws of war. In this regard the Herbert case remains both disturbing and revealing.

Herbert contended, apparently accurately, that although he witnessed and reported the most flagrant abuses of captured Vietnamese suspects, the only effective response he was able to obtain from his military superiors was his own dismissal from command responsibility. A remarkable feature of his personal misfortune is that despite his extraordinary military record—Herbert was the most decorated soldier in the Korean War and had received a steady stream of commendations in his various assignments—no one high in the military or civilian structure intervened on his behalf (although admittedly, doubts about Herbert's adequacy as a military commander began to arise prior to the controversy provoked by his allegation of war crimes).

Herbert seems unusual in his ability to have maintained some feeling for limits under the dehumanizing and brutalizing pressures of combat duty in Vietnam. Calley represents a more typical, if perhaps extreme, instance of the American soldier's sensibility in Vietnam, barring those who either opted out via drugs or turned against the conflict by accepting an antiwar position. Calley's outlook is vividly described in his own words about the situation in My Lai:

> [If] those people weren't all VC then prove it to me. Show me that someone helped us and fought the VC. Show me that someone wanted us: one example only! I didn't see any . . . Our task force commander—well, the Colonel's dead and I'd rather not say. His staff, though, said it's a VC area and everyone there was a VC or a VC sympathizer. "And that's because he just isn't young enough or old enough to do anything but sympathize." I even heard a brigadier general say, "My God! There isn't a Vietnamese in this goddam area! They are all VC!" I believed it, and as soon as I understood it, I wasn't frustrated anymore.[31]

While these sentiments may carry the logic of counterinsurgency beyond the zone of normal perceptions, without strenuous interventions at the command level the extreme tactics of My Lai were virtually certain to be used. And they frequently were, especially in low-visibility contexts.

Other counterinsurgent tactics and methods—more impersonal but hardly less indiscriminate and total—also helped set the climate for atrocity. This was particularly true of such military actions as obliterating villages by air or artillery attack; random or computer firing of long-distance artillery and bombing missions; harassment-and-interdiction patterns of fire power deployment; and naval bombardments set by computers to saturate wide areas with a rain of destructive explosives.[32]

Under the circumstances of technological and ethnic distance presented in Vietnam, it is easy to understand how the "enemy" grew to encompass the entire civilian population, and how the most extreme tactics of abuse gained high levels of combat acceptance. The atrocities in the counterinsurgent context of Vietnam had a poignant irony because they were often committed in the hope of winning the "hearts and minds" of the civilian population—what came to be called the "other war" or "pacification." In a tragic distortion of military logic and overall political strategy, the civilians who were the main focus of the "other war" became the principal victims of methods and tactics designed to benefit them.[33] Additional counterinsurgent tactics and methods could be described, but they would merely reinforce the overall analysis that maximum technological ingenuity was used to inflict pain on the "enemy," targeting was necessarily indiscriminate, and the civilian population was forced to bear the brunt of the cruelest tactics.

The insurgents' contribution to the belligerent setting should not be overlooked, of course. Vietcong soldiers intermingled with the general population and conducted their own extensive efforts to persuade, intimidate, and assassinate civilians. In many respects there were notable similarities between the combat behavior of insurgents and counterinsurgents. But the insurgents necessarily operated at a much lower level of technological capability, while they also had far more authentic links with the land and the people.[34] Consequently, the foreign-directed counterinsurgencies in Vietnam and Laos were particularly extreme in their tendency to subordinate the interests of the civilian population to considerations of military effectiveness.

Wherever the political and geographical terrain can support an insurgent movement whose goals include the country's liberation from foreign rule, it is difficult to avoid combat tendencies of the sort used by the NLF. Under these circumstances, the foreign supplier of counterinsurgent weaponry is almost certain to be aligned with the state's most regressive forces—those forces that identify their interests with continued dependence on foreign rule and with the existing structures of economic and political exploitation. This point is important for understanding how the population as a whole becomes the "enemy" of the governing groups, and why only the most extreme military tactics and methods can offset the relation of forces between the contending political factions within the country. It is this imbalance that leads the incumbent government, despite its inherent advantages in a world order system of statist organization, to turn over its own war effort to a foreign government. The incumbent government thereby relinquishes both the symbols and the actuality of self-determination and national sovereignty, in order to maintain the appearance that its particular ruling group is still ascendant on the national level.

## Role of International Law

What can international law achieve in such a setting? There is some temptation to accept the genocidal view of counterinsurgent warfare and to pronounce the entire enterprise as "criminal." But international lawyers have long been reconciled to the pursuit of modest ends. To forbid counterinsurgency is not to prevent it.[35] The most persuasive interpretation of political trends suggests that many wars of this kind will occur in the years ahead. As matters now stand, the foreign policies of most principal governments involve military commitments to governments facing insurgent challenges. This pattern of commitments is partly statist, partly quasi-imperialist, and partly reflective of alliance policies in a world of rival coalitions. In important countries reorientations of policy will therefore have to be brought about, if at all, by domestic political movements.[36]

With respect to issues of individual responsibility, the United States seems already to have gravely compromised the expectations it helped to create at Nuremberg.[37] There is no realistic prospect that the Nuremberg approach will be applied in the Vietnam context. Individual responsibility has been imposed, reluctantly and conservatively, on a few combat soldiers who participated directly in highly publicized killings or abuses. But official policies have not been scrutinized by Congress in relation to the laws of war; judicial redress has been denied in a number of court cases; and no private action has been taken to discredit the main war planners. Both the means and the ends of large-scale externally financed and directed counterinsurgent operations in Vietnam received official endorsement to the very end of American involvement.

A large-scale counterinsurgent effort carried out in a foreign country produces five consequences relevant to the role of international law. First, counterinsurgent methods and tactics of the kind used in Vietnam violate on a massive scale both specific legal prohibitions and the general principles of the laws of wars. Second, there is no organized, influential international effort to condemn these methods and tactics. Indeed, many principal governments in the world depend on counterinsurgent capabilities to maintain their rule at home and to pursue their interests abroad. Third, there is a considerable prospect of continued counterinsurgent warfare throughout the world in the years ahead. Fourth, individual responsibility for war crimes in a counterinsurgent context is likely to remain narrowly confined to participants in face-to-face atrocities.[38] But fifth, the Nuremberg ethos is likely to motivate some individuals to assume responsibility in defiance of governmental directives. The militant antiwar resistance movement in the United States was profoundly influenced by the "wider logic" of Nuremberg.[39]

The fundamental legal challenge of counterinsurgency, however, involves the basic dynamics of large-scale counterinsurgent warfare in situations where, as in Vietnam, a substantial segment of the population provides a shield for the insurgent cause, whether voluntarily or not. The question is not one of effecting legal reform in the sense of establishing workable standards of conduct, but rather one of determining practical and normative issues of individual responsibility. For various reasons, large-scale counterinsurgent warfare like that in Vietnam may not appear to be "aggression" in the Nuremberg sense. The struggle is centered in a single country. There is no border-crossing except for purposes incidental to the war itself. The external actor's role is usually veiled with an invitation, whether genuine or engineered, to enter the conflict. Indeed, the insurgent actor may have itself initiated the struggle, possibly even at the behest of another external actor.[40] Furthermore, the statist bias of the system of world order heavily favors the claims of the constituted regime over those of the insurgents.

For a number of reasons, it is equally complicated to apply the laws of war to the conduct of a large-scale counterinsurgent movement. Because insurgent methods and tactics are inevitably illegal, they tend to vindicate a government's recourse to effective responses, including its request for external military assistance. Yet counterinsurgent weaponry and tactics have been developed only relatively recently, in the context of rapidly widening gaps—technological, bureaucratic, and geographic—between policy-makers and battlefield soldiers.[41] In any event, international law is generally accorded a very limited sphere of applicability in relation to a largely internal war.[42] As a result of all these considerations, American citizens mounted only a very weak effort to shift the appraisal of the Vietnam War beyond the sphere of prudence to that of individual accountability for immoral, illegal, and criminal activities.

What should be done about this apparent suspension of the laws of war in relation to what may well become the most pervasive form of conflict in the latter portion of the twentieth century? There is obviously an urgent educational need to bridge the gap between the cool rhetoric of policy-making and the horror of battlefield execution. But beyond this, there is a need for more formal action, which might usefully include the following steps. An international effort should be made to clarify the conditions under which an externally based insurgency or counterinsurgency would qualify as an aggressive war in the Nuremberg sense. A world conference of governments under United Nations auspices might then seek to establish permissible limits on methods and tactics of counterinsurgency; these limits should apply to all actors, but especially to external participants, in counterinsurgent wars. One possible topic for such a conference would be the threshold limits involving troops, but not equipment.[43] If such a conference were to follow the Hague model of public visibility rather than the Geneva model of technical working sessions of experts, it would serve to illuminate the interplay of legal, political, and moral factors involved in governing the conduct of war.

A domestic reassessment of the methods and tactics of large-scale counterinsurgency is also badly needed to address a number of issues, including the traditional moral and legal conventions of warfare, and the costs of brutalizing and demoralizing American soldiers. At all levels of the military establishment as well, a much greater effort must be made to inculcate knowledge and respect for the laws of war, and a duty to report, investigate, and prosecute apparent violations. In addition, this country should initiate a series of domestic reforms designed to lift the veil of secrecy from United States interventionary diplomacy, including its counterinsurgent operations. Such reforms would enable the Congress, the courts and the public to exercise a greater review function in relation to executive branch initiatives affecting war and peace. And finally, it would be desirable to initiate a series of structural reforms at the international level, designed to improve impartial fact-finding in relation to externally abetted insurgence and counterinsurgency.

These initiatives are not likely to be effective without a fundamental reappraisal of world-wide counterinsurgent activities. This reappraisal can proceed from many angles. However, one specific issue that must be confronted is the impossibility of waging high-technology counterinsurgency in accordance with the limiting principles of discrimination, proportionality, necessity, and humanity. Unless these limiting principles are taken seriously, there can be no meaningful effort to apply law to the conduct of war.

America, with a new political consciousness activated by the bitter experience of the Vietnam War, may seem less prone to engage in a brutal quest for victory. But beleaguered ruling groups all over the world are likely to make maximum use of counterinsurgent methods, with ever more indiscriminate effects. Pakistan's treatment of the East Pakistan uprisings in 1971 provided an ugly foretaste of internally centered counterinsurgency and its tendency to generate international warfare. Unless international society organizes its sentiments and capabilities to oppose these "crimes" carried out against the innocent, the prospects for a just world order are virtually nonexistent. Up to now, we have failed to face squarely the question of individual responsibility in relation to large-scale counterinsurgency. The low profile of this issue may yet turn out to be a critical indication of the decay and disintegration of the present system of world order, which openly acquiesces in the absolutist prerogatives of national sovereignty with respect to internal military and paramilitary challenges. The legal traditions of limitation and accountability are virtually meaningless so long as these statist prerogatives go unquestioned.

Undeniably, certain reforms might be made on both the domestic and international levels to mitigate the character of large-scale counterinsurgent war. However, the more fundamental question concerns the extent to which high-technology weaponry should be used at all against a civilian population or a low-technology insurgent, in order to uphold the power of a foreign ally.

Although much of this analysis is couched in general language, it is primarily a reflection on the American involvement in Vietnam. We need more broadly-based comparative studies of counterinsurgent operations.[44] Also, I have purposely focused on the primary impacts of belligerent operations, rather than on a technical interpretation of the scope of positive rules and the prospects for their extension or revision.[45] Furthermore, it seems clear that the existing law of war embodies the homocentric bias present in all pre-ecological legal and political thought. It therefore fails totally to deal with issues of environmental warfare and "ecocide" or, more restrainedly, with obligatory aspects of man's relation to nature during a war.[46] And finally, much more thought must be devoted to ways of sensitizing public consciousness to the concepts of individual responsibility in relation to the initiation and conduct of counterinsurgent warfare. New procedures must also be developed to make these concepts relevant for legal testing and enforcing. At the present time the Nuremberg idea appears to be repudiated, although its essential claims remain as valid today as most Americans regarded them to be at the end of World War II.[47]

# 6 | Ecocide and the Case for an Ecocide Convention

Indochina during the sixties provided the first modern case where the environment was selected as a "military" target appropriate for comprehensive and systematic destruction. This decision was one of many expressions of the insensitivity of high-technology planners to the consequences of their war policies. It also involved carrying the logic of counterinsurgency warfare to its conclusion when the insurgent threat arises in a tropical locale. Recourse to deliberate forms of environmental warfare was part of the wider military conviction that the only way to defeat the insurgent was to deny him the cover, the food, and the life-support of the countryside. As a result of this conviction, bombers and artillery sought to disrupt all activity, so as to make it more difficult for insurgent forces to mass for effective attack. Such policies led in Indochina to the destruction of vast tracts of forest land and to the so-called "crop-denial programs." Although the United States government eventually altered its tactics, shifting from chemical herbicides to Rome plows as the principal means to strip away the protective cover of the natural landscape, the basic rationale remained: to separate the people from the life-support of their land. In order to succeed, such policies must be coupled with the more familiar counterinsurgency tenet that calls for drying up the sea of civilians in which the insurgent fish are attempting to swim. This drying-up process is translated militarily into making the countryside unfit for civilian habitation. Thus, the military in Vietnam undertook a series of steps—including the establishment of free-fire zones, search and destroy operations, and forcible relocation of villagers into secure areas—which were consciously and deliberately designed to compel peasants to flee their ancestral homes and to turn Indochina into a sea of fire. Therefore, environmental warfare is linked in critical ways to the overall tactics of high-technology counterinsurgency warfare, and extends the indiscriminateness of warfare to the land itself.

It may be more than coincidental that this extraordinary enterprise of deliberate environmental destruction in Indochina confronted us at just the historical moment when we were discovering the extent to which man's normal activities are destroying the ecological basis of life on the planet. These conscious and unconscious tendencies need to be linked in any adequate formulation of the challenge for world order confronting mankind. So far, moreover, environmental warfare has been concentrated in the Third World, a sector of world society that has largely relegated ecological concerns to the bottom of its priorities. Environmental warfare serves as a dramatic reminder that the planet as a whole must mobilize a response to the ecological challenge. Furthermore, through consideration of environmental warfare, Third World leaders and peoples may more readily grasp the relevance of ecological issues for their own societies and may thereby become less short-sighted regarding environmental protection.

On a more technical level, several related questions should be considered. First, to what extent do patterns of environmental warfare violate existing legal criteria? Second, how can we best develop new law that both reflects the uniqueness of recent developments and anticipates future dangers? Clear legal prohibitions respecting environmental warfare might be particularly helpful in shaping future governmental conduct. Many governments, reluctant to protest United States activities in Indochina, have avoided concerning themselves with environmental warfare. However, at this stage it should be possible to formulate a series of public demands that a combined movement of peoples, governments, and world institutions could support in a joint effort to change the situation.

A consideration of the relevance of international law to environmental warfare must cover several points: the connection between treaties and customary international law; the role of world community consensus in interpreting the requirements of international law; the importance of principles of customary international law for interpreting the legal status of disputed tactics of warfare; the importance of moral considerations in determining permissable behavior for governments and their officials; and the significant distinction between the illegality of governmental conduct and the criminality of individual conduct, whether or not in the line of official duty.

## Treaties and Customary International Law

Governments have tended improperly to confine the scope of the law of war to treaty law. Even the United States Army Field Manual 27-10 acknowledges that customary international law complements treaty rules. Because weaponry and battlefield tactics have evolved dramatically since the basic treaties were formulated at the turn of the century, it is important to understand that customary norms do exist and continue to apply, even in a modern high-technology setting. The broad treaties of 1907 bearing on the law of war were themselves specific embodiments of the attempt to relate general principles of belligerent restraint to contemporary war technology tactics. These customary principles, more than the treaty rules to which they gave rise, still remain the primary legal basis for the law of war. Certainly new treaties would be desirable, because they could generate agreement on specific ways of relating modern weaponry and tactics to the customary principles underlying the law of war. In addition, new treaties could authoritatively demarcate legal state behavior. Furthermore, new treaties would be more likely to engender respect, for contemporary government officials who participated personally in the reformulation process would have renewed their commitments by participating in the solemn treaty-making rituals. But in the absence of a new round of Hague-type conferences, the best ground that exists for legal judgment is provided by customary principles of international law. These general principles are very important for understanding the legal status of the various dimensions of environmental warfare and can also provide a framework for examining specific belligerent practices.

## Role of World Community Consensus

The increasing number and diversity of actors on the international scene, and the complexity of international life in general, make it more difficult to assume that procedures based on governmental consent can either develop binding new interpretations of old rules or generate new rules of international law. Therefore, a consensus of governments acting within the scope of formal procedures is increasingly viewed as capable of generating authoritative interpretations and standards. The most significant arena wherein these newer procedures of law creation have been used is the General Assembly of the United Nations. The status of its resolutions remains controversial, especially among the more sovereignty-oriented governments, but the record of reliance on such resolutions, especially in the areas of arms control, space, and human rights, seems to support the contention that these resolutions can, when so intended by a large majority of governments, declare and create law. It is true that the degree of authoritativeness and effectiveness of such lawmaking activity depends on a number of factors, including the strength and quality of consensus, the strength and quality of dissent, the specificity of demand, and the willingness to implement conformity with prior legal and moral expectations. The basic point is

that the General Assembly now possesses a quasi-legislative competence that must be seriously considered whenever it is relevant, especially when it sets forth a prevailing interpretation of a legal rule which
has previously been agreed to.

## Principles of Customary International Law

The four principles of customary international law provide guidelines
for interpreting any belligerent conduct not specifically covered by valid
treaty rule. To recapitulate, they are: the principle of necessity—no
tactic or weapon may be employed in war that inflicts superfluous suffering on its victims, even if used in the pursuit of an otherwise reasonable military objective; the principle of discrimination—no weapon or
tactic may be employed in war that fails to discriminate between military and nonmilitary targets, or that is either inherently or practically
unable to discriminate between combatants and noncombatants; the
principle of proportionality—no weapon or tactic may be employed in
war that inflicts death, injury, and destruction disproportionate to its
contribution to the pursuit of lawful military objectives; and the principle of humanity—no tactic or weapon may be employed in war that is
inherently cruel and offends minimum and widely shared moral sensi-
bilities.

Admittedly, it is difficult to apply these general principles to the
complexities of the battlefield. However, a rule of reason can be used to
identify patterns, as distinct from instances, of clear violation—patterns of weaponry and tactics that simply cannot be reasonably construed as compatible with these principles of overriding constraint.
These principles also reflect the minimum moral intent that underlies
the whole enterprise of a law of war: to strive for a mitigating framework of restraint within the admittedly horrible context of war.

Because of war's dynamic character, customary principles of international law are especially important in relation to the law of war. The
underlying commitment of governments to restraint depends on the
interplay between good-faith adherence to these four principles and the
actualities of war. The famous Martens clause inserted in the Hague
Conventions acknowledged this importance: "Until a more complete
code of the laws of war has been issued, the high contracting Parties
deem it expedient to declare that, in cases not included in the Regulations adopted by them, the inhabitants and belligerents remain under
the protection and the rule of the principles of the law of nations, as
they result from the usages established among civilized peoples, from
the laws of humanity, and the dictates of public conscience."[1]

Widely ratified treaties, such as the 1925 Geneva Protocol on Gas, Chemical, and Bacteriological Warfare, may also attain the status of customary international law by virtue of a consensus among governments active in the world community, even if the consensus falls short of unanimity. Such treaties may thereby bind even nonparties. The reason is analogous to that which explains the potentially authoritative status of General Assembly Resolutions purporting to interpret a treaty. Resolution 2603A (XXIV), for example, which extends the coverage of the Geneva Protocol to tear gas and herbicides, illustrates an effort both to make a binding interpretation of a treaty rule and to extend the treaty's coverage to the entire community, including nonparties. In the text of this resolution the General Assembly "called for the strict observance by all States of the principles and objectives of the Geneva Protocol" and "Declares as contrary to the generally recognized rules of international law as embodied in the Geneva Protocol" the use of tear gas and chemical herbicides. The point is that the United States is bound by "the principles and objectives" of the Geneva Protocol, including the General Assembly's interpretation of its scope, even though the United States itself has not ratified the treaty. In essence, this conclusion implies that an impartial third party—for instance, the International Court of Justice— would adjudge the United States to be bound by the Geneva Protocol and by the United Nations interpretation of its scope. This prediction may be made either because the resolution is itself law-proclaiming and authoritative, or because it is indeed an accurate declaration of the proper meaning of the Geneva Protocol, and a parallel norm in customary international law.

As a practical matter, United States ratification may still be important because much of the international law of war depends for effective application on self-enforcement, especially when the actor is a major state not in conflict with, and hence not deterred by, another major state. Accordingly, the United States would be much more likely to respect the Geneva Protocol if it explicitly ratified the treaty, although it is nevertheless bound by its terms even without such ratification.[2]

A final point concens the common contention that governments have generally used whatever weapons and tactics seemed militarily advantageous, paying little if any heed to restraining principles of customary international law or treaty law. In fact, however, this is not necessarily so. For example, evidence suggests that in the Pacific theater during World War II, the United States—even though not itself a party to the Geneva Protocol—respected legal restraints on the use of gas, despite the military advantages that might have been gained by its use. There is even a common misunderstanding that a claim of military necessity overrides legal restraints. In reality, the agreed understanding of governments embodied in the law of war is that legal restraints have been formulated with due regard for military necessity, and that any further unilateral abridgments are violations. To say that the law of war is frequently violated is simply to affirm that governments are not very law-abiding in this area, and may indeed be criminally disposed, especially when their vital interests are at stake. This conclusion demonstrates the need merely for devising better law enforcement—perhaps spearheaded by a law-minded citizenry—but not surely for suspending or negating these international rules.

## Moral Factors

The law of war attempts to reconcile minimum morality with the practical realities of war. This reconciliation is best summarized in the four principles of customary international law. These principles, which embody the moral sense of the community, provide a legislative direction for the expansion and application of international law. No activity is more relevant to international law than war, if one contends that the law does and should reflect what ought to be done or not done by governments and their representatives. In this way, morality attempts both to fill the legislative vacuum created by the institutional deficiencies of international society and to adapt law somewhat to the rapidly changing realities of war. Although the growth of the international law of war may therefore contain a greater element of retroactivity than constitutional systems of domestic society, the retroactivity exists only on a legalistic plane. The Nuremberg initiative provides the most dramatic illustration of a legislative spasm in international law that rested on the firmest grounds of shared morality, but which aroused criticism from legalistically inclined observers.[3] Given the public outrage over the desecration of the land at the time of rising environmental consciousness, the Indochina experience presents an opportunity comparable to Nuremberg. Surely it is no exaggeration to consider the forests and plantations treated by Agent Orange as an Auschwitz for species of trees such as the mangrove tree or nipa palm. And just as the Genocide Convention came along to formalize part of what had already been condemned and punished at Nuremberg, so an Ecocide Convention could help to carry forward into the future a legal condemnation of environmental warfare in Indochina.

## Distinction Between Government and Individual

International law is characteristically concerned with regulating the behavior of governments. The laws of war are binding on governments, although national legal systems generally make the laws of war binding on combat personnel, with criminal sanctions applicable in the event of violations.[4] The Nuremberg approach makes individuals criminally liable for violating the laws of war even if the violations were committed in the line of duty and in deference to orders issued by bureaucratic or military superiors. That is, the Nuremberg approach to international law directs that individual adherence to the laws of war take precedence over normal obligations to domestic law or military commands. The practical consequences of this directive have presented conscientious Americans with many difficulties during the Indochina War. The Nuremberg obligation may be taken more seriously in the United States than elsewhere because of the tradition respecting individual conscience and because the war crimes trials after World War II were so much a product of American initiative. Daniel Ellsberg and Anthony Russo, draft evaders and tax resisters, and an expanding national movement of civil disobedience, all draw support from the wider logic of Nuremberg. This wider logic implies that a citizen is bound by duty to refuse participation in illegal war policies or an illegal war; it also creates a legal basis for individual action to prevent governmental crimes of war.

Now it is possible to assess the legality of the principal components of the environmental warfare waged in Indochina. It is important legally to distinguish between weapons or tactics that are designed specifically to damage the environment, and tactics or weapons (such as bombs) which are designed to strike human or societal targets but which may also, as a side effect, damage the environment. In addition, specific instances of environmental warfare must be distinguished from persistent patterns of warfare whose cumulative effects on ecosystems can properly be called "ecocide." Finally, it is necessary to decide whether the scope of environmental warfare includes the effects of these weapons on humans. On one level, the issue is whether for this purpose man is to be conceived as an integral element of the "environment"; on a more practical level, the issue is whether human side-effects of chemical weapons like 2, 4, 5-T are to be included in a discussion of environmental warfare. The problem with the more expansive definition is that all forms of warfare are detrimental to man and his artifacts. In this sense all warfare could be conceived as environmental or ecological warfare, thereby missing the distinctive feature of American warfare in Indochina and the specific dangers of ecosystem destruction posed by high-technology counterinsurgency warfare, especially in tropical settings. At the same time, it is artificial to ignore altogether the specifically human concerns, and it seems appropriate to orient the subject toward a concept of human ecology, wherein bonds between man and nature provide an essential focus for inquiry. Environmental warfare, therefore, is defined to include all those weapons and tactics that intend either to destroy the environment per se or to disrupt on a sustained basis the normal relationships between man and nature. The focus is on environmental warfare only as practiced by the United States in Indochina, rather than on the full gamut of weaponry detrimental to environmental values, which would certainly include as well biological, radiological, and nuclear weapons. The weapons or tactics used in Indochina whose legal status is considered are herbicides, deforestration, bombardment and artillery fire, and weather modification.

## Herbicides

There is extensive information available on the use of herbicides in the Indochina War, principally in South Vietnam.[5] The major chemicals used as military herbicides were Agent Orange (a mixture of 2,4-D and 2,4,5-T), used against forest vegetation; Agent White (a mixture of 2,4-D and picloram), also used primarily against forest vegetation; and Agent Blue (cacodylic acid), used against rice and other crops. Defense Department figures disclose a steady escalation in the use of chemical herbicides from 1962 through the early months of 1968, with a slight tapering off through the middle of 1969, when the final figures on usage in the war were released. In this period, 4,560,000 acres of forest land and 505,000 acres of crop land were sprayed, amounting to a total acreage of 5,065,000, or more than 10 percent of the entire area of South Vietnam. The rate of application was roughly thirteen times the dose recommended by the United States Drug Administration for the occasional domestic use of herbicides as weed killers.

President Richard Nixon reportedly terminated the use of herbicides for crop destruction in the Indochina War and announced a phase-out of the defoliation efforts in 1970. But defoliation was not halted by Nixon. Instead, the military task was taken over by plows, which from an ecological point of view achieve even more disastrous results than chemicals.

The environmental damage caused by defoliants still cannot be fully assessed. However, strong evidence suggests that some varieties of trees in South Vietnam, particularly nipa palms and mangroves, were not merely defoliated but destroyed by a single application; multiple applications killed other trees. A study sponsored by the respected American Association for the Advancement of Science (AAAS) concluded that half of the hardwood trees north and west of Saigon were damaged. Arthur Westing, a professor of botany and a specialist on environmental warfare, estimated that by December 1970, 35 percent of South Vietnam's dense forests had been sprayed: 25 percent once, 10 percent more than once. Madame Nguyen Thi Binh, speaking in Paris on behalf of the Provisional Revolutionary Government of South Vietnam, alleged that between 1961 and 1969, 43 percent of arable land and 44 percent of forest land had been sprayed at least once and in many cases, two, three, or more times. In this process, over 1,293,000 persons were "directly contaminated."[6] John Lewallen, an environmentalist with several years' duty as a civilian volunteer in Vietnam, concluded: "The forests of South Vietnam have not been merely damaged for decades or centuries to come. Nor have they simply been deprived of rare tree species. It is probably that many areas will experience an ecosystem succession under which forest will be replaced by savanna."[7] Often elephant grass overwhelms a forest area that has been so heavily defoliated, and reforestation is then prevented altogether.

There is ample evidence, then, that military herbicides were used extensively throughout South Vietnam, especially along rivers and estuaries, on village and base perimeters, and on suspected base areas and supply trails. Defoliants were generally sprayed from the air in specially fitted C-123 cargo planes, often near populated areas; wind factors significantly spread their dispersal beyond the intended areas. Consequently, the herbicides contaminated crops, which were then either destroyed or passed on teratogenic effects to unborn children. Numerous authenticated reports cited human and animal poisoning throughout the course of the war.

The basic military justification for the massive defoliation program was the need to deny the NLF protective cover, thereby guarding defensive positions against ambush and surprise attack, and improving target identification for offensive operations. The destruction of crops was justified as an effort to deny food to the NLF forces in areas under their control.

The legal rationale of the United States government was formulated by J. Fred Buzhardt, then general counsel to the Department of Defense, in a letter dated April 5, 1971, to Senator J. William Fulbright, who was chairman of the Senate Foreign Relations Committee:

> Neither the Hague Regulations nor the rules of customary international law applicable to the conduct of war prohibit the use of anti-plant chemicals for defoliation or the destruction of crops, provided that their use against crops does not cause such crops as food to be poisoned by direct contact, and such use must not cause unnecessary destruction of enemy property.

The Geneva Protocol of 1925 adds no prohibitions relating either to the use of chemical herbicides or crop destruction to those above. Bearing in view that neither the legislative history nor the practice of States draw chemical herbicides within its prohibitions, any attempt by the United States to include such agents within the Protocol would be the result of its own policy determination, amounting to a self-denial of the use of weapons. Such a determination is not compelled by the 1907 Hague Regulations, the Geneva Protocol of 1925, or the rules of customary international law. [8]

In essence, the United States government claimed that no existing rules of international law prohibit the military use of herbicides.

It seems clear, however, that an overwhelming majority of governments hold the view that the prohibitions of the Geneva Protocol bind nonparties as well as parties, and extend to military herbicides. The protocol is binding because it enjoys the status of customary international law, a status that the United States has not seriously challenged. Indeed, the United States government has avowed its adherence to the terms of the protocol, contending only that these terms do not extend to military herbicides or riot-control gasses. In submitting the protocol to the Senate Foreign Relations Committee for ratification in 1971, Secretary of State William Rogers provided an accompanying statement that said: "it is the United States' understanding of the protocol that it does not prohibit the use in war of riot-control agents and chemical herbicides." [9]

Such an understanding of the scope of the protocol is not shared by the international community as a whole. United Nations General Assembly Resolution 2603A (XXIV), supported by a majority of 80-3, with 36 abstentions, indicated its express intention to dispel "any uncertainty" over the scope of the protocol and contained the following operative statement: "*Declares* as contrary to the generally recognized rules of international law as embodied in the Geneva Protocol the use in international armed conflict of any chemical agents of warfare: chemical substances, whether gaseous, liquid, or solid, which might be employed because of their toxic effects on man, animals, or plants." [10] This declaration of law provides a dual basis for disregarding the more restrictive interpretation advanced by the American government. First, Resolution 2603A constitutes evidence of what most governments regard as the scope of the prohibition. Second, the consensus supporting the resolution is itself enough to give its law-declaring claims an authoritative status, by virtue of the quasi-legislative competence enjoyed by the General Assembly.

The broader view of the scope of the Geneva Protocol, derived from positive international law, also accords with the emerging moral consensus and community expectations relating to environmental quality.[11] Since the scope of this treaty rule is under question, it is desirable to seek a determination that accords with unfolding community sentiments. On the level of customary international law, the broad principles of discrimination and proportionality disqualify the novel claim to attack vast areas of forest land in order to deprive an adversary of natural cover. It is questionable whether the basic character of a high-technology counterinsurgency warfare waged against a low-technology opponent can ever be reconciled with the framework of restraint provided by the four principles of customary international law. In this sense the problems raised by claims to use military herbicides are part of a larger set of legal concerns.

On balance, the conclusion is inescapable that the American use of military herbicides in Indochina violated the Geneva Protocol, which is both a treaty and a standard of prohibition that enjoys the status of customary international law. This assessment of existing law could be confirmed by requesting the International Court of Justice to formulate an advisory opinion on the status and scope of the Geneva Protocol. Such an advisory opinion is not really necessary, but if, as expected, it did confirm the interpretation of the protocol embodied in Resolution 2603A, it would once and for all lay the American contention to rest.

With respect to crop destruction, the prohibition against military herbicides rests on even stronger legal ground. As one academic expert on the laws of war, Tom Farer, pointed out, such tactics are "at best indiscriminate, and they may in fact discriminate against civilians because, even if the food supply which survives defoliation was distributed evenly, in absolute terms civilians would suffer disproportionately in that there are more of them and many civilians, the young, for instance, have particularly intense needs for certain foods."[12] Indeed, government studies have convincingly shown that crop destruction as an intentional military tactic had the principal effect of reducing the food available to civilians, because NLF food requirements were given priority in areas under their control, and were small enough in relation to the food available to be satisfied. A former high official in the so-called "pacification" program in Vietnam, L. Craig Johnstone, described the effects of crop destruction:

> In the course of investigations of the program in Saigon and in the provinces of Vietnam, I found that the program was having much more profound effects on civilian noncombatants than on the enemy. Evaluations sponsored by a number of official and unofficial agencies have all concluded that a very high percentage of all the food destroyed under the crop destruction program had been destined for civilian, not military use. The program had its greatest ef-

fects on the enemy-controlled civilian populations of central and northern South Vietnam. In Vietnam the crop destruction program created widespread misery and many refugees.[13]

Such effects on the civilian population were evidently a central ingredient of counterinsurgent strategy vis-à-vis the countryside. Therefore, crop destruction was fully consistent with other war policies that aimed at generating and then "pacifying" refugees, such as free-fire zones, harassment and interdiction, artillery fire, forcible removal of refugees, and search-and-destroy missions. The use of chemical herbicides to destroy crops destined for civilian consumption provides a focal point for dual allegations of ecocide and genocide.

## Deforestation

A second major form of warfare waged directly against the environment was to clear the land of vegetation by means of systematic plowing or bulldozing. According to Paul R. Ehrlich, the author on population and environmental policy, and John P. Holdren, his collaborator:

> Perhaps the crudest tool the United States is using to destroy the ecology in Indochina is the "Rome plow." This is a heavily armored D7E caterpillar bulldozer with a 2.5 ton blade. The Rome plow can cut a swath through the heaviest forest. It has been used to clear several hundred yards on each side of all main roads in South Vietnam. In mid-1971 five land clearing companies were at work, each with some thirty plows, mowing down Vietnamese forests. By then some 800,000 acres had been cleared and the clearing was continued at a rate of about 2,000 (3 square miles) daily.[14]

E. W. Pfeiffer and A. H. Westing, two highly respected scientists, concluded that by 1971 Rome plowing "had apparently replaced the use of herbicides to deny forest cover and sanctuary to the other side." They also concluded that Rome plowing was more effective than chemicals and "probably more destructive of the environment." This tactic was used to "scrape clean the remaining few areas of the Boi Loi Woods northwest of Saigon." Pfeiffer and Westing visited an area of forest that had been plowed several years previously and found it covered with cogon grass which, according to these experts, makes "further successional stages to the original hardwood forest very unlikely."[15] It is clear that such plowing inflicted ecological damage that may last for a very long period of time, perhaps even permanently.

As far as I am aware, no attempt has been made to defend Rome plowing as a legitimate tactic of war. A legal defense of this practice, if attempted, would undoubtedly rest on the alleged military legitimacy of denying protective cover to the enemy, and on the absence of specific prohibitions in either treaty law or customary international law.

The existing law of war reflects its pre-ecological origins. Therefore, none of its standards or rules could anticipate a military strategy designed to destroy the environment as such. But Article 22 of the Annex to the Hague Convention on Land Warfare is relevant here in stating that "the right of belligerents to adopt means of injuring the enemy is not unlimited." And the Supreme Court's interpretation of Constitutional norms often reflects an evolving sense of limits within the world community, especially when its interpretations must be applied to conduct not contemplated at the time of ratification. Nevertheless, it is not easy to conclude that Rome plowing, however offensive to ecological consciousness, constitutes a violation of existing standards of international law. This difficulty points up the need for formulating clear standards of prohibition in a new protocol on environmental warfare.

Finally, it is possible to view such environmental devastation as "a crime against humanity" in the Nuremberg sense, suggesting again the quasi-legislative potentialities created by a situation of moral outrage. The destruction of Vietnamese forests is likened to crimes against humanity by way of "human ecology," for the environment is organically interrelated with human existence. Indeed, some relatively hard evidence supports this inference. The official history of the United Nations War Crimes Commission reported:

> During the final months of its existence the Committee was asked in a Polish case (Commission No. 7150) to determine whether ten Germans, all of whom had been heads of various Departments in the Forestry Administration in Poland during the German occupation (1939-1944), could be listed *as war criminals on a charge of pillaging* Polish public property. It was alleged that the accused in their official capacities caused the wholesale cutting of Polish timber to an extent far in excess of what was necessary to preserve the timber resources of the country, with a loss to the Polish nation of the sum of 6,525,000,000 zloty. It was pointed out that the Germans, who had been among the first as a nation to foster scientific forestry, had entered Poland and willfully felled the Polish forests *without the least regard to the basic principles of forestry.* The Polish representative presented a copy of a circular signed by Goering under the date of 25th January, 1940, in which were laid down the principles for a policy *of ruthless exploitation of Polish forestry.* It was decided by the Committee that prima facie existence of a war crime had been shown and nine of the officials charged were listed as accused war criminals.[16]

## Bombardment and Artillery Fire

Pfeiffer and Westing summarized the general information available through 1971:

> In the seven years between 1965 and 1971 the U.S. military forces exploded 26 billion pounds (13 million tons) of munitions in Indochina, half from the air and half from weapons on the ground . . . For the people as a whole it represents an average of 142 pounds of explosive per acre of land and 584 pounds per person . . . most of the bombardment was concentrated in time (within the years from 1967 on) and in area. Of the 26 billion pounds, 21 billion were exploded within South Vietnam, one billion in North Vietnam, and 2.6 billion in Southern Laos.[17]

Later bombing augmented these awesome statistics still further. Unlike herbicide and deforestation practices, bombardments were not designed per se to destroy the environment. But although the element of intentionality was probably absent, on the basis of past experience the environmental consequences of bombing patterns could not have been unknown to the war planners. Available evidence indicates that three distinct patterns of ordinance use should be separately considered for purposes of legal analysis: craterization, "daisy-cutter" super-bombs and electronic or systematic bombing, and free-fire zones.

Pfeiffer and Westing estimated that 26 million craters were made, covering an area of 423,000 acres and representing a displacement of about 3.4 billion cubic yards of earth. Much of the cratering was caused by 500-pound bombs dropped from high altitude B-52 flights or from large artillery shells. Such a bomb typically produces a crater that is thirty-to-forty feet wide and five-to-twenty feet deep, depending on topographical conditions, although larger craters have been reported. The craters have numerous effects on the Vietnamese terrain and people. Arable and timber land were withdrawn from use virtually indefinitely. Unexploded bombs or fragments made the neighboring land unsatisfactory for normal use and caused injury to man and animals. Craters that penetrated the water table became breeding grounds for mosquitoes, increasing the incidence of malaria and dengue fever. Craters also displaced soil and, especially in hilly areas, accentuated soil runoff and erosion, causing laterization of the land in and around craters. And finally, bombardment of forest areas harmed the timber industry, either by outright destruction or by weakening the trees with metal shards and making them vulnerable to fungus infection.[18]

The legal rationale for the bombardment is that it involved legitimate targeting of suspected concentrations of enemy troops or supplies. Environmental damage was an unintended side-effect that was in no way regulated by existing international law. The bombing is subject to independent attack only to the extent that it was indiscriminate. The demonstration of environmental damage adds little to the legal analysis of the Indochina bombing patterns.

This rationale is correct to the extent that no explicit rules of prohibition seem available to assess the legal status of craterization. However, the scale and magnitude of bombardment raises special issues under Article 22 of the Annex to the Hague Convention on Land Warfare, and in relation to the Crimes Against Humanity as specified at Nuremberg.

It does seem desirable, nevertheless, to devise new legal rules and principles to deal explicitly with the environmental side-effects of standard war policies. It is also necessary to regard belligerent action that exceeds the enviroment's capacity quickly to absorb and respond as constituting the independent crime of ecocide.

Until these crimes are specified, one might ask whether a Nuremberg tribunal convened today to assess the liability of American leaders for the craterization in Indochina would convict on this count. It is difficult to predict the outcome on this issue, because the law is murky and because American civilian and military leaders apparently had no direct intention of destroying the environment.

After mid-1971 gigantic bombs called "daisy-cutters," weighing 15,000 pounds, were dropped at an estimated rate of two per week in South Vietnam to establish instant clearings for fire-base helicopter landing areas. According to some accounts these bombs were also dropped on areas of suspected troop concentrations. Such bombs kill all animals and people within a quarter-mile radius, and also completely deforest the area they "clear."

The legal rationale for these bombs is that their damage is incidental to a valid military purpose, in a context where no rule of prohibition exists. The specific action does not, in fact, seem to violate positive norms of international law. The condemnation of it is partly an expression of outrage in relation to the overall devastation of Indochina, and partly an expression of an emerging ecological consciousness. Again, the legal retroactivity of any prohibition in a Nuremberg type of setting would be more than offset by a sense that such bombs are indiscriminate and hence violate the prohibition against indiscriminate warfare which is a tenet of customary international law.

The other bombing patterns, which included electronic battlefields, saturation bombing, and free-fire zones, were indiscriminate with respect to all that breathed and moved. The saturation bombing also devastated the land and tended to depopulate the area under attack.

Fred Branfman described in agonizing detail the total destruction of the idyllic and prosperous agricultural subsociety of 50,000 in the Plain of Jars in Laos.[19]

There is no legal rationale for these practices. The facts have therefore been officially repressed or distorted by the United States government. When these war policies involved attacks on civilian targets, such as rural villages, they were in clear violation of international law. The legal status of separate acts of environmental destruction is, at present, more problematic. When an inhabited ecosystem such as the Plain of Jars was devastated by direct action, the United States government committed a crime against humanity in the spirit of the Nuremberg findings.

## Weather Modification

There is increasing indication that the United States seeded clouds over Laos in order to increase rainfall. The military rationale for this tactic was to muddy or flood the network of roadways constituting the Ho Chi Minh trail. A cloud-seeding plane, like a reconnaissance plane that drops flares, could accomplish its mission by dropping 35-to-100 pounds of silver iodine over a six-hour period. The Defense Department shrouded the subject in secrecy and refused to make any statements of unequivocal denial or confirmation. Nevertheless, a series of collateral accounts, including references in the Pentagon Papers and some leaked information that appeared on March 18, 1971 in a news column by Jack Anderson, create a strong basis for believing that weather modification was used as a deliberate weapon of war in Indochina.[20]

Such tactics, because of their relative covertness and potentially devastating impact on the target area (and perhaps on global weather patterns as well), pose a very great danger to the future of world order. It is vital to arouse public concern at this time and to seek a clear-cut prohibition on weather modification for military purposes.

Because of the secrecy that surrounds this activity and because of its very novelty, it is virtually impossible to carry legal analysis any further at this stage. Even more than poison gas and bacteriological weapons, weather modification for military purposes poses dangers of indiscriminate and uncontrollable damage. It is clearly a menacing genie that must be recaptured and confined for all time, hopefully through the adoption of an absolute legal prohibition.

The legal status of the main elements of environmental warfare in Indochina highlights two distinct sets of tasks. First, steps must be taken to strengthen and clarify international law with respect to the prohibition of weapons and tactics that inflict environmental damage, and with respect to the designation as a distinct crime of those cumulative war effects that do not merely disrupt but substantially and irreversibly destroy a distinct ecosystem. Second, steps must be taken to rectify the ecological devastation of Indochina, to censure the United States for these actions, to impose on the United States a minimum burden of making available ample resources to permit ecological rehabilitation to the extent possible in the shortest time and in the most humane manner, and to assess fully the various ecological effects of the war on Indochina.

To accomplish the first objective of clarifying international law, I propose taking the kind of action illustrated by the following draft instruments: An International Convention on the Crime of Ecocide (Appendix 2); A Protocol on Environmental Warfare (Appendix 3); and A Petition on Ecocide and Environmental Warfare, to be signed by individuals and nongovernmental organizations, addressed to the Secretary-General of the United Nations (Appendix 4). To deal with the more specific problems generated by the Indochina War, I propose adopting measures based on the following draft document: A Peoples' Petition of Redress on Ecocide and Environmental Warfare, addressed to governments and to the United Nations (Appendix 5).

Special difficulties pertain to taking appropriate legal action concerning the environmental devastation in Indochina. First of all, as a preeminent state in the world system, the United States is able to block serious inquiry into this subject. In fact, this obstructive capability probably accounted for the failure to inscribe the issue of environmental warfare on the agenda of the United Nations Conference on the Human Environment. The second difficulty is closely related to the first: the United Nations is not able to pursue effective initiatives without the assenting participation of its most powerful members, especially the United States. The organization's silence through a decade of warfare in Indochina is a shocking revelation of the Charter's impotence whenever its violation is primarily attributable to one of the superpowers. Third, the United States did not lose the Indochina War in the way in which Germany lost World War II. Consequently, its leaders and policies were never subjected to critical review by an independent commission of inquiry, nor by an intergovernmental tribunal.

Because of these realities, it is necessary to develop an action plan with some prospect for success. Such a plan has to discount the possibilities of relying on governments or intergovernmental organizations, although governments that are willing to formulate a critical response—as did Swedish Premier Olaf Palme's at the Stockholm Conference on the Human Environment in June 1972 when he denounced the practice of environmental warfare in Vietnam—help greatly to document the failure of governmental institutions to safeguard the common heritage of humanity. Similarly, petitions seeking redress of grievances signed by individuals and directed at institutions entrusted with formal responsibility help to reveal institutional responses that sustain or acquiesce in the practice of environmental warfare and ecocide. Such efforts to present petitions emphasize the need to stimulate a world populist movement, both nationally and internationally, as a way of eroding the power of governments over human and ecological destinies.

The most important arenas of action may be nongovernmental. At some point it may even be desirable to organize a peoples' commission of inquiry and redress that seeks to focus on the facts of environmental devastation and ecocide in Indochina, and to formulate appropriate demands for censure and relief.

On a more fundamental level, the issues of environmental warfare are peculiarly resistant to intergovernmental collaboration because of their apparent link with counterinsurgency warfare. It is the counterinsurgent who tends to pursue the tactics and rely on the weapons most damaging to the environment. That is, governments have a particular interest in being able to use their technological advantages to neutralize whatever advantages of dispersal and maneuverability an insurgent may enjoy. In Indochina, because of this technological and tactical gap, almost all the serious environmental damage was inflicted by the forces aligned with the incumbent government. It can even be argued that without military herbicides, Rome plowing, and massive air power, battlefield outcomes would have decisively favored the insurgent forces. Therefore, environmental devastation seems to be a virtually inevitable byproduct of a sustained campaign of counterinsurgency, especially if carried out in the tropics against insurgent forces that enjoy a strong base of popular support. Under such circumstances, not only must the sea be drained to imperil the fish, but its life-supporting ecology must be destroyed as well. Because of the prospect of future insurgent challenges, it is unlikely that governments will assent to legal prohibitions that would foreclose military options for counterinsurgent response—not, at least, without the pressure of a major populist campaign.

These considerations suggest wider grounds for skepticism as to legal responses. Even in the Third World there is a large technological gap between the weaponry and tactics of a constituted government, and those available to internal challengers. Throughout the world most governments are confronted by insurgent challenges and seek to overcome such threats with any and all effective means. This common governmental predisposition is abetted by arms sales and transfers, which make all governments increasingly dependent on high-technology military establishments. From this dependence the willingness and capability to wage environmental warfare is almost certain to follow.

It should be understood that international law, by and large, continues to reflect the perceived self-interest of governments. In terms of its formulation and its implementation, international law is a consensual system. It presupposes that reciprocal interests will uphold voluntary compliance. When these interests do not exist or are not perceived to exist, then it is difficult to generate new law or enforce old law in international affairs. This is peculiarly true for the law of war, which raises vital questions of governmental survival. Because the insurgent actor, unlike sovereign states, is unrepresented in the international legal order, the law is likely to be shaped to serve the perceived military interests of governments, that is, to serve actual and potential counterinsurgents.

Such conclusions reinforce the view that the state system is inherently incapable of organizing the defense of the planet against ecological destruction. Therefore, the prospects for ecological protection are intimately linked with the prospects for initiating a world populist movement that can incorporate the ecological imperative while simultaneously working to secure equity for all men on earth.

# 7 | A Nuremberg Perspective on the Pentagon Papers Trial

The most celebrated case brought by the United States government against domestic opponents of the Vietnam War arose from the release in 1971 of major portions of the so-called Pentagon Papers by Daniel Ellsberg and Anthony Russo. Because the government's misconduct in *United States v. Russo* eventually led to the dismissal of the charges, important questions embedded in the litigation concerning the application of international criminal law were never resolved, although interim rulings by Judge Matthew Byrne suggested their disposition at the trial level.[1] In particular, the defendants Ellsberg and Russo tried to argue that the disclosure of the Pentagon Papers was a reasonable and effective method of terminating their complicity in a war whose conduct violated international law.

International law imposes criminal liability for complicity in crimes against the peace. It can be argued that this potential liability of Americans has been officially recognized as part of the American law. Hence, fairness to potential defendants makes it essential that they be allowed to rely on any defense that arises out of their accountability under international law standards. In addition, the substantive merits of international criminal law make it desirable to encourage national implementation, including a recognition that individual action undertaken to prevent the consummation of international crimes should be accorded precedence over conflicting dictates of national law.

These issues are paramount in *United States v. Russo*. The released portion of the Pentagon Papers contained strong evidence to support a reasonable belief that the United States had pursued and was continuing to pursue in Vietnam a policy which violated international law, and that the defendants, Ellsberg and Russo, could reasonably infer that they were accessories to the formulation and execution of public policies which violated international law. Furthermore, the defendants could have been internationally indicted for these acts in accordance with precedents established by the Allied prosecutions of German citizens at Nuremberg following World War II.[2] Therefore, by partially disclosing the contents of the Pentagon Papers, the defendants were making a reasonable effort to terminate their complicity in such illegal acts.[3] Furthermore, the "superior orders" dictated by domestic law in the form of classification restrictions to prohibit the disclosure of such information would not act as a bar to international prosecution or conviction based on the alleged violations of international criminal law. Consequently, a national prosecution should allow defendants to demonstrate that their actions, which might appear illegal if judged exclusively by national standards, were undertaken in accordance with the standards of a higher applicable law, namely, international criminal law. To disallow such a demonstration in an American court seems to deny defendants a fundamental ingredient of due process.

Beyond these considerations of procedural fairness in criminal cases lies a fundamental issue of public policy. To encourage nonviolent acts of conscience based on a reasonable belief of the sort taken by the defendants in the Pentagon Papers case in fact serves the national and global interest. That is, there is more at stake here than fairness to the defendants; what is really at issue is whether civilians should be any more beholden to "superior orders" than are soldiers confronted by unlawful battlefield commands. To accept the Nuremberg defense in a national trial setting is one way of rejecting any such dichotomy. To accept such a defense as permissible is *not*, however, to vindicate any or all specific actions attributed to a particular defendant. A defendant's reliance on the claim that he was opposing the commission of an international crime is subject to an appraisal of reasonableness. To succeed with the Nuremberg defense, a defendant must show two things:—first, that he acted on the basis of reasonable belief that an international crime had been committed; and—second, that his action was a reasonable and prudent way of either terminating his own complicity in the criminal conduct *or* seeking to terminate the criminal conduct itself.

In other words, theoretically the Nuremberg defense is not restricted to those who, like Ellsberg and Russo, had been participants at some stage of the allegedly criminal enterprise. It can be invoked by any citizen who has a reasonable belief that an international crime has been or is being committed. However, the fact of complicity should be considered in determining whether there are sufficient objective and subjective bases for such a reasonable belief.

The case involving Karleton Armstrong is an apt example. By his own admission, Armstrong participated in exploding a bomb in the Army Mathematics Research Center at the University of Wisconsin on August 24, 1970. Despite precautions taken by the defendant to assure that the building would be unoccupied at the hour planned for the explosion, the bomb accidentally killed Robert Fassnacht, a research physicist then present in the building. Armstrong pleaded guilty in a Wisconsin state court to charges of second-degree homicide but was allowed to raise the Nuremberg defense during an extensive hearing held to determine the proper sentence.[4] Although a complete record on the Nuremberg defense was made in the *Armstrong* case, his sentence was reduced from the maximum only by the amount of time he had already spent in jail pending disposition of the case. The *Armstrong* case illustrates the relevance of the Nuremberg defense in a noncomplicity context but indicates that allowing the Nuremberg defense to be made does not by itself ensure its influence on the outcome of a trial proceeding or even on the extent of punishment imposed on a criminal defendant.

## Applicability of International Criminal Law

Article VI, paragraph 2, of the United States Constitution provides that rules of international law embodied in treaties made under the authority of the United States are part of the "supreme Law of the Land." Mr. Justice Gray, in the Supreme Court decision of *The Paquete Habana,* concluded that even in nontreaty contexts: "International law is part of our law, and must be ascertained and administered by the courts of justice of appropriate jurisdiction, as often as questions of right depending upon it are duly presented."[5] The application of treaty international law by domestic courts has never been seriously challenged, although complexities arise from the question of whether the treaty is non-self-executing or has been superceded by subsequent inconsistent acts of Congress. That this procedure extends to nontreaty norms such as those associated with the Nuremberg Principles seems equally clear. Even the assistant general counsel for international affairs of the Department of Defense, Benjamin Forman, acknowledged that "from an international criminal law point of view . . . the Nuremberg norms are part of our municipal law and may be enforced by our courts."[6]

In recent years the Nuremberg defense has been asserted in domestic courts in a variety of contexts, principally tax and selective service cases arising from the Vietnam conflict. The courts have relied on various legal doctrines in an effort to avoid examining the applicability of international criminal law. However, none of these doctrines was entirely applicable to the special claims put forward by the defendants in *United States* v. *Russo.* The first such doctrine holds that the defendant lacks standing to assert the international law argument.[7] But where the defendants argue, as in the *Russo* case, that it was necessary for them to take steps to dissociate themselves from the circle of complicity because they themselves were accessories to violations of international law, it seems clear that the legal interest asserted is direct and concrete, not hypothetical (as when the argument is advanced by a draftee seeking to avoid future complicity in an illegal act) or indirect (as in the case of a taxpayer seeking to withhold that portion of his taxes which would be used to finance the illegal actions). Ellsberg and Russo clearly had a personal stake in the controversy over the applicability of international law.[8]

The second legal doctrine used by the courts to sidestep the application of international law concerns the issue of justiciability, particularly whether there is a sufficiently close causal connection between the actions that the defendants took and the alleged violation of international law that they assert. Three legal scholars, Anthony A. D'Amato, Harvey L. Gould, and Larry D. Woods, have stated:

> An American soldier who refused to obey an order to torture a prisoner of war would face no difficulties defending himself before a court-martial. Clearly he would have a valid "Nuremberg Defense" based on the argument that the international law of war crimes on this matter is part of American law, that his military obligation is only to obey "lawful" orders, that the order given him is unlawful, and the so-called defense of superior order is not available to him. He would face no serious procedural hurdles nor any questions of justiciability.[9]

Ellsberg and Russo claimed that their actions were analogous to that of an American combat soldier who refuses to obey an illegal order. Civilians subjected to criminal prosecution should be able to demonstrate the reasonableness of their contention that, under the circumstances in which they acted, the domestic claims or regulations amounted to "illegal" superior orders.

In *United States* v. *Russo* it was also unnecessary for the court to determine whether the United States government actually did violate international law. Rather, the court had only to determine whether the defendants reasonably believed that such violations occurred, and whether partial disclosure of the Pentagon Papers by the defendants was a reasonable act in light of that belief. In this sense, the *Russo* case is based on a closer causal connection between the acts done by the defendants and the alleged violation of international law than are the cases of those who withheld war-related taxes or destroyed selective service records.[10] There was reason to believe, for instance, that disclosure of the Pentagon Papers would erode Congressional and public support for the Vietnam War more effectively than would isolated acts of individual resistance. A case raising the justiciability of such limited issues, focusing on the attitude and perception of the defendant vis-à-vis the allegedly unlawful governmental action, would create far less difficulty and embarrassment to the courts than would a case seeking to have the court pass on the legality of the conduct itself. Consequently, in a case such as *United States* v. *Russo* judicial abstention on the ground of nonjusticiability of the issue would be inapposite.

The third device employed by courts to avoid the application of international law in the Vietnam War context is the view that courts should refrain from adjudicating such an issue because its resolution is a so-called "political question" upon which Executive determination is authoritative.[11] However, even the most orthodox view of this political question doctrine would not require its application to the specific facts of *United States v. Russo*, where the defendants were seeking their day in court with respect to a criminal indictment charging them with violation of domestic laws in releasing the classified Pentagon Papers. Surely, it would have been reasonable—and indeed necessary—to determine whether the laws that the defendants violated were, as applied to the facts of the case, "illegal superior orders," especially given the defendants' credible contention of acting to end complicity in the underlying violations of international law. Nothing about this defense touched on the allocation of powers or on the Executive's prerogatives in foreign affairs. Indeed, as Judge Charles E. Wyzanski, Jr., indicated in *United States* v. *Sisson,* it would violate a defendant's right to due process if the court excluded basic issues relevant to his defense merely by invoking the political question doctrine.[12]

On a more fundamental level, the propriety of judicial deference to Executive policy in the area of war and peace is subject to serious question. This pattern of deference evolved from cases decided in the pre-Nuremberg context, when special circumstances existed and there were no clear legal limitations on governmental conduct. However, since World War II a reasonably definite set of legal criteria has developed by which to appraise challenges to Executive action.[13]

There is no longer any justification for the political question doctrine, which rests on the notion that the judiciary cannot displace Executive discretion. Now that international law has constrained Executive discretion, it seems appropriate for courts to implement these constraints. Indeed, it would seem inappropriate for the courts to act as though no such constraint existed, which would be the effect of applying the political question doctrine to a given situation. At a minimum, a court should reconsider the applicability of the political question doctrine to the war-peace area in light of the post-World War II international legal developments. To date, however, courts have hidden beneath the political question cloak without even addressing themselves to the substantial issue of whether this mode of deference is still appropriate in view of recent shifts in international law.

The portion of the Pentagon Papers that was covered in the indictment of Ellsberg and Russo contained evidence which supported at least an inference that the United States government was guilty of several major violations of the international law that applied to its conduct throughout the course of its Vietnam involvement after 1954. This evidence was relevant to the defendants' arguments because it formed the basis of their belief that they were both entitled and obligated to act to dissociate themselves from the continued prosecution of such policy. Furthermore, the disclosure of this evidence to the public and to Congress could be reasonably calculated to increase and substantiate opposition to the continued prosecution of the war.

The Pentagon Papers disclosed established patterns of activity by the United States government that appear inconsistent with fundamental obligations which are embodied in international law and which are therefore binding on national governments. The United States violated international law in at least three respects: by failing to respect international agreements seeking to secure international peace; by failing to seek peaceful settlement of international disputes; and by intervening in the internal affairs of a foreign state. In each of these legal contexts extensive support exists for the contention that the United States government is subject to relevant obligations of international law.

## Failure To Respect International Agreements

There is a legal duty to respect international agreements seeking to establish peace. This is one aspect of the wider legal duty to refrain from the use of force in international relations except in self-defense or under the authority of the United Nations. It is also a special case of the general legal duty to respect valid international agreements.[14]

The General Treaty for the Renunciation of War, known as the Treaty of Paris or the Kellogg-Briand Pact, signed on August 27, 1928, is a fundamental assertion of these legal duties, and it has been validly ratified by the United States. Article I reads: "The High Contracting Parties solemnly declare in the names of their respective peoples that they condemn recourse to war for the resolution of international controversies, and renounce it as an instrument of national policy in their relations with one another."[15]

The character of this obligation was specified in the so-called London Agreement of August 8, 1945, governing the prosecution and punishment of major war criminals of the European Axis. Article VI (a) defines crimes against peace as: "Planning, preparation, initiation or waging a war of aggression, or a war in violation of international treaties, agreements or assurances."[16] This same definition of crimes against peace was incorporated in Control Council Law No. 10, signed in Berlin by the four Allied commanders on December 20, 1945 and used as the basis for prosecuting persons below the highest levels of the German leadership.[17]

Several of the volumes of the Pentagon Papers cited in the indictment of Russo and Ellsberg reveal an intention by policy-makers in the United States government to wage war in violation of the Geneva Accords, a set of validly concluded international agreements ending the French War in Indochina in July 1954. The United States filed a declaration at Geneva stating that it "will refrain from the threat or use of force to disturb" the Geneva Accords and "would view any renewal of the aggression in violation of the aforesaid agreements with grave concern."[18] Even without such a declaration, the United States, along with all other governments, would be legally obligated not to disturb a peace agreement. As a member of the United Nations, the United States has a legal obligation to respect its Charter, especially the principles concerning international peace set forth in general terms in Article 2.

However, the Pentagon Papers Task Force Summary characterizes the United States response to the Geneva Accords as follows:

> It is charged that the U. S. tried to sabotage the Geneva Conference, first by maneuvering to prevent the conference from taking place, then by attempting to subvert a settlement, and finally, by refusing to guarantee the resulting agreements of the conference. The documentation on this charge is complete, but by no means unambiguous. While "sabotage" may be a strong word, it is evident that the U. S. by its actions and statements during this period did seek to down-play the conference, disassociate itself from the results, and thereby did cast doubt on the stability of the Accords.[19]

In the years following 1954 the Geneva Accords were not implemented, and their collapse led to the renewal of warfare in Indochina. The United States, through its support of Ngo Dinh Diem, the prime minister of South Vietnam who refused to implement the critical provision of the Accords relating to general elections for a government of a reunified Vietnam, played a major role in assuring the collapse of the Geneva arrangements. Article 7 of the Final Declaration at the Geneva Conference called for general elections in July 1956, preceded by consultations between the representatives of the two zones of Vietnam commencing on July 20, 1955. The Pentagon Papers confirm that "backed by the United States, Diem refused to open consultation with the North Vietnamese concerning general elections when the date for these fell due in July, 1955."[20] Yet France and Britain clearly realized that the collapse of the Accords would lead to a renewal of war: "the French Government urgently sought to persuade Diem to accept consultations about the elections scheduled to begin in July 1955. Britain wanted to prevent any public repudiation of the Accords and joined France in urging Diem to talk to the Vietminh. But Diem had not changed his view of the Accords: he had refused to sign them and continued to insist he was not bound by them."[21]

In a sense, the elections issue was used by Diem and the United States as a symbolic demonstration of their refusal to implement the Geneva arrangement beyond the very minimal extent of dividing Vietnam into two separate states, one communist, one anticommunist. Even this minimal acceptance of the Geneva solution cannot be understood as a tactical position responsive to geopolitical realities. There are indications that Saigon, as well as Hanoi, nurtured dreams of reunification, and the post-1954 paramilitary penetration of North Vietnam gives tangible evidence of these dreams at a time prior to any claim by Saigon or Washington of North Vietnamese activity in the south.

The United States support for Diem was a natural sequel to its opposition to a negotiated settlement of the war between the French and the Viet Minh, and to the concomitant belief until the 1970s that United States interests in the conflict were more effectively served on the battlefield than at the peace talks, despite the adverse military situation. American policy was operating in a context where substantial military gains could not be contemplated. Yet on those occasions where military gains had been reported or claimed, the main orientation of civilian policy-makers was that, in view of the favorable military situation, peace talks were less necessary than ever. That is, the mood shifted between arguing that the military situation was so bad that negotiations would merely ratify defeat or that it was so favorable that negotiations were an unnecessary interference with the prospects for military victory. The Pentagon Papers quote from President Eisenhower's personal message to Winston Churchill to demonstrate the attitude of the United States government toward peaceful settlement: "I can understand the very natural desire of the French to seek an end to this war which has been bleeding them for eight years. But our painstaking search for a way out of this impasse has reluctantly forced us to the conclusion that there is no negotiated solution of the Indochina problem which in its essence would not be either a face-saving device to cover a French surrender or a face-saving device to cover a Communist retirement."²² It is also important to note that the Pentagon Papers reported that North Vietnam adhered to the Geneva Accords and was prepared to allow the future to be governed by their terms.²³

Even more revealing of official intentions is the authoritative policy statement of the National Security Council of August 20, 1954 (NSC 5429/2), which set forth United States policy toward Vietnam and openly planned a campaign of paramilitary disruption of the recently concluded peace agreements. "Covert operations on a large and effective scale" were urged so as to make "more difficult the control by the Viet Minh of North Vietnam." This document provides other clear indications of the official determination of the United States government to pursue its objectives in Vietnam without exhibiting any regard for the basic peace-restoring provisions and intentions of the Geneva Accords.²⁴

Even though the United States was not a combatant in the Indochina War between France and the Viet Minh, it opposed the Geneva negotiations from the outset and disapproved of their outcome. Subsequently, it supported Diem policies that avowedly defied the Geneva Accords, and it proposed and undertook covert paramilitary actions designed to disrupt Viet Minh control in North Vietnam, as well as to invite retaliatory actions by North Vietnam which could then serve as a pretext for further escalation and militarization of the conflict. These various actions led to a collapse of the Geneva Accords and to a renewal of large-scale and prolonged warfare.

The United States government, then, seems clearly implicated in a pattern of behavior based on failure to respect a validly negotiated agreement restoring international peace. As the Task Force Summary makes clear, "Geneva might have wrought an enduring peace for Vietnam if France had remained a major power in Indochina, if Ngo Dinh Diem had cooperated with the terms of the settlement, and if the U. S. had abstained from further influencing the outcome."²⁵ It is also evident that the United States blocked the French desire to adhere to the Geneva Accords. "The GVN [Government of Vietnam] remained adamantly opposed to elections and neither the U. S. nor any other western power was disposed to support France's fulfillment of its responsibility to the DRV [Democratic Republic of Vietnam]."²⁶

## Failure To Seek Peaceful Settlements

In addition to its obligation to respect international peace agreements, the United States is obligated to seek a peaceful settlement of any international dispute likely to endanger international peace, and to seek a peaceful settlement of any ongoing conflict involving the use of force. Article II of the Treaty of Paris recites the agreement of the contracting parties that "the settlement or solution of all disputes or conflicts of whatever nature or of whatever origin they may be, which may arise among them, shall never be sought except by pacific means."[27] This obligation of pacific settlement is an integral aspect of the underlying obligations to renounce war as an instrument of national policy, and it was so understood by the Nuremberg and Tokyo war crimes tribunals.

In addition, the United Nations Charter is a duly ratified treaty of the United States and, as such, forms part of the supreme law of the land. The Charter obligates its member states to pursue pacific means of settlement and imposes the complementary obligation to renounce the use or threat of force as an ingredient of diplomatic persuasion.[28] These obligations were reaffirmed in 1970 by the United States government through its acceptance of the Declaration on Principles of International Law concerning Friendly Relations and Co-operation among States as adopted by the United Nations General Assembly.[29]

An analysis of those volumes of the Pentagon Papers covered by the indictment of Ellsberg and Russo shows that this legal obligation to seek peaceful solutions to international disputes was persistently violated by the United States government. The Pentagon Papers exhibit both an official American preference for military as opposed to pacific settlement methods in Vietnam, and a tendency to use negotiating contexts either to create an illusion of respect for pacific settlement or to channel threats of force in the event that a settlement was not reached in terms satisfactory to the United States. In both respects the Pentagon Papers provide an authoritative basis for assessing, and then rejecting, the United States government's contention that it was negotiating in good faith and that it at all times sought a peaceful settlement of the Vietnam War.

The papers disclose that the opposition of the United States government to pacific settlement dates back to the immediate post-World War II period. Ho Chi Minh's several letters appealing to the United States government to play a diplomatic role that would avoid a war of independence were ignored.[30] In 1954, during the closing months of the French war in Indochina, the official American position, as summarized in the Task Force Study, was "to attempt to steer the French clear of the negotiating table pending substantial military gains on the battlefield . . . In general, the U. S. sought to convince the French that military victory was the only guarantee of diplomatic success."[31] The

United States government then supported Diem when he refused to open consultations with the North Vietnamese concerning general elections as required by the Geneva Accords.[32]

The "negotiating volumes" of the Pentagon Papers also make clear that the United States often used negotiations either to relay threats or to create a false public expression of interest in peaceful settlement, thereby evidencing a failure to negotiate in good faith.[33] When the Canadian diplomat J. Blair Seaborn was preparing to leave on a negotiating mission to Hanoi in 1964 at the behest of the United States, the United States ambassador to France, C. Douglas Dillon, conveyed to the French government for transmission to Hanoi a number of threats directed at North Vietnam. These maneuverings formed the background of Seaborn's mission. The basic message to Hanoi was that the "devastation" of North Vietnam would result unless the United States succeeded in confining it to the "territory allocated to it" at Geneva in 1954 and in securing the "writ" of the South Vietnam government throughout its own territory by suppressing the guerrilla activity. In fact, it was clearly stated that "Seaborn should get across to Ho and his colleagues the full measure of U. S. determination to see this thing through. He should draw upon examples in other parts of the world to convince them that if it becomes necessary to enlarge the military action, this is the most probable course that the U. S. would follow."[34]

A cable dated May 15, 1964, from the United States ambassador to South Vietnam, Henry Cabot Lodge, to President Johnson underscored the intimidation aspects of Seaborn's mission by suggesting that, "If prior to the Canadian's trip to Hanoi there has been a terroristic act of proper magnitude, then I suggest that a specific target in North Vietnam be considered as a prelude to his arrival."[35] Lodge went on to suggest a "selective use" of South Vietnamese air power to accomplish this effect, so as to avoid provoking Chinese or Soviet responses. He also noted, as a way of supporting limited air strikes, that "if you lay the whole of the country to waste, it is quite likely that you will induce a mood of fatalism in the Viet Cong." The purpose of the "negotiations" was not to search for mutually satisfactory solutions but to change the behavior of the North Vietnamese by the threat of intensified application of force unless American war aims were realized.[36] As put by Ambassador Lodge "it is . . . a relatively simple concept to go out and destroy North Vietnam. What is complicated but really effective, is to bring our power to bear in a precise way so as to get specific results."[37]

Secretary of State Dean Rusk indirectly confirmed the coercive intent of the diplomatic mission when, in a cable of May 22, 1964, he acknowledged the Canadian reluctance to deliver messages to Hanoi "that they will be punished." Although Rusk informed Lodge that the proposed air attacks on the DRV would "simply not be feasible," he accepted Lodge's approach to negotiations as an occasion to intimidate rather than to come to terms. As Rusk expressed it when referring to the covert armed missions being carried out in North Vietnamese territory by GVN forces under specific United States direction, "We do recognize that something a little stronger . . . might be carried on on the basis you propose." Seaborn's final negotiating instructions from Dean Rusk and other United States officials were to tell Hanoi that unless it stopped military activity, including that of the Viet Cong, within a week, "the U. S. will initiate action by air and naval means against North Vietnam."[38]

The same kind of reasoning underlay the bombing pauses between 1965 and 1968 that allegedly were made to encourage a settlement of the conflict. The Pentagon Papers show that these pauses were viewed partly as public relations efforts to quiet public opinion and partly as a new means of conveying threats of further escalation.[39] In fact, some policy-makers in Washington evidently concluded that this threat strategy would itself end the war and obviate the need for formal negotiations. Thus, the supposed negotiating contexts were really alternative means by which to convey battlefield objectives coupled with threats of further escalation in the event that these military objectives were not accepted by the North Vietnamese.

The missions of the Canadian diplomat Chester Ronning to North Vietnam in 1966 for the ostensible purpose of exploring the basis for peace negotiations also were seen by American policy-makers as an opportunity to provide a public relations foundation for a planned escalation of the air war.[40] Canadian officials expressed concern that it would "appear the U. S. used Ronning as a means of obtaining a negative readout on negotiations which would justify escalation." This was indeed the case. Secretary of State Rusk had already informed Secretary of Defense Robert McNamara: "If he [Ronning] has a negative report, as we expect, that provides a firmer base for the action we contemplate and would make a difference to people like [the United Kingdom's Prime Minister Harold] Wilson and [the Canadian Prime Minister Lester] Pearson."[41]

In relation to the contact with North Vietnam known by the code name Marigold, the subordination of the negotiating prospect to the bombing effort was made explicit in United States government correspondence. Attorney General Nicholas deB. Katzenbach cabled the United States ambassador in Warsaw, John A. Gronouski, that the "present bombing pattern has been authorized for some time and we do not wish to withdraw this authorization at this time." Katzenbach also conceded that the bombing pattern "may well involve some targets which Rapacki [the Polish foreign minister] will insist represent further escalation."[42] According to Gronouski, the Polish diplomats seeking to convey the American position to North Vietnamese leaders accused the United States of deliberately provoking breakdowns of the negotiating contacts.[43] In a cable of December 15, 1966, Gronouski stated that if the escalated bombing produced a breakdown, the Soviet Union, Poland, and North Vietnam "will have no trouble convincing the leadership in every capital of the world that our stated desire for peace negotiations is insincere."[44]

## Intervention in Internal Affairs

An important development in international law since World War II has been to acknowledge the rights of national self-determination and to emphasize, as a legal duty, the prohibition against one state's intervention in the internal affairs of another. This emphasis has found expression in a series of documents that are declaratory of customary international law.

The Declaration on the Inadmissibility of Intervention in the Domestic Affairs of States and the Protection of their Independence and Sovereignty was adopted as a United Nations General Assembly Resolution on December 21, 1965, by a unanimous vote, including the vote of the United States. Among its other provisions, the Declaration proclaims that "no State has the right to intervene, directly or indirectly, for any reason whatever, in the internal or external affairs of any other State. Consequently, armed intervention and all other forms of interference or attempted threats against the personality of the State or against its political, economic and cultural elements, are condemned."[45]

In 1970 The General Assembly adopted without vote the Declaration of Principles of International Law Concerning Friendly Relations, which elaborates the duty of nonintervention and the related right of self-determination. In light of the developing Vietnam experience, this Declaration amended the earlier Declaration on the Inadmissibility of Intervention by adding to the notion that intervention was a violation of international law, the further notion that the scope of the prohibition was broad enough to include groups of states acting in concert.[46] This prohibition against intervention is undoubtedly vague and has been manipulated by governments to serve their political preferences in a wide series of global situations. Nevertheless, the basic nonintervention norm clearly seems to form part of customary international law, and the concept has been given a rather authoritative statement in the widely endorsed United Nations resolutions. This basic norm has two elements: first, military intervention in foreign societies is not permissible; second, the invitation of one party in a civil strife does not suspend the nonintervention norm unless it has also been endorsed by a consensus of members in a formal act of the United Nations.

In Vietnam, then, it would seem that the United States action violated a most minimal concept of the nonintervention norm. Throughout the Pentagon Papers runs evidence of an American commitment to frustrate national self-determination, first by helping France to prevail in its war against the Viet Minh, and then by taking over the French role in South Vietnam. Indeed, at first the United States tried to persuade France not to relinquish its presence in Vietnam and sought to organize a procolonialist collective intervention on behalf of France even while the Geneva talks were underway in 1954.[47] Subsequently, on numerous occasions the United States intervened in a variety of ways in Vietnamese internal affairs, both in relation to an ongoing civil war and in disregard of the sovereign rights of the Saigon government that it was supporting.

The United Nations Declaration of Principles explicitly taints intervention on behalf of a colonial government as interference with the rights of national self-determination.[48] Military intervention in a foreign country, without the justification of individual or collective self-defense permitted by the United Nations Charter or in the absence of a specific act of endorsement by the Security Council or General Assembly, also violates the more general Charter prohibitions against the use of force. Article 2(7) of the Charter even prohibits intervention by the United Nations itself "in matters which are essentially within the domestic jurisdiction of any state" except under the carefully specified conditions involving United Nations "enforcement measures" authorized by the Security Council.[49]

The Pentagon Papers contain considerable documentary and interpretative evidence to support the inference that the United States military intervention in South Vietnamese affairs violated the nonintervention principles of international law. The entire pattern of military involvement in the ground war in South Vietnam from 1965 onward clearly substantiates the allegation of United States military intervention in an ongoing civil war in South Vietnam.

Beyond this, even in the diplomatic relations between Saigon and Washington there is much evidence that the United States government deprived South Vietnam of its legal right of political independence. For instance, as early as 1954, American officials acted as if they were entitled to select the leadership of South Vietnam's government. The Task Force noted that during the Diem regime in 1954-1955, "Secretary [of State] Dulles and the Department of State in general seemed disposed to consider favorably suggestions that an alternative leader for the Vietnamese be placed in power."[50] General Lawton Collins, while acting as special American envoy to Vietnam charged with overseeing all United States operations, persistently urged Washington to accomplish Diem's removal from power. For a short period in the spring of 1955, Collins succeeded in persuading his superiors in Washington to consider shifting support to other potential leaders.[51]

The Pentagon Papers also indicate that American military involvement during the immediate post-Geneva settlement period included playing interventionary roles in various internal struggles in South Vietnam.[52] Such indications contradict the claim that American policy was concerned with protecting the Saigon administration against external attacks. The Task Force Study also confirms the contention that the establishment of the Southeast Asia Treaty Organization (SEATO) and its later invocation to support American involvement were regarded as little more than cosmetic ways of disguising the unilateral pursuit of American interests by military means in Vietnam.[53]

The volumes of the Pentagon Papers disclose further American interventionary pressure on the Diem regime in its later years. The United States ambassador to South Vietnam, Elbridge Durbrow, proposed that Washington consider alternatives to Diem in order to assure the overriding objective of securing a "strongly anti-communist Vietnamese government" in South Vietnam.[54] By definition, this American objective directly violated the nonintervention and self-determination legal norms, for the essence of political independence lies in a state's ability to choose its own government.

In 1963, when the United States participated in the overthrow and assassination of Diem, the interventionary role became a matter of complicit deed as well as wish. The United States had been asking Diem "to forego independence by accepting the wisdom of American recommendations for reform." For example, "Diem was warned that Nhu must go."[55] By mid-1963 the United States government had chosen to support antigovernment efforts in South Vietnam, which led to the coup by a group of generals in December of that year.[56] In assessing the American role in that event, the Task Force concluded:

> For the military coup d'etat against Ngo Dinh Diem, the United States must accept its full share of responsibility. Beginning in Au-

gust of 1963 we variously authorized, sanctioned and encouraged the coup efforts of the Vietnamese generals and offered full support for a successor government. In October we cut off aid to Diem in a direct rebuff, giving a green light to the generals. We maintained clandestine contact with them throughout the planning and execution of the coup and sought to review their operational plans and proposed new government. Thus, as the nine year rule of Diem came to a bloody end, our complicity in his overthrow heightened our responsibilities and our commitment in an essentially leaderless Vietnam.[57]

Taken alone, the sections of the Pentagon Papers which formed the basis for the indictment in *United States* v. *Russo* clearly supported an inference that United States policy in Vietnam violated international law. This view was reinforced by evidence contained in other sections of the Pentagon Papers not included in the indictment but which formed the essential legal context in which Daniel Ellsberg made his decision to release portions of the papers. These additional sections encompass the role of the United States in relation to the use of covert force in North Vietnam and Laos, especially during the period 1963-1965; the reprisal raids in North Vietnam associated with the Tonkin Gulf incident in August 1964; and the decision to initiate the sustained bombardment of North Vietnam starting in February 1965.

In sum, then, the United States violations of international law as evidenced in the Pentagon Papers could have led to the indictment and conviction of individuals, civilian as well as military, for criminal acts arising out of their connection with the United States involvement in Vietnam. Furthermore, both defendants in *United States* v. *Russo,* Daniel Ellsberg and Anthony Russo, occupied positions for which a presumption of legal jeopardy was not unreasonable if one were to assume an American willingness or an international capability to implement relevant portions of international criminal law.

The defendants, independent of their jeopardy, may also have had a legally protected right to disclose information that they might reasonably have calculated would bring an illegal war to a close. In this context, Ellsberg's prudence in seeking the most effective means of disclosure compatible with preserving American interests at stake, namely, withholding the negotiating volumes, is relevant to a determination of reasonableness. To emphasize the defendants' right of exculpation is really to take a minimalist position on the Nuremberg obligation. A maximalist position would seek to identify occasions other than those arising out of prior complicity, in which individuals might justifiably violate domestic law in order to oppose an illegal war or illegal conduct in the course of conducting a war.

## Criminal Liability for Violations of International Law

The United States recognized the principle of individual responsibility for violations of international law when Roosevelt, Churchill, and Stalin signed the Moscow Declaration of 1943 declaring the intention of the Allied Powers to prosecute Germans for violations of international law in initiating and waging World War II.[58] This intention was implemented by the London Agreement of August 8, 1945, which specified the charter that was to govern the International Military Tribunal (IMT) convened at Nuremberg.[59] The Allied commanders in Berlin then issued Control Council Law No. 10 on December 20, 1945, to provide a framework governing the prosecution of individuals charged with criminal violations of international law.[60] This document, mirroring the London Agreement, defined "Crimes against the Peace" as the "planning, preparation, initiation or waging of a war of aggression, or war in violation of international treaties, agreement or assurances."[61]

Control Council Law No. 10 also sought to identify the range of individuals who could be held responsible for criminal violations of international law:

> Any person without regard to nationality or the capacity in which he acted, is deemed to have committed a crime as defined in paragraph 1 of this Article, if he was (a) a principal or (b) was an accessory to the commission of any such crime or ordered or abetted the same or (c) took a consenting part therein or (d) was connected with plans or enterprises involving its commission or (e) was a member of any organization or group connected with the commission of any such crime or (f) with reference to paragraph 1(a), if he held a high political, civil or military (including General Staff) position in Germany or in one of its allies, co-belligerents or satellites or held high position in the financial, industrial, or economic life of any such country.[62]

The fact that an individual "acted pursuant to the orders of his government or of a superior" could not free him of culpability, although it could be considered in mitigation.[63]

Similarly, with reference to a Japanese cabinet minister, the Tokyo War Crimes Judgment decreed that persons in high political positions would not be held responsible for violations of international law that occurred outside the scope of their official function unless:

> (1) They had knowledge that such crimes were being committed and having such knowledge they failed to take such steps as were within their power to prevent the commission of such crimes in the future, or (2) they are at fault in having failed to acquire such knowledge . . .

(and) if such a person had, or should, but for negligence or supineness, have had such knowledge he is not excused for inaction if his Office required or permitted him to take any action to prevent such crimes.[64]

It follows logically and as a matter of policy implication that anyone with the knowledge of illegal activity and an opportunity to do something about it is a potential criminal defendant unless he takes affirmative steps to "prevent the commission of such crimes in the future."

The case law developed in the war crimes trials after World War II established that the zone of individual responsibility for crimes against the peace extended well beyond principal policy-makers and state leaders.[65] The responsibility of secondary figures for war crimes generally turned upon whether they had voluntarily aided and abetted illegal acts in a situation in which such persons had or should have had adequate knowledge of the character of these acts. The basis of potential legal responsibility rested on the extent of complicity as reflected in actions and knowledge. Many of the war crimes cases support the conclusion that a defense of necessity was admissible only in cases where the defendant had no practicable way to dissociate himself from the criminal features of German or Japanese war policy.

Furthermore, it was established that the legal duty to comply with international law was not confined to public officials or political and military leaders. The *Flick* case involved indictments brought against German industrialists, in which the tribunal had to face squarely the issue of civilian responsibility for violations of international criminal law:

> [I]t is urged that individuals holding no public offices and not representing the state, do not, and should not come within the class of persons criminally responsible for a breach of international law. It is asserted that international law is a matter wholly outside the work, interest, and knowledge of private individuals. The distinction is unsound. International law, as such, binds every citizen just as does ordinary municipal law. Acts adjudged criminal when done by an officer of the government are criminal when done by a private individual. The guilt differs only in magnitude, not in quality. The offender in either case is charged with personal wrong and punishment falls on the offender in *propria persona. The application of international law to individuals is no novelty.*[66]

Different issues of civilian responsibility were presented in the *Zyklon B* case, in which the civilian defendants were charged with supplying Zyklon B or prussic acid for use in concentration camps. The defendants argued that Zyklon B could be used in beneficial as well as harmful ways and that they had no specific knowledge that the supplies which were being sent to the government were being used to administer lethal poison to inmates of concentration camps. The judgment in the case dealt explicitly with the liability for criminal complicity as applied to civilian defendants.

> [T]he present case is a clear example of the application of the rule that the provisions of the law and customs of war are addressed not only to combatants and to members of state and other public authorities, but *to anybody who is in a position to assist in their violation.*
>
> The activities with which the accused in the present case were charged were commercial transactions conducted by civilians. The military court acted on the principle *that any civilian who is an accessory to a violation of the laws and customs of war is himself also liable as a war criminal.* [67]

The incorporation of the principles established by the Nuremberg and Tokyo war crimes trials into the permanent body of international law was considered a priority item in the postwar world. President Harry S. Truman, in an address to the United Nations General Assembly, affirmed the Nuremberg Principles and declared that they pointed "the path along which [international] agreement might be sought, with hope of success."[68] Accordingly, the United States delegation introduced a resolution before the General Assembly to make the principles a permanent part of international law. This resolution, which "Affirm(s) the Principles of International Law recognized by the Charter of the Nuremberg Tribunal," was adopted unanimously on December 11, 1946.[69]

These principles of international law were restated in 1950 by the International Law Commission. Principle II states: "The fact that internal law does not impose a penalty for an act which constitutes a crime under international law does not relieve the person who committed the act from responsibility under international law."[70] Principle IV recognizes that superior orders are no defense against complicity in violations of international law. The scope of actions for which individual responsibility attaches is defined by Principle VI. Principle VII notes that complicity in the commission of these crimes constitutes a violation of international criminal law. These principles, having become part of international law, are by virtue of such a development a valid part of the domestic law of the United States. In a due process sense, whether or not international law has developed to supercede domestic law, it may be a valid defense in a criminal prosecution, such as *United States* v. *Russo*, if the defendants have adequate reason to believe that the domestic legal norms under which they have been charged with illegal acts have been superceded by international legal norms.

## Vulnerability to Prosecution and Conviction As Accessories

Given the premise of potential individual liability for violations of international law, and in light of the evidence contained in the indictment volumes of the Pentagon Papers that such violations did occur, it was not unreasonable for the defendants in *United States* v. *Russo* to regard themselves as implicated in a criminal enterprise from which they had a responsibility to dissociate themselves. If one were to imagine a procedure of accountability in the United States for the Vietnam War comparable to that which was used after World War II, establishing individual responsibility for violations of international law, then the two defendants in this case, especially Daniel Ellsberg, could have been indicted. Both defendants occupied positions for which a presumption of legal jeopardy was not unreasonable if one were to assume an American willingness to implement relevant portions of international criminal law.

Ellsberg, as a prominent policy adviser to the assistant secretary of defense and as a senior analyst with The Rand Corporation, exerted a direct role on the formation of American military policy in Vietnam. His role in policy formation included work relating to the implementation of "Rolling Thunder," the sustained American bombardment of North Vietnam that was carried out in direct violation of international law.

Defendant Anthony Russo, as a staff employee of The Rand Corporation was entrusted with specific studies related to battlefield operations, including the crop destruction program practiced by the United States in South Vietnam during the 1960s. Russo came to realize that this program of crop destruction involved a war tactic whose principal impact was to deprive Vietnamese civilians, especially women, children, and the aged, of food. The program's purported target, the National Liberation Front, enjoyed priority access to available food supplies. Russo was aware that the crop destruction program continued to be maintained even after the United States government had ample evidence that its impact was primarily on civilians.

The defendants' affiliation with The Rand Corporation in many respects resembles the position of the defendants in the *Zyklon B* case, who were civilian employees of a private company that supplied their government with products enabling it to violate international criminal law. In the instant case, The Rand Corporation was a quasi-public entity closely linked to United States government war policies. The products it supplied were policy analysis and information rather than prussic acid. The critical point is that Ellsberg and Russo were "in a position" to assist in the violation of international law with respect to the initiation and conduct of war.

## Obligation To Terminate Complicity

The key factors in the case of Ellsberg and Russo are that the United States government had violated international law in the conduct of its Vietnam policy, that international law assesses individual responsibility for the commission of such crimes against the peace, and that the professional roles of the defendants as defense policy specialists supported their belief that they were implicated in a criminal enterprise and thus subject to a hypothetically plausible indictment and conviction. Under these circumstances, international law imposed an obligation on the defendants to take such action as was available to them to terminate their complicity in the illegal activity and to attempt to prevent the continued commission of such crimes. "If such a person [in a high political or civilian position] . . . had such knowledge [of crimes against the peace] he is not excused for inaction if his office required or permitted him to take any action to prevent such crimes."[71]

Ellsberg and Russo determined that the release of the Pentagon Papers was the one action available to them which would most likely eliminate or substantially diminish their potential liability. The Pentagon Papers contained official government documentation of the illegality of the war and evidence that the violations of international law were causally linked to their own roles in the war effort. The evidence contained in the papers also had contributed to the formation of their own belief that they had to take action to dissociate themselves from the continued prosecution of the war. Most important of all, the disclosure of the Pentagon Papers to the Congress and the public could be calculated to establish the illegality of the war and to secure support for efforts to ensure its speedy conclusion.

In a more general sense, the defendants acted in the spirit of the message sent by President Franklin Roosevelt to the German people in 1944: "I ask every German and every man everywhere under Nazi domination to show the world by his action that in his heart he does not share these insane criminal desires . . . I ask him to keep watch, and to record the evidence that will one day be used to convict the guilty."[72] As citizens of a country with a democratic tradition, we should welcome a doctrine that confers on citizens a responsibility and a duty to take steps to terminate an illegal war or illegal war tactics. At a minimum we should allow individuals to make available information to the public that confirms the illegal character of a war so that the elected members of Congress can properly exercise their functions, including the obligation to respect the international law as part of the law of the land.

The prosecution in *United States* v. *Russo* relied on statutes, regulations, and classification procedures that allegedly prohibited the disclosure of the Pentagon Papers. To the extent that these statutes and regulations applied to the papers, the defendants were seemingly caught between contradictory legal duties. On the one hand, they were obligated to respect the secrecy status accorded the Pentagon Papers. On the other hand, they were compelled to terminate their complicity in the illegal war and to speed the war's conclusion by releasing the papers.

The contradiction was resolved by one of the most fundamental Nuremberg Principles, namely, that continued complicity in international crimes is not excused by a continued deference to the requirements of municipal law. The so-called defense of superior orders is not available to defendants accused of war crimes. The International Law Commission has provided guidance in this area in its restatement of the principles of law recognized at Nuremberg.[73] Daniel Ellsberg and Anthony Russo's release of the Pentagon Papers was a reasonable interpretation of their primary legal duty, regardless of administrative or municipal legal inhibitions.

Courts presume, as a matter of law, that domestic legislation must be construed in conformity with relevant rules of international law, wherever such a construction is possible. It would violate the fundamental principles of fairness and due process of law guaranteed by the Fifth Amendment of the United States Constitution to subject the defendants to contradictory legal claims on their behavior. To interpret those claims protecting governmental secrecy as precluding the disclosure of information where such disclosure is justified under relevant principles of international law would be to deny the defendants due process of law. Administrative regulations, such as the classification procedures, are subordinate to international law under the supremacy clause of the Constitution and a fortiori could not have been construed as prohibiting the defendants' actions. In addition, inhibitions on public disclosures of information are themselves devalued to the extent that they involve placing unnecessary burdens on First Amendment freedoms.

In sum, the case of *United States v. Russo* raises several significant and related issues. First is the question of whether the basic provisions of international criminal law are incorporated into national law in such a way as to be operative in domestic courts. Second is the constitutional question of due process, or more generally of fairness, as to whether civilian defendants are to be denied a Nuremberg defense for determining that they have a duty to oppose illegal "superior orders"—in this case in the form of secrecy regulations. Third is the broad question of the extent to which governmental control over the use of force in international affairs can be penetrated by according legal status to opposing claims of individual conscience.

One legacy of the Vietnam War should be to vindicate the argument that national security is helped, not hindered, by heeding the conscience of the citizenry. In large, depersonalized bureaucracies it is difficult for individuals to act responsibly or to be held accountable in the complex settings of war-making. The locus of action is too diffuse and dispersed. It is particularly necessary, then, to encourage and protect individuals who do make responsible claims on behalf of individual conscience. If these claims are expressed as acts of resistance, a domestic court should examine in context the reasonableness of such claims, rather than dismissing them out of hand by invoking mechanically applied labels such as lack of standing, nonjusticiability, or the political question doctrine. An inquiry into the reasonableness of such claims should include the following six guidelines: the extent to which international law experts had written or spoken about the illegal character of a war; the degree to which individuals were familiar with such an international law analysis; the extent to which the act of resistance was reasonably calculated to bring the official illegality to an end; the extent to which the individuals had tried to rectify the official illegality by peaceful and acceptable means before resorting to resistance activity; the extent to which the act of resistance was developed to minimize the disruption of domestic "law and order," given the situation and opportunities available to the claimant; and the extent to which the resistance activity avoided physical violence and damage to property, especially to third parties. In my judgment, had such a checklist of factors been used in the case of *United States v. Russo,* the decision of defendants Daniel Ellsberg and Anthony Russo to release the Pentagon Papers would have been indicated, regardless of prohibitions on the disclosure of classified materials and national security information.

# 8 | A Nuremberg Perspective on the Trial of Karl Armstrong

There is considerable disagreement over the extent of the Nuremberg obligation, especially when it is used to justify opposing an illegal war, as was attempted on a number of occasions by Americans resisting the United States involvement in Indochina. At issue in particular is the claim of an ordinary citizen to engage in violent acts of resistance, illegal under domestic law, in opposition to a war that can reasonably be considered to violate international treaties and to defy basic moral precepts. The broader question is whether a movement for global reform, which includes among its goals the elimination of the war system, should, as one of its operative principles, renounce reliance on violent tactics.

In the years since the Nuremberg judgment of 1945, no official attempt has been made to apply the Nuremberg Principles to the concrete circumstances of violent conflict. An unofficial and symbolic application of the Nuremberg idea underlay the proceedings of the Bertrand Russell War Crimes Tribunal held in 1966-1967 in two Scandinavian countries. The proceedings of the tribunal depict accurately the basic pattern of combat violations of the laws of war characteristic of the early years of heavy American involvement in Vietnam.[1] Aside from this single controversial incident, there has been no effort by governments, international institutions, or public opinion to take seriously the justly celebrated American pledge at Nuremberg of the chief prosecutor for the United States, Justice Robert H. Jackson: "If certain acts in violation of treaties are crimes, they are crimes whether the United States does them or whether Germany does them, and we are not prepared to lay down a rule of criminal conduct against others which we would not be willing to have invoked against us."

Even as Justice Jackson uttered these sentiments on behalf of the United States, there were grounds for suspicion. After all, the Allied powers after World War II did not allow inquiry into the legal status of their own war policies, even though their obliteration bombing of cities in Germany and Japan and the atomic bombing of Hiroshima and Nagasaki could not easily be reconciled with prevailing views of the restraints embodied in rules of international law applicable at the time. The long dissent by the Indian jurist Radhabinod Pal to the majority opinion in the Tokyo war crimes trials argues that the whole judicial exercise of prosecution and conviction was a kind of pompous farce.[2] Indeed, a Japanese domestic court some years later did conclude, after an exhaustive and soul-searching inquiry, that the atomic bombings violated international law.[3] In an apparent effort to avoid any impression of self-righteousness, the Japanese court released this decision on December 7, the anniversary of Japan's surprise attack on Pearl Harbor.

Furthermore, the governments that initiated the Nuremberg experiment have exhibited no disposition to implement standards of accountability in subsequent contexts. Even in bitter warfare, where evidence of atrocities exists, there is little support for a war crimes approach. After the Indo-Pakistan War of 1971, there was some demand from Indian and Bangladesh leaders for war crimes trials.[4] However, it is doubtful whether any trials will ever be held, despite the capture of many of those who had played an active part in the genocidal repression of East Pakistan in the period prior to the war. In general, then, the Nuremberg Principles seem neither to have had a deterrent impact on leaders nor to have motivated any community insistence on the formal prosecution of those who violate such principles.[5]

Is it appropriate, then, to repudiate the Nuremberg Principles and to write off the Nuremberg and Tokyo experiments as little more than a pretentious form of "victors' justice?" Not in my view. In a series of conflicts, but especially during the American involvement in Indochina, the Nuremberg idea has provided conscientious citizens with a legal and moral foundation for condemning official policy, and has facilitated citizen demonstrations of governmental lawlessness. As such, the Nuremberg orientation provided certain elements of the American antiwar movement with a legal rationale for their rage, a rationale that could be conveyed with increasing credibility to the general population and to a wide spectrum of leaders. The My Lai disclosures in late 1969 helped to dramatize the criminal side of America's combat role in Vietnam, and also gave war critics a larger audience for their view that My Lai was only the tip of the atrocity iceberg. That is, My Lai was only one of many massacres, and was only a more spontaneous assault on the civilian population than such premeditated official counterinsurgency policies as crop denial, the Phoenix Program, free-fire zones, herbicidal destruction, area bombing, the massive use of antipersonnel weaponry, and the forcible removal of civilians from their homes.[6] It is difficult to calculate the extent to which reliance on the Nuremberg idea lent strength to a variety of antiwar stands. Mainstream opposition to the war was developed on a far more pragmatic basis, with the war being generally characterized as a mistake; liberals shied away from the drastic implications of concluding that national leaders were indictable as war criminals by Nuremberg standards. More radical postures toward the war did generally embody an acceptance of the central Nuremberg postulate that wrongful resort to military power was a criminal act for which the responsible officials were accountable. After the release of the Pentagon Papers in June 1971, it became difficult for an even broader segment of public opinion to resist the conclusion that American policy-makers directly and illegally intended to carry the violence in South Vietnam across international boundaries. Perhaps the prima facie criminality of America's war policies did eventually firm up liberal opposition to the war and finally undergird a belated congressional willingness to impose the August 15, 1973, cutoff on Cambodian bombing. But such a supposition is highly speculative and probably far too charitable.[7]

The most direct significance of Nuremberg thinking involved its impact on resistance activity. In a wide variety of contexts, antiwar groups premised their actions, especially their defiance of enacted law, on an acceptance of the right or even the duty of citizens to resist an illegal and criminal war. Draft resisters, tax resisters, and other militant opponents of the war justified their position in this way. The members of Redress, a loosely organized group of professionals in the arts and letters, based their willingness to confront Congress and go to jail for a symbolic interval on this principle. More significantly, Daniel Ellsberg and Anthony Russo so justified their release of the Pentagon Papers, as did various religiously oriented groups intent on stopping the flow of munitions by obstructing rail and ship passages. In other words, the plausibility of the Nuremberg obligation in the context of resistance activities became crystallized as the Vietnam War proceeded, providing a moral and legal thread that ran through a wide variety of such activities.

Such a norm-related concept of resistance seems highly relevant for any serious global reform movement. Drastic and progressive global reform will come about, if at all, only when coalitions of progressive or change-oriented individuals in the highly-industrialized countries (plus perhaps an occasional government) work together along parallel political lines with the more militant governmental and nongovernmental elements in the Third World. Such populist tendencies need to anchor their opposition to prevailing policies and structures through an association with widely shared and potentially planetary community principles of decency. The Nuremberg Principles enjoy such a stature, as well as the nominal adherence of virtually every government in the world.[8]

## The Resistance Claim

The circumstances that condition the effectiveness of acts of resistance vary greatly: what is an effective act of resistance in one national setting may be meaningless or worse in others. Norman Morrison's martyrdom when he set fire to himself on the steps of the Pentagon in 1967 is virtually unknown among Americans, but it had a surprisingly strong resonance for the Vietnamese, inspiring songs, poems, and postage stamps.

Did Morrison's act of suicide overstep the limits of effective resistance? Can we identify such limits? It is a complicated matter to characterize an act of political suicide. Most generally it is viewed as a self-destructive action designed to bear witness in an extreme form. But sometimes its intention is to provoke others of similar persuasion to undertake action, even violent action, to rectify the perceived wrong. In any case, although suicide is not itself an act of violence against another person or even against property, its very extremity provokes the most serious thought and inquiry on the question of whether violent acts of resistance can effectively be justified in contexts like the Vietnam antiwar movement. The elemental character of this issue emerged during the course of Karl Armstrong's trial in Madison, Wisconsin, for his admitted participation in the bombing of the Army Mathematics Research Center at the University of Wisconsin on August 24, 1970. The 3:00 A.M. bombing accidentally caused the death of Robert Fassnacht, a research physicist whose work was totally unrelated to the war. Armstrong pleaded guilty to charges of second-degree homicide, carrying a maximum punishment of twenty-five years, in exchange for an assurance that a full-scale hearing on motivation would be permitted and taken into account by the sentencing judge. At this hearing the war was put on trial by a variety of witnesses—including antiwar veterans and such well-known opponents of the war as Robert Jay Lifton, Gabriel Kolko, Senator Ernest Gruening, Howard Zinn, Daniel Ellsberg, and Philip Berrigan—who were not constrained by the rules of evidence which had largely kept such testimony out of earlier antiwar trials around the country.

The deeper question presented by the trial was whether Armstrong had transgressed the limits of resistance and ought to be held accountable, despite the fact that he was motivated by antiwar sentiments and had reason to believe that the building was unoccupied when the

bomb exploded. It may seem as though Armstrong's motivation, whatever its moral status, has no relationship to the application of the
criminal law. In one narrow sense such a view is correct. In the course
of appraising guilt or innocence, a judge or jury is not supposed to go
behind the intended consequences of a criminal defendant's actions. In
other words, motivation is irrelevant. But on this, as on many other
legal issues, the quick answer is not always very helpful, especially in illuminating the choices posed by a difficult case. For one thing, as the
legal philosopher Ronald Dworkin argued in another context, the
prosecutor enjoys a large measure of discretion over whether to prosecute and, if so, at what level of criminality. As Dworkin suggested with
regard to the related area of draft resistance, the moral features of a
technical violation of enacted law ought properly to enter into a prosecutor's decision.[9] Furthermore, the issue of motivation is properly
taken into account in affixing the level of punishment; indeed, it is one
of the principal justifications for the considerable judicial discretion
that is allowed at the sentencing stage. Finally, it is at least arguable
that juries do in fact take such considerations into account in reaching
verdicts, and that such tempering of the letter of the law is not only desirable but is even encouraged by the fact that juries are not asked to
disclose the reasoning by which they have arrived at their verdicts.
These elements of discretion all operated in the antiwar contexts
created by draft resistance. As the motivation of antiwar defendants
won wider approval in the community, there was a tendency for the
courts to defer or avoid criminal prosecutions, or to proceed half-
heartedly or even apologetically, and there was a corresponding tendency toward greater judicial leniency at the sentencing stage than had
been true in similar cases earlier in the war. In sum, then, "the law"
encompasses a far wider set of issues than whether given acts violate the
statute in question.

In cases of resistance there is a further complication that has not
been adequately identified in most discussions of this subject. Resistance claims have been generally treated as examples of civil disobedience. Consequently, there is a disposition to evaluate particular
acts of resistance in relation to certain criteria that have come to be
widely, though not universally, accepted in the civil disobedience tradition. For instance, the philosopher John Rawls defines civil disobedience "as a public, nonviolent, conscientious yet political act contrary to law usually done with the aim of bringing about a change in the
law or policies of the government."[10] In contrast, the political historian
Howard Zinn, extending civil disobedience to the antiwar context that
evolved during the period of United States involvement in Vietnam,

contends that it is "a fallacy" to condition the legitimacy of a claim of civil disobedience by an absolute requirement of nonviolence. Zinn argues that the validity of an act of resistance depends on a variety of contextual factors, including the harm being perpetrated by the policies which have occasioned the resistance, and the prospects for mounting effective opposition to these same policies.[11] However, even Zinn's broader concept of the civil disobedience tradition allows room for Armstrong's act to be variously interpreted as valid or invalid.

A clearer and more appropriate approach to the Armstrong case is provided by the Nuremberg tradition, where the context of resistance is characterized by conflicting sets of obligations, at least if one grants Armstrong's basic contentions that the Nuremberg Principles are part of international law, that international law is part of the law of the land, and that he, Armstrong, reasonably believed that the United States government's prosecution of the Vietnam War was in flagrant violation of international law. If one accepts these assertions, then the reasonableness of Armstrong's resistance claim depends on whether he acted or believed he was acting in accordance with an applicable law, namely, the legal duty of individuals to oppose wars believed to be wars of aggression. Unlike the traditional practitioner of civil disobedience, who deliberately oversteps the bounds of legal conduct because he intends his behavior as a symbolic form of resistance to alleged injustices, but whose acts involve no harm to other persons or to property and are carried out with full acceptance of the anticipated legal consequences, the resister may be opposing in a substantive rather than a symbolic way those policies that he considers abhorrent. Americans applauded this form of substantive opposition when citizens of many foreign countries engaged in violent resistance to Nazi rule during World War II. Indeed, most Americans would have been morally offended if those resisters had been apprehended after the war and subjected to prosecution, even though their actions clearly violated domestic statutes of criminal law and in some instances resulted in injuries to innocent third parties.

I believe it is within this tradition of resistance that Armstrong's action should be evaluated. Because resistance can properly be substantive rather than symbolic, it does pose grave threats to the security of the community; and certainly there are many potential claims of resistance that we would not want to endorse as legitimate extensions of the Nuremberg tradition. Stringent tests of reasonableness must be developed, especially when the claimant acts violently against people or property. But to argue in favor of such tests is to acknowledge that under certain circumstances the Nuremberg tradition does provide a legal basis for giving legal protection to acts of resistance even as extreme as Armstrong's, or at least justifies a more lenient approach at the sentencing stage. Admittedly this argument is speculative, but it warrants serious consideration as part of an effort both to make effective the rules of international law in the area of war and peace and to restore a measure of balance into the relationship between a citizen and his government. At a minimum, such a tradition of resistance might encourage the courts to pronounce upon the constitutional and international legal status of a controversial war that exacts a heavy toll in human casualties, imposes serious financial burdens, and may even risk the stability of world society. In effect, the Nuremberg argument can be thought of as a technique to extend the doctrine of "checks and balances" to the relationship between citizen and government in the critical area of war and peace. Even if the province of a valid claim of resistance is kept very small, the resister can exercise a populist "check" on the powers and pretensions of the government.

Finally, the growing interdependence of the contemporary world makes the territoriality of a particular claim seem much less relevant. Thus, although the antiwar movement was attempting to change policies which emanated from Washington but whose direct effects of death and destruction were felt only in Vietnam, the movement's attempt was no less valid than if these same effects had been felt within the United States itself. The hard question to ask is whether an act of resistance which is reasonable in other respects is plausibly linked to opposing or changing the policies it seeks to repudiate.

On one level it is easy to argue, as many defense witnesses did, that Karl Armstrong's rage against the criminality of the war had no effective nonviolent outlets of the sort available to intellectuals, officials, or even soldiers; this would help us understand and perhaps even excuse his act, but not necessarily accord it our approval. More relevant from a legal angle is the argument that the prosecution in this case was so tainted by its own criminality arising from the war that it was in no position whatsoever to arrange for the punishment of any resister.[12] Certainly this view would justify the decision to testify on behalf of Armstrong, but it still does not clarify the moral and political status of his kind of act. On this point it can be argued persuasively that as of September 1970, Armstrong could have no reasonable expectation that nonviolent modes of antiwar activity would be effective, nor that Congress, the courts, or even the media were effectively available to someone with his views about the war. Furthermore, the harm inflicted on the Indochinese during that period was of such a magnitude that exceptional actions of resistance were appropriate. This position is not refuted by the suggestion that such random violence was or might reasonably have been thought to be "counterproductive," in the sense of vindicating government repression and turning public opinion against resisters rather than against the war. Less drastic means had been tried with no apparent success, and it is at least possible now to contend that one source of pressure to end the war, although difficult to calculate and never officially acknowledged, was a sense that the fabric of American society was unraveling, a sense created largely by resistance actions at the extreme.[13]

A more provocative and less equivocal kind of support came from Van Ba, a representative of the Provisional Revolutionary Government of South Vietnam, who lauded Armstrong's deeds at an August 1972 rally against the war: "The bombing of the Army Math Research Center was a heroic act, not on the fringes of North American left extremism, but in the center of a world-wide revolutionary struggle."[14] This contention is forceful. Armstrong's act was an expression of deep conviction, involving risk-taking of the sort that is characteristic of genuine revolutionary struggle. Armstrong was thus in close solidarity with the National Liberation Front, which itself might not hesitate to bomb civilian buildings if such acts could be related to its war aims. In Vietnam these aims included disrupting the tranquillity of urban populations in South Vietnam, who sought to remain uninvolved in the struggle. Furthermore, the extremity of Armstrong's act created the kind of transnational bond with Indochinese victims of the war that more restrained forms of resistance could never achieve. In this regard, Armstrong to some extent transcended his national identity as an American by acting as if he had as much at stake as a Vietnamese patriot. It is difficult to know whether these considerations dominated Armstrong's state of mind at the time of his controversial act, but Armstrong's own explanations are consistent with this possibility, and wide-ranging testimony from many sources supports his exceptional sincerity. Armstrong's father, a factory worker in the Madison area, was moved by his son's sincerity to the point of being able to comprehend sympathetically an act that he had previously viewed with abhorrence.[15] Of course, Van Ba's enthusiasm for Armstrong's act arises from its objective quality as an extreme form of opposition to the war and as an acceptance by the actor of risks somewhat comparable to those taken by participants in the struggle within Vietnam.

But even if Armstrong's act can be explained on moral grounds and from certain political perspectives morally endorsed, that does not resolve the question of whether it can also provide a general precept for resistance or radical reformist action. This issue is fundamentally the question of whether the best strategy for a movement of resistance and drastic global reform is to be found within a framework of violent or nonviolent action. Richard Goldensohn, an editor of *Liberation* magazine, argues that the Armstrong bombing should be viewed as a case of terror—"We understand terror to be a political tactic which relies upon instilling fear of personal harm in part or all of a population in order to motivate it to act in a particular way. Ultimately it is a threat." Goldensohn distinguished such terror from "revolutionary violence, which—so it can be argued anyway—can at least be directed toward a particular 'enemy' or object with the purpose of destroying a specific obstacle to the success of a movement."[16] He maintained that the bombing of the research center was, in effect, "a symbolic warning that, if the war did not end, yet another installation might be next, and so on"; it was terror rather than revolutionary violence, because it sought to frighten the American people into opposing the war, rather than to destroy the war machine itself. This distinction is not persuasive. Van Ba's enthusiasm for the bombing seems credible precisely because he viewed it as a pure instance of revolutionary violence. The research center was a war-related facility, contributing research designs and models relevant to the electronic battlefield,[17] and the death of Robert Fassnacht was an unintended as well as highly unlikely side-effect. The main question, therefore, is whether violence can be considered the best resistance tactic, when all relevant factors are taken into account.

I think not. I am increasingly convinced that from a global perspective, violence creates at least as many problems as it solves, that it sets in motion and feeds destructive processes over which we have less and less control. Because violence almost always begets violence, its use initiates a vicious cycle that deprives a progressive movement of one of its principal strengths, its moral superiority over opponents. Furthermore, in military contexts the use of violence is increasingly indiscriminate, whether considered from the nuclear or from the insurgency/counterinsurgency end of the violence spectrum, and tends to inflict so much damage and suffering as to negate any possible advantage.

We must distinguish the moral quality of an act of resistance that is motivated by a reasonable belief in its necessity and proportionality, from its political quality as an act likely to elicit wider support or to bring about increased pressure on policy-makers. In the American context, it is important for political reasons to repudiate Armstrong's act, while it is important for moral reasons to protest his punishment and imprisonment. My reasons for politically repudiating this act stem in part from an adverse appraisal of the relation of forces between revolutionary and repressive constituencies in American society. That is, violence which is endorsed and encouraged on the Left provides the government with a more plausible case for employing repressive tactics of its own, and nurtures an indulgence for violence emanating from the extreme Right. In effect, then, if we vindicate violent claims of resistance even within the Nuremberg framework, we are also creating a climate for other forms of violence that are likely to have greater wellsprings of support in American society, at least at the present time.

This appraisal of Armstrong's defense of violent resistance leads to several conclusions. First, the state itself was sufficiently discredited that Armstrong's prosecutors lacked legitimacy. This dubious status of the prosecution is legally relevant to the controversial procedure of trying to determine what the law should have been if correctly applied to the war policies in Vietnam (although less relevant to the conventional procedure of accepting what authoritative interpreters of the law, such as the Supreme Court, declare the law to be).

Second, the violent element of the action was less deserving of punishment because the premeditated target was property rather than life; the death which resulted in this case was an unforeseeable and completely accidental side-effect. While it is generally true that criminal accountability is extended to the harm that actually results from illegal acts of violence, it is also true that the intent to avoid inflicting personal harm is relevant at the sentencing stage. Admittedly, to be relevant is not necessarily to be decisive. Surely, a judge who must weigh various legal factors and social priorities might reasonably conclude that a heavy sentence is required in cases like that of Armstrong because the kind of violence involved has implicit within it a risk to life as well as to property. Again, however, if the Nuremberg concept of legitimated resistance is to be accorded any status, acts of resistance must be appraised in context. It is worth recalling once more the anti-Nazi resistance claims, in order to underscore the contention that even violent claims may win general approval if the political and moral climate is supportive.

Third, although Armstrong's specific acts are potentially justifiable within the Nuremberg tradition, any grant of actual support, to whatever extent and from whatever source (including private observers like myself or the sentencing judge), necessarily depends on an overall evaluation of the reasonableness of the acts undertaken. Such an evaluation could lead to an eventual rejection of the claim altogether, or to various degrees of accepance, including mitigation of the sentence. Since Armstrong pleaded guilty to second-degree homicide, in a technical sense the only issue before the court was whether the judge should be more lenient when passing sentence, because the actions in question reasonably fit the Nuremberg tradition. Moreover, the Armstrong action seemed, for those who identified with the revolutionary claims of the National Liberation Front, like an appropriate extension of the arena of revolutionary struggle beyond the territory of South Vietnam. The action had a depressant impact, however on progressive politics and militancy in the United States, and thereby contributed unwittingly to official designs to pacify America. The ultimate moral status accorded to Armstrong's action depends on one's overall views as to the role of violence or its renunciation with regard to progressive politics. Yet in the wider setting of global reform, it seems desirable at the present time to orient opponents of the war system around a nonviolent ethos, for several reasons: to gain an audience in a war-weary world, to avoid becoming sucked into the war-making cult even while opposing it, to take comparative advantage of moral assets, and to expose the reliance of most rulers on violence and cruelty.

A distinction should be drawn between Armstrong's plight as a political prisoner and the moral, legal, and political status of his role in detonating bombs at the Army Mathematics Research Center in 1970. Regardless of one's appraisal of the latter, Armstrong seems to have been victimized on a number of grounds that qualify him as a political prisoner. For one thing, Armstrong was found in Canada and returned to the United States following a request for extradition. Political crimes are explicitly categorized as nonextraditable in the relevant treaty, yet the Canadian judge concluded that Armstrong was subject to extradition because the acts with which he was charged did not qualify as political crimes. This conclusion seems arbitrary and unfortunate. I doubt that many Americans would advocate that violent resisters from other countries who have found sanctuary in the United States should be turned over by the United States authorities for prosecution by their respective governments. In other words, the capacity to prosecute Armstrong was itself based on a dubious interpretation of an extradition treaty that contained a provision expressly exempting politically motivated behavior from procedures designed to facilitate transnational cooperation for enforcing domestic criminal law.

Even more fundamental than jurisdictional competence, however, is the question of legitimacy presented by a governmental and prosecutorial system that was itself tainted through its involvement in violent crimes of war. The judicial system, too, by its failure to pass judgment on issues of legality and criminality raised with respect to the Vietnam War, was not likely to provide a fair context for considering the kind of claim that Armstrong was trying to make. This particular claim could be fairly appraised only in a tribunal not tied to the American governmental system, unless Congress had previously directed American courts to consider the Nuremberg Principles as part of the law of the land whose relevance must be taken into account. As it was, Armstrong was judged by the ordinary rules of law applicable to any incendiary incident, and the claim that acts of resistance might, under certain exceptional circumstances, be entitled to legal protection was completely put aside.

The Armstrong case raises important, difficult, and controversial questions about which reasonable people might disagree. Above all, it raises questions of how we really feel about the Nuremberg precedent as operative law when its teachings are turned inward. These questions go to the essence of global reform, for what is at stake is whether the nonviolent processes of the law will at least give a hearing to individuals engaged in conscientious acts of resistance designed to curb the war-waging propensities of a sovereign state. It is true that Armstrong's violent act has anarchic potential and that violence always poses threats to bystanders, but this does not dispose of the underlying contention that we are legally required by the Nuremberg Principles to look beyond the confines of domestic criminal law, however circumspectly, whenever an appropriate claim of resistance is reasonably made. If the state system is ultimately to be eroded, it will be partly as a consequence of reinvigorating the individual citizen as an actor whose perspectives have legitimacy and relevance in the delicate process of balancing justice and order in world affairs.

Nevertheless, although the Nuremberg argument should be taken into consideration in determining a fair sentence for Armstrong, I believe that his act of exploding bombs should not be granted legal exoneration in toto. That is, the Nuremberg argument is persuasive enough for leniency, but not for complete exoneration. My conclusion rests on two principal reasons. First, the burden on the claimant to show that violent resistance was both warranted and effective was not adequately sustained by Armstrong. Second, a resistance claim of the Armstrong sort should be reserved for a situation of objective desperation where all legal paths of opposition are blocked off. These legal paths were certainly obstructed at the time Armstrong acted in 1970, but it is not reasonable to conclude that a situation of objective desperation existed.

Despite my acceptance of these lines of objection to Armstrong's action, I can envisage an altered historical and moral setting in which violent tactics would be efficacious for resistance purposes or reformist ends, and in which the ethical ambiguities of renouncing violence might be so great as to tip the scale in the other direction. At this stage in world history, however, nothing could be more revolutionary than a militant nonviolent movement for drastic global reform in which adherents exhibited discipline, courage, and tactical ingenuity.

# 9 | Nuremberg Reconsidered

"What happens in Nuremberg, no matter how many objections it may invite, is a feeble, ambiguous harbinger of a world order, the need of which mankind is beginning to feel."[1] These words, addressed by the philosopher Karl Jaspers to the German people shortly after the end of World War II, have a peculiarly vivid relevance to the situation of Americans in relation to the momentous issues of war crimes and individual responsibility presented by the American involvement in the Indochina War.

In 1970, with the publication of his book *Nuremberg and Vietnam: An American Tragedy*, Telford Taylor helped greatly to move the issue of war crimes and individual responsibility toward the center of public consciousness in this country when he contended that the United States involvement in Vietnam was, in many respects, criminal in the Nuremberg sense. Earlier efforts to demonstrate the same conclusion, directed at mobilizing antiwar sentiment, had been easily shrugged off,[2] but Taylor's timing was fortunate. He rode the crest of indignation, confusion and concern created by the sensational disclosures of the My Lai massacre in late 1969, the subsequent prosecution of some of the leading participants, and the eventual conviction of William Calley. At the same time, antiwar veterans were beginning to describe in public combat experiences that had routinely involved intentional killing and cruelty toward innocent Vietnamese civilians. Finally, Taylor's argument appeared at a time when prowar sentiment had virtually vanished from the American scene, and the political debate was confined to disagreement over exit strategies.[3]

As the war went on, Taylor further developed his position, especially in discussions stimulated by the publication of his book. Taylor implied that General William Westmoreland, the American military commander in Vietnam during most of the Johnson years, appeared subject to criminal prosecution if his relation to battlefield atrocities was appraised by the standards used to assess the personal responsibility of a rather comparable Japanese military commander, General Yamashita, after World War II.[4] In the late spring of 1971 a portion of the so-called

Pentagon Papers was placed in the public domain.[5] These documents dissolved many cherished ambiguities about the motives, intentions, and objectives of Washington's leading policy-makers with respect to United States involvement in Indochina. The full corpus of Secretary of Defense Robert McNamara's task force study of the history of this involvement established two propositions having a direct and important bearing on the criminality of the United States government. First, there is clear proof that American civilian and military leaders did not consider the specific effects on the civilian society of Vietnam of their decision to bring high-technology weaponry to bear in massive fashion on a low-technology society.[6] Second, the case against the United States on the aggressive war issue is strengthened by the availability of authoritative documentary evidence as to the intentions of the policy-makers.[7]

But even before release of the Pentagon Papers, the issue of war crimes had developed independently. The public outcry against Lt. Calley's conviction and imprisonment was partly occasioned by the belief that he was the little guy selected as a scapegoat for policies adopted at the highest civilian and military levels of policy planning. Furthermore, the irony of rewarding putative "war criminals" (first-line policy-makers such as the Bundy brothers, Dean Rusk, Robert McNamara) with jobs of prestige and influence in American society was not lost on the widening antiwar community in this country, nor was the further irony of treating those who had struggled to bring the war to an end as "enemies of the people," criminals, exiles, or traitors. The public became conscious that war crimes had been committed on a large scale by American officialdom. The public also became aware that those who had participated or conspired with these "war criminals" still remained in control of the system. As a result, tension developed between, on the one hand, the clarity of the facts and the law on the war crimes issue and, on the other, the inability to bring this clarity to bear on policy, even to the extent of hastening an end of the war.

These matters are still unsettled. They call for a reconsideration of the post-World War II approach toward the individual criminal responsibility of German and Japanese war leaders. In essence, we need to determine whether those war crimes trials can be viewed as precedents in an evolving legal tradition of individual responsibility. Or must they be seen instead as special events, associated with the conditions of victory in World War II, which as a result of ensuing patterns of statecraft have by now been denied any status as legal precedents? Naturally this issue cannot be resolved in a decisive way. But the question of the evolving meaning of the Nuremberg idea underlies any discussion of the individual responsibility of American leaders in connection with the Vietnam War.

## Nuremberg Controversy Renewed

In the context of the 1970s people are skeptical about the moral stature of international law in the Nuremberg area. There has, indeed, been a rebirth of cynical realism, often proclaimed under the peculiar contention that excessive moralism and an exaggerated rhetoric of moral concern, rather than immorality or even amorality, indirectly produced the most serious excesses of American battlefield practices in Vietnam. The conviction of American leadership that its attempt to defeat the Communist challenge in Vietnam was a morally righteous enterprise seems to have contributed to an atmosphere in which the human costs of the war for the Vietnamese civilian population were put aside without qualms of conscience. Such thinking certainly seems to exemplify the adage that "the end justifies the means."

This kind of moralizing induced reactions of various kinds. Arthur Schlesinger, Jr., sought to revive an emphasis on the national interest, seeking thereby to discourage policy-makers from invoking moral arguments to support unwise policies that constituted unsuccessful uses of national power. In Schlesinger's words: "Until nations come to adopt the same international morality, there can be no world law to regulate the behavior of states. Nor can international institutions—the League of Nations or the United Nations—produce by sleight of hand a moral consensus where none exists. World law must express world community; it cannot create it."[8] On this basis Schlesinger restricted morality to ideas of prudence rather than notions of right, and condemned the American war in Vietnam as "immoral" only because the scale of the commitment

> burst the limitations of national interest. Our original presence in South Vietnam hardly seems immoral since we were there at the request of the South Vietnamese government. Nor does it seem necessarily contrary to our national interest; conceivably it might have been worth it to commit, say, 20,000 military advisers if this could preserve an independent South Vietnam. But at some point the number of troops, and the things they were instructed to do, began to go beyond the requirements of national interest. This point was almost certainly the decision taken in early 1965 to send our bombers to North Vietnam and our combat units to South Vietnam and thus Americanize the war.[9]

According to Schlesinger, it was the wrong-headed morality of the architects of escalation who believed that the rightness of their cause vindicated any degree of devastation and suffering, which "intensified senseless terror till we stand today as a nation disgraced before the world and before our own posterity."[10] In essence, this approach associates the immorality of the war primarily with the disproportion of the means adopted, given a reasonable construction of the geopolitical ends in view. Had the policy-makers engaged in such calculations, rather than in missionary claims relating to "freedom," "commitment," and "communism," then presumably the threshold of immorality would never have been crossed. There is an apparent paradox here: immorality arises because moral claims are made to justify a line of policy. Schlesinger overcame this paradox by asserting that statist imperatives of rival national governments prevent the formation of any moral consensus in world society; moral considerations invoked to justify national policy are therefore best regarded as a form of self-serving moralism, which prevents the operation of the only true kind of morality possible on an international level, namely, the prudential calculation of means and ends. Within such a framework, law follows morality, its role being confined to reinforcing the logic of the moral order. It is then appropriate to limit the role of law to questions of means, not ends.

But this denies Nuremberg as a basic orienting tradition. At Nuremberg, three categories of offenses were regarded as punishable crimes under international law:

a. Crimes against peace:
   (i) Planning, preparation, initiation or waging of a war of aggression or a war in violation of international treaties, agreements or assurances;
   (ii) Participation in a common plan or conspiracy for the accomplishment of any of the acts mentioned under (i).
b. War crimes:
   Violations of the laws or customs of war which include, but are not limited to, murder, ill-treatment or deportation to slave-labour or for any other purpose of civilian population of or in occupied territory, murder or ill-treatment of prisoners of war or persons on the seas, killing of hostages, plunder of public or private property, wanton destruction of cities, towns, or villages, or devastation not justified by military necessity.
c. Crimes against humanity:
   Murder, extermination, enslavement, deportation and other inhuman acts done against any civilian population, or persecutions on political, racial or religious grounds, when such acts are done or such persecutions are carried on in execution of or in connexion with any crime against peace or any war crime.

This is the formulation relied on in the Nuremberg charter and judgment and carried forward in the Nuremberg Principles as set forth by the International Law Commission in 1950. There is no reason to question its authoritativeness so far as what was decided at Nuremberg; the authoritativeness of Nuremberg itself is a separate matter.

Clearly, the logic of Nuremberg rests on a moral order in which the ends of policy are crucial, and in which means are assessed according to their intrinsic character as well as their proportional relationship to ends. The prime effort at Nuremberg was to regard "aggressive war" both as illegal in itself and as entailing individual criminal responsibility for its principal planners. In the language of the judgment: "To initiate a war of aggression, therefore, is not only an international crime; it is the supreme international crime differing only from other war crimes in that it contains within itself the accumulated evil of the whole."[11] This position takes the view that the very nature of the war policies themselves, and not their proportional relationship to the national interests at stake, must form the basis of moral and legal appraisal. In Schlesinger's terms, Japan's effort to expand its zone of economic and security control by means of war should be considered a reasonable, if ultimately disastrous, calculation of means in relation to ends in the context of national interest. The Tokyo Tribunal, however, held that Japan committed aggression because it initiated war by military attacks.[12] And certainly this view of the central teaching of Nuremberg underlay Taylor's application of legal criteria to war policies. But oddly enough, even Schlesinger argued that "the Charter, Judgment, and Principles of the Nuremberg Tribunal constitute, along with other treaties, rudiments of an international consensus" that warrant enforcement: "Such documents outlaw actions that the world has placed beyond the limits of permissible behavior. Within this restricted area a code emerges that makes moral judgment in international affairs possible up to a point. And within its scope this rudimentary code deserves, and must have, the most unflinching and rigorous enforcement."[13]

This approach confuses the significance of Nuremberg, and also endorses substantive rules and standards that are inconsistent with the main plea for a calculus of means and ends as the basis of a moral foreign policy. Schlesinger did note that "these international rules deal with the limits rather than with the substance of policy" and, as such, "do not offer grounds for moral judgment and sanction on normal international transactions (including, it must be sorrowfully said, war itself, so long as war does not constitute aggression and so long as the rules of warfare are faithfully observed)." But even the most morally and legally inclined position would contend this much. Schlesinger thus wrote about "moral absolutism" as a "malady" that "may strike at any point along the political spectrum," and "[f]rom the standpoint of those who mistrust self-serving ethical stances, the heirs of John Foster Dulles and the disciples of Noam Chomsky are equal victims of the same malady. Both regard foreign policy as a branch of ethics."[14] Presumably, Schlesinger intends here to link Dulles and Chomsky because, despite their dramatic political differences, their views share a concern with the intrinsic moral and legal status of American foreign policy and can thus be compared with the more pragmatic view that a moral foreign policy is one that brings means, ends, and national capabilities into approximate balance. In the context of Indochina, Chomsky and his unnamed disciples did nothing more than to document Schlesinger's own conclusions about the aggressive character of the war and the barbarous tactics by which it was waged. Schlesinger cannot explain his Vietnam position as merely one of the degree of violence used to crush the National Liberation Front. One can, to be sure, contend that carrying the war beyond a certain point was stupid ("counterproductive," as the authors of the Pentagon Papers tend to put it), but surely it did not become "aggression" at some point merely because of an increase in its magnitude.[15]

The legal philosopher Richard Wasserstrom attacked Taylor's approach to the laws of war by emphasizing its failure to insist on the moral status of its own principles. Taylor ended his book with the kind of statement that epitomizes Wasserstrom's objection: "One may well echo the acrid French epigram and say that all this 'is worse than a crime, it is a blunder'—the most costly and tragic national blunder in American history."[16] Wasserstrom countered that "crimes are much worse than blunders."[17] He objected to the basic sentiment that underlies this kind of bias toward pragmatic judgments about what was wrong with America's policy in Vietnam. The objection is fundamental. Those who opposed the war on intrinsic grounds, contending both that it was a crime and that crimes of this sort are far worse than blunders or mistakes, were kept outside the counsels of decision, whereas those who merely differed with policy, even if strenuously, did not cut themselves off from discourse. In the war crimes context this latter attitude causes some confusion, as it analyzes notions of criminality in a framework that it regards as susceptible only to prudential criticisms.[18]

This kind of ambivalence between morality and legality is one characteristic of a period of transition within international life itself. The controversy about the Nuremberg tradition is characteristic of the transition process from statist imperatives of the Westphalia tradition to the communitarian drift of the Charter tradition.[19] The Westphalia tradition is a shorthand description of the system of world order that has prevailed in international life since 1648, when the Peace of Westphalia was concluded at the end of the Thirty Years War. The main characteristic of this system is the acknowledgment of the sovereignty of national governments in domestic and international affairs. The Charter tradition, far weaker and of more recent origin, seeks to qualify the discretion of sovereign governments in the area of war and peace by establishing rules of restraint and creating international institutions of review. The convergence of these two approaches to the organization of international life exposes a number of contradictions between sovereign discretion at the national level and community judgment at the global or regional level. The present structure of power and authority in the world system is heavily weighted on the Westphalia side of the seesaw. The world's strongest military capabilities are effectively controlled by principal national governments. The political organs of the United Nations function mainly as instruments of statist diplomacy, rather than as the exponents of world community envisaged by the authors of the United Nations Charter. On one level, then, it appears naive and misguided to invoke the Nuremberg tradition as a basis for judging the dominant actors in world affairs. There is no point in trying to oppose the mighty and powerful with moral and legal fulminations. Given this outlook, the only realistic hope for shifting attitudes among leaders and their publics is to persuade the strong that it is contrary to their own welfare to wage wars which do not promote national interest. Hence the practical appeal of Schlesinger's plea for amorality and a sober calculation of national interest. Hence also Taylor's confusion of the military failure of the Vietnam War as an exercise in intervention, with its normative status as an aggressive war involving criminal tactics. By his own acknowledgement, for example, Taylor "until 1965 supported American intervention in Vietnam as an aggression-checking undertaking in the spirit of the United Nations Charter"; then he, like Schlesinger, altered his attitude essentially because of that year's drastic changes in "the nature, scale and effect of intervention."[20] It is important to realize that by 1965 more than a year had passed since the assassination of Ngo Dinh Diem, the Geneva Accords had been partially repudiated, an overt United States role in a large-scale counterinsurgency war had been revealed, the Gulf of Tonkin incident had occurred, and the resolution bearing that name had been passed.

This ambivalence is embedded in the Nuremberg experience itself. Only the victorious nations participated in setting up the tribunal and passing on the charges.[21] More important, ghastly wartime actions of the Allies, such as the destruction of Dresden, the fire bombing of Tokyo, and the atomic bombing of Hiroshima and Nagasaki, were kept outside the orbit of war crimes inquiry. Standards of negative reciprocity were used at the Nuremberg bar of international justice: leaders of the defeated states were not charged with any such actions that were also commonly practiced by the victorious side, such as unannounced submarine attacks or aerial bombardment of enemy cities. Such forbearance can be interpreted to mean that anything the victor does is beyond condemnation as criminal, and that a defendant might succeed with a *tu quoque* argument. So interpreted, Nuremberg is deeply flawed as moral education. However, there is more to Nuremberg than its judgment. Certainly the Nuremberg trial contributed to an international learning experience on world order, representing a precedent whose significance would, with the passage of time, reach beyond the original circumstances of its application. Part of the ideology of Nuremberg itself was contributed by Justice Robert Jackson in his assertion that, "If certain acts in violation of treaties are crimes, they are crimes whether the United States does them or whether Germany does them, and we are not prepared to lay down a rule of criminal conduct against others which we would not be willing to have invoked against us."[22] Taylor's book represents an effort to insist on the relevance of the Nuremberg idea even in a context where the accused government officials were neither on the enemy side in a war nor beaten into submission on the battlefield.[23] The United States was not defeated in Indochina in anything like the way that Germany was defeated in World War II. Although the military mission failed and has been widely discredited, United States military and economic prowess remains preeminent in world affairs. Nuremberg has reached beyond its original dimensions when applied to Vietnam, because in 1945 there was no prospect of its subsequent intergovernmental application; hence, this moral extension, so to speak, was implicit within its initial historical dimensions.

Those who are working for a new system of world order based on some form of effective central guidance in matters of war and peace reject as obsolescent and regressive the "realism" of national interest approaches to foreign policy. There is a new realism emerging out of the need to adapt the state system to the multiple challenges of war, population pressure, global pollution, resource depletion, and human alienation.[24] This new political consciousness insists on regarding United States involvement in the Indochina War as illegal and immoral from the beginning, in the late 1940s and early 1950s. This assessment can be made more authoritatively since the publication of the Pentagon

Papers.[25] But the main point is that the world is in a situation of transition from one system of order to another—from a statist logic that is no longer adequate, to a normative logic associated with the United Nations Charter and the Nuremberg Principles that does not yet pertain. In the midst of such a process of transition, rigid distinctions between what the law "is" and what it "ought to be" obscure the central reality of movement from one position to another. Those who identify with a progressive vision of world order are primarily agents of value change. In this sense, to pass judgment on one's own government, to discredit those who for so many years planned and waged aggressive warfare in Vietnam, and to seek an application of the Nuremberg concept, is to embody the future in the present to some small extent. We become, in a normative way, what we do.

## Problems of Application

The available facts show that the United States violated the Nuremberg Principles, and that its chief policy-makers could be prosecuted before a Nuremberg-type court for crimes in all three categories. The question arises as to what kind of action is appropriate in the absence of a proper adjudicating tribunal. Since evidence is increasingly available to support allegations of criminality, the nonavailability of an adjudicating forum is now the most crucial policy issue.

The Nuremberg concept presupposed an Allied victory in World War II. In the context of the Vietnam War, there was no prospect that a United States military surrender would enable either North Vietnam or the National Liberation Front to convene a tribunal that would hear charges against United States military and civilian leaders.[26] Moreover, the organized international community has neither the will nor the capability to proceed against the most powerful country in the world. There is no prospect, in other words, of bringing United States leaders before the bar of international justice, even in the imperfect manner of Nuremberg.

Some legalistic observers have argued that the inability to convene an international war crimes tribunal should put to rest, once and for all, allegations about war crimes. Taylor was somewhat ambiguous on this point. On the one hand, he argued that at the end of the war crimes trials after World War II, the United States government "stood legally, politically and morally committed to the principles enunciated in the charters and judgments of the tribunals. The President of the United States, on the recommendation of the Departments of State, War and Justice, approved of the war crimes programs . . . The United States delegation to the United Nations presented the resolution by which the General Assembly endorsed the Nuremberg Principles. Thus the integrity of the nation is staked on those principles."[27] In short, the United States created a precedent intended to bind itself in the future. On the other hand, on the difficult issue of application in the altered setting of the American involvement in Vietnam, Taylor came down hard against entrusting United States domestic courts with any role in assessing the legal status of American involvement or battlefield tactics. Thus, despite his reasonably clear set of judgments that our role in Vietnam created a Nuremberg problem, Taylor provided absolutely no guidance as to what can (or should) be done about it. In response to this criticism, Taylor has said that he regards the question of applications as "a political one," outside the scope of his technical competence. And I suppose it is "political" in the sense of involving the mood of public opinion. Obviously, if 90 percent of the American public (rather than a tiny number, say one percent) clamored for war crimes trials against American leaders in the Vietnam War, including Westmoreland, Abrams, Rusk, Rostow, and others, then there would be a powerful movement in this country to constitute some sort of tribunal.

Serious legal questions, however, are also involved. The growth of international law has always depended on the vigor of its domestic enforcement. The absence of an international tribunal does not prevent serious judicial treatment of war crimes issues. After all, the *Eichmann* case was heard before a domestic court in Israel, and there is a Security Council Resolution calling on nations to use their domestic legal systems to punish World War II war criminals.[28] In a variety of areas, ranging from the apprehension of international pirates (and more recently hijackers) to the enforcement of antitrust and expropriation norms, domestic courts have performed valuable functions when international tribunals were nonexistent or unable to act.[29] Furthermore, a particularly strong case for the development of a more active judicial role could be made in light of certain tendencies to downgrade Congress' constitutional role.[30] The expansion of executive prerogatives has eroded the constitutional scheme envisioned by its framers and has led to other undesirable effects.[31] In particular, presidential ability to maintain secrecy and to manage the release of news has virtually nullified the development of legal restraints on war-making at the global level.[32]

In Taylor's view, "[a]fter five years of bloody and costly war sustained by Congressional appropriations, if the President's course is to be checked by another branch of the Government, it is the Congress and not the Court that can and should be the checking agent."[33]

This line of argument is very statist in character, for it overlooks the degree to which the legitimacy of government is undermined when standing and judicial relief are denied to individual citizens who raise these legal issues.[34] The efforts to gain judicial relief in relation to the Vietnam War, for example, arose from refusals to enter the armed forces or pay taxes—in other words, refusals to contribute to the war. The "wider logic of Nuremberg" supports such individual efforts, for they are based not on the Nuremberg decisions strictly construed, but rather on the concept of Nuremberg as a set of directives about individual responsibility in relation to aggressive war-making.[35] In this regard the "wider logic" includes such actions in the Nuremberg setting as President Roosevelt's appeal of 1944 to the German citizenry on the issue of war crimes: "Hitler is committing these crimes against humanity in the name of the German people. I ask every German and every man everywhere under Nazi domination to show the world by his action that in his heart he does not share these insane criminal desires. Let him hide these pursued victims, help them to get over their borders, and do what he can to save them from the Nazi hangman. I ask him to keep watch, and to record the evidence that will one day be used to convict the guilty."[36] There is an implicit civic responsibility to resist and oppose any war which it seems reasonable to believe is aggressive and, hence, whose furtherance involves the commission of crimes against peace.

Part of the "wider logic" also involves the generalized responsibility of all actors at every level of social organization to implement the basic Nuremberg directives. The United Nations Security Council has urged governments to facilitate the prosecution of World War II war criminals. By preparing the Nuremberg Principles—merely a codification of what was decided at Nuremberg—the United Nations has set forth general standards of responsibility that pertain to all who hold high public office.[37]

And finally, the "wider logic" has to do with giving effect to the Nuremberg concept in contexts other than the prosecution of those leaders responsible for the policy. The attempt by war resisters to turn the legal system against illegal and criminal warfare involves a symbolic effort to use these ideas of personal responsibility to inhibit unrestricted sovereign discretion in the area of war and peace. The United States is not Nazi Germany, and precisely for this reason, the vulnerability of the war-making apparatus may lie in the potential responsiveness of its institutions to the values embedded in Nuremberg thinking, rather than in its susceptibility to battlefield defeat.[38] The "wider logic" explores the possibilities of enforcing Nuremberg in a situation where "victor's justice" is unavailable, and where the war machine and its underlying criminality persist.[39]

Taylor advanced five reasons for concluding that a domestic court should not inquire into the legality of the American involvement in the Vietnam War. He based his arguments either on constitutional grounds of executive usurpation of congressional privilege, or on international law grounds of incompatibility with treaty obligations to refrain from nondefensive (or aggressive) uses of force. It is important to emphasize the distinction between the "illegality" and the "criminality" of a war. Domestic courts have been asked by litigants to rule only on the issue of illegality as it impinges on their rights as citizens. Such rulings are quite different from a determination that particular government leaders are "guilty" of war crimes and, by Nuremberg reasoning, should be held individually responsible.

Taylor argued, first, that to resolve the issue would require "the examination of hotly controverted evidentiary questions" for which much relevant material is unavailable; these questions involve the quantum and timing of infiltration from North to South Vietnam, the status of the 1954 Geneva Accords, and the relevance of the SEATO Treaty. Second, unlike the situation after World War II, the perception of who was "the aggressor" in the setting of Vietnam is very difficult to adjudicate because even the issue of "who attacked whom" is factually and legally murky; moreover, governments through the years have been unable to evolve an agreed definition of aggression. Third, in Nuremberg and Tokyo it was possible for the prosecution to establish intent and motivation by relying on the "proven intentions and declarations" of the defendants. Fourth, Congress had endorsed the war by means of the Tonkin Resolution in 1964 and by voting appropriations since that time. And fifth, the judicial capacity to act in the area of foreign affairs is severely restricted, even if it is not entirely clear whether this is a matter of constitutional requirement or judicial self-restraint.[40] On these bases Taylor concluded that "the Supreme Court *is not authorized* to render judgment on the validity of our participation in the Vietnam War under the Nuremberg Principles or international law in general."[41]

Taylor's five points can be dealt with individually: His first point concerns the lack of evidence of criminal behavior. Since publication of the Pentagon Papers, however, ample documentary material has appeared on which to assess the central issue of whether the United States government waged a war of aggression in Indochina.[42] Some difficult issues of interpretation remain, but these issues are not inherently more difficult than those confronting courts in many other areas of the law, nor do they seem to hamper greatly the prospect of reaching a clear conclusion. On the issue of war crimes and crimes against humanity there is less documentary evidence, but there is also less need for it, as alternative sources of reliable evidence exist. For instance, many Vietnam veterans, who at times themselves participated in specific massacres, are willing and eager to testify about the tactics, methods, and weapons of warfare used. There is no longer any reasonable doubt, if indeed there ever was, about the main United States patterns of warfare in Vietnam that have been challenged as illegal.[43] The evidence is there.

Taylor's second point has to do with the ability to identify an aggressor. The setting of the Vietnam War, however, is not significantly different from that of World War II. The extension of the combat zone to North Vietnam in 1965, and the character of the interventions by both sides in South Vietnam, seem susceptible to legal analysis and inference. Indeed, proadministration and antiadministration legal scholars have long shared the conviction that the law and the facts are clear enough to support an inference of aggression, though they do not agree on who the aggressor is.[44] Under such circumstances it should be possible for a court to make a comparable assessment. Indeed, the government as a whole seems estopped from even contending that it is impossible to identify the aggressor in the Vietnam context, since it has itself so frequently argued that it was acting in defense against aggression.

The failure of governments to reach an agreement on the international definition of aggression is surely not a plausible obstacle for a domestic court that seeks to reach a determination in relation to specifically challenged conduct. This assertion takes on more weight with the realization that the growth of American law has proceeded on the assumption that the content of general concepts has generally depended on a case-by-case development, rather than on the application of a definition agreed to in advance. Indeed, the United States has been a leading opponent of international attempts to define aggression, and has consistently opposed the definitional initiatives of the Soviet Union and others on these general grounds of legal policy. Finally, there was enough clarity about the character of aggression at Nuremberg and Tokyo to permit authoritative inferences of aggression in the absence of a definition. It is not at all clear that to strike first is a decisive indicator of the aggressor's identity. Consider, for example, the legal debate about the outbreak of the 1967 Middle Eastern War, or the American threat to use force, if necessary, to prevent the deployment of Soviet missiles in Cuba in 1962. Nor is it clear that in World War II there was an undisputed chain of aggressive actions by Germany and Japan and of defensive responses by the Allied Powers.[45]

The third objection to a judicial review of the Vietnam War concerns the lack of evidence of intentions, which here too is undercut by the publication of the Pentagon Papers. Even if these documents are incomplete or one-sided, as claimed by most of the principal officials depicted therein, a prima facie case has still been made, and a burden to come forward has still been imposed on those who would repudiate the available evidence of intentions. Furthermore, the issue before domestic courts would not be the criminality of specific government officials, for which the question of intent is relevant, but rather the legality of state action, for which the question of intent is not relevant. If the first two concerns are dissipated, then this one seems immaterial in many contexts where judicial redress has been sought. This issue of intent seems relevant only to the formation of some Nuremberg-type operation against specifically identified defendants.

The fourth block to judicial review is the fact of congressional endorsement. By now, however, there is ample indication that the passage of the Tonkin Resolution should not be viewed as an endorsement of the legality of the war as a whole, any more than its later repeal should be viewed as a repudiation of the war.[46] Several prominent senators who voted for the Tonkin Resolution had been outspoken opponents of the war for several years and have denied their intention to give the President blanket authority to expand the combat theater. The argument on appropriations seems even weaker, since it has been made abundantly clear by many congressmen and senators that votes for appropriations reflected an overriding concern for the physical welfare of Americans in the battlefield. However misconceived and implausible such a rationale may be—for example, the welfare of American soldiers could best have been safeguarded by earmarking appropriations "for withdrawal purposes only"—it nevertheless suffices to establish the view that a vote for appropriations cannot properly be construed as a vote for the war.[47] In any event, congressional approval of the war is not strictly relevant to its legal status. Congress might (and often has) given its formal approval to executive policy that courts have later deemed unconstitutional. The doctrines of judicial review and of constitutional supremacy, as developed in American legal history, presuppose that courts have the last word on issues of this kind. Obviously, the need for a court to reach a decision that challenges fundamental policy of both coordinate branches poses very delicate political problems for a society that prides itself on popular sovereignty and representative government, but these difficulties are not properly viewed as obstacles to adjudication. Especially where individual issues of life and death and collective issues of war and peace are concerned, the right of judicial redress seems to take clear precedence over the prospect of potentially harmful clashes among coordinate branches of government.

The fifth objection to judicial scrutiny of the Vietnam War asserts the judicial incapacity in the area of foreign affairs. There have been very few tests, however, of the scope of judicial power in the area of foreign affairs, and these have been in relation to special circumstances favoring judicial prerogatives. The "political question doctrine" as a basis for deference seems to be the most persuasive ground on which to urge courts to side-step the legal issues raised by the Vietnam War, but even this argument is not very strong. As the landmark decision of *Baker* v. *Carr* made clear in an apportionment context, there is no fixed context for a "political question."[48] In the present context, there seems to be a powerful basis in law and policy to reverse past court dispositions to treat all issues of foreign policy as falling within the domain of executive discretion and outside the domain of judicial scrutiny. Until the Kellogg-Briand Pact of 1928, no effort was ever made to outlaw aggressive war, but since that time numerous events have confirmed the growth of this prohibitive rule of law. There are no technical difficulties in the Vietnam type of context to prevent applying this rule of international law, which is central to the United Nations Charter, and its implementation by domestic courts seems desirable. The incapacity of the political organs of the United Nations to proceed effectively against a principal state, and the general unavailability of an adjudicating tribunal on the global level, make it especially important to establish the responsibility of domestic courts in this area. Generally, in fact, domestic courts have been far more important than international courts in developing and upholding international law. The contemporary situation, in which the United States is the most powerful actor on the world scene and is deeply involved in foreign military operations, makes it evident that if legal limits are going to have any relevance at all, they will have to be generated on a domestic level. Since the executive part of the government is already engaged in evolving the policy, normally with the acquiescence of Congress, the courts provide the only conceivable arena in which a serious legal challenge can be mounted. Admittedly, such a position requires "a new patriotism" in which the national interest in law-abidingness in international undertakings is given an unprecedented priority.[49]

The strength of the Nuremberg imperative within our political culture is apparent in relation to the overall impulse by individuals and groups to invoke the Nuremberg Principles when governments fla-

grantly disregard the standards established at Nuremberg.[50] Without
the wider logic, Daniel Ellsberg would probably not have been motivated to act as he did. It is significant that Ellsberg spoke of himself as
a war criminal warranting prosecution *before* he apparently decided
that he had a duty to unlock the secret files.[51]

The issues of separation of powers and "political question" seem an
insufficient basis for judicial passivity. Legal criteria now exist by which
to appraise a challenge directed at war policies.[52] The flow of power
from Congress to the executive in the area of war and peace has badly
distorted the constitutional notion of checks and balances. Where Congress fails to act and a clear issue of urgent national welfare is at stake,
the courts have an obligation to act.

Obviously, it is tempting for an American court to dispose of such issues as belonging to the executive province, or as having been resolved
by subsequent congressional action that governs judicial action. But to
yield to such a temptation is to consign American institutions to a state
of impotence during times of emergency. The differences between Nazi
Germany and the United States need to be stressed when considering
the benefits and burdens that would result if the courts were allowed to
deal with this conflict within the public consciousness. To shut off judicial redress leaves conflict to the streets; to control the streets is to
initiate a program of "pacification" at home that seriously endangers
the fragile institutions of a democratic polity.[53]

## Nuremberg and the Present

In writing about the waning impact of the Pentagon Papers, Walter
Pincus suggested that "Daniel Ellsberg may look back and wonder why
he did it."[54] As with the invasion of Cambodia in May 1970, the My Lai
disclosures, and the Calley trial, the revelations of the Pentagon Papers
generated a temporary furor in the country but did not exert any decisive influence on either public opinion or government policies.[55] In
each instance, the war persisted, bureaucratic momentum was maintained, public apathy returned, and the bipartisan elite that had conceived and executed the Vietnam intervention remained in or close to
power. There has been a turn against neither the war, nor the war-
makers, nor even against the military-industrial complex. To be sure,
there are ripples of discontent, but the dominant mood of the country
appears to stress the continuity between the recent past and the hoped-
for future.[56]

If this evidence of continuity is considered from the perspective of the
Nuremberg tradition, the implications are extremely discouraging. In-

terpreting Nuremberg for the benefit of German society in 1947, Karl
Jaspers wrote, "The essential point is whether the Nuremberg trial
comes to be a link in a chain of meaningful, constructive political acts
(however often these may be frustrated by error, unreason, heart-
lessness and hate) or whether, by the yardstick there applied to mankind,
the very powers now erecting it will in the end be found wanting."[57]
The United States failed to abide by the Nuremberg tradition both
with respect to the use of its military power against a foreign society and
with regard to attitudes toward individual responsibility. Despite the
evidence of war crimes, crimes against peace, and crimes against
humanity, one detects neither public indignation of any magnitude,
nor efforts to hold the main policy-makers accountable in any degree
for the moral consequences to Vietnam and to the United States of the
involvement. Accountability could also be achieved by paying reparations to the peoples of Indochina or by exonerating those who engaged
in nonviolent acts of war resistance. An atmosphere of reconciliation
might be established by offering amnesty to war criminals, both as an
acknowledgment of political reality and as a way of dealing with these
questions on some nonpunitive level of concern. What public indignation there is decries the cost and the failure, namely, that the war
plans were too expensive, given the interests at stake, and that these
plans did not accomplish the mission of securing South Vietnam for an
anticommunist Saigon regime. To discredit policy-makers for their
failure to achieve stated goals is a normal accompaniment of any democratic system of political accountability. But it represents only a
pragmatic, not a normative, basis of judgment, for such criticism
happens also when the means and goals of policy were admirable.[58]

This American repudiation of the Nuremberg tradition is part of a
more general pattern of international behavior. The Soviet interventions in Eastern Europe, the French colonial wars in Indochina and
Algeria, and the Anglo-French cooperation in the Suez campaign are
examples of international conduct that appear to be criminal if measured by Nuremberg standards. These examples of criminality show
that none of the powers that sat in judgment at Nuremberg has kept
the implicit promise of establishing a precedent for the future. Indeed,
it is a tribute to the public consciousness of the United States that the
Nuremberg issue has been raised at all, although this consciousness
also reflects the length, the frustrations, and the overall failure of the
American effort in Vietnam. The basic international reality, tragic
from the perspective of Nuremberg, is that world public opinion, at
least as it has crystallized in the setting of the United Nations, neither
expects nor insists on carrying forward the Nuremberg tradition. This

is partly because the pattern of repudiation seems so pervasive, and partly because there is no international capability to pass judgment on the actions of a state that has not been utterly defeated in a war.[59]

The failure of Nuremberg is a matter both of behavior and of public consciousness. On both levels the Nuremberg tradition has been virtually repudiated by the governments that dominate international life. The only open question is whether some popular movement could revive and sustain this tradition in defiance of the statist logic that prevails in international life. It is for this reason that unorganized efforts by "peace criminals," peace groups, and journalists seem so important. They are important because the future of world society ultimately depends on keeping the promises of Nuremberg. For, to again quote from Jaspers, "Ever since European nations have tried and beheaded their monarchs, the task of the people has been to keep their leaders in check. The acts of states are also the acts of persons. Men are individually responsible and liable for them."[60] Jaspers' words are especially relevant today, because he was so keenly aware that an external judgment like Nuremberg was not an adequate means of resolving for German society the genuine issues of coping with the Nazi experience. These issues have their proper locus within the national consciousness of the state that has acted in such a criminal fashion. The external judgment, by its very externality, tends to divert attention from the need to emphasize internal processes of renewal.[61]

## Keeping the Nuremberg Idea Alive

Some lines of constructive initiative to preserve the Nuremberg Principles are possible. It may well be impractical and undesirable to press for formal trials of those American political and military leaders principally responsible for both the overall drift and the main battlefield tactics of the Vietnam involvement. But the formation of an American commission of inquiry that would assemble evidence and draw conclusions on the issue of war crimes could have a constructive impact.[62] It also seems essential for the moral status of law in American society that steps be taken to exonerate draft resisters, tax evaders, and others who committed nonviolent "crimes" to manifest their opposition to the Vietnam War. There seems to be an ample basis for the United States to pay reparations to Vietnam as well as to Laos and Cambodia, to help them overcome the war damage that has been done. These reparations should be gathered on as public a basis as possible, perhaps being collected from a one percent income tax surcharge for a number of years, and from cuts in the counterinsurgency portion of the Defense

Department budget. In any event, the idea that the United States has some ongoing responsibility to those war-ravaged societies seems essential for America's civic health. This assertion of an American responsibility does not imply direct participation in postwar Indochina. Funds should be channeled through an international trust arrangement and given to the Indochinese governments to spend according to their own priorities.

Other steps could also be taken, even in face of the low state of public consciousness in these matters. Governments could press for a new world conference, on the order of the effort to codify a modern law of war at the Hague Conferences in 1899 and 1907, so as to establish new laws of war that would incorporate, to whatever extent possible, both the normative developments (such as the Nuremberg experience and the United Nations Charter) and the technological developments of the last several decades. It may not be realistic to suppose that governments would be willing to participate in such an endeavor, given the widespread practice of counterinsurgency warfare. It may also be questioned whether the statist bias that would be likely to underlie such a world conference might not produce a code that was heavily weighted in favor of counterinsurgent preferences. These are real concerns, but not of sufficient weight to nullify the effort to inhibit the relapses into barbaric behavior that now occur whenever a large-scale war of counterinsurgency takes place and relies on high-technology weaponry.[63] At a minimum the process of preparing for such a conference would vividly heighten awareness of many of the relevant issues.[64] Participation by governmental delegations would reaffirm the validity of legal and moral restraints on the discretion of government officials, and the pressure to produce something tangible might lead to a renewal of the law of war on a realistic and effective basis. The international climate seems somewhat receptive to an initiative of this type, in view of such bloody struggles as those in Indochina, Nigeria, Pakistan, and the Middle East.

Another area of change could involve structuring the American governmental system to make it more responsive to normative restraints in relation to warfare.[65] Congress could clarify its own relation to the presidency and establish definite procedures to authorize limited objectives within fixed times and periods; in other words, except for an emergency response to a sudden attack, recourse to war should be based on specific congressional declaration, although it need not be technically treated as a declaration of war.[66] If the President acted without such authorization or exceeded its express terms, then he could be made subject to a series of congressional remedies ranging from censure to impeachment, and any member of Congress should be given judicial access to seek declaratory, and possibly injunctive, relief. Congress could also grant the courts an express mandate to hear arguments about the legal status of any war, and could confer standing upon individuals to seek judicial redress for alleged infringement of personal and property rights.

Of great potential importance would be the creation of some post within the government that would have responsibility for conforming the action of the country to the requirements of international law. This post could be conceived of as an attorney general for international affairs, or as an under-secretary in a yet-to-be-created department of peace. The function of this job would be to report privately to the President on the legal status of any contemplated undertaking by the United States, and to report publicly any doubts about the legal status of ongoing policies. Such a public official would serve notice on the President that legal consequences of foreign policy activity would receive explicit attention. Of course, there are many difficulties with such a proposal. For example, how does one prevent the government official entrusted with the task of being an international law watchdog from becoming a presidential lap dog? How does one take account of reasonable differences of opinion as to the requirements of international law, requirements that are often controversial in the extreme, especially in determining "aggression," "armed attack," and "self-defense"? How can such a public official gain access to the facts on which a persuasive legal appraisal depends? How can an international law argument prevail in relation to a determined President, a militant Congress, or a mobilized electorate? How would such legal judgment be enforced? How should account be taken of the failure of "the other side" to show comparable respect for the restraints of international law?

All these difficulties are generally characteristic of efforts to bring law to bear on human behavior. Pitfalls, weaknesses, and ambiguities are unavoidable at any level of social and political organization. Nevertheless, the legal approach seems a valid method of inhibiting aggressive war-making and discouraging criminal methods of warfare. The national and human peril of allowing the discretion of governmental centers of power and authority to determine the occasions and character of warfare seems clear. We need to build barriers against warmaking carried on in the name of national populations who are often victimized by the process without ever participating in it. The next great movement of mankind needs to involve decisive action by the public "to keep their leaders in check" in the area of war and peace.

The steps here outlined are intended only to indicate a sense of direction on the most immediate level of response. In more fundamental terms, I am persuaded by the view held by the philosopher J. Glenn Gray that "to resolve the problem of warfare, civil or international," requires that "a transformation of a deepgoing inner sort will have to come over men."[67] I also share his view that "a changed attitude toward our habitat must precede—or at least accompany—a changed attitude toward our fellow man."[68]

Law is largely a dependent variable in both accomplishing and sustaining change, although it may symbolize emerging human aspirations and precede a wider social adjustment to new challenges. The Nuremberg idea needs to be understood as a statement both of aspiration and of necessity. The American indebtedness to Telford Taylor, Daniel Ellsberg, and the Berrigans is essentially the same: they remind us of our ideals in a period of national and international danger. Taylor further demonstrated that in earlier days of triumph, Americans even acted to translate these ideals into norms of judgment and conduct. The question before all of us, at this time, is whether we who originally lit the Nuremberg torch can keep it aflicker in these times of barbarism. This question will not be answered affirmatively by governments, but only by popular forces who are committed to building a new world order in which tenderness toward nature and fellow men is the basis of organization and action. It is this greater struggle that is being prefigured by the debate surrounding Nuremberg and Vietnam.

# Part Three: Analytic Modes

# 10 | The United Nations: Constitutional and Behavioral Tendencies

Popular perceptions of the United Nations have tended to be increasingly negative about the organization's role in international society. These perceptions are heavily influenced by the gap that separates the goals proclaimed for the United Nations in its own Charter from the observable facts of international life. They are also influenced by a gap between the needs of world order and the capabilities of the organization. These two gaps appear to be widening over time, and they confirm the view that the sovereign state continues to be the only significant political actor in international society.[1]

Even the late Secretary-General U Thant was led to say, in the Introduction to his *Annual Report* for 1968, "this document must make gloomy reading."[2] U Thant evidently shared, to some extent, the widespread pessimism that has arisen as a result of the organization's inability to close the gap between international behavior and Charter goals. U Thant's later views seem to be somewhat negative about United Nations accomplishments and prospects. He said in 1970 that "the United Nations born of the Charter has done well, but it has not done well enough."[3]

The Secretary-General made plain his view that the prime deficiencies of the United Nations are not of a sort that call, at least initially, for organizational reform: "Nor is the structure of our world Organization, although admittedly imperfect, incapable of performing the tasks assigned to it. Indeed the machinery for international cooperation is as yet largely untested and untried." In his message on United Nations Day in 1970, U Thant urged that "It is time for Governments to make a fresh start and to lift themselves again to the same high level, if not a higher level, of vision and determination as that of the authors of the Charter. We must give the Charter a real chance at last. We must pass from words to deeds." U Thant apparently believed that the deteriorating United Nations situation results from the nonsupportive attitudes and patterns of behavior on the part of many national governments. In a similar vein, Emilio Arenales, President of the 23rd session of the General Assembly, said that a pes-

simistic view of the United Nations "is unfair and ought to be recti-
fied."[4] Arenales' assertion embodies the view that the United Nations
should be primarily understood as an instrumentality of governmental
action, rather than as an autonomous actor with tasks that it either
does or does not perform.

More specialized commentary takes account both of the gaps between Charter aspiration and United Nations actuality, and of the extent to which the sovereign state persists as the dominant actor in international society. Ernst Haas wrote that "the United Nations system is
hyperdependent on its environment." Stanley Hoffman expressed the
same kind of judgment, observing that "the efficiency and authority of
the organization depend ultimately, not on its Charter, but on the state
of the world outside."[5] Such an acceptance of environmental deter-
minism avoids the question of whether the United Nations has failed in
conception or execution.[6] It also encourages a specification of those
aspects of environment that determine the kinds of tasks that the
United Nations can perform under various sets of international circumstances.[7] The Charter framework has become virtually irrelevant to
most close students of United Nations behavior; recently academic effort has concentrated on trying to evolve functional categories of explanation that identify the tasks which the United Nations has actually
performed.[8] A newer generation of specialists has affirmed the concrete,
if modest, accomplishments of the organization and regards the more
grandiose conceptions of Charter goals or world community needs as
generally incapable of further realization in the present international
system.[9] Thus, while United Nations civil servants, peace groups, and
public officials tend to keep alive the sense of "the two gaps," more
specialized scholars tend to redefine inquiry so as to maintain a descriptive and analytic focus on the organization as an evolving
actuality.[10]

My aim is to lay a foundation for disciplined inquiry into the adequacy of a given arrangement of power and authority on a global scale
in relation to such objectives as the maintenance of peace and stability,
the gradual reduction of poverty and economic inequity, the protection
and promotion of human rights, the achievement of national self-
determination, and the maintenance of ecological balance through
both resource conservation and environmental protection. "World
order" is increasingly used as a descriptive term in the social sciences to
link considerations of global arrangements of power and authority in
relation to these normative issues.[11]

Social science can contribute to problem-solving by careful analysis
of issues and solutions.[12] The false utopianism of the past character-

istically proposed a new system of world order and then assumed that the progressive role of reason in human affairs would assure its adoption.[13] Few people now believe that the future will be an automatic improvement over the present—quite the contrary. In fact, the loss of hope is so widespread and immobilizing that we must now demonstrate that the future can be beneficially shaped at all.[14] This essay takes the position that an evaluation of the United Nations properly combines descriptive analysis with normative appraisal. It is part of the scholarly function to clarify what has taken place; it is also part of this function to appraise performance in light of explicit goals and to recommend courses of action that might bring future behavior into closer conformity with preferences.

## The Two Gaps

In several important respects, the Charter conception of the United Nations is distinct from the United Nations as an operative political entity. For convenience I refer throughout to the "United Nations" as though there were a concrete entity to which the label corresponds. Except as a convenience, such a form of reference is a misleading kind of reification. The United Nations consists of many distinct organs and organizational settings. Also, the specific organ does not "act" in any way analogous to the way a person acts. Instead, actions are taken in accordance with established procedures by individuals who are assigned different roles that they play in quite different ways. This concreteness and specificity of event should be kept continually in mind, although the discussion is conducted at a higher level of abstraction. The interaction between Charter goals and United Nations action is highly relevant and can be used as the basis for mobilizing certain types of political attitudes and support. It is in this respect that an official of the United Nations, such as U Thant, invokes the gap between Charter language and statecraft to mobilize public and elite opinion in favor of more moderate international behavior. Furthermore, the United Nations has had a different center of organizational activity at each of the various stages of its existence. Therefore, there is an analytic need to differentiate these stages, especially by reference to shifts in coalition patterns and the bearing of these patterns on the prospects for implementing various categories of interacting national claims and counterclaims to act in specified ways that are asserted by states within the United Nations, and which constitute the essence of international disputes.[15]

The second gap is created by the distance between the United Nations as an operative system and the problems of world order that were set forth in Articles 1 and 2 of the Charter. This second gap does not imply organizational deficiencies but rather takes account of those features of the international environment that identify the limits of United Nations capacity. It calls attention to the capacities that would be needed to attain certain goals of world order involving the minimization of violence, the maximization of human dignity, and the promotion of social and economic progress.

An awareness of these two gaps helps to orient inquiry into the significance of the United Nations in the present world, and evokes such questions as, what would be likely to change if the United Nations were to be removed from the world scene? Or what would be the impact on world affairs of a greatly strengthened United Nations?[16] Such questions are unrealistic, however, to the extent that unidentified changes in the global setting would have to occur to set the occasion for the actual removal or strengthening of the United Nations.[17]

Despite the dependence of the United Nations on its setting, the organization has a distinct identity, as well as certain autonomous and semiautonomous roles. These roles were probably not fully envisioned by the drafters of the Charter, and their character has changed from one stage to another in the history of the organization. Furthermore, the United Nations as an actor builds up a certain momentum of its own, which produces an organizational identity that influences to varying degrees, on varying issues, the attitudes and behavior of its members.[18]

The United Nations is an integral part of the complex pattern of international politics. To observe that the United Nations is highly dependent on the character of the international setting implies that the main currents of political conflict influence the action of its main organs, particularly the more political ones. However, there is a discernible pattern of an opposite sort, namely, a refraction effect, such that the setting of the United Nations itself may also influence the ways in which conflicts are conducted and justified. The prospect and actuality of United Nations discussion seems to have had a marginal moderating and conditioning impact on the behavior of governments in most instances of armed conflict since World War II, although this assertion is difficult to prove and must be regarded as vague and speculative. Convincing evidence will be difficult to obtain until foreign office archives are available. The assertion is based mostly on impressionistic indications of influence, though it is supported by the recollections of participants in such international crisis situations as the Cuban missile crisis of 1962 and the Suez campaign of 1956. This refraction effect has a differential impact, depending on the government concerned, the issue area presented, and the concrete setting of a particular concern. Also, patterns of refraction effect vary with the specific traditions of different institutional arenas within the overall United Nations setting.[19]

The susceptibility to environmental influences also varies in extent and quality from organ to organ within the United Nations system. Of the principal organs, the International Court of Justice is probably the least responsive to the international environment, and the General Assembly the most responsive. The voting procedures in the General Assembly, based on the principle of sovereign equality, do not accurately reflect the grossly unequal distribution of power within the overall international system. Therefore, the General Assembly often tends to reflect environmental shifts in an unreliable or partial fashion. For instance, the collapse of colonialism has apparently not increased the international system's pressure on South Africa to abandon apartheid nearly so much as it has increased the scope and magnitude of the General Assembly's concern and pressure. This situation illustrates the refraction effect created by the ability of the Afro-Asian states to dominate, increasingly since 1955, the agenda of and the mobilization of support for positions in the General Assembly, while remaining unable to command the capabilities that would assure implementation of the claims endorsed by the Assembly.[20] To vote in favor of a course of action is quite different from taking steps to obtain the desired results, such as providing the resources needed to make effective or merely credible a position that engenders support from even an overwhelming majority of states.[21] The influence of the international environment in the General Assembly is so great that the membership itself has become cynical. Failure to implement claims that have often received the support of an overwhelming consensus calls dramatic attention to the limits of United Nations enforcement capability.[22] The disjunction between words and deeds encourages the view that the United Nations is, "at most, a debating society" and, what is more destructive, lends some credence to the position that justice claims—those advanced by groups to change their relative status, wealth, or power within the political system and supported by appeals to the justice of their demands—will only be satisfied to the extent that they can be enforced by violent means. Failures of peaceful implementation by the United Nations encourage independent strategies of violent implementation.[23] The Goa model of social change is instructive in this respect: India's years of futile effort to eliminate the Portuguese colonial presence in Goa through United Nations intervention offer a sharp contrast to the efficacy of India's violent takeover of that area in December 1962. The Goa incident illustrates a double failure of implementation, which led both sides in the dispute to criticize the United Nations: the Afro-Asian side was critical because of the prolonged inability of the organization to secure compliance with the anticolonial demand put forward by India; and the conservative states criticized the inability and unwillingness of the organization to take steps on behalf of a member state, Portugal, who had been the victim of "aggression" directed at its territorial boundaries.

Given the absence of autonomous capabilities on the part of the United Nations, efforts by the organization to alter patterns of behavior must be correlated with the prospects for a reasonably prompt and effective implementation, as well as with the capacity to muster a constitutional majority in support of a United Nations resolution.[24] The quality of this double-dimensioned correlation is difficult to assess in particular instances, because there may be a variety of objectives underlying the assertion of a claim, including the creation of some kind of legitimizing basis for recourse to violence outside the United Nations framework. Recourse to the United Nations in search of a persuasive solution is part of the contemporary process of exhausting all pacific remedies before recourse to violent remedies. Nondefensive recourse to force for legislative purposes that have been approved by the world community is not explicitly allowed by the Charter or positive international law, but such recourse does seem to enjoy some status to the extent that formal and authoritative expressions of the will of the international community can now be regarded as the fundamental law-creating process. Careful research is needed, as well as analysis of the effects of different degrees of correlation between the Charter and the United Nations response for different issues at different stages of United Nations history.[25]

To regard the United Nations as an actor within the international organization can transform international politics without endowing the organization with military and police capabilities and missions.[26] At the same time, United Nations arenas are to a variable and uncertain extent separated from national arenas and are therefore capable of inducing a sum greater than their parts. A shared allegiance to an agreed set of norms shapes the communication of national positions even within highly political organs, influences their rhetorical style, and may gradually socialize the participants toward more cosmopolitan values.[27] Furthermore, an international civil service is built up over time, in the secretariat of each international institution, and these international civil servants interact with the nationally oriented missions of the membership. Such data may not yet appear significant, but they seem to reinforce the efforts of cosmopolitan constituencies within nation-states to diminish reliance on sovereign prerogatives and to build up confidence in the prospects for a world community. These constituencies appear especially active within the liberal democracies in the developed countries of the world at this time.[28] But socialist and centralized societies might experience a sharp shift of outlook in reaction to the growing evidence that mankind cannot long expect to endure the hazards and costs attendant on "a world of sovereign states."[29]

## Multiple Roles and Functions

More often than not the performance of the United Nations is judged by its success or failure in the area of war and peace. The United Nations emerged as a direct consequence of World War II, just as the League of Nations was established as a reaction to the breakdown of international order in 1914.[30] The Preamble of the Charter talks of "saving succeeding generations from the scourge of war," and both utopian and cynical perceptions of the United Nations converge on its role as an agency of war prevention. Perceptions more attuned to the global setting of the United Nations emphasize that the organization is poorly endowed to maintain peace and that the international environment does not reinforce these Charter goals, except in those very special and limited circumstances where the principal states perceive their interests as converging in an endorsement, or indulgence, of a peace-keeping or peace-enforcing role for the United Nations.

But during its history the United Nations has acquired functions other than the maintenance of peace and security; its new functions have, in fact, grown to be its main preoccupations. These functions are: the promotion of social change, such as decolonialization or economic development; the aggregation of claims by the newer states for the reform of the international economic order; the facilitation of forms of technical cooperation, including standard-setting and the exchange of information; the publication and censure of certain classes of violation of human rights, such as apartheid; and the formulation of a world public interest with respect to subjects of global dimension, such as the status of nuclear weapons or pollution. Each of these complex objectives is more successfully pursued by certain United Nations organs than by others, and is more prominent at some stages of United Nations history than at others. Here too careful research and analysis is needed to present a sophisticated profile of the multidimensional role of the United Nations.

Within the organization, there is always the possibility of bargaining, and this potential encourages a search for compromises and tradeoffs. For instance, the United States for many years lent some support to antiapartheid resolutions partly with the hope of obtaining African support or abstention on the issue of Chinese representation. Such bargains may be tacit, implicit, or explicit. It is difficult to gain insight into the dynamics of this bargaining process, and virtually impossible to acquire data on specific bargaining patterns. Nevertheless, the bargaining process that takes place in various United Nations arenas determines to a great extent the shape of action that is undertaken.[31] Often the bargaining involves only an exchange of verbal commitments, thereby accentuating the problems associated with a failure of implementation, and calling dramatic attention to the disjunction between the implementing capabilities within and outside the organization.

As a quasi-dependent international actor, the United Nations is far more apt to reflect changes elsewhere in the international system than it is to initiate changes by its own existence and undertakings. It is primarily an instrument of confrontation and cooperation for member states. In addition, it has certain active potentialities that encourage viewpoints to coalesce; these potentialities can also help to create a moral presence in areas where a vacuum might otherwise exist. Indicators need to be developed to draw attention to changes in the international environment that are likely to have significant impacts on United Nations operations.[32]

## Correlation with International Political System

For example, the effectiveness of the United Nations is likely to vary directly with the correlation between its own authority patterns and the distribution of power in international society.[33] The greatest significance of this correlation is for issues of peace and security. The achievement of a positive correlation between power and authority within the United Nations is impeded by four factors. First is the postulate of sovereign equality, especially in the General Assembly, which gives states of greatly unequal power an equal influence in the formulation of authoritative policy.[34] The second impediment is the fact that permanent membership on the Security Council is reserved to the principal members of the alliance that achieved victory in World War II, which gives status to states of diminished importance in the present world, such as Great Britain and France, and excludes more important states from participating on a permanent basis, such as India, Brazil, and the United Arab Republic. This authority pattern fosters the anachronistic idea that the major European states are among the most important actors on the international scene.[35] The third factor is the prolonged period of exclusion of mainland China from participation in the affairs of the United Nations and the willingness for so many years to indulge the Cold War fiction that the Taiwan regime represents China for United Nations purposes. And the fourth factor is the failure to confer some sort of direct United Nations status on regional and possibly transnational functional, cultural, or even ideological actors who might be far better suited than are separate sovereign states to present the most meaningful political perspectives on many international issues.

These four negative correlations between the organizational structure of the United Nations and the structure of the international political system within which the United Nations must operate suggest some of the reasons why the organization has not assumed greater importance. There is also a basic circularity here: the United Nations has the structure that it does partly in order to ensure that its role will in fact be marginal.[36]

The scale and character of United Nations operations is very much confined by the budgetary and other resources at its disposal. Limits on assured resources generally exclude the United Nations from playing an autonomous and central role in major international conflicts. Under special circumstances, an ad hoc political consensus may form to assign a mission to the United Nations and even to provide some confidence that the mission can be financed. Shortly after Belgium granted national independence to the Congo in 1960, violence broke out in the new state. Opposing factions in the Congo looked to the Soviet Union and the United States to support their respective causes. The prospect of competitive interventions by these two superpowers encouraged recourse to the United Nations. The Congo operation was the consequence, a United Nations peace-keeping operation in the early 1960s, initially supported by all principal governments and arriving on the scene with an invitation from the Congolese government. The collapse of that government and the more conservative orientation of its successor led to a collapse of the consensus at the United Nations. Indeed, the Soviet Union charged that the United Nations peace-keeping force had played a pro-Western interventionary role in the Congo and had exceeded the original mandate. As a consequence, the Soviet bloc refused to accept any financial responsibility for the Congo operation even though the undertaking had been formally approved by the organization, including a special assessment. The Soviet Union also contended that the Secretariat was biased in a pro-Western direction and made its troika proposal to reorganize the United Nations Secretariat by having three Secretaries-General to represent Western, socialist, and neutralist approaches to world politics. These disputes over financing and organizational reform illustrated the outer limit of such an ad hoc operation, within a setting where the political consensus authorizing the mission disguised sharp disagreements among principal states over the character and outcome of the United Nations role. The learning experience provided by the Congo operation had induced a sense of modesty about what might be expected from the United Nations in situations where the scale and stakes of the conflict are sufficiently great to undermine the stability of the initiating consensus.[37]

The lack of autonomous United Nations capabilities is itself a way of maintaining the preeminence of principal sovereign states and of sustaining traditional modes of diplomatic interaction. The search for peace and security, economic development, or human rights, involves undertakings of such a magnitude as clearly to exceed normal United Nations capabilities, so that the organization's role is certain to be both subordinate and marginal. The United Nations tends to stress roles and discharge functions that are not concerned with the direct resolution of conflicts and controversies which imperil peace. These roles and functions make use of the organization as a facility for articulating and exchanging claims and conducting conference diplomacy at various levels of overtness.[38] Therefore, the importance of the United Nations at any given time, as one of a variety of diplomatic forums available in international society, depends directly on the degree to which diplomacy within the United Nations appears propitious to either parties or observers. A judgment of censure is one way to use the political arenas of the United Nations when other modes of adverse response seem both too dangerous and too costly.[39]

The capabilities for coercive action remain heavily concentrated within the principal states of the world. The refusal of these states to endow the United Nations with a greater measure of complementary capabilities is a clear expression of their unwillingness to depart from a system of largely decentralized management for the vital affairs of international society. This unwillingness is deep-seated and was, in fact, embodied in the original Charter drawn up by the victorious powers in World War II during a period in which these governments seemed to share a commitment to world peace. Therefore, the meager powers assigned to the United Nations cannot be adequately attributed to the patterns of intense conflict that subsequently emerged.

## *Secondary International Conflicts*

The United Nations was not intended to resolve intense conflicts between its principal members. However, it was hoped that the organization might keep secondary international conflicts within tolerable limits, or even bring them to an end. The United Nations has performed this role with varying degrees of success.

The factor most critical for determining United Nations success in this role is the extent to which the disputing parties are prepared to accept a solution involving political compromise. The United Nations lacks autonomous capabilities and, since the Congo operation, has not enjoyed enough confidence among enough of its membership to take a major part in matters of peaceful settlement. Its most characteristic role in the years ahead is likely to involve assisting parties to maintain a stalemate or to establish a negotiated compromise.[40] The political organs will also serve to register world reactions to particular complaints about violations of sovereign rights, and perhaps in certain cases to mobilize different publics for or against one side in an international controversy. Since June 1967 the United Nations, especially the Security Council, has served in this capacity in relation to the conflict in the Middle East, arousing sentiments in favor of the Arab countries and increasingly putting Israel in a position of diplomatic isolation.[41]

Moderation in the scope, means, and ends of a conflict facilitates all forms of nonviolent resolution, including those modes involving varying degrees of United Nations participation. The existence of irreconcilable conflicts—those in which the minimum terms of the revisionist actor are clearly unacceptable to the status quo actor—appear to be least susceptible to settlement by United Nations intervention, unless possibly the organization can be mobilized to take one side in the conflict.[42] Such mobilization is likely to be most effective when the principal states of the organization agree about the direction, rate, and outcome of influence to be exerted. The attack on apartheid provides an example of irreconcilable conflict. Although the United Nations has taken sides and the principal states share an original consensus as to the character of change that is desirable, this consensus hides contradictory attitudes toward the rate and outcome of change and toward the appropriate limits of external influence.[43] The conflicts between the Arab countries and Israel and between India and Pakistan over Kashmir also seem to be of an irreconcilable nature. The United Nations might nevertheless help in these settings to prevent a deterioration of the status quo or to restore a condition of nonviolent confrontation by facilitating and sustaining a cease-fire.

Another kind of immoderateness results from hegemonic claims exerted by principal states over dependent or lesser states situated within a clearly delimited zone of influence. In settings like Eastern Europe and the Caribbean, the United Nations is denied an active role by the preemptive presence of a state with the capabilities to enforce its will, subject only to challenge by another principal state willing to risk a major conflagration.

If any major state pursues an expansionist policy by overt military means, then there is likely to be little role for the United Nations in the area of peace and security.[44] Serious challenges to the present distribution of power in international society continue to be dealt with through increasing defense spending at the national level and intensifying cooperative efforts at the alliance level. It is hardly surprising that the Soviet occupation of Czechoslovakia in August 1968 had a far greater impact on United States-Soviet relations and on NATO-Warsaw Pact relations than it did on the operations of the United Nations.

## Exclusions, Withdrawals, and Nonmembers

The authority of the United Nations depends considerably on its claim to be a universal organization representing the whole of international society. Significant nonparticipation by states, regardless of reason, weakens this claim. Furthermore, nonparticipating states are likely to be strongly opposed to accepting a United Nations role in disputes to which they are a party. The opposition of China and North Vietnam to any United Nations role in settling the Vietnam War is one salient demonstration of the effects of nonparticipation on the willingness of states to use the United Nations as a problem-solving agency.

Existing approaches to the United Nations emphasize various types of distinction: between the Charter as a formal concept and the United Nations as a network of political actors; among successive phases of United Nations operation; and among distinct issues of United Nations concern. Each of these distinctions should be stressed in order to form an adequate conception of the United Nations role at any particular time.

However, there has been little discussion of how to specify the dominant aggregate trends of United Nations activity. A preliminary attempt is here made to specify the principal modes of operation, both as contemplated in the Charter and as exemplified by the organization's experience with distinct, substantive concerns and during distinct phases of its history. Each main pattern is characterized as a "system."[45] The objective is to facilitate comparison among distinct issues and time periods. The various systems are themselves delineated to highlight distinctive patterns of expectation and operation. They can be conceived either in analytical terms as hypothetical alternatives, or in sociohistorical terms as condensations of United Nations history.[46] Because the clarity of the boundaries between systems is often exaggerated, it is desirable to make intrasystemic as well as intersystemic comparisons.[47] My purpose is to outline an approach to United Nations studies through the conceptualization of these main systems, in the hope that this approach, in combination with other efforts, can produce greater analytic clarity and substantive understanding about the United Nations.

A basic distinction is made between the formal system embodied in the instrument of incorporation and the life history of the resultant organization.[48] The instrument of incorporation, the United Nations Charter, is susceptible to multiple perceptions and interpretations because of its complexity, its inclusion of contradictory and complementary norms and procedures, and its vagueness about the relative priority of concerns. In part, a formal instrument of incorporation is intended only to sustain a minimum original consensus among the founding members of an organization, in order to create a frame for action within which different lines of development, depending on the political climate, can unfold. The formal level of system planning is important in any project to strengthen the United Nations. The Charter system establishes certain constraints and opportunities for behavior, although under some circumstances the constraints will be eroded and under others the opportunities will go unused. Several points follow from the distinction between Charter systems and United Nations systems: the clear separation between the idea of the United Nations and its actual realization; the complex interactive relationship between the idea and its realization through time; the limited capacity to predetermine the behavioral patterns of a political actor by agreeing on an instrument of incorporation; and the shaping role of the overall environment within which an actor operates.[49]

The following presentation differentiates a series of systems—one Charter system and five United Nations systems—which are outlined with a clarity not reproduced in actual experiences. In reality, the boundaries of these systems are often blurred, because observers approach them with distinct preconceptions, assess them on the basis of different readings of facts and preferences, and bring to bear quite different ideas about evaluating the behavior of the United Nations.

## Charter System I

The United Nations Charter establishes a series of norms, procedures, and institutions that incorporate a set of political assumptions and expectations about the resulting organization. The document is coherent in itself and can be understood without any further consideration of United Nations history.[50] The Charter's basic goal is to contribute to the maintenance of peace and security in international society. The basic political assumption is that an international institution can be set up for this purpose only if the powerful states of the world are assured that the organization will not act against their wishes, and that harmony can be attained within a framework of orderly cooperation among sovereign states. The principal victors of World War II were designated the states of primary rank.[51] The main device used to assure deference to these states was to confer on them alone permanent membership in the Security Council. Permanent members were given the veto power within the Security Council, which was in turn entrusted with exclusive decision-making authority and with primary competence on matters of peace and security. The organization was endowed with almost unlimited potential authority to implement any consensus of the victorious states of World War II, including the competence to undertake further action against the defeated countries, promote a build-up of United Nations enforcement machinery, or intervene in the affairs of smaller countries.

The Charter also embodied several central ideas of normative constraint: a prohibition on the discretionary right to use force, an insistence that claims to act in self-defense be subject to community review by the Security Council, and an obligation to use procedures of pacific settlement in the event of a dispute. There were certain inadequacies in this pattern of normative constraint, aside from the political problems of implementation: no clear delimitation of the idea of self-defense, no assured procedure for passing judgment on an alleged recourse to self-defense, no prospect of impartially determining claims about aggression and self-defense, and no assured policing procedures to impose the will of the Security Council.[52]

Geopolitical calculations and ideological solidarity proved to be far stronger influences than a nation's commitment to adhere to the United Nations framework of action. States voted in the United Nations in light of these traditional affinities and often did not allow their positions to be shaped by the merits of a controversy. The strongly political content of the deliberations led states in minority positions in the United Nations into an adversary relationship with the organization; real credibility was never established for the Charter claim that the organization would act on behalf of some neutral and transcendent world interest, as specified by the Charter in normative terms. The rivalry and tension of the world political setting was not excluded from the United Nations arena; indeed, it is possible to maintain that this atmosphere of intense rivalry defeated Charter expectations and made it impossible for the United Nations to carry out its intended role. However, the Charter was never intended to transform the structure of international society, and there was no reason to suppose that severe international conflicts would not emerge after 1945. The Charter embodied only a commitment to create a flexible instrument of collective action that would be continuously readapted to the dominant trends of international life.

Several developments shaped the role of the United Nations in directions not fully anticipated in the explicit terms of the Charter. First, the postwar political alignments split the permanent membership of the United Nations.[53] Second, the development of a nuclear missile technology established a clearly delimited international hierarchy of power and introduced an element of moderation into adversary relations among principal states. Third, liberation movements and civil strife came to have a central and controversial role in international society. Fourth, the unexpectedly rapid decolonialization of Asia and Africa, and the concomitant entry into international society of a large number of new states, altered the balance of political influence within the United Nations. Fifth, the outcome of the Chinese civil war and the continuing representation of China by the Western-oriented Chiang regime in the organization distorted its authority structure.

These developments partly explain why the enforcement provisions of the Charter were never carried out. There was no continuing political consensus that could sustain cooperation among the permanent members of the Security Council. The United Nations was denied autonomous capabilities, and the main issues of peace and security were handled by the traditional Westphalia methods of national defense, alliances, and spheres of influence, as well as by newer regional arrangements of a quasi-institutional variety.[54] During this same early United Nations period, the United States' political dominance of the organization led to its partial conversion into an instrument of American foreign policy on issues of peace and security.[55] Therefore, some ex parte missions were entrusted to it, most notably to conduct the defense of South Korea. A rather indefinite United States-Soviet convergence on some aspects of an anticolonialist position has also been evident in certain United Nations action.

The Charter distribution of functions between the General Assembly and the Security Council was altered by the following two developments. One was the desire of the United States to circumvent the Soviet veto and obtain a United Nations mandate for its international policies. The other was the growing insistence by Afro-Asian states that issues of human rights and residual colonialism be given prime attention.[56]

Several conclusions can be stated about this Charter system. First, it was based on a set of normative imperatives that were at sharp variance with Westphalia modes of international behavior. Second, there was no serious effort to evolve procedures within United Nations settings for implementing these normative imperatives. Third, several sharp discrepancies between the Charter conception of international society and its empirical character became apparent during the first decades of the United Nations existence. And fourth, the net effect of these two kinds of discrepancy has resulted in a marginal role for the United Nations in the area of peace and security, a role restricted to moderating conflict and facilitating social change.[57] As a result, it has become all too plain that the organization is not able to secure compliance with its Charter's own prescriptions about international behavior.[58]

Could a more useful or effective United Nations be derived from a new and different Charter? The answer depends on whether it is practical to suppose that it would be possible to negotiate a new Charter, given the present composition of the organization and the current international environment. In the contemporary world political climate, it would be impossible to agree on a Charter at all, much less a greatly different one. There are no indications whatsoever that governments of principal states would endow the community of states or a political majority of states with the competence and implementing resources to override sovereign discretion on central matters of security and development. Nor does it appear likely that principal governments would even encourage the autonomy needed for the organization to evolve over time a world position of its own on vital questions of war and peace. It was only the war-sustaining consensus that provided the degree of solidarity needed to bring the United Nations into being. If the project had been put off until the 1950s, it would be hard to conceive of the Soviet Union and the United States agreeing on joint sponsorship of a world peace organization of even such modest proportions as the United Nations.

The Charter system is not seriously inadequate, given the character of international society. There is no consistent evidence of governmental disposition either to create stronger implementing machinery or to abandon altogether the normative ideals of a world without war. The

Charter has been flexible enough to accommodate itself to an international system differing in key respects from what had been anticipated. Without a strong disposition to dissolve or reconstitute the framework established by the Charter, its system seems to be a durable, if ambiguous and uncertain, element of the current international system.[59] Part of this durability arises from the capacity of the United Nations to alter its main forms of behavior within the Charter framework. The cost of such flexibility is a weak tradition of constitutional adherence, itself a factor inhibiting the growth of real authority over behavior. However, weakness in this particular respect may not interfere with the role of the organization as a forum for communication, political mobilization, and interest articulation.

## United Nations System I

During the first ten years of its existence, the United Nations was dominated by a Western alliance led by the United States. The organization operated principally as an instrument of United States foreign policy in relation to the issues of war and peace that arose from a competitive bipolar relationship with the Soviet Union. The Soviet role in the United Nations was to obstruct the organization from operating at more than a verbal level and to sustain the existence of an open forum for the assertion of its position. The United Nations also provided a channel for continuing communication and diplomacy among rival governments at any desired level of overtness or covertness, ranging from propaganda to secret talks. In the Korean War the United Nations provided the American-led Western alliance its full and unqualified support. The American military operation in defense of South Korea was formally categorized as a United Nations undertaking under a United Nations military command. Chinese intervention in the war in defense of North Korea (and possibly of its own territory as well) was condemned as "aggression" by the United Nations. Clearly, the United Nation's role in the Korean War was the most extreme example of the organization's use as a partisan instrument for executing the foreign policy directives of its leading member state. This use of the United Nations was not solely a consequence of United States ability to mobilize a sufficient number of votes to assure that its political preferences would prevail. The nature of the United States position in the Korean controversy also seemed consistent with the Charter's basic normative imperative about force—the prohibition against aggressive force and the toleration of defensive force—as well as with the organization's commitment to fight on the side of a victim of aggression. Thus, the foreign policy of the United States in the Korean War could be understood as fulfilling the Charter conception rather than distorting it. More controversial instances of the partisan manipulation of United Nations machinery include the successful United States efforts for so many years to deny mainland China access to United Nations affairs, and the related ability to maintain the Chiang regime as China's representative in the Security Council.

The point is that one main United Nations system of operation has been to execute in selected instances the foreign policy of the politically preeminent member, over the opposition of other members accorded a veto power. Clearly, this system is not in accord with Charter principles or procedures. The financing dispute in the mid-sixties illustrates one set of limits on this United Nations system. France and the Soviet Union refused to pay special budgetary assessments that had been imposed by the General Assembly in connection with peace-keeping operations arising out of the 1956 war in the Middle East and the Congo operation. The United States pressed hard for enforcement, supporting recourse to the International Court of Justice for an advisory opinion. The legal case was won in 1962 by those insisting that the assessments were proper and hence, that failures to pay constituted a default for which voting privileges could be suspended. However, the United States effort to force payment was finally abandoned in 1965 as a futile and even counterproductive policy, as it weakened the United Nations by placing the organization in a confrontational relationship with the Soviet Union and France. In net effect, the countries objecting to Assembly assessments established, at least, their right to be financially exempt from Assembly initiatives in the peace-keeping area, thereby protecting to some extent their Security Council veto. The United States concomitantly lost out in its cold war effort to circumvent the Soviet veto. But more recently, the United States has repudiated this effort, even making severe admonitions against a "tyranny of the majority" in the Assembly (in the words of John Scali, United States ambassador to the United Nations, in a speech before the 29th General Session in 1974). The United States has so far been able to avoid United Nations censure for such uses of force as its Dominican intervention of 1965 or its involvement in Vietnamese affairs after 1954. The United States has been far less subject to United Nations criticism on bipolar issues connected with the cold war than has the Soviet Union.[60] On Afro-Asian issues such as the Security Council debate in 1964 on the propriety of the Stanleyville operation undertaken by the United States in cooperation with Belgium and Great Britain to rescue white hostages in the midst of the Congo strife, or the sanctions against the

Smith regime in Rhodesia, there is growing evidence that the United States political capability in the United Nations has recently been declining.[61]

Afro-Asian control of the General Assembly since the late 1950s has made this arena less available for partisan United States manipulation than is the Security Council. Although the availability of the Soviet veto prevents formal substantive decisions from being reached in the Council, this forum can always be used prominently to express an international mood of censure.

## United Nations System II

The convergence of United States and Soviet policy perspectives and interests leads to occasional or sporadic cooperation in the United Nations on the part of these two dominant rivals. Both in response to the Suez campaign of 1956, when the United States joined with the Soviet Union in condemning the joint British-French-Israeli invasion of Egyptian territory in retaliation against Nasser's nationalization of the Suez Canal, and in the early stages of the Congo operation in 1960, bipolar cooperation also initially occurred but was quickly dissipated. Under such circumstances, there is a greater tendency to evolve an autonomous and central United Nations role. However, because of the complexity of executing this role, before long the United Nations is likely to disappoint one or the other of the superpowers, or even both. Such was the case during the long period in which the United Nations sought to terminate the strife in the Congo. This kind of cooperative role is most likely to endow the United Nations with the sort of functions suggested by an optimistic view of the potentialities of Charter System I. Successful implementations, if sustained and not interspersed with serious reversions to United Nations System I, might create more confidence in the positive potentialities of the organization, leading to an expanded budget, more assigned tasks, greater deference to claims, and a generally enhanced stature.

The United Nations as an arena for bipolar cooperation varies with issue and time period. United Nations System II, in the presence of serious forms of United States-Soviet cooperation, could allow the United Nations to become an instrumentality to facilitate and disguise bipolar hegemony. The quality of this system depends in part on the extent to which bipolar cooperative steps accord with or appear to violate the normative framework embodied in Charter System I, as well as on the way in which particular forms of cooperation interact with the sentiments, interests, and capabilities of other groupings of states.

One conclusion is clear: given the bipolar political structure on matters of strategic security, a closer correlation between the structure of power in international society and the assertion of United Nations authority seems to result from United Nations System II than from United Nations System I. Of course, to the extent that the United States becomes the preeminent world power and bipolarity is supplanted by unipolarity, the correlation between power and United Nations authority will be established for United Nations System I, but at the expense of any normative pretense of a cooperative universal and pluralistic framework. The tendency of United Nations System I is to convert the organization into a hegemonic political alliance of the dominant states, with the resultant loss of authoritativeness for United Nations decisions and recommendations. [62] One positive consequence of Afro-Asian participation in the United Nations has been to diminish the relevance of System I to peace-keeping operations. The attitude of nonalignment is sufficiently dominant to discourage United States policy-makers from making partisan use of the General Assembly. [63]

United Nations System II has most chance of controlling the situation in those settings where the United States and the Soviet Union have distinct, but convergent, interests that each feels can be safely or usefully advanced under United Nations auspices. [64] The establishment of standards with respect to arms developments, such as the demilitarization of outer space, and the management of intraregional conflicts, as in the Middle East or India and Pakistan, are areas in which United Nations System II might achieve prominence in the near future. The scope and significance of this system reflects the orientations of the domestic regimes and foreign policies that prevail in the United States and the Soviet Union at a particular period of time. These respective orientations include the United Nations role deemed appropriate by each government and the extent to which these governments hold convergent perceptions of key foreign policy objectives.

## United Nations System III

United Nations System III has emerged as a consequence of the Afro-Asian control of the General Assembly and the voting majority at the disposal of a caucus of the poorer countries. It represents the claims made on behalf of the organization and expressed by a consensus of the General Assembly—at least two-thirds of it. United Nations System III posits demands, asserts interests, seeks to mobilize public opinion, and tries especially to induce the more powerful and rich states to make more of their resources available for economic development in the poorer ones.

The most typical illustration of United Nations System III is the crusade against apartheid, which has been carried on in various ways through almost the entire history of the United Nations.[65] The Afro-Asian priority schedule involves putting pressure on the white regimes of southern Africa, on the ground that these regimes are racist and colonialist. The Soviet voting bloc endorses these Afro-Asian demands, but there has as yet been little Soviet willingness to endow the United Nations with the capabilities needed to implement them. The United States position is similar, although its government shows a greater deference to Charter System I and may be more concerned with sustaining the credibility of actions of censure under United Nations System I. The resolution of this set of issues will involve a greater conflict of interest for the United States, as a consequence of its heavy investments in that part of Africa and because those regimes are anticommunist. At the same time, the dynamics of the rivalry with the Soviet Union for Third World allegiance, as well as the problems of domestic race relations, mount pressure on the United States government to lend increasing support to Afro-Asian objectives.

The Afro-Asian position, generally reinforced in recent years by the Latin American countries in the areas of aid, trade, and investment, is also much concerned with finding ways to overcome national and regional poverty, mass misery, and economic backwardness. The United Nations Conference on Trade and Development (UNCTAD) is a product of United Nations System III, as is the increasing emphasis on the framework of a new international economic order. In fact, since 1957 the agenda and acts of the General Assembly have been increasingly governed by this system.

United Nations System III embodies a maximum disjunction between the power capabilities and authority claims of the organization. This disjunction engenders disrespect for the United Nations on the part of those who assess its success or failure by reference to the successful enforcement of its authority claims.[66] This disrespect is deepened concomitantly with the failure of United Nations Systems I and II to operate in relation to peace and security issues. In United Nations System III the organization does not usually attempt to deal with the grave war-and-peace issues of the day, except to propose general goals and standards concerning the status of nuclear weapons or the desirability of drastic disarmament. One problem with this system is that the only apparent outcome of the political process is to intensify verbal demands. There is neither a gradual build-up of commensurate capabilities, nor any genuine prospect of such a build-up. In this system there is also some indication of a tacit willingness by the principal states to concentrate action functions in the Security Council, where the voting rules work against the operation of United Nations Systems I and II. And because considerable intersystemic bargaining takes place from time to time within the United Nations, the United States has supported some of the projects of United Nations System III in exchange for Afro-Asian support of some of its own projects, such as Chinese representation, which it insists on treating as a United Nations System I issue.

The future of United Nations System III depends very much on the extent to which the Afro-Asian majority begins to command the capabilities, whether within or without the organization, that might make some of their major claims credible or successful. The Afro-Asian attitude toward the United Nations as a whole will be largely determined by whether this system begins to operate beyond the threshold of interest articulation. If implementation by United Nations Systems II or III projects takes place, then the relevance of the organization to Afro-Asian affairs is probably assured. If not, Afro-Asian disenchantment with the United Nations may lead to an increasing emphasis on regional and special diplomatic forums. The continuing possibility also remains that the more militant or dissatisfied Afro-Asian states might form a counterorganization comparable to that proposed by Sukarno after Indonesia's brief period of withdrawal from the United Nations in 1965.[67]

United Nations System III represents the most serious explicit assault on Charter System I, because some of its claims involve direct violations of such basic Charter norms as deference to sovereignty, respect for domestic jurisdiction, and renunciation of nondefensive uses of force. Above all, the Afro-Asian majority demands the use of coercion to achieve social change and to topple constituted regimes in southern Africa in the process. Such objectives can be somewhat reconciled with the human rights provisions of the Charter, but the proposed means of attainment cannot. In this sense, then, the implementation of United Nations System III involves the most severe strain on Charter System I. The diplomatic representatives of South Africa have pointed to this strain as part of their overall contention that United Nations System III is in its totality "unconstitutional" and *ultra vires.*

A serious implementation of this system in relation to either self-determination or economic reform issues would create a de facto revision of the Charter.[68] The abridgment of domestic jurisdiction, as a result of the United Nations use of force to implement legislative claims, would amount to a major modification of Charter expectations.[69] In contrast, United Nations System II lies clearly within the scope of Charter System I, while United Nations System I is substantively, if not procedurally, compatible with Charter System I. The whole effort of the United States to engineer a shift of emphasis from the Security Council to the General Assembly was designed to circumvent the Soviet veto and enable United Nations actions despite the opposition of a permanent member of the Security Council.[70] This intended redistribution of functions was a precondition for the operation of United Nations System I, but it is difficult to reconcile with the expectations of Charter System I. It should be understood that the constitutional criterion is certainly not the decisive one in assessing United Nations developments.[71]

## United Nations System IV

There is a less obvious area where United Nations decisions are reached after an assessment of the merits of contending claims, and with primary reference to the relations between Charter norms and behavior. United Nations System IV is characterized by the search for an impartial determination of the facts in dispute. In United Nations Systems I, II, and III the violation of Charter norms by the target country may well intensify the claim and is a factor taken into account during debate, but the nature of the decision and voting behavior are largely shaped by patterns of political affiliation that persist outside the halls of the United Nations. By hearing which state is making what sort of claim, it is possible to predict who will vote how.

On peace and security issues, especially prior to the heavy Soviet involvement since 1965, the Middle East has provided a context in which the political organs of the United Nations have often and largely behaved in accordance with the postulates of United Nations System IV. The most dramatic example of this kind of behavior was the joint United States and Soviet insistence that Great Britain, France, and Israel restore the status quo ante after the Sinai campaign of 1956. The United States failure to uphold its prime allies and its possible sacrifice of geopolitical advantage on that occasion was widely scored as a gesture of "legalistic" deference to the Charter.[72] Supporters of the United Nations in the area of peace and security have always hailed United Nations System IV as the optimal mode of behavior for members for the organization. This system entails a measure of depoliticization of state behavior within the political organs of the United Nations. Depoliticization has not generally occurred except in instances where the comparative geopolitical merits of a dispute were either clouded or marginal for principal states. The expansion of United Nations System

IV would require international politics to become increasingly sub-ordinate to a more law-oriented approach to the settlement of disputes. Such a transformation of behavioral patterns would seem first to re-quire a shift in priorities and traditions at the national level, and at present no such trend seems apparent. Up to this time, therefore, United Nations System IV has come into play only in exceptional cir-cumstances.

Nevertheless, states attempt to solicit support for their respective positions by talking as if the organization normally functioned ac-cording to the terms of United Nations System IV. Political decisions by national governments are reached through the operations of United Nations Systems I-III, whereas the debate is carried on with reference to United Nations System IV. This incongruence facilitates the re-jection of a United Nations claim by a target state. South Africa, Israel, and the Soviet Union have all been repeatedly subject to adverse votes that reflected their minority status, given the operation of United Na-tions Systems I-III at certain times for certain issues. These votes were political expressions of preference couched in legal and moralistic rhet-oric taken from the Charter and cannot be regarded as a fair applica-tion of Charter norms after impartial and full-scale inquiry.

The International Court of Justice is an arena wherein United Na-tions System IV prevails to a far greater extent than elsewhere in the or-ganization. It is not possible to predict how most of the judges will vote merely by looking at the geopolitical status of the adversary positions, and there is no strong correlation between the judicial behavior of a judge and the foreign policy of his country.[73] The fact that most in-ternational disputes are not deemed suitable for judicial settlement is one expression of the minor role accorded this system in the present in-ternational political system.[74] The exceedingly unpopular outcome in the Southwest Africa Cases aroused Afro-Asian resentment about the way in which the International Court of Justice was using this system. The Afro-Asian countries expected that the International Court would reach a result in accordance with the political logic of United Nations System III, regardless of the perception of the relative merits of the contending factual and legal arguments.[75] It seems clear that a United Nations institution cannot achieve importance unless it is somewhat responsive to the political dimensions of international society, and that the International Court of Justice—even if it allows political factors to exert more influence on the recruitment of judges in the future—is un-likely to be entrusted with a major role in settling politically significant disputes. Governments are reluctant to entrust vital issues to tribunals, not so much because they are concerned about biased decisions being rendered against them but because they are unwilling to risk an adverse outcome of an unbiased decisional process. The real point is that national adversaries are still unwilling to allow their vital concerns to be compromised by third-party procedures, no matter how reliable these procedures may appear to be. Naturally, if the outcome of a United Nations System IV inquiry is likely to vindicate a national position, then it is good politics to advocate and accept such an approach; or if, as in South Africa, the likely outcome of the political process is so much worse that the worst plausible result of a United Nations System IV approach, then it may make sense to accept the International Court of Justice as a forum for decision even if an adverse result is expected.[76]

In short, given current behavior patterns, states will seldom approach important controversies in the spirit of United Nations System IV, although part of the myth of Charter System I is the general prevalence of United Nations System IV in the organization's operations. Whereas United Nations Systems I-III are mainly ways of formulating claims to control behavior, expressive of the political sentiment of a voting majority, these claims may or may not be consistent with the results that would be reached by a United Nations System IV approach. Finally, the implementation of a United Nations System IV outcome is by no means assured if the result is an unpopular one. The continuing primacy of politics in world affairs thus leaves a minor role for United Nations System IV. It is not possible to expand the scope of this system until other changes in attitude and behavior lead principal governments to depoliticize international society.[77]

## United Nations System V

There are recent indications that the United Nations may be increasingly useful to mobilize world political opinion on general issues of global concern, such as pollution, population policy, and resource conservation. In this setting there is less effort to resolve conflicts than to clarify international concern about an existing situation. The claims posited by the organization are likely to be made under the leadership of middle-rank moderate states such as Sweden, Canada, and Japan, which have accepted as their function the responsible articulation of urgent matters of interest to the world community. The development of this range of concerns was not really anticipated by the Charter as a major United Nations activity.

These issues are likely to attract growing attention as their seriousness to national and world welfare becomes more apparent. United Nations System V will probably work initially to clarify the objective situation and then proceed toward the recommendation of cooperative action on behalf of a global interest. Within a decade one can imagine the declaration of "a world ecological emergency."[78] By the end of the century United Nations System V is likely to become the most important activity of the organization.

These concerns with the fundamental conditions of human existence should be sharply distinguished from issues of technical cooperation that have been handled by functional international agencies since the formation of the International Telecommunications Union of the Universal Postal Union in the nineteenth century.[79] United Nations System V should also be distinguished from the broad efforts at standard-setting and knowledge dissemination that have been made by the International Labor Office and UNESCO. United Nations System V will undoubtedly generate various kinds of political pressures, especially because the issues will tend to point up the need for greater political integration at the world level.[80] Therefore, formal acts of this system are likely to impinge upon sovereign prerogatives to an increasing extent. However, the character of the issues likely to concern the system may lead to the suspension of the predominant influence of normal political alignments. It is also hard to tell whether the main governments will find that the United Nations provides a useful set of arenas within which to cope with these problems, and whether United Nations actions will proceed beyond the stage of fact-gathering and interest articulation.[81]

## Projected Charter and United Nations Systems

It is possible to contemplate the adoption of a new Charter designed to shift capabilities to international institutions. The Clark-Sohn plan and the Chicago proposals are two prominent examples. Both propose to convert the United Nations into a form of limited world government, with the latter emphasizing the regionalization of political influence to a far greater extent than the former.[82] Constitution-building as an intellectual exercise, as distinct from a political proposal, may clarify alternatives to the present structure of international society, as well as give some sense of content and direction to a strategy of change. Normally such constitutional models are put forward as mere exercises in advocacy with no discussion of political obstacles or consideration of how to accomplish the transition. Consequently, there is a considerable tendency to dismiss such a Charter system as wishful thinking.

In addition, existing limits on the usefulness of the United Nations do seem to result more from the character of the international environment than from the deficiencies of Charter System I. In fact, Charter

System I seems to have established an adequate framework to facilitate growth or contraction of United Nations activity, depending on the relative weight of political pressure on a given issue or at a particular time. At present there is no political disposition to adopt another Charter system that would do away with the existing behavioral patterns. The main issue posed for reformers of world order is how to generate a political disposition favoring change in national orientation and international structure. The projection of a new Charter system may help to clarify the reorientation that would be required, but it does not constitute any evidence that such a reorientation is at all likely to occur. As in Frederick the Great's time, the successful creation of world government still awaits a crop of political leaders who have experienced a complete conversion to cosmopolitanism "and a few other trifles." However, the emerging imperatives of United Nations System V, combined with the persisting, if not increasing, danger of nuclear warfare and other varieties of catastrophe, emphasize the unprecedented vulnerability of the present basis of human organization. Nothing less than the survival of the human species may be finally at issue. Charter projections, then, are part of a new political terrain on which world reform movements might be expected to play an increasingly significant role.

It would also be necessary to project the main implementing systems that would be likely to result from the adoption of the main alternative conceptions of a Charter system. Obviously one system of importance would be some kind of autonomous structure of United Nations administration in the area of peace and security. As shown by current United Nations operations, a realistic assessment of the role of the organization should be closely associated with the prevailing patterns of political influence and their correlation with implementing capabilities. The same effort at projection might improve the understanding of how alternate systems of world political organization might be expected to operate.[83]

The purpose of analyzing variations in systems is to help identify the principal modes of United Nations operation and to facilitate comparison with past and future practices of international organizations. The focus on distinct systems of operation suggests the importance of consensus patterns, implementation prospects, and national strategies of participation to an understanding of how the United Nations works in relation to a given issue during a particular phase of its existence. These initial mapping exercises need to be continued and refined, thereby making possible a gradually sharper discernment of principal patterns.

The entire orientation stems from an acceptance of the primacy of political factors in explaining United Nations activity. The approach of this chapter holds that the explanation of these political factors is not antithetical to the United Nations idea, as formal legalists tend to argue, but that politics must inevitably be at the root of whatever role international institutions play in world affairs, and therefore must be understood. At the same time, a formal instrument of incorporation such as the Charter, and a special sense of normative mission, condition at least the rhetoric and possibly also the behavior of its member states. The United Nations provides a distinctive set of arenas for the conduct of international politics, and it remains necessary for students of the subject to develop appropriate methods of interpretation.

A social scientist has special skills, complementary to those of the political analyst, diplomatic historian, legal analyst, and commentator, which should be brought to bear on the task of building up a conceptual environment for the classification and presentation of the mass of information generated by the complex network of the United Nations. This conceptual environment aspires to be at once parsimonious and comprehensive. As greater conceptual sophistication is achieved, it becomes desirable to obtain statistical and other forms of empirical verification by formulating and testing propositions about principal processes. A series of case studies would provide evidence about the usefulness of the hypothetical systems outlined here to describe the main forms of United Nations activity.

At present, one high priority for social science is to promote disciplined inquiry without indulging in formalistic or sentimental modes of analysis. Discussion about whether the United Nations has been or is likely to be a success or a failure are not likely to be illuminating unless the criteria of judgment are put forward in a challenging fashion. Similarly, narrations of the formal procedures by which United Nations organs have dealt with a controversy or an issue are not likely to promote understanding unless tied to a theory of United Nations politics, which in turn needs to be interpreted as one subsystem of the overall international political system.

# 11 | Geopolitics and World Order

Various structures of political domination exist in the world today. Some of these structures are internal to a single national society; they may involve the systematic suppression of a part of the population (such as apartheid), or even the entire population (such as totalitarianism). Other structures of domination are external, relying on colonial title, economic pressure, or periodic intervention to control or manipulate foreign policies, institutions, and attitudes.

Structures of domination are sustained by the threat or use of force. There is no voluntary acquiescence in these structures, even though the dominated people may at times have such a strong sense of alienation that they accept their inferior status as inevitable or even foreordained. In any case, dominant groups usually evolve myths to justify their power. Furthermore, in many political contexts modern propaganda techniques facilitate public compliance, while improved police technology increases the effective ability to maintain a structure of domination even when opposition persists.

In today's world, the preeminent structures of domination are those administered by the main governmental centers of power: the United States and the Soviet Union. One such structure is the "sphere of influence," an area of foreign states over which a larger sovereign nation claims and exercises special prerogatives to interfere. This structure of domination has been incorporated into the prevailing idea of world order. Mutual respect for its boundaries prevents the outbreak of general war in the nuclear age and thus contributes to the stability of the existing system.

But stability of this sort, although less catastrophic than warfare, is nevertheless undesirable. My principal objective in this chapter is to demonstrate that despite the legitimacy that this pattern of relationships now enjoys within the existing world order system, this structure of domination nevertheless produces negative consequences.[1]

In general terms, "world order" refers to the aggregation of norms, procedures, and institutions that give shape and structure to international society at any given time. There is no implication that a particular system of world order either prohibits the recourse to war or is successful as a peace system, although it may accomplish either of these things. There is also no implication that a system of world order is committed to the promotion of human justice, although the degree of justice may be one element in assessing the quality of a given system of world order. Many systems of world order can be isolated in the history of international relations, and many more systems can be projected as alternatives for the future. In essence, what these systems of world order have in common is a concern with the varying roles of norms in the process by which power is managed in international life. But a rule of positive law is only one kind of norm. Other norms arise from behavioral regularities that are expressed in terms of claims and counterclaims on the part of the principal actors.

Likewise, the use of the term "legitimacy" is to identify attitudes toward what is permissible at any given time. These attitudes may be established by formal agreement, as through a treaty, or by more tacit and indirect means, as through resolutions in the General Asembly of the United Nations. Because the several perspectives bearing on the legitimacy of a specific claim to act may be inconsistent with one another, it is important to regard a particular claim as more or less legitimate, rather than as either legitimate or illegitimate. Legitimacy is a matter of degree.

There are two principal negative consequences. First, dependent states are denied opportunities for autonomous development, and their dignity is seriously infringed. Dependent populations are accorded a kind of secondary status, which inevitably generates humiliation and resentment. Consider this statement of a Bedouin clan leader to an Israeli reporter: "Do you want me to tell you the truth? I hate you. Yes, I know before you came I was much worse off. Now I have a herd of camels. I live in a real hut instead of a *husha* and all my sons are working and earning good money. We have, I admit, never been so well off. But we hate you all the same. We would rather be oppressed by our people than continue to live under you."[2] This attitude is characteristic of subordinate peoples. Israelis may proclaim that Arabs are better off in Israel than in any Arab country, just as South Africans tell the world that "their" blacks have a higher standard of living than any other black Africans. But people do not consider themselves "better off" if they must be dependent. Conversely, men who are free to determine their destiny will seldom accept the inferior status conferred by a structure of domination.

Second, the existing structures of domination inhibit orderly adaptive change in the world community. Because these structures rest ultimately on the army and the police, they encourage violence in fundamental ways: violence to keep the structure intact, and violence if the structure is ever to be overthrown. This cycle virtually precludes the possibility that significant changes can be brought about through peaceful means, for the alignments are too rigid. Therefore, structures of domination are maintained only at the cost of political flexibility, as institutions are rendered less capable of adapting nontraumatically to change. On a global level, the use of military power for purposes other than self-defense both reinforces and perpetuates the existing hierarchical, largely decentralized system of world order. However, this system has itself become outmoded, increasingly less able to assure adequate security and welfare for most of the world's human communities. Consequently, rigidity characterizes the international political system precisely when structural reform is urgently needed. By examining what are roughly known as bloc relationships in contemporary international society, I hope to contribute something toward both evolving a suitable method of inquiry for this subject and clarifying the task of transforming the system of world order.

## Geopolitical Dimension of World Order

Recent years have seen a major effort to liberate the study of world order from its double heritage of utopian wishful thinking and cynical disregard. This effort would be strengthened by incorporating into our conception of world order certain geopolitical patterns of interaction which have not, by and large, been treated satisfactorily by either international lawyers or by specialists in foreign policy.

The standard juridical approaches to world order continue to focus on the rights and duties of formal political entities in international society. Sovereign states and international institutions are regarded as the principal such entities, and they are seen as carrying out their respective roles within an international setting formally circumscribed by various doctrinal notions. Juridical analysis continues to be dominated, in particular, by the assumption that the territorial sovereign state is the basic actor in world affairs.

States are regarded as a homogeneous class of actors, except in the United Nations context where permanent members of the Security Council are distinguished from the others. Although inequalities of power and differences in domestic public order systems are widely noted, their specific implications for the character of world order are generally ignored. The vocabulary and method of international lawyers have not been generally sensitive to the structures of authority that rest on inequalities of power, especially if these structures have not been explicitly authorized to act in a particular way. One difficulty with juridical approaches is their insistence on a sharp separation between law and politics. But geopolitical reality presupposes certain intermediate kinds of relationships that have some of the definiteness, but not all of the formal attributes, which are associated with a legal regime.

In contrast, the principal approaches of specialists in foreign policy, military strategy, and international relations have not been sensitive to the relevance of geopolitical norms to the management of power. They have shown a tendency to write about the world from a particular actor's point of view, and then to recommend an action strategy based on the relative capabilities and goals of the actor in question. American policy-makers and their advisers have consistently disavowed any systematic exploitation by the United States of its preeminent position within international society. American foreign policy pronouncements typically assert not imperial claims, but rather commitments to universally beneficial principles of world order. However, such statements may be coupled with a self-serving but unconvincing manipulation of these principles to fit the actualities of American foreign policy.[3]

Some of the more perceptive commentators on the recent course of American foreign policy place heavy emphasis on the decision-making process within the national government, the various pressures brought to bear on the executive branch, and the various styles of presidential response. But the "bureaucratic politics" perspective has not so far extended to the informal structures of authority in international society. And in any case, this approach takes no cognizance of normative considerations. Except for the emphasis on nuclear bipolarity as a distinctive and fundamental premise of peace in our era, little attention is given to the consequences of geopolitical patterns for world order.

In the field of international relations, a new body of literature is attempting to give a systematic account of the ways in which power is and should be managed in international society. Some of this literature has noted geographical factors, especially in connection with a concern over the relationship between the global and regional systems or subsystems of politics. This literature follows upon earlier geopolitical interpretations of world order under prenuclear conditions.

A geopolitical interpretation is here offered for one set of important relationships that have emerged in the early decades of the nuclear age. These are the relationships between a dominant state, the United States or the Soviet Union, and certain secondary—that is, subordinate—states. This set of relationships is differentiated from those between the superpowers *inter se*, and also from those between the superpowers and weaker states with no clear subordinate affiliation. A primitive set of terms is supplied in order to simplify the description, to establish the basis for more comprehensive lines of interpretation, and to show the links between hegemonial and other relationships in international society. This analysis can provide both a simple taxonomy more useful than alternative modes of analysis in designating a certain category of dependency relationships in international society; and a better understanding of certain international relationships, which will in turn heighten sensitivity to the patterns of action and reaction that can be anticipated. Although the presentation makes no claim to enable automatic behavior predictions, some refinement of the analysis should facilitate a kind of forecasting comparable to early weather predictions.

The United States and the Soviet Union are classed as Zone I actors because of their military and economic preeminence in the world political system. Secondary states subject to supervisory domination by either the United States or the Soviet Union are identified as Zone II actors, whereas secondary states subject to no clear line of hegemonial domination by either Zone I actor are labeled as Zone III actors. And states such as France, Switzerland, Japan, and Sweden, which enjoy national autonomy in the sense of relative freedom from the threats of military interference by either Zone I actor, are identified as Zone IV actors.

The main patterns of relationship can be put in the form of a simple tabulation:[4]

| States | Mandatory alignment | Discretionary alignment or nonalignment |
|---|---|---|
| Major | I | IV |
| Minor | II | III |

Zone I status is conferred on the basis of capability, intention, and conduct.[5] The distinction between Zones II and III is primarily jurisdictional: countries are assigned to Zone II if they possess the formal attributes of sovereignty but are nonetheless subject to unrequested supervisory interventions by a Zone I actor.

Zone II is characterized by a long-standing tradition whereby a dominant actor enjoys within a weaker state certain prerogatives of claim, control, and geopolitical access. This tradition establishes a line of dependence so strong that a supervisory intervention can occur without the "target government's" consent, or when a Zone II actor has no possibility of establishing a government that might withhold its consent.

As of 1974, such a narrow definition of Zone II excludes all but the countries of Central America, including the Caribbean, and Eastern Europe. These states are clearly subject to hegemony and potential intervention by one and only one Zone I actor, whereas countries in Zone III may be subject to periods of hegemony and military intervention by states in Zone I, Zone IV, or even Zone III.

These conditions do not necessarily require geographical proximity between Zone I and its sector of Zone II, but such proximity does in fact characterize present interzonal relationships. Although in this postcolonial age the Zone I tradition is no longer embodied in juridical form, the regionalist mantle may still serve to establish a quasi-juridical basis for relegating certain smaller countries to Zone II status. There are interesting parallels between the Soviet reliance on an alleged consensus of "the socialist Commonwealth" to justify its 1968 action in Czechoslovakia, and the United States claims of "collective responsibility" in the Caribbean theater. [6]

Zone II may also be described as an extension, in diluted form, of the domestic jurisdiction of a Zone I actor. That is, on certain limited occasions the dominant actor may treat its sector of Zone II as though the latter were part of its own national domain. [7]

As control over proximate territory becomes increasingly less vital for the security needs of the two preeminent actors, one might expect the importance of Zone II status to diminish accordingly, if not to disappear altogether. However, other socioeconomic, ideological and psychological factors may contribute to motivate these actors to maintain their control over political developments in neighboring countries. For example, a Zone I actor might want to expand its sector of Zone II to encompass new geographical areas. Nor would it be hard to imagine another Dominican-style or Chile-style intervention by the United States to prevent a Castroist or Allende-type takeover in, say, Colombia or Venezuela, or to prevent a radical left regime from emerging in several of the presently noncommunist countries of Asia.

In any event, at the present time the critical variable that distinguishes a Zone II situation from other dependent country relationships is the unsolicited, and perhaps opposed, exercise of military power by a dominant state actor over another constituted government. Other actors may censure such assertions of military power, and in fact a Zone I actor may even renounce its own competence to intervene. But there is no serious external effort to challenge the intervention when it actually occurs, provided that it occurs within the boundaries of an acknowledged sector of Zone II.

There is an intentional circularity here: the conditions that determine a country's Zone I status are in fact the product of this very status. The circularity arises from the fact that the boundaries of Zone II are drawn expressly to accord with the claims and behavioral patterns of the Zone I actor; the Zone II setting in turn limits the potential success of any possible counterclaims or countervailing behavior.

Specialists in international relations have long recognized the existence of spheres of influence, blocs, and other hegemonial patterns. However, these traditional approaches have tended not only to be impressionistic but also to posit bloc relationships in opposition to, rather than as integral aspects of, the prevailing conception of world order. But once acknowledged, the role of hegemonial patterns in sustaining world order can overcome, to some extent, the sharp and artificial separation between the realms of law and politics.

Supplementing national boundaries with geopolitical boundaries implies nothing whatsoever about the homogeneity of each zone's membership, nor about the uniformity of intrazonal relationships in general.[8] Nor does the inclusion of hegemonial patterns within the concept of world order imply an unqualified approval of such arrangements. It is useful simply to recognize that the exercise of unilateral prerogatives by the most powerful states in international society may impose discernable restrictions on the discretion of subordinate states.[9] It would also be useful, although beyond the scope of this chapter, to compare the motivations, techniques of control, occasions of military intervention and withdrawal, claims and effects, of various Zone I policies, as well as the interactive relations between each Zone I actor and its sector of Zone II.

Another useful focus for study would be the evolution of Zone I policy over time. In the contemporary setting a broad comparison of Soviet and American policies would have to emphasize, among other factors, the degree of economic development in the target countries of Zone II, the scale of the Zone II units, logistic access of the Zone I actor to dependent political units, and the extent to which the demands of the Zone I actor influence the quality of political, economic, and social life in Zone II.

One objective here is to delineate the Zone II structure of domination from a perspective of world order. That is, Zone II is treated as one component of the global postwar pattern for the management of power. Zone II is also assessed in relation to the prospects for creating a system of world order better suited to the objective needs of the international community. The central arguments are, first, that because Zone II is part of the present system of world order, its status and operation must be understood, as well as its relationship to other parts of the existing system; and second, that the existence of Zone II significantly impedes the creation of a world order system which could better satisfy widely professed values and enhance longer term prospects for human survival, peace, and welfare.[10]

## Zone II As a Geopolitical Boundary

In the aftermath of the Czech occupation of 1968 James Reston wrote, "The trouble is not that Moscow and Washington have defined their spheres of influence, but that they haven't." Reston argued essentially that international stability depends on the existence of clearly delimited and mutually acknowledged geopolitical boundaries.

Part of the difficulty in openly drawing such boundaries arises from an inconsistency between the character of Zone II and the main tradition of international affairs involving an acceptance of a mutual obligation to respect the sovereignty of states, including their political independence and territorial jurisdiction, regardless of size. An explicit acknowledgment of Zone II is discouraged, particularly by the doctrine of sovereignty and derivative ideas such as equality of states, domestic jurisdiction, and nonintervention.[11] The nature of world order in the modern world since 1648 has usually been identified closely with the voluntary arrangements agreed upon by national governments to regulate world affairs.

These arrangements do include the establishment of various international institutions. But the character even of international institutions, along with their legal powers and procedures, is generally traceable directly to the formal consent of sovereign states. This emphasis on the formal aspects of sovereignty has long led to artificial descriptions of interstate relations by international lawyers, descriptions that have failed to take account of certain well-grounded patterns of behavior involving reciprocal assertion of and deference to the exercise of superordinate power in international society. In fact, however, the behavior patterns, tacit understanding, and expectations that demarcate Zone II may become almost as clear boundaries of national discretion as are the more familiar territorial ones.

Zone II consists of sovereign units whose political independence is qualified by the expectation that they may be subject to control by a preeminent actor (Zone I) and that this control cannot and will not be effectively opposed. A Zone II actor, then, will normally acknowledge limits on its own discretion to pursue certain lines of domestic or foreign policy, and will almost certainly be limited in its freedom to enter into certain kinds of arrangements with the principal adversaries of the superordinate Zone I actor. A few examples illustrate this situation. The Cuban government under Castro was not free to allow the Soviet Union to deploy missiles on its territory. Czechoslovakia under Dubček was not allowed to pursue certain domestic policies of liberalization, to allow its press to criticize other socialist states, or to encourage the expression of political dissent. In the Dominican Republic in 1965, the domestic play of opposing forces was not allowed to determine the nation's own political outcome; Zone I control was similarly imposed in Guatemala in 1954, as well as in Hungary and Poland in 1956.

Two principal elements are evident in the basic relationship between countries of Zone I and Zone II. The first element is a fairly clear conception, on the basis of past history, geography, logistical access, and relative capabilities, of what the relationship involves for both the dominant and the dependent actors. In other words, both parties must understand the operational content of their relationship; each must know what actions it can realistically expect from the other.

More specifically, on the basis of past dealings with their respective sectors of Zone II, both the United States and the Soviet Union seem to have established key guidelines or parameters for Zone II actions. Because of these implicit guidelines, a Zone II nation may not adopt the adversary's ideology, nor may it affiliate with the Zone I adversary on matters of security. In addition, both Zone I actors endorse certain rules of disaffiliation arising from their common, if highly qualified, contention that Zone II status is voluntarily sustained. Efforts at disaffiliation or suspected disaffiliation by constituted regimes in Zone II characteristically provoke suppression, as in Hungary in 1956, Czechoslovakia in 1965, and the Dominican Republic in 1965. Occasionally, disaffiliating regimes will be toppled, such as Guatemala's in 1954, or merely "destabilized," as was Chile's in the 1970-1973 period. Regimes that succeed in disaffiliating and then reaffiliating may continue to be threatened by their original Zone I overseer, as is the case in Cuba since 1960. The case of Yugoslavia is exceptional, for she managed to attain Soviet acquiescence in her disaffiliation and her subsequent enjoyment of Zone III status. The United States toleration of deviational initiatives by a Zone II actor was tested and strained in the case of Cuba; the American reaction was ambivalent, but culminated finally in the Bay of Pigs operation. This modified Zone I intervention was unsuccessful, in part because of the desire to maintain a veneer of American nonparticipation.[12] The learning experience of the Bay of Pigs was reflected in the explicitness of the Dominican intervention. The rationale itself used in the Dominican case—the weakly alleged need to protect foreign nationals—would probably be made only in relation to a Zone II country.

In addition to a fairly clear and mutually understood definition of what constitutes the Zone I-Zone II relationship itself, such relations require as their second principal element a fairly clear, if normally tacit, mutual acknowledgment of the Zone I actor's predominance, coupled with an unwillingness to challenge it with credible counter-vailing instruments.

Under standard conditions—that is, the usual conditions within an effective structure of domination—the government elite of a Zone II country confines its behavior well within the mandatory limits presumed or known to be insisted on by Zone I actors as the condition of their nonintervention. The sanctioning role of the Zone I actor is normally implicit and inhibitory, rather than explicit, directly evident, or coercive.

Nor is the hierarchical relationship between these zones significantly altered if Zone II actors change their tacit acquiescence to a formal acknowledgment of Zone I's predominance. Zone II actors cannot so easily attain the rank of alliance partners, for voluntary affiliation is not normally accompanied by any concomitant right of voluntary disaffiliation.

It is when the parameters in Zone II status, or the fact of Zone II status itself, are only dimly perceived, or when Zone I demands become too burdensome, that the sanctioning procedures of the Zone I actors are likely to be tested. In the first instance, communications relative to the assertion of authority have broken down, whereas in the second instance, the burden of authority has prompted rebellion, even in the face of overwhelming odds. An illustration of the first pattern is the various acts and undertakings by the Arbenz government in Guatemala in 1953-1954 to displace American influence by soliciting Soviet help, including even the purchase of Soviet armaments, and of the second is the sporadic efforts by Eastern European countries to break the yoke of Soviet dominance.

Since Zone II states are by definition essentially required to accede to Zone I domination, a state would not normally be reduced to Zone II status in the first place if its capabilities or scale could prevent a Zone I actor from quickly and effectively imposing its will. A state may avoid Zone II status if its government can mobilize a credible resistance, if its terrain and size make occupation difficult, if it is geographically or lo-gistically remote, or if for other reasons the anticipated political and military costs of imposition appear to outweigh the gains.

For example, it is virtually inconceivable that, despite ideological af-finities, the Soviet Union would purport to exercise the same prerogatives of control in either China or Cuba as it has in Eastern Europe since the close of World War II. In China the sovereign unit is neither small nor weak enough to qualify for Zone II status; its capabilities are not sufficiently inferior to those of the potential Zone I actor to be vulnerable to policing action. In some ultimate test of military power the Soviet Union could possibly devastate China through its superiority in nuclear weapons, but this ultimate potentiality cannot be readily brought to bear in the course of normal relations. The ultimate power ratio—the expected outcome of a war—does not necessarily shape normal interstate relations, even in the event of severe political conflict.

It also seems clear that in a state with established Zone II status, as the prospects of rapid police-style enforcement decline, then either the parameters set on the discretion of Zone II actors are relaxed, or these parameters must be maintained through the use of indirect and covert means. A mixture of relaxation with indirect and secret control increasingly characterizes the United States role throughout Latin America.

In short, the two basic features central to the successful exertion of hegemonial power by Zone I actors are a mutually understood definition of the Zone I-Zone II relationship itself, and the unwillingness or inability of Zone II seriously to challenge the Zone I actor's predominance. These "rules of the game" apply specifically to relations between Zone I actors and their respective sectors of Zone II. The effort to impose the policies of a Zone I actor on the units situated in a rival Zone II, or even more dramatically, in the adversary Zone I, would almost certainly endanger world peace and create an immediate prospect of World War III. More concretely, consider what might have happened had the Soviet intervention of 1968 in Czechoslovakia or the American intervention of 1965 in the Dominican Republic been undertaken in other, less "appropriate" geopolitical settings.[13]

Notable asymmetries between the two Zone I actors should also be considered, for the underlying notion of Zone I parity is misleading if taken too literally. Each of the Zone I actors has quite different capabilities for handling an array of Zone II situations. Moreover, the policing styles used by Zone I actors should be compared in terms of their imposition, technique, and effect. Many of these differences reflect the contrast between the liberal democratic ideology underlying American foreign policy, and the post-Stalinist brand of moderated totalitarianism underlying Soviet foreign policy.[14] Other differences arise, however, because the Zone I actors adhere to different strategies of security and hold different concepts of what constitutes the essence of international conflict.

There are also borderline situations where a country or region does not fit neatly into any of the three principal zones. Some of these borderline situations involve Zone I actors in dependency relationships similar to those subsumed within the idea of Zone II. For example, a Zone I actor may have certain exclusive prerogatives in a foreign country. But these particular prerogatives may fall short of entitling the Zone I actor to exercise or even claim the authority to police on behalf of the local status quo, should the dependent government come under severe challenge. The role of the United States in Western Europe has often had this character; the relation of the United States to the Middle East under the Eisenhower Doctrine, and the Soviet relation to the Middle East since the June war of 1967, both demonstrate similar principles. One can imagine the use of Zone I capabilities in these settings to complement the policing capability of a constituted regime, or as part of an effort to sustain a government confronted by domestic or even regional opposition. In these intermediate situations, great stress is placed on the request for intervention, and the intervener is far less disposed to bypass the explicit will of the dependent government. Even when a dependent government has been helped to power by the superordinate actor, the weaker government retains considerable leverage precisely because the Zone I actor is not likely to claim the same interventionary prerogatives that it would in its own sector of Zone II. The United States relationship to several of the smaller Southeast Asian states has this quality: despite the actual political and other dependence of these states, the United States accords great deference to their expression of their sovereign will. In these situations the Zone I actor may be providing the resources, and possibly the military capability, to sustain a regime confronted by an insurgent challenge.

The so-called divided countries, especially Korea and Vietnam, present dangerous intermediate settings. China and Germany, two other divided countries, are of sufficient scale to qualify for Zone IV status. The Zone I actors have been playing special defensive roles in relation to the weaker units—the Soviet Union by securing East Germany, the United States by securing Formosa. However, East Germany can be considered part of the Soviet sector of Zone II, whereas Formosa, although a dependent client regime of the United States, cannot properly be perceived in Zone II terms. The United States would probably respect the expressed will of the Formosan government, even if a series of domestic convulsions should bring a pro-Peking regime to power.

The two principal cases of warfare since 1945 have involved the divided countries of Korea and Vietnam. In both instances, Zone I actors became committed to maintaining an inherently unstable status quo in a setting with important resemblances to a Zone II situation. In a di-

vided country with a reasonably well-developed sense of national identity, the pressures to reestablish unity are strong. If the division is
coupled with severe ideological antagonism, then the governing elite in
each half has both an incentive to avoid unification by the opponent,
and a contradictory incentive to satisfy the national aspirations for
unity. The nature of the conflict between divided country elites may
often approach a zero-sum situation, especially to the extent that it is
aggravated by the unsatisfactory character of an indefinite standoff.
This generic characterization of divided countries of Zone II rank does
not take account of certain sociohistorical factors that may in some
cases make the status quo more or less acceptable.

The Korean context was a complex one, with some revisionist danger
from the South and evidently some expectation that a Northern military
initiative would not engage a full United States commitment to defend
the South. The Korean case would seem to indicate that the stability of
Zone II relations depends very much on a clear communication of intentions on the part of Zone I actors. Any ambiguity may activate Zone
II pressures for change, thereby initiating a chain of violent actions and
reactions culminating in war. However, it is also conceivable that under
special circumstances ambiguity of status could deter intervention by a
Zone I actor—because it is uncertain of the repercussions—or could
deter disaffiliation by a Zone II actor—because it cannot be sure that
military intervention will not follow.

In several respects, the Vietnamese context is even more complicated
than the Korean one. In Vietnam the domestic polity was less clearly
divided. In fact, between 1946 and 1954 the anticolonial forces successfully fought a long war of independence. After 1954, the domestic
balance of social and political forces in Vietnam seemed strongly to
favor the transfer of power from the French to the Viet Minh, and no
reasonably viable South Vietnamese alternative had emerged in Vietnam. Then the United States, with no prior tradition or experience in
Vietnam, transformed the southern portion of the country into a dependent ally with many Zone II traits. In the years following the French
defeat, the Vietnamese elite that governed South Vietnam was both
oppressive and incompetent, the logistics of a successful American
military involvement seemed formidable, and there was no evident
reason for North Vietnam, China, or the Soviet Union to defer to the
American claims to convert South Vietnam into a Zone II affiliate.[15]
Thus, the Vietnam War illustrates the dangers that arise whenever
Zone I actors reach contradictory conclusions about the status of a
politically volatile society.

These dangers are somewhat mitigated, vis-à-vis the threat of general warfare, by the relatively small scale of a dependent society, and by the adherence of political rivals to certain game rules for internal wars.[16] But in smaller divided countries the situation is so unstable partly because efforts to alter the status quo are not nearly as inhibited by the threat of nuclear war as they would be in principal Zone II countries or unambiguous Zone II situations. Thus, the various Berlin crises or the Cuban missile crisis appeared to bring the world closer to the brink of general nuclear war than did sustained warfare in Vietnam.

Several distinct points bear upon an understanding of the status of divided countries vis-à-vis Zone I. First, Zone I actors appear committed to avoiding, by force if necessary, revisions of the jural status quo unfavorable to the position of their affiliate unit. Second, in a divided country situation, the jural status quo may be subject to severe revisionist pressure of a relatively one-sided or two-sided character. Third, procedures for negotiating revisions of the jural status quo are exceedingly difficult and inadequate, owing to poor prospects for reconciling the parties and lack of areas for compromise or trade-offs. Fourth, the nuclear threshold inhibits revisionist pressure in relation to divided countries of a scale too large to qualify for Zone II rank. And fifth, the perception of whether or not a country is divided is not always clear or universally shared. For example, Korea and Germany present clearer cases than China and Vietnam.

In summary, Zone I actors often, although not invariably, exert comparable control over events within their affiliate units in divided countries as they do over their respective sectors of Zone II. In both cases, this control results in the considerable erosion of an "ally's" political independence. However, certain situations preclude Zone II treatment, whether the country is unified or divided. The unit may be too large to qualify for Zone II rank (such as West Germany and China), or it may be too remote and autonomous to give a Zone I actor access (such as North Vietnam and North Korea). But most typically the sovereignty of a divided country shades off in the direction of a Zone I actor, when an affiliate elite cannot by itself sustain the jural status quo and requires substantial military support from Zone I. The Saigon regime is the divided-country affiliate most subject to Zone I domination, although the national regimes centered in East Berlin, Taipei, and Seoul are also dependent regimes which can, in several but not in all respects, be included in the Zone II category.[17] But the main feature that distinguishes Zone I relations with affiliated elites in divided countries from their relations with Zone II is Zone I's apparent deference to the will of the formally constituted government. No matter how great its covert manipulation of political forces in a divided country, the Zone I actor normally claims no prerogative to override the will of the local government.

For example, although both the military conduct of the Vietnam War and the political decision to seek a negotiated settlement were apparently determined more or less unilaterally by American policymakers, the United States always placed great emphasis on the Saigon regime's request for defensive support. Saigon's leverage seemingly depended on how much the United States cared about securing the regime's formal participation, or acquiescence, in decisions made in Washington. Thus, the case of South Vietnam exemplifies a Zone I attempt to thwart the domestic play of forces in a divided country by preventing the exertion of revisionist pressures. In juridical terms, this constitutes an effort to prevent the forces of national self-determination from shaping control.

From the preceding discussion of the characteristic relationships between Zone I and Zone II, as well as of the closely related situations posed by divided countries, it seems evident that in a juridical sense some states are neither colonies nor truly independent political entities. The existence of these relationships contradicts the normative ideology of world order affirmed by both Zone I actors. But the orthodox juridical account of Zone II is misleading and even dangerous, for the expectations that it encourages about international behavior are unrealistic.

It seems far more appropriate to treat Zone II as one of those "more or less clearly discerned patterns of coercion and submission, and influence and submission," present in every period of history.[18] But unlike the colonial period, when gradations of submission were translated into clearly conceived legal categories, the existence of Zone II is acknowledged only tacitly at most, and then primarily in relation to competing interpretations of Zone I prerogatives, as when Zone I/USA is supported and Zone I/USSR is condemned, or vice versa. By making more explicit the contours and significance of Zone II, I hope to bring the realms of international law and international politics into closer alignment.

## Legitimacy and Zone II

The fundamental character of world order reflects the degree and form of consensus prevailing among principal actors on the international scene regarding the standards that govern the threat or use of military power.[19] At various historical moments, the consensus has produced collective procedures of sovereign states, such as the Holy Alliance in Europe following the Congress of Vienna, or the Allied opposition in World Wars I and II. At other times the consensus has led to the allocation of spheres of exclusive concern, as in the colonization of Africa following the Congress of Berlin in 1885. At the present historical juncture, Zone II deserves to be included in a description of the contemporary system of world order.

In the period since 1945, only the nuclear superpowers have been in a position to shape the basic jural order by mutual consent. But their intense rivalry on moral and ideological grounds has prevented effective recourse to either collective procedures or explicit allocational arrangements. At the same time, neither state has often wanted to challenge the jural order severely enough to produce or even seriously threaten general war. Therefore, low-visibility consensus-generating devices like the "hot-line" have evolved, to assure the possibility of direct communication between rival governments during periods of crisis. The ability to communicate tends to facilitate policy coordination, which in turn helps to induce tacit patterns of deference to allocational arrangements within Zone II. The perimeters of Zone II have been reasonably stable except in those marginal situations where the jural order was itself being challenged by opposing revisionist movements, each sponsored by a Zone I actor—the divided country situation for states of Zone II rank.[20]

It should be recalled and underscored that "world order" implies neither the maintenance of world peace nor the justice of the system in being. The character of world order at any given time is created, as already indicated, by the rules, procedures, and institutions—both formal and informal—which attempt to regulate behavior and confine conflict within tolerable limits, and which attempt particularly to minimize the risk of large-scale, irreversible violence in the relations among principal states. In the present historical period, a central concern of world order is to prevent the use of nuclear weapons, especially in the relations of Zone I actors with one another. Part of this concern is expressed through the tacit acceptance of Zone II relationships, even when these relationships result in the violent suppression of a group adhering to the ideology of the rival sector of Zone I.

Henry Kissinger wrote that "a generally accepted legitimacy" characterized the procedures used to moderate conflict in the period of European history after 1815. Kissinger pointed out that his use of the term legitimacy "means no more than an international agreement about the nature of workable arrangements and about permissible aims and methods of foreign policy."[21] Legitimacy, then, can be said to pertain to an international arrangement, whether explicit or implicit, when a careful observer can delineate its contours and define the nature of tacit consensus creating an orbit of effective authority in geographical space.

Within this intellectual framework, Zone II appears entitled to consideration as one distinct component of the current system of world order: it represents an area of tacit agreement whose implicit rules form part of the process by which world order is maintained. A "violation" of these "rules" would probably make conflict difficult to confine if, for example, the United States should decide to use force to interfere with Soviet policing efforts within the Soviet sector of Zone II. It is only the normative taboos associated with an absolute respect for national sovereignty and for national self-determination of all states, regardless of their size or geopolitical locus, which prevents Zone I actors from acknowledging the existence of Zone II.

France, during the 1968 United Nations debate on the Czech intervention, referred to the Soviet occupation as the outcome of "the policy of blocs" which had dominated the European scene since the end of World War II. But such an explicit, and therefore derogatory, identification of the prevailing pattern of control could only be made by an opponent of this pattern. The practitioners of Zone I diplomacy share an aversion to any overt acknowledgment of a symmetrical pattern; instead, they vigorously condemn the behavior of their rival, while equally vigorously defending their own. [22]

One cost of resting world order partially on patterns of control that cannot be acknowledged by their own creators is to cast into cynical disrepute the entire enterprise of law and order in world affairs, except for marginal issues of world security. Therefore, it is important for specialists, at least, to admit that Zone II does possess generally accepted legitimacy within the existing system of world order. [23] Kissinger again provides a germane formulation: " 'Legitimacy' as used here should not be confused with justice." Many structures of domination ranging from colonialism to slavery have enjoyed legitimacy, but no one would automatically ascribe justice to each of them. However, in international affairs the case still remains that a peace treaty which amounts to a *diktat* can convert a de facto conquest into a de jure expansion of territory. [24] The primary concern of world order is legitimacy. Although it can be argued that a legitimate order will be more or less stable to the extent that it accords with the prevailing sense of justice, the justice or injustice of a legitimacy arrangement is only one of several principal factors which should be taken into account in assessing its contribution to the maintenance of world order.

The legitimacy of Zone II can now be assessed with reference to factors relating to the extent to which Zone I prerogatives are mutually accepted in Zone II and challenges to them would be provocative and dangerous. However, no effort will be made to assess the relative importance of these factors in different situations. Such factors can best be considered by visualizing a Zone I actor's claim to assert police (or military) authority in relation to a country situated within its sector of Zone II. More concretely, consider the type of assertion of United States authority in the Dominican Republic since 1965 and the type of assertion of Soviet authority in Czechoslovakia since 1968. These two occurrences are not here discussed in historical terms; rather, they are used to indicate the international status of Zone II.

Legitimacy is not equivalent to the exercise of naked power, or to compliance with enacted law; nor is it necessarily compatible with prevailing or posited standards of justice. In fact, what is legitimate may be very undesirable in net effect, as it is with Zone II diplomacy. The legitimacy of a particular set of actions is a matter of degree, as well as a consequence of weighting and interrelating a series of factors. Various criteria can be used to assess relative legitimacy, and to relate the control of Zone II to other dimensions of the present system of world order. These criteria provide a framework for organizing material rather than a calculus for drawing a clear conclusion. The twelve factors bearing on the legitimacy of Zone II dependency are:

1. The perceived relationship of compatibility or incompatibility of claimed Zone I prerogatives with other authoritative norms of behavior;

2. The perceived relationship of compatibility or incompatibility of claimed Zone I prerogatives with the prevailing regional or global sense of justice;

3. The perceived relationship of particular Zone I claims to the prevailing expectations in the rival Zone I government and in the regional and global arenas of diplomatic interaction;

4. The response of the Zone II victims, the Zone I adversary, and global or regional opinion to the Zone I claim;

5. The minimization of violence in the execution of the Zone I policy in Zone II;

6. The relative effectiveness of the claim;

7. The degree, credibility, and timing of collective participation in the assertion of control by a Zone I actor;

8. The persuasiveness of the claim;

9. The outcome of community review at the global level;

10. The stability of the Zone I claim and the subsequent behavior of the Zone I actor;

11. The Zone I claims as precedents for the future of Zone II; and

12. The disruption of the normal structure of relations between Zone I and Zone II.

*1. The perceived relationship of compatibility or incompatibility of claimed Zone I prerogatives with other authoritative norms of behavior.* Zone I claims to act within Zone II depend on both threatened and actual uses of military force. Such claims violate basic postulates of the two dominant explicit normative systems of international society: the norms of territorial sovereignty underlying the Westphalia system, and the norm prohibiting nondefensive military action underlying the Charter system. In this respect, then, Zone I military prerogatives in Zone II appear to be highly "illegitimate," especially when the military force is used overtly, unilaterally, and in the face of violent resistance. The attempts by both the Soviet Union and the United States to collectivize such claims acknowledges, in part, the gross incompatibility between the claims and this factor in the legitimacy scale. There is also an effort by Zone I to invest regional actors with the authority to implement its policies. To the extent that it succeeds, this effort to create regional counternorms to the Charter is both legislative in character and subversive of the United Nations role.

*2. The perceived relationship of compatibility or incompatibility of claimed Zone I prerogatives with the prevailing regional or global sense of justice.* Some national claims to use or threaten force are not even condemned in global arenas if their assertion satisfies the prevailing sense of justice. Clear examples are presented by India's use of force in 1962 to acquire control of Goa from Portugal, and the threatened use of force by African countries and regional institutions to end the rule of colonial and racist regimes in Southern Africa. But claims by Zone I that its military intervention in Zone II countries will uphold justice generally lack wide support in formal arenas of world opinion, as well as in impartial professional circles. There is a sliding scale of perceived injustice depending on the evaluation of the circumstances that prompt the Zone I claim, the efficiency and effectiveness of its assertion, the stability of its effects, and the time span during which Zone II sovereignty must be violated.

*3. The perceived relationship of particular Zone I claims to the prevailing expectations in the rival Zone I government and in the regional and global arenas of diplomatic interaction.* To a certain rhetorical extent, Zone I military assertions in Zone II are always subject to criticism and censure, because they violate the theoretical notion that Zone I governments adhere to the prevailing norms (factor 1) and the prevailing sense of justice (factor 2). However, an assertion of military power is normally accompanied by a rationale whose general formula implies claims to act in the future. Both the Soviet military occupation of Czechoslovakia and the American intervention in the Dominican Republic were widely felt to violate expectations about permissible behavior. These violations related to the settings that induced the governments of Zone I to assert their military power: in the Dominican case, the possibility that a Castroite regime would prevail; and in the Czech case, the pursuit of a set of official policies aimed at domestic liberalization. There are important asymmetries: Czechoslovakia was well administered, whereas the Dominican Republic was in the midst of a struggle for control of the regime; Czechoslovakia is bigger, more developed, and more closely connected with principal Soviet security and domestic policies, whereas the Dominican Republic is a minor unit in Zone II with no clear course of political leadership.[25] The provisional effect of the Soviet intervention was to terminate Czechoslovakia's liberal domestic policies without altering the composition of the administrative elite. In contrast, the American intervention probably converted a rebel victory into a rebel defeat, enabling the accession to power of a governing elite quite different in personnel and policy orientation.[26]

In any case, the relation of the Zone I claim to expectations elsewhere in the world (factor 3) depends on the setting rather than the structure of the claim. The general stature of the Czech leadership, the dignity, discipline, and gallantry of its population, the long struggle of the country for national autonomy, its strategic location in the heart of Europe, and the dampening of prospects for an all-European settlement made the Soviet acts in Czechoslovakia far more disruptive of governing expectations than were the American acts in the Dominican Republic.[27]

*4. The response of the Zone II victims, the Zone I adversary, and global or regional opinion of the Zone I claim.* The spectrum of possible responses to an adversary Zone I interventionary operation ranges from acquiescence to counterviolence. The Hungarian resistance to Soviet military power in 1956 may have been based partly on the expectation of or hope for American military support. It is reasonable to speculate that the Czech refusal to use violent means of resistance, no matter what, was based at least in part on what had been learned in Hungary about the structure of relations within the Soviet sector of Zone II. Similarly, the Soviet refusal to become involved when United States military power has been used to thwart the domestic balance of forces in Latin America is probably included in the calculations of various revolutionary groups.

Even the most serious exercises of Zone I power in Zone II, if measured by factors 1-3, have not provoked reactions that represented major dangers to world peace. The major dangers have arisen in contexts such as small divided countries, where it was ambiguous whether Zone II considerations applied to the maintenance of the jural status quo, and where each Zone I actor felt itself "committed" to react with counterviolence. But when Zone I power is charted within an undisputed, unambiguous sector of Zone II, although world tension might rise and feelings of spontaneous outrage and frustration might mount, there is no serious danger of violent confrontation.

Cuba represents a special case, for it successfully rejected Zone I prerogatives at least temporarily, and then shifted its allegiance to the adversary Zone I actor.[28] Once the shift of allegiance had occurred, the Soviet involvement conformed more closely to prevailing rules of competition. Cuba had apparently escaped from the American sector of Zone II and was therefore now eligible for protection against former Zone I prerogatives. The Cuban missile crisis, unlike the Bay of Pigs operation of 1961 in which the CIA backed an abortive invasion of Cuba in an attempt to topple Castro, caused intense danger to world peace because the United States was still attempting to maintain minimal residual Zone I prerogatives in relation to Cuba. Specifically, the United States insisted on the right to interdict the deployment of nuclear missiles on Cuban territory by its Zone I rival. It seems highly doubtful, however, that the United States would have interdicted missile deployment within the clearly established contours of the Soviet sector of Zone II.[29] The relationships of Cuba with both the United States and the Soviet Union since 1959 suggest the tension and potential danger inherent in the sudden erosion of zonal boundaries and affiliations. The problem is accentuated by the absence of any procedure by which to differentiate a Zone I actor's attempt to prevent disaffiliation, from its action taken to punish a Zone II actor that has successfully achieved a new affiliation. In the former setting, normal deference patterns allow the Zone I actor to assert its control with no adverse reaction stronger than protest or community censure. In the latter setting, the rival Zone I actor is likely to perceive a new status quo in which the disaffiliating state is entitled to the option of reaffiliation, or at least of political autonomy, whereas the former hegemonic actor is less likely to perceive or acknowledge the diminished status of its zonal prerogatives. In either case, changed circumstances generally tend to encourage the selective perception of critical facts.

5. *The minimization of violence in the execution of the Zone I policy in Zone II.* The relative unacceptability of Zone I policies in Zone II depends to a great degree on the amount of violence used and the

amount of bloodshed caused. It also depends on how hard Zone I tries to avoid provoking international reactions above a certain threshold (factor 4). In relation to factor 5, the Bay of Pigs and the Cuban missile crisis again provide a useful contrast in United States policy. The United States displayed a certain callousness in its Bay of Pigs operation, which was conducted with much violence and loss of life. This operation nevertheless proved to be an ineffectual assertion of power (see factor 6), with no resultant policing effect. In the missile crisis, however, maximum precaution was taken to avoid recourse to violence during the assertion of Zone I's claim of authority. This extreme precaution was demonstrated first by the claim itself, and second by the overwhelming capability that was brought to bear in order to deter Soviet miscalculation. The immense size of the Soviet occupation force in Czechoslovakia (over 600,000) may also be interpreted partly as an effort to deter Hungarian resistance. In any event, the degree of legitimacy attaching to Zone I prerogatives in Zone II is deeply affected by the degree to which violence is minimized.

The basic infringement on the autonomy of Zone II actors is continually sustained by threats, informal structures of influence, and nonmilitary means of coercion. Only the test case provided by a direct challenge or accidental misunderstanding of Zone I imperatives provokes military intervention. An effective system of communication is therefore one key element in the successful administration of Zone II. The Zone I actor can effectively use its overwhelming military superiority and its threat of intervention only if it conveys to the elites of Zone II countries the restrictions it is willing to enforce on their discretion.

Under some circumstances, radical elites in a Zone II country might welcome a confrontation to expose a Zone I actor's willingness to disrupt with naked force the processes of national self-determination that it purports to respect. Under typical circumstances, however, the uncertainty of Zone I parameters of tolerance is what induces military interventions in Zone II. And it is difficult for Zone I actors clearly to communicate the parameters that demarcate their partial hegemony precisely because the reality of their hegemony so obviously contradicts their own avowed norms regarding the proper basis of world order (factor 1) and their own assertions respecting the voluntary basis of their alliances. It is ironic that in recent years the most brutal suppressions of national autonomy have occurred among states with supposedly strong bonds of friendship, ideology, interest, and propinquity.

6. *The relative effectiveness of the claim.* Any legal order will eventually work to accommodate the effective assertion of power.

Under normal conditions, the authoritative is a fairly accurate reflection of the effective. Therefore, the success with which Zone I actors pursue their supervisory goals is important both for making these goals adequately understood and for deterring defection by members of Zone II. The capacity to administer authority effectively is obviously a significant principle of order.

The assertion of ineffective Zone I claims by the United States tends to unite the liberal and conservative domestic opposition to the government. The Soviet government, unimpeded by a free press and vigorous internal dissent, is apparently much less vulnerable to repercussions from an ineffective and controversial assertion of its authority.

7. *The degree, credibility, and timing of collective participation in the assertion of control by a Zone I actor.* Problems posed by factors 1-3 have led Zone I actors to obscure these issues by acting within a wider framework of decision in policing Zone II. Hegemonial regionalism—where the Zone II members of the sector more or less comply with the will of the Zone I leader—are attempts to endow Zone I claims with some explicit legitimacy. A decision to enforce the regional will on an intraregional deviant is alleged to be compatible with Charter norms of collective responsibility. Both the United States and the Soviet Union generally seek to obtain some kind of regional endorsement for the use of force within Zone II. These endorsements themselves may be more or less genuine, and may also be more or less influential in moderating Zone I behavior. It is necessary to assess the additional margin of legitimacy that may be conferred by a regional rather than unilateral framework of authority. The genuine regionality of the claim must also be evaluated. Relevant considerations include the degree of regional participation in the formulation and execution of the decision, and the degree to which specific Zone II interests (as distinct from Zone I interests) are visible in the operation. For instance, it is clear that several Zone II members supported and perhaps even insisted on Zone I initiatives against Czechoslovakia in 1968 and against Cuba in the post-Castro years.

There is no question, however, that the normative issues raised by factor 1 are blurred to an extent if some sort of regional consensus can be mobilized in support of Zone I military action in Zone II. The normative traditions underlying both Westphalia and Charter conceptions are based on the rules restraining states in their conduct with one another. The extent to which these norms also constrain action by a regional actor is far less clear, although there is a nominal insistence that regional competence be subordinated to the normative framework of the United Nations Charter.[30]

*8. The persuasiveness of the claim.* The Zone I claimant almost always seeks to vindicate its supervisory actions with supportive arguments. These arguments may vary from contentions regarding the needs of the region (for example, that its welfare and security depend on an ideological solidarity which is threatened by domestic developments in a Zone II target country), to allegations about the regional competence to resist extraregional political and military penetrations. Most efforts at persuasion may be classed as legal arguments, moral arguments, or security arguments. The rhetoric of law, morality, and security is persuasive to the extent that there exists a reasonably close correlation between the control claims advanced and the general appreciation of the facts to which the claims supposedly pertain. Occasionally, the standards are themselves controversial, as when the United States and the Soviet Union claim a regional mandate to uphold certain minimum conditions of ideological solidarity within their respective sectors of Zone II. For example, Marxism-Leninism is no more incompatible with human welfare if adhered to by Castro's Cuba than by Tito's Yugoslavia. Yet Cuba was expelled from the Inter-American System in 1962 on the grounds that her Marxist-Leninist ideology was incompatible with the ideals of the hemisphere, as if ideological orientation was per se correlated with peacefulness or a capacity for international cooperation.

There is some connection between this factor and factors 1-2. The stress here is on the pattern of justification invoked by the Zone I actor, rather than on the perceived relationships between the Zone I claim and legal norms or the prevailing sense of justice. The very willingness to justify Zone I claims in a global forum is itself a significant element of accountability, which may over time socialize the Zone I actors toward accepting broader concepts of international propriety. Therefore, to appraise the form and substance of the arguments with which Zone I actors seek to support their military interventions in Zone II is of interest—although of no great significance; Hitler, after all, advanced legal, moral, and security arguments for German aggression during the 1930s.

Consistency of argument can suggest the strength and sincerity of a Zone I claim. For instance, the Soviet Union's original contention that its 1968 actions were in response to a Czech invitation, or the original American contention that its Dominican intervention sought merely to protect the safety of its nationals, were later abandoned or muted in favor of slightly more plausible, if even less generally acceptable, justifications. The Soviet argument shifted to an idea of the responsibility of the socialist community to prevent certain kinds of regressive social and political behavior, and the American argument came to focus on the need to frustrate alleged communist efforts to take advantage of political chaos.

9. *The outcome of community review at the global level.* Closely related to, but far from coincident with, a claim's intrinsic persuasiveness is the judgment passed on Zone I action by the political organs of the United Nations. When voting majorities in the United Nations exercise review functions, they characteristically reflect political alignment and ideological orientation, rather than an impartial assessment of a particular Zone I claim. The comparatively greater political control of the United Nations machinery by the United States, especially during the earlier years of the organization, has meant that American Zone II military operations have fared much better in the United Nations than have comparable Soviet operations. In fact, it is possible to argue that even relatively persuasive Soviet claims (as measured by normal criteria) would be censured by the United Nations, whereas the most unpersuasive United States claims would not likely be subject to censure. Because of this disparity of political support within the United Nations, the organization's conclusions on what Zone I actors do in Zone II cannot be taken as impartial determinations on the merits of a Zone I claim.

It may be that the Soviet Union and the United States have an inverse relationship regarding global and domestic criticism. The Soviet control over its sector of Zone II is subject to censure in the United Nations but is relatively free from opposition pressures at home, whereas the American government's situation is just the reverse. The shifting variables of domestic and global settings are significant, however, in assessing these inhibitions on Zone I discretion in Zone II.

10. *The stability of the Zone I claim and the subsequent behavior of the Zone I actor.* The assertion and implementation of Zone I patterns can control the situation for the indefinite future without the reassertion of military power or the recourse to violence. Following the Hungarian uprising, for instance, there was a kind of liberalization of domestic policy that did not transgress the Soviet-sanctioned parameters and yet satisfied some of the 1956 aspirations. Since Soviet troops left Hungarian soil in 1956, there has been no recurrence of violence and no further military intervention. Nor has there been any evidence of acute economic exploitation or intimidation by the Zone I actor—two issues prominent among the original grievances. It appears that the Zone I actor can allow reform to take place if its minimal demands for Zone II allegiance are still met. But the Zone I actor can also choose to repress the domestic balance of forces in a variety of ways, either directly or through a

client regime. The United States has more than adequately proved this point by its brutal and pervasive disregard of the popular welfare in South Vietnam.

The consensus that Zone II constitutes a legitimate arrangement of world order rests on its role in maintaining the tolerable level of stability which is essential to survival in the nuclear age. Therefore, the extent to which peace prevails within Zone II is an important criterion for evaluating Zone II's impact on international affairs. Of course, there are other criteria as well, including the impact of Zone II status on national self-determination, on minimum human rights for individuals and groups, and on raising standards of living, health, and education among the Zone II population.

*11. The Zone I claims as precedents for the future of Zone II.* In a sense, this factor incorporates all the others. Zone I claims can perpetuate the infringement of Zone II's independence and discretion. And changes in the personnel and policy of a Zone I government can lead past claims to be abandoned, moderated, or extended. World opinion was shocked by the 1968 Soviet occupation of Czechoslovakia partly because of the strong international presumption that the Hungarian case no longer served as precedent for Soviet policy. Certainly some significant segments of American public opinion would not regard the Dominican precedent of 1965 as a continuing claim for the future.

Nevertheless, the claims of the past remain one significant means for communicating to Zone II actors the operative restrictions on their discretion. These claims may be more or less significant, depending on how well they embody continuing lines of policy for the Zone I actor. In this sense, the United States defense of South Korea in 1950 appears to be a far stronger precedent than the post-1954 United States "defense" of South Vietnam.[31] The Vietnam claim seems weaker than the Korean one in almost every relevant respect (compare factors 1-10).

*12. The disruption of the normal structure of relations between Zone I and Zone II.* If a Zone I actor began to commit genocide in its sector of Zone II, would the rival Zone I actor refrain from counterviolence? This question concerns the sense of justice (factor 2) and suggests that there may be restrictions on the discretion of Zone I actors even when they are operating within their own sectors of Zone II.

The restrictions on Zone I discretion are more readily apparent in relation to events within the adversary's sector of Zone II. The United States response to the Soviet intervention in Czechoslovakia or the Soviet response to the American intervention in the Dominican Republic are good illustrations. Different factors govern response when the military activity of a Zone I actor occurs in a Zone III or Zone IV situation.

The fluid character of these restrictions is suggested by the kinds of Soviet and American involvement in various states of Congolese strife and in the Nigerian civil war. To react to a Zone II conflict as if it were a Zone III conflict would very likely endanger peace in a serious way. Similarly, to treat a Zone II conflict as if it were a confrontation between Zone I actors would almost certainly create a major crisis. That is, if the United States had reacted to the occupation of Czechoslovakia in the way that it did to the Berlin blockades, then the danger to world peace would indeed have been great. The Berlin blockades could be viewed as a careful test of wills related to the jural status quo, whereas a neutralizing United States intervention on behalf of the anti-Soviet Dubček regime in Czechoslovakia during 1968 (even assuming that one had been requested) would have represented an attempt significantly to revise the strategic status quo. A particular move does not have to be either good or bad from the perspective of justice in order clearly to disrupt the existing consensus on the "legitimacy," in Kissinger's sense, of Zone I prerogatives in Zone II.

These twelve factors offer a tentative framework both for understanding the character of the relationship between Zone I and Zone II, and for assessing the quality of any particular claim by a Zone I actor to assert its military control over a country within its sector of Zone II. The distinctive feature of Zone II dependency is the continuing prospect of military intervention by the Zone I actor in possible defiance of the will of the Zone II government. The two principal elements in this dependency relationship are the military dimension of the control and the acceptance of the claim by the only actors capable of challenging it. Zone I administration accords with tacit expectations, even though it contradicts the world community values embodied in both positive international law and the United Nations Charter.

## Zone II and the Future of World Order

The character and modes of operation of Zone II have lessons to teach for building a system of world order better than the one that presently exists.[32] Zone II constitutes a structure of domination that exists by virtue of the threat and use of Zone I's military power. As with any structure of domination, the basic limits on behavior are made effective through a credible intent to impose superior force in the event of violation. The motives of the Zone I actor may range from moderate altruism to extreme exploitation. The predominant actor may seek to uphold the autonomy of the units in its sector of Zone II, especially if these units really are vulnerable to external penetration or to internal takeover by regressive elites (regressive, that is, by world community standards). A Zone I actor may also seek to assure its own security by preventing the rise to power in Zone II of any elites that are hostile to it or friendly to its adversary Zone I actor.

Both the degree of domination and its arbitrariness depend on the circumstances that originally prompt Zone I to interfere within a Zone II state. The Soviet intervention in Czechoslovakia was so disturbing because the Dubček regime had firm control of its own society and had embarked on a widely admired social and political program. The Soviets blatantly rejected Czech autonomy, requiring the Prague government to deny its own population freedom of action and expression.[33] Clearly, there was very little bilaterality in the Czech-Soviet relationship of 1968.

The same conclusion applies, although somewhat less obviously, to the relationship between the United States and many Central American countries. American economic support, military assistance, and covert military interference are required to sustain the power of governments that neither represent the domestic balance of forces within their countries nor conform to liberal ideas of progressive government. When subtler forms of maintaining hegemony do not achieve their aims, cruder forms of Zone I control are imposed. This escalation can be seen in the evolution of American policy in both Cuba and the Dominican Republic.

The balance sheet of Zone I dominance is difficult to draw up. Mutual deference to Zone I prerogatives in respective sectors of Zone II clearly helps to prevent certain international conflicts from provoking general war. Without such patterns of insulation, the use of military power by Zone I actors in Zone II might create major international crises.

However, because of this insulation, Zone II states are denied the benefits of national self-determination. Zone II subordination is especially unfortunate in countries where the domestic balance of forces would otherwise be able to produce stable and progressive government. It may be less unfortunate for Zone II countries that might otherwise experience prolonged civil strife or extremely repressive government. In this respect, Nigeria is arguably worse off in Zone III than it might have been if located in Zone II. And it was precisely those groups concerned with the human rights of the black majority who demanded in the months after the Unilateral Declaration of Independence in 1965 that Great Britain assert Zone I-type control over Rhodesia. In other words, countries of lesser scale are not necessarily better off if they are shifted from Zone II to Zone III. However, it does seem that the Eastern European and probably the Central American countries, including the Caribbean, would benefit from the loss of Zone II status, or at least from a more permissive conception of the range of national discretion vis-à-vis Zone I.

Some states may receive certain economic or even political benefits from Zone II status, if Zone I states pay more than mere lip service to their special obligations to safeguard security and promote economic development within Zone II. Unfortunately, the record of these security guarantees and economic relationships does not confirm that special advantages necessarily accrue to Zone II countries. Often the security of a Zone II country is threatened only by the Zone I actor that has taken custody.

The drive of national societies to achieve the dignity of genuine political autonomy is a major part of the contemporary scene. For many disadvantaged claimants, the ethics of actual participation are replacing the ethics of theoretical equality. Both the strength of decolonizing pressures and the rise of the Black Power movement bear witness to this very strong drive for participation. One principal cost of Zone II status is the forfeiture of national independence in international arenas. Zone II members of the United Nations generally vote in accordance with the will of their Zone I leader. Their separate membership is virtually nominal, entailing no meaningful right of independent participation. The consequence is a general loss of prestige, what the Chilean sociologist Gustavo Lagos calls *atimia*. [34]

But perhaps the severest cost of legitimizing Zone II as a structure of domination is to weaken the energies of transformation at work in international society. Given the objective case for transformation, and given the role of military power in maintaining Zone II, Zone I actors have strong incentives to resist system-changing proposals so long as their own prestige, security, and welfare are connected with Zone II. Therefore, it is important to make clear both that Zone II exists as a major structure of domination in international society, and that the existence of such structures of domination inhibits the prospects for system-adaptive change. [35]

It might become possible to transform Zone II, and to persuade the governments of Zone I countries to renounce all, or most, of their prerogatives in their respective sectors of Zone II. In both Zone I countries, in fact, there are strong currents of domestic opposition to the exercise of these prerogatives. World opinion opposes the assertion of hegemonial claims. Such claims seem incompatible with the whole movement away from the cold war and toward detente. The defense of Zone I countries depends far less now than in the prenuclear period on controlling their adjacent lands and seas. Consequently, the old geopolitical arguments have lost much of their functional justification. The aggregate impact of these considerations is difficult to assess at this point. A clearer awareness on the part of Zone I elites of their own need for changes in the global system may induce some efforts to dissolve the separate sectors of Zone II. However, a general heightening of bipolar tensions, or the acquisition of power by more repressive elites in either the Soviet Union or the United States (or both), would undoubtedly strengthen both internal and external structures of domination, including Zone II.

# Part Four: A Vision for the Future

# 12 | Reforming World Order: Zones of Consciousness and Domains of Action

In 1971 U Thant, then Secretary-General of the United Nations, told the twenty-sixth session of the European Economic Commission: "If the great French philosopher Descartes were alive today he would probably revise his celebrated rules for good thinking and add two new principles: the principle of global thinking and the principle of thinking well ahead into the future."[1] Such explicit imperatives reflect a widespread appreciation that we live at a time of danger and opportunity, not just as Americans or Nigerians or Frenchmen, but as human beings concerned with the destiny of our species and the welfare of our planet. This aroused concern has generated an unprecedented effort to achieve a planetary perspective on human problems and prospects.

There is, as yet, no consensus about how to achieve such a planetary perspective, beyond the elementary need to detach oneself as much as possible from too firm an anchorage in the particularities of time and space. One approach to universal thinking is to move from considerations of quality to considerations of quantity. Numbers are more objective than words, data more persuasive than opinions, charts more convincing than speculations or prophecy. The scientific temper of the times reinforces this effort to evolve a valid planetary perspective by so-called objective methods; indeed, a whole subdiscipline of sorts has grown up under the label "futurology."[2]

The essence of futurology is the attempt to acquire knowledge about the future through the projection of trends, accompanied by speculation about likely consequences of various lines of development. Such exercises typically include collecting data about the past and present, using sophisticated charts and tables, and constructing scenarios for the future. It is difficult to evaluate the results of these exercises in futurology. Perhaps if considered as an early stage in a critical effort to marshal enough understanding of the present world to permit intelligent planning for the future, these exercises represent a promising beginning. However, unless they are viewed in this light, even the most influential and ambitious works of futurology seem rather disappointing,[3] which is to say no more, perhaps, than that we continue to lack sufficient knowledge and understanding of the present to be able either to explain or to predict, let alone to control, the course of future developments.[4] Our disappointment with the futurologists arises in part, I think, because we are led to expect more guidance than they are able to provide.

Another source of difficulty lies in a cultural tendency to accept quantitative assertions, particularly if reinforced with the authority of a computer, more readily than normative assertions. If one's views on a probable or preferred future can be presented as the product of trend projections or computer printouts, they will be endowed in our culture with greater credibility than would similar conclusions sustained by qualitative forms of analysis and interpretation. In effect, if our soft knowledge about the future can be cloaked with a relatively hard appearance, its accompanying message will be more sympathetically received. For this reason, there is an enormous temptation to rely on futurology as a vehicle for transmitting an action message.

The Club of Rome represents perhaps the most significant effort to date to gain a hearing for an interpretation of the future presented in quantitative forms and offered as new knowledge. The Club of Rome was founded several years ago by Aurelio Peccei, a former top Italian executive of the Fiat Company. Peccei feared that uneven technological development in the advanced industrial world, resulting from the anticipated American dominance of Europe, would lead to global disaster unless nongovernmental actors could mobilize to conceive a dramatic transnational response.[5] Peccei understood that the dynamic interplay among pollution, population pressure, and resource depletion was placing the future of the human race (and of Europeans in particular) in early jeopardy. His key insight was the recognition that the world's major governments seem incapable of making the necessary institutional and behavioral adjustments urgently demanded by these irreversible pressures. Therefore, in 1968 Peccei conceived the project of organizing a group of individuals dedicated to the special mission of alerting the public to the need for confronting these planetary dangers. The Club of Rome was the result.[6]

The Club of Rome has a membership of about one hundred prominent individuals, drawn from various nations and professions, but has no physical plant, no bureaucracy, and no budget. Its purpose is to sponsor work that arouses public opinion to the point of generating pressure on governments and other institutions of authority and influence.[7] The club has associated itself with a particular interpretation of the present world crisis, namely, that global society is now exhibiting the strains of unsustainable economic, demographic, and related forms of growth. The group's primary aim has been to commission studies that document this interpretation as convincingly and effectively as possible.[8] To this end, the Club of Rome commissioned in 1970 a series of studies with the title "Project on the Predicament of Mankind." These studies were carried out by a group of young scholars at MIT, working within the framework of systems analysis pioneered by Jay Forrester, and their purpose was to design a world model for computer analysis organized around the interactions of dynamic processes such as resource use, food production, population growth, capital investment, and industrial output.[9] Under the leadership of Dennis Meadows, this project resulted in the publication of a popular book entitled *The Limits to Growth* (1972), which did in fact stimulate the kind of public discussion that Peccei had in mind. The book summarized computer applications of the basic conclusion that the dynamics of economic growth, especially in conjunction with population growth, were creating pressures beyond the earth's capacity to respond, pressures which were leading toward some form of catastrophic breakdown timed to occur probably at some point in the next century, but possibly much earlier. As was to be expected, such alarming conclusions provoked sharp controversy, and some critics attributed the severity of these predictions to incomplete data, questionable assumptions about the interplay of factors, and a persistent underestimation of the capacity of human institutions to adapt should matters in fact become that serious. Indeed, a counterattack of sorts was mounted to show that "the computer was crying wolf," diverting human energies from the challenges of poverty and development.[10]

Futurology is intrinsically flawed by the tension between its methodology and its policy recommendations. The method is not presently capable of producing a convincing argument unless it is supplemented by subjective factors—judgments, values, preferences. But the whole enterprise of arousing a dormant public is premised upon the effectiveness of making policy recommendations appear as objective as possible. Such a search for objectivity, however, means that the subjective side of the case is not stated at all, or is presented in an understated, possibly even disguised form. For the perceptive reader, this subjective or normative inadequacy of a policy statement actually diminishes the persuasiveness of its argument. Hence, there is a justifiable suspicion that the elaborate apparatus and technique of presentation are designed to disguise the insufficiencies of our present knowledge.

The Club of Rome has undertaken a laudatory mission, and I share its sense of urgency; moreover, I think this group has succeeded in alerting the public to danger. At the same time, an insufficient emphasis on the ethical and political dimensions of its interpretation has made its presentation vulnerable to counterattacks. Also, the techniques of *The Limits to Growth* could be used to produce quite a different image of the future, with contradictory policy consequences, if different subjective factors were included in the construction of the basic computer program. Nevertheless, if one is sensitive to the limits of futurology and of other quantitative efforts in systems analysis, its investigations can be helpful in the organization and presentation of knowledge. What is dangerous, and what can discredit the message of an enterprise such as the Club of Rome, is to exaggerate the claims of knowledge. In fairness, Peccei, as well as the authors sponsored by the club, have in subsequent work been sensitive to these lines of criticism.[11]

From a bold perspective of cultural history, William Irwin Thompson has provided a brilliant critique of these technocratic forays into the future.[12] Thompson described Peccei as a "new post-industrial manager" with the "institutional corporate politics of a Catholic Cardinal." Peccei believes we need a better understanding of the problems of technological society in the present context of danger. Such an understanding is expected to help shape appropriate forms of managerial oversight. Thompson disagrees. He has no confidence either in rationality as a source of guidance, or in managerial capabilities as a mode confronting the challenges facing human society. Indeed, Thompson believes that if Peccei's projects for transnational managerial coordination were to be realized, they would produce a kind of bureaucratic imperialism, because they would simply embody at more general levels of social and economic organization the ways of thought and action that are presently embedded in the state system.[13] Thompson believes that a new consciousness, based on a new spiritual awareness and appreciation of the realities of planetary culture, is a necessary precondition for any kind of successful response to the world order crises now being acknowledged even by statesmen. As Thompson put it, "If you are going to humanize technology, you're not going to be able to do it within the limited terms of books and civilization and other older containers. You've got to go very far out."[14]

In order to go "very far out," Thompson proposed an effort to bring about a reunion of scientific and mystical thinking in small-scale institutions that embody a vision of the future.[15] In my view such an orientation, although preliminary and tentative, provides solid ground on which to build a relevant consciousness about the future--a consciousness that is receptive to knowledge and wisdom, yet oriented toward change and decency. There is some danger, of course, that such an enterprise might remain too aloof from felt needs for peace and justice, and might deteriorate into self-satisfying but self-indulgent explorations into oneself. It may be important for some sensitive individuals to withdraw from the world during periods of tumult in order to preserve what is valuable and to concentrate on spiritual development, but such withdrawals should be constantly animated by the concerns and tested by the risks of the outside world, at least to sustain the claim that such an enterprise can indeed contribute to wider social, economic, and political reform. A classical questioning along these lines is contained in Herman Hesse's novel *Magister Ludi*, which poses in a variety of profound ways the connection between the perfected aloofness of Castalia and the imperfections of the outside world.

Those who choose to be more remote from direct participation in society have a special obligation not to ignore the world of hunger and bloodshed. We cannot become trustworthy about the future unless we show signs of being trustworthy in the present. For Americans, at least, it is morally and hence intellectually impossible to propose a new Jerusalem and yet at the same time remain agnostic or indifferent about genocide and ecocide in Indochina. That is, the dichotomy between future goals and present responses suggests a form of distancing which is disturbing in its human consequences. At issue is also the matter of personal responsibility, its extent and character. In this sense, all human beings share a responsibility to act to stop war crimes like those of the Indochina War. The affirmation of this universal bond of involvement and accountability is the most significant outcome of the Nuremberg judgment and of what has more recently come to be called the Nuremberg obligation.

These comments about a new consciousness are designed to set the stage for an inquiry into the future of world order. I accept fully the mandate for a planetary, future-oriented perspective, but seek to avoid any dogmatic assumptions that its realization depends on objective or detached knowledge. In this sense, the unity of thought and feeling is an essential ingredient of a relevant approach to the future. With these considerations in mind, it still seems possible and desirable, indeed necessary, to propose new ways of envisioning—really revisioning—the future so as to break the bonds of present constraints on moral and political imagination. My primary purpose is therefore educational, to awaken man's reason to the idea of wholeness as the basis for individual or collective sanity. Just as the biologist tends to focus on survival as a normative touchstone,[16] so the social scientist should be concerned with conditions of collective health and welfare. Seneca observed, "Between public madness and that treated by doctors the only difference is that the latter suffers from disease, the former from wrong opinions."[17] This analogy should be central to efforts to determine the ingredients of a preferred future capable of rekindling hope and hence of remobilizing energies for action. Unlike Seneca, however, I believe that public madness is a result of far more complex forces than mere wrong opinions. To put it differently, wrong opinions rest on cultural and philosophical underpinnings that cannot be removed merely by argument or evidence.

For instance, the American involvement in Indochina illustrates an extreme form of public madness, but there is something very functional about its persistence, given the realities of American culture. Kurt Vonnegut, Jr., emphasized that Americans are winners in a world of scarcity and misery: "The single religion of the Winners is a harsh interpretation of Darwinism, which argues that it is the will of the universe that only the fittest should survive." By inuring itself to the fighting in Vietnam for so many years, American society could acquire the moral hardening needed in a world of growing inequity and desperation. To quote Vonnegut once more: "The Vietnamese are impoverished farmers, far, far away. The Winners in American have had them bombed and shot day in and day out, for years on end. This is not madness or foolishness as some people have suggested. It is a way for the Winners to learn how to be pitiless." And this toughening of the winners is necessary, despite America's present prowess and prosperity, because the winners understand "that the material resources of the planet are almost exhausted, and that pity will soon be a form of suicide."[18]

Vonnegut's perception of the psychology of the ruling group suggests that what is public madness on one level (the waste of resources, internal dissent, loss of international prestige — in other words, the whole gamut of arguments that turned liberals against the Vietnam War) is on another level the very essence of rulership.[19] This relationship points up the central issues in the present context of world order: Are the prescriptions of the winners necessary or desirable? What are the alternatives?

To pose these questions somewhat differently, is the Darwinian ethos adaptable to the contemporary situation? Does the notion of the survival of the fittest provide sound operating guidelines for the existing centers of power and authority? There is no doubt that profound challenges are being posed by the crowding of the planet and the depletion of its resources. These challenges are intensified by the destructive technology of warfare that is being spread throughout the world, as well as by the vulnerability of the postindustrial world to well-conceived disruption. We face a world crisis of unprecedented magnitude, involving the risk of irreversible ecological decay because of the accumulating pollution, the phenomena of mass famine and pandemics, and the possibility—never more than an hour away—of catastrophic war.

In such circumstances, to recall Seneca's precept, we are confronted by a prime necessity to identify "wrong opinions" as quickly as possible. This necessity can be approached from many angles. From the viewpoint of reforming world order, the goal is to try to determine what changes are desirable and possible within the next several decades. We must find the most effective ways to think about world order change so as to conceive of real alternatives, in a manner that is the captive neither of present clichés nor of prospective fantasies. These issues should be approached with the social scientist's respect for evidence and discipline, yet with sensitivity to the criticism that "scientific method," as it has been understood by Western social scientists, excludes many realities which must inform the politics of transformation. William Irwin Thompson, Doris Lessing, or Kurt Vonnegut are thinkers of relevance in this context precisely because they are "open" to these nonrational sources of insight into the present and future.

This approach to the reform of world order is based on two orienting imperatives, the methodological and the normative. Each of these imperatives requires some explanation.

## The Methodological Imperative

To fashion meaningful designs for the future will require disciplined inquiry, systemic comprehensiveness, and continuous revision. To be concerned with world order is to be concerned with the basic relations of power and authority that operate throughout the planet. Such relations are not exhausted by an analysis of state sovereignty in the modern world, although such an analysis is of great significance. In addition to national governments, there are many other actors on the world scene that must increasingly be taken into account. The activities of the multinational corporations, international institutions, transnational associations (whether of airline pilots or of Red Cross officials), and reform-oriented social movements of any scale or scope are important components of the world system and condition its potentiality for change.

Of basic significance is the hypothesis that authority is related to power, and that in today's system of world order power is concentrated in a relatively small number of large national governments and closely affiliated corporate entities. This hypothesis has tactical implications. It implies, for one thing, that changing the world system depends on altering the perceptions, values, and personality features of ruling groups in these key components, or in replacing these ruling groups with new elites having different perceptions, values, and personality features. As far as method is concerned, there is a corresponding need to concentrate on the activities of domestic social movements, especially in the largest states, as well as on the shape of struggle, if any, between territorially-based political power and market-based economic power — in other words, between government leaders and multinational managers.[20]

This approach reverses the emphasis of traditional reformers of world order, who tend to concern themselves with external relations among the governing elites presumed responsive to the common interests of world society. These reformers have posited designs for new arrangements of power based on an idealistic image of peace and good will on earth.[21] But their designs have never seemed relevant because they lacked a theory of change and were based on an ethos antithetical to the conflict-oriented ethos that naturally results from the workings of state sovereignty in a laissez-faire market framework conditioned by centralized national restraint and regulation. When laissez-faire has prevailed within national societies, it has been a policy; but within international society it is an inherent condition. Often these designs have involved "world government" based on "law," an outlook embodied in the most influential modern variant of traditional thinking about world order.[22] Traditional reform consists of convincing influential individuals that a particular set of proposals for world order is desirable. However, completely contrary to observed fact, this persuasive strategy presupposes that the existing structure of world order is administered by reasonable men of good will who are in fact susceptible to persuasive techniques of influence.

After World War I, but even more after the atomic explosions at Hiroshima and Nagasaki in World War II, the plea of world order reformers has rested on a claim of alleged necessity. In other words, their argument for reform is founded on the assertion that the existing system is heading for destruction, given the possibilities for catastrophic war.[23] This warning has been bolstered recently by a declaration of ecological emergency on many fronts.[24] Here again, however, it is clear that such a plea has no capacity to induce fundamental world reform. Indeed, the main impact of ecological pressure may be to exacerbate the Darwinian tendencies of the present world system, encouraging an even more explicitly imperial arrangement by reducing the number of relevant political and economic centers of decision, and by widening the gap between winners and losers. There are various ways of responding to an objectively dangerous situation for world order. It is simply not methodologically accurate to assume that "reform" must necessarily take a progressive direction, even given an idealistic outlook on man and the world. The spectrum of future patterns for world order must include alternatives that convey a sense of choice and of process.

At the present time there is a consensus among the powerful that adjustments in the world order system are needed to maximize the short- and middle-term interests of the strongest and richest governmental actors. The shape of this design was implicit in the diplomacy of Richard Nixon and Henry Kissinger, as well as of Leonid Brezhnev, and must be understood for what it is: a reform of world order engineered by and for the winners.[25] At the present time there is insufficient evidence to demonstrate that it will not work for the next few decades, if it seeks specifically to maximize the security, wealth, and influence of these dominant actors and of those aligned with them. However, the successful transfer of wealth to the oil producers, the Indian nuclear explosion, and the economic chaos of the advanced industrial countries have seriously undermined the confidence of the winners among nations in their own capacity to keep the old game going.

## The Normative Imperative

There are a number of plausible models for world order reform. Each model could be realized within the next several decades, and each has its own immediate implications for policy, action, tactics, and belief systems. There is no objective way to demonstrate which model is preferable; we are obliged to operate within the determinate realm of moral choice.

Given the existing resource scarcity, widespread misery, and danger of war, the fundamental normative choice is between an actor orientation and a community orientation with respect to world order reform. An actor orientation means that the policy of each national center of power and wealth is oriented toward maintaining a preeminent position vis-à-vis others in the system (potential rivals) by reliance on threats, force, and cunning. This reliance is exhibited in international policy by stressing alliances, by intervening in foreign societies to assist sympathetic elites in their efforts to retain or acquire power in struggles against potentially hostile elites, and by ideological rationalizations that convey to one's own population a higher motive than maintaining one's position in the structure of international power, wealth, and prestige. These ideological mystifications are often so potent that they can even entrap political power-wielders in their own claims, thereby inducing poor calculations based on "principles" rather than "interests." Henry

Kissinger's critique of foreign policy-making during the Kennedy-Johnson presidencies illustrates this problem.[26] Underneath the pious rhetoric, which serves to distract attention from the real or operational code of behavior, there is no true concern for those who are suffering or who are denied the fruits of participation. Indeed, there is a constant vigilance against challenges from the dispossessed, accompanied by a ruthless willingness to repudiate their claims and to repress or persecute their spokesmen. This is the significance for world order, of the American role in Indochina and of the Soviet Union's willingness—despite its rival geopolitical perspective in the conflict—to accommodate its foreign policy to such outrages.

A community orientation means that the basic relationships of power and authority must become increasingly contractual and voluntary in character. Such goals mean that the problems of human existence on the planet must be approached without deference to artificial boundaries, whether of states, races, classes, or castes. This orientation means that issues of poverty, pollution, and repression are essential concerns for world order, to be confronted in accordance with a vision of human community in which men live in harmony with each other and with their natural habitat. This outlook can be implemented by various models of world order, the choice reflecting issues of feasibility and of time horizon. There is no federalist scheme buried in the normative imperative that underlies a community orientation. Again, as with the basic concern over reform prospects, it is helpful to set forth contrasting alternatives, and to choose among them on the basis of principled judgment. The sequel to thought must be action. Every assertion of preference, whether it relates to the goals or the tactics of transition, should be continuously reconsidered in light of further developments, so that it can be adapted to subsequent experiences and to changing forms of consciousness.

The permanent element in the normative imperative is an insistence on thinking about welfare in terms of wholes—of the human species, the earth, the overall pattern of linkage between man and earth, as well as between the present and the future. It is their insistence on the coherence of the whole that makes the normative and methodological imperatives compatible, and which creates the basis for substantive investigations of the present prospects for reforming world order.

## Alternative Systems of World Order

The failures of the present system of world order suggest the need for alternatives. Specialists could make an important contribution by designing credible alternative systems that could plausibly be realized within the relatively near future, say by the first decade of the twenty-first century. Such design concepts have in the past—within the wider tradition of utopography—been harmed by two basic defects: they have generally lacked a concept of transition linking the present to the future, and they have failed to envision solutions other than global replications of those concentrations of power and authority that now dominate the existing system of world order.

I propose a new social science approach to the design of future systems of world order, which not only overcomes these defects but posits three other orienting conditions. First, the future system will itself be one step in an ongoing process of political development on a global scale. Because unfulfilled aspirations and projects for change are essential for individual and social health, there can be no final solution of the problem of world order, but only a series of transitional solutions. Each utopia, once achieved, generates its own new horizon of aspirations.

Second, the search for a new system of world order depends upon mobilizing support for a series of explicit values. Solving the transition problem requires achieving and implementing a normative consensus.

And third, this normative consensus is animated by an overriding concern for initiating a process of coping humanely with the problems that stem from crowding, depletion of resources, and poisoning of the biosphere. As Jay Forrester suggested, "Civilization is in a transition zone between past exponential growth and some future form of equilibrium."[27] The focus of inquiry, then, should be on developing dynamic equilibrium models of world order that can be achieved without undue trauma and which can be sustained without recourse to repression. The ethical dimensions of such models must encompass attitudes toward violence, toward satisfying basic human needs, and toward fostering social and political conditions that will be compatible with a sense of human equality and with an affirmation of individual worth.

I can here provide only a sense of direction.[28] The basic framework of thought that has been developed in response to these three orienting conditions are set forth in Figures 1 and 2. Figure 1 depicts a basic set of concepts for developing a systematic method of thinking about future systems of world order $(S_1, S_2, S_n)$, and of conceiving the transition path from the system at point of origin to the point at which the new system emerges, a transition that can be represented as $S_0 \rightarrow S_1$ (either in analytic terms of $t_1, t_2, t_3$, or in temporal terms of $t_{1970s}, t_{1980s}, t_{1990s}$). Figure 2 suggests one line of transition in relation to value priorities of

System level
$(S_0 = S$
at origin)

$$S_{-1} \longleftarrow S_0 \longrightarrow S_1 \longrightarrow S_2$$

System level
(chronological
subscripts)

$$S_{1914} \longleftarrow S_{1975} \longrightarrow S_{2000} \longrightarrow S_{2050}$$

Transitional stages
for the interval
$S_0 \longrightarrow S_1 \longrightarrow S_2$

$$S_0 \xrightarrow[\;(t_1)\,(t_2)\,(t_3)\;]{} \qquad S_1 \xrightarrow[\;(t_4)\,(t_5)\,(t_6)\;]{} S_2$$

Transitional stages
for the interval
$S_{1975} \longrightarrow S_{2000}$
with chronological
subscripts

$$S_{1975} \xrightarrow[\;(t_{1975})\;(t_{1980})\;(t_{1990})\;]{} S_{2000}$$

Figure 1.  Transition Conceptions

peacefulness, social and economic welfare, environmental quality, and human dignity. This transition path emphasizes several sequences of development that seem to be necessary preconditions for the emergence of $S_1$ (on the level of action the correlation is between consciousness and $t_1$ or $t_{1970s}$, between mobilization and $t_2$, or $t_{1980s}$, and between transformation and $t_3$ or $t_{1990s}$; on the level of primary institutional arenas a similar sequence of correlations with $t$ intervals is depicted). The basic purpose of Figure 2 is to embody a conception of global change that will have to accompany any serious process of designing and achieving a new system of world order. The number of stars in each box signifies the additional emphasis that builds upon the achievements of preceding intervals. Thus, by the end of $t_2$ both war and social and economic welfare considerations have six units of cumulative change. The distribution of stars is meant to be only a rough approximation of relative degrees of effort and achievement at the various stages of the transition process. It should be understood that this is a conception, or at most a prescription, rather than a prediction. In these conceptual terms it is possible, even likely, that $t_1$ will never come to an end; the point is simply that one way to move from $S_0 \rightarrow S_1$ is to proceed along this path of sequenced transition. The proposed transition process is only one of an infinite series; an alternative transition path $S_0 \rightarrow S_1$ can and should be studied as part of a broader inquiry into comparative systems of world order.

To make clearer the point that $S_1$ is itself a transitory solution to the

Figure 2. Transition Path $S_O \longrightarrow S_1$

| Transition stages | | Problem focus: Change orientation: Institutional Focus: | War Consciousness Domestic arena | Poverty Mobilization Transnational and regional arenas | Pollution Transformation Global arena | Human rights Transformation Global arena |
|---|---|---|---|---|---|---|
| Temporal subscripts | Analytic stages | | | | | |
| | $t_{1970s}$ | $t_1$ | ****[a] | ** | * | |
| | $t_{1980s}$ | $t_2$ | ** | **** | *** | * |
| | $t_{1990s}$ | $t_3$ | * | *** | **** | *** |

a. The number of asterisks in each box is proportional to the degree of emphasis in each $t$ interval.

Figure 3.  Transition Path $S_1 \longrightarrow S_2$

| Temporal interval | | Positive goal:  Creativity | Self-realization | Joy |
|---|---|---|---|---|
| $t2010s$ 2020s | $t_4$ | ***[a] | ** | * |
| $t2030s$ | $t_5$ | ** | *** | ** |
| $t2040s$ | $t_6$ | * | * | *** |

a. The number of asterisks in each box is proportional to the degree of emphasis in each $t$ interval.

challenge of world order, a subsequent process of transition $S_1 \longrightarrow$ $S_2$ can be depicted (Fig. 3), showing a similar suggestive profile of sequenced transition. The figure merely suggests the more personalist sequel to a successful effort to save the planet from extreme danger and misery. In a sense, $S_O \rightarrow S_1$ is concerned with a rescue mission for world order, whereas $S_1 \rightarrow S_2$ is concerned with the positive task of building a system of world order capable of fulfilling human potentialities for growth and satisfaction.

The only element that remains to be portrayed is some conception of the various structural outcomes which the transition process might produce. What will be the basic arrangement of power and authority as an organizing energy in planetary affairs? Again, the objective is to suggest a mode of thinking rather than to argue on behalf of a particular configuration of power and authority. At the same time, if dynamic equilibrium is the fundamental prerequisite, it is possible to set forth four models of world order, which correspond with various relevant lines of real-world preference and prediction: the pentagonal model (Fig. 4), two doomsday models (Figs. 5 and 6), a world government model (Fig. 7), and an $S_O \longrightarrow S_1$ model (Fig. 8).

The basic attribute of the pentagonal model of world order reform (Fig. 4) is the notion that existing centers of industrial capability, and hence military potential, are capable of providing a stable and acceptable system of world order for the indefinite future. This system rests on moderation of means and ends among the five dominant actors, who will work out patterns for efficient cooperation and limited competition, based on a general acceptance of the geopolitical and geoeconomic status quo. The pentagonal model places little empha-

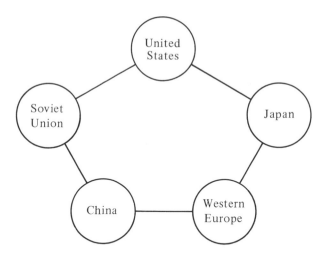

Figure 4. Pentagonal Model

sis on social and economic justice; it is also pre-ecological to the extent that it assumes the capacity of competing national units to behave in a manner compatible with ecological balance. While the notion of a concert of dominant actors may avert short-term breakdown, it hardly provides a satisfactory response to the negative threats posed by the present crisis; nor does it offer any prospect of fulfilling the positive potential for human social and individual development.

The disarray variant of the doomsday model (Fig. 5) depicts the breakdown of the present system of world order ($S_O$) into a series of gravely weakened and uncoordinated units. These units may or may not possess a statelike formal identity, but in either case they will face a loss of internal cohesion and a virtual collapse of any capacity to enter into stable external relationships. The state system will have disintegrated into a condition of world anarchy or chaos, and no compre-

Figure 5. Doomsday-Disarray Model

Figure 6.  Doomsday-Tyrannical Model

hensive political organization will exist. Poverty, violence, and disease
will be rampant, with no prospects for recreating conditions of order
and justice that are even comparable to $S_O$.

In the other main line of response to the collapse of $S_O$, the tyrannical
variant of the doomsday model (Fig. 6), the remaining power is
concentrated at a single focal point. Because planetary resources are
exceedingly scarce, relative to human needs, privation is widespread. A
small elite runs the world in a highly dictatorial, repressive fashion. No
opposition is tolerated. The system of world order resembles a police
state of the sort now associated with the worst national tyrannies.

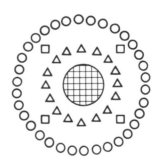

Global government structure

△     International institutions of a functional
character (e.g. regime for sea beds or
environmental quality)

□     Regional institutions (e.g. European Economic
Community)

O     State actors

Figure 7.  World Government Model

In effect, the collapse of $S_O$ is likely to accentuate either the centrifugal tendencies (Fig. 5) or the centripetal tendencies (Fig. 6). By comparison with either eventuality, the present system of world order, with all its deficiencies, looks like a utopia. It is important to understand that regression, as well as positive change, can occur in relation to the future of world order.

A world government response to the inadequacies of the present system can be depicted in crude terms (Fig. 7). Some constitutional conception of this sort has dominated the visionary literature of world order for centuries. The notion of world government seems to satisfy a basic human craving for unity and order. As such, it captures something fundamental about the essential direction of world order reform. At the present stage of international relations, however, a world government solution does not seem attainable except in the course of reconstruction subsequent to a doomsday situation; the more likely world order system in this setting of catastrophic breakdown is a dysutopia of the doomsday-tyrannical sort (Fig. 6). In other words, there is no credible transition path to be followed over the next several decades that could lead reliably toward world government of a benevolent character.

Furthermore, governmental solutions to human problems have not often worked with success at a national level. Many more potential dangers would inhere in a huge global bureaucratic presence, especially if it were combined with the sort of technological apparatus that will be available. Serious problems could arise from domination, conformism, and excessive administration, as well from overconcentration of military capabilities and political powers at this stage in the growth of social relations among human societies.

A compromise between the state system and world government is found in the $S_O \longrightarrow S_1$ solution (Fig. 8). I regard this compromise as the most desirable conception of world order that is also both attainable within a reasonable length of time and does not rely on transitional trauma. For this reason the model is called the preference model for the transition from $S_O$ to $S_1$. The special quality of this preference model is to increase greatly the central guidance capabilities of the present system of world order for functional purposes, while endeavoring simultaneously to diminish the bureaucratic intrusions on individual human existence below the state level. The overall objective is to evolve a new planetary community capable of benign self-management and of improving the conditions for individual and group respect. The basic constitutional principles embodied in the profile of $S_1$ seek to achieve maximum coordination and guidance on the basis of minimum

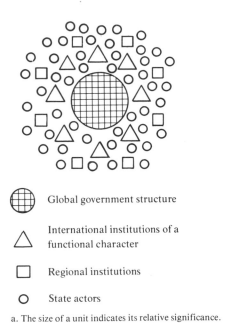

|  | Global government structure |
|---|---|
|  | International institutions of a functional character |
|  | Regional institutions |
|  | State actors |

a. The size of a unit indicates its relative significance.

Figure 8. The $S_O \longrightarrow S_1$ Preference Model

coercion and bureaucratic intrusion. Great emphasis is placed on diminishing the existing power apparatus in the superstates, rather than in transferring power upward, and on incorporating into the structure numerous checks and balances, as well as upward avenues of influence and participation.[29] Figure 8 does not indicate the presence of transnational groupings, which will probably be very important in $S_1$, especially given the altered political consciousness that must precede the shift from $t_1 \longrightarrow t_2$. In fact, transnational economic, cultural, and political groupings may even provide an emerging focus for human loyalty, circumventing and gradually displacing the symbolism of national patriotism.

These are the skeletal elements of a new way of thinking about the future of world order. This way of thinking is shaped by a normative orientation toward what is desirable in human relations and political arrangements. The approach amounts to a plea for restructuring inquiry into international relations in the direction of a newly conceived academic discipline of comparative systems of world order—"comparative" in relation to past, present, and possible future arrangements of power and authority in human affairs; "systemic" in the sense of being as rigorous as possible with respect to the totality of behavior embraced by the subject matter, and "world order" in the sense of adopting a normative orientation toward the performance or desirability of a particular global authority, both in relation to tasks performed (such as human needs, peace, and the conservation of resources and in relation to responsible future projects (conditioning goals by feasibility studies of transition prospects).

In the past, the dichotomies between thought and feeling, on the one hand, and between thought and action, on the other, have often engendered sterile analyses of world order that conveyed the impression of either intellectual aridity or political futility. On the intellectual basis set forth here, a new conception of world order can begin to emerge, which is sensitive to the role of thought and reason in facilitating an essential fusion between feeling and action.

# Appendices

# Notes

# Index

# Appendix 1.    The Nuremberg Principles, 1946

*Principles of International Law Recognized in the Charter of the Nuremberg Tribunal and in the Judgment of the Tribunal.*

As formulated by the International Law Commission, June-July 1950.

*Principle I*

Any person who commits an act which constitutes a crime under international law is responsible therefor and liable to punishment.

*Principle II*

The fact that internal law does not impose a penalty for an act which constitutes a crime under international law does not relieve the person who committed the act from responsibility under international law.

*Principle III*

The fact that a person who committed an act which constitutes a crime under international law acted as Head of State or responsible government official does not relieve him from responsibility under international law.

*Principle IV*

The fact that a person acted pursuant to order of his Government or of a superior does not relieve him from responsibility under international law, provided a moral choice was in fact possible to him.

*Principle V*

Any person charged with a crime under international law has the right to a fair trial on the facts and law.

*Principle VI*

The crimes hereinafter set out are punishable as crimes under international law:

a. Crimes against peace:

(i) Planning, preparation, initiation or waging of a war of aggression or a war in violation of international treaties, agreements or assurances;

(ii) Participation in a common plan or conspiracy for the accomplishment of any of the acts mentioned under (i).

b. War crimes:

Violations of the laws or customs of war which include, but are not limited to, murder, ill-treatment or deportation to slave-labour or for any other purpose of civilian population of or in occupied territory, murder or ill-treatment of prisoners of war or persons on the seas, killing of hostages, plunder of public or private property, wanton destruction of cities, towns, or villages, or devastation not justified by military necessity.

c. Crimes against humanity:

Murder, extermination, enslavement, deportation and other inhuman acts done against any civilian population, or persecutions on political, racial or religious grounds, when such acts are done or such persecutions are carried on in execution of or in connexion with any crime against peace or any war crime.

*Principle VII*

Complicity in the commission of a crime against peace, a war crime, or a crime against humanity as set forth in Principle VI is a crime under international law.

# Appendix 2.  A Draft International Convention on the Crime of Ecocide

The Contracting Parties,

Acting on the belief that ecocide is a crime under international law, contrary to the spirit and aims of the United Nations, and condemned by peoples and governments of good will throughout the world;

Recognizing that we are living in a period of increasing danger of ecological collapse; acknowledging that man has consciously and unconsciously inflicted irreparable damage on the environment in times of war and peace;

Being convinced that the pursuit of ecological quality requires international guidelines and procedures for cooperation and enforcement,

Hereby agree:

*Article I*

The Contracting Parties confirm that ecocide, whether committed in time of peace or in time of war, is a crime under international law which they undertake to prevent and to punish.

*Article II*

In the present Convention, ecocide means any of the following acts committed with intent to disrupt or destroy, in whole or in part, a human ecosystem:

a. The use of weapons of mass destruction, whether nuclear, bacteriological, chemical, or other:

b. The use of chemical herbicides to defoliate and deforest natural forests for military purposes;

c. The use of bombs and artillery in such quantity, density, or size as to impair the quality of soil or to enhance the prospect of diseases dangerous to human beings, animals, or crops;

d. The use of bulldozing equipment to destroy large tracts of forest or cropland for military purposes;

[*253*]

e. The use of techniques designed to increase or decrease rainfall or otherwise modify weather as a weapon of war;

f. The forcible removal of human beings or animals from their habitual places of habitation to expedite the pursuit of military or industrial objectives.

*Article III*

The following acts shall be punishable:
a. Ecocide;
b. Conspiracy to commit ecocide;
c. Direct and public incitement to ecocide;
d. Attempt to commit ecocide;
e. Complicity in ecocide.

*Article IV*

Persons committing ecocide as defined in Article II or any of the acts described in Article III shall be punished, at least to the extent of being removed for a period of years from any position of leadership or public trust. Constitutionally responsible rulers, public officials, military commanders, or private individuals may all be charged with and convicted of the crimes associated with ecocide as set forth in Article III.

*Article V*

[This article may be the most controversial provision in the proposal and could be either deleted altogether or appended as an optional protocol, to enhance the prospects for ratification of the basic Convention.]

The United Nations shall establish a Commission for the Investigation of Ecocide as soon as this Convention comes into force. This Commission shall be composed of fifteen experts on international law and assisted by a staff conversant with ecology. The principal tasks of the Commission shall be to investigate allegations of ecocide whenever made by governments of States, by the principal officer of any international institution whether or not part of the United Nations Organizations, by resolution of the General Assembly or Security Council, or by petition signed by at least 1000 private persons. The Commission shall have power of subpoena and to take depositions; all hearings of the Commission shall be open and transcripts of proceedings shall be a matter of public record. If after investigating the allegations, the Commission concludes by majority vote that none of the acts described in Article III has been committed, it shall issue a dismissal of the complaint accompanied by a short statement of reasons. If after investigating the allegations, the Commission concludes by majority vote that acts within the scope of Article III have been or are being committed, then it shall issue a cease and desist order, a statement recommending prosecution or sanction of specific individuals or groups, and a statement of reasons supporting its decision. It shall also recommend whether prosecution should proceed under national, regional, international or ad hoc auspices. Regardless of the decision, minority members of the Commission may attach dissenting or concurring opinions to the majority decision. In the event of a tie vote in the Commission, the Chairman shall cast a second vote. The Commission shall have rule-making capacity to regulate fully its operations to assure full realization of the objectives of this Convention but with due regard for the human rights embodied in the United Nations Declaration of Human Rights.

*Article VI*

The Contracting Parties undertake to enact, in accordance with their respective Constitutions, the necessary legislation to give effect to the provisions of the present Convention and, in particular, to provide effective penalties for persons guilty of ecocide or any of the other acts enumerated in Article III.

*Article VII*

Persons charged with ecocide or any of the other acts enumerated in Article III shall be tried by a competent tribunal of the State in the territory of which the act was committed, or by such international penal tribunal as may have jurisdiction with respect to those Contracting Parties which shall have accepted its jurisdiction.

*Article VIII*

Ecocide and the other acts enumerated in Article III shall not be considered as political crimes for the purpose of extradition.

The Contracting Parties pledge themselves in such cases to grant extradition in accordance with their laws and treaties in force.

*Article IX*

Any Contracting Party may call upon the competent organ of the United Nations to take such action under the Charter of the United Nations as they consider appropriate for the prevention and suppression of acts of ecocide or any of the other acts enumerated in Article III.

*Article X*

Disputes between the Contracting Parties relating to the interpretation, application, or fulfillment of the present Convention, including those relating to the responsibility of a State for ecocide or any of the other acts enumerated in Article III, shall be submitted to the International Court of Justice at the request of any of the parties to the dispute.

*Article XI*

The present Convention, of which the Chinese, English, French, Russian, and Spanish texts are equally authentic, shall bear the date of . . .

*Article XII*

The present Convention shall be open until . . . for signature on behalf of any Member of the United Nations and of any nonmember State to which an invitation to sign has been addressed by the General Assembly.

The present Convention shall be ratified, and the instruments of ratification shall be deposited with the Secretary-General of the United Nations.

After the date of . . . the present Convention may be acceded to on behalf of any Member of the United Nations and of any nonmember State which has received an invitation as aforesaid.

Instruments of accession shall be deposited with the Secretary-General of the United Nations.

*Article XIII*

Any Contracting Party may at any time, by notification addressed to the Secretary-General of the United Nations, extend the application of the present Convention to all or any of the territories for the conduct of whose foreign relations that Contracting Party is responsible.

*Article XIV*

On the day when the first twenty instruments of ratification or accession have been deposited, the Secretary-General shall draw up a *procés verbal* and transmit a copy of it to each Member of the United Nations and to each of the nonmember States contemplated in Article XIII.

The present Convention shall come into force on the ninetieth day following the date of deposit of the twentieth instrument of ratification or accession.

Any ratification of accession effected subsequent to the latter date shall become effective on the ninetieth day following the deposit of the instrument of ratification or accession.

*Article XV*

The present Convention shall remain in effect for a period of ten years from the date of its coming into force.

It shall thereafter remain in force for successive periods of five years for such Contracting Parties as have not denounced it at least six months before the expiration of the current period.

Denunciation shall be effected by a written notification addressed to the Secretary-General of the United Nations.

*Article XVI*

If, as a result of denunciations, the number of Parties to the present Convention should become less than sixteen, the Convention shall cease to be in force as from the date on which the last of these denunciations shall become effective.

*Article XVII*

A request for the revision of the present Convention may be made at any time by any Contracting Party by means of a notification in writing addressed to the Secretary-General.

The General Assembly shall decide upon the steps, if any, to be taken in respect of such request.

*Article XVIII*

The Secretary-General of the United Nations shall notify all Members of the United Nations and the nonmember States contemplated in Article XII of the following:

a. Signatures, ratifications, and accessions received in accordance with Article XII;

b. Notifications received in accordance with Article XIII;

c. The date on which the present Convention comes into force in accordance with Article XIV;

d. Denunciations received in accordance with Article XV;

e. The abrogation of the Convention in accordance with Article XVI;

f. Notifications received in accordance with Article XVII.

*Article XIX*

The original of the present Convention shall be deposited in the archives of the United Nations.

A certified copy of the Convention shall be transmitted to all Members of the United Nations and to the nonmember States contemplated in Article XII.

*Article XX*

The present Convention shall be registered by the Secretary-General of the United Nations on the date of its coming into force.

## *A Resolution Relating to the Study by the International Law Commission of the Question of an International Criminal Jurisdiction*

The General Assembly,

Considering that the Discussion of the Convention on the Prevention and Punishment of the Crime of Ecocide has raised the question of the desirability and possibility of having persons charged with ecocide tried by a competent international tribunal,

Considering that, in the course of development of the international community, there will be an increasing need of an international judicial organ for the trial of certain crimes under international law,

Invites the International Law Commission to study the desirability and possibility of establishing an international judicial organ for the trial of persons charged with ecocide or other crimes over which jurisdiction will be conferred on that organ by international conventions;

Requests the International Law Commission in carrying out this task to pay attention to the possibility of establishing a Criminal Chamber of the International Court of Justice.

# Appendix 3.   A Draft Protocol on Environmental Warfare

Considering that environmental warfare has been condemned by public opinion throughout the world and that the deliberate destruction of the environment disrupts the ecological basis of life on earth;

Mindful of the extent to which the future of mankind is linked with the rapid development of protective attitudes toward environmental quality;

Conscious of the extent to which existing and prospective weapons and tactics of warfare, particularly counterinsurgency warfare or reliance on nuclear weapons, disrupt ecological patterns for long periods of time and destroy the beneficial relationship between man and nature;

Recalling the prior expressions of collective concern with the general effects of war embodied in General Assembly Resolutions 1653 (XVI) and 2603A (XXIV);

We, as representatives of governments and as citizens of the world community, do hereby commit ourselves as a matter of conscience and of law to refrain from the use of tactics and weapons of war that inflict irreparable harm to the environment or disrupt fundamental ecological relationships.

This Protocol prohibits in particular:

1. All efforts to defoliate or destroy forests or crops by means of chemicals or bulldozing;

2. Any pattern of bombardment that results in extensive craterization of the land or in deep craters that generate health hazards;

3. Any reliance on weapons of mass destruction of life or any weapons or tactics that are likely to kill or injure large numbers of animals.

We, as undersigned, will seek to gain as many individual and institutional accessions to this Protocol as possible.

The Protocol shall come into effect after the first five signatures, and is binding thereafter on all governments of the world because it is a declaration of restraints on warfare which already are embodied in the rules and principles of international law.

Violation of this Protocol shall be deemed an international crime of grave magnitude that can be charged and considered, by fair trial proceedings, wherever an alleged culprit can be apprehended; in cases of extreme necessity trials in absentia are authorized.

Done in Stockholm, Sweden, June, 1972.

# Appendix 4.   A Draft Petition on Ecocide and Environmental Warfare

The undersigned,

Mindful of their concern with the ecological quality of this planet and with the purposes and principles of the Charter of the United Nations;

Gravely concerned by the evidence of ecological devastation in Indochina and by the spread of counterinsurgency weaponry and doctrine to governments throughout the world;

Fearful of the further willingness of governments to conduct their operations without due deference for the conditions of ecological welfare, especially during periods of armed conflict;

1. Declare that:

a. The commission of acts of ecocide is an international crime in violation of the spirit, letter, and aims of the United Nations and, as such, is in direct violation of the Charter of the United Nations and violates the sense of minimum moral obligation prevailing in the world community;

b. The protection of man's relation to natural ecosystems is a legal and moral obligation deserving of the highest respect and directly related to the prospects for human survival and social development;

c. Any government, organization, group, or individual that commits, plans, supports, or advocates ecocide shall be considered as committing an international crime of grave magnitude and as acting contrary to the laws of humanity and in violation of the ecological imperative;

2. Request that the Secretary-General of the United Nations take the following steps:

a. Convene an emergency session of the Security Council to order the United States to cease and desist from all war policies responsible for the ecological devastation of Indochina;

b. Compile a report on the ecological damage done in Indochina and urge the establishment of a commission of inquiry composed of experts that would submit periodic reports to the General Assembly of ecological effects of the war on Indochina and courses of action, together with funding, available to secure maximum rehabilitation of ecological quality;

c. Request the International Law Commission to prepare an International Convention on Ecocide, a Protocol on Environmental Warfare, and a Code on individual and collective responsibility relative to the crime of ecocide;

d. Convene a conference of governments during 1974 to take appropriate legal steps to outlaw ecocide and to provide the legal framework needed to prohibit environmental warfare, including principles and procedures to assess responsibility and to enjoin activity destructive of environmental values.

# Appendix 5.    A Draft Peoples' Petition of Redress on Ecocide and Environmental Warfare

The undersigned,

Recognizing that modern weapons of mass destruction are capable of causing widespread and enduring devastation of the human environment;

Concerned by the evidence of long-term, extensive ecological damage caused in Indochina by a variety of weapons, including bombs, napalm, herbicides, plows, and poisonous gases, used principally and massively by the United States in the course of waging the Indochina War;

And further concerned by reports of the supply and sale of these means of waging war by the United States to other governments, including the Saigon administration of South Vietnam and the government of Portugal;

Do hereby petition all governments to renounce weapons and tactics of war designed to inflict damage to the environment as such.

We call especially on the Government of the United States of America immediately to stop the sale and transfer of weaponry designed primarily to carry on environmental warfare;

And call upon the United Nations to take steps immediately to investigate and report the full extent of ecological damage resulting from the Indochina War, to consider and recommend steps that could be taken to restore the environment in Indochina as rapidly as possible, and to assess responsibility for ecological damage and to call for appropriate reparations from the government(s) responsible after the termination of hostilities.

We further appeal to the United Nations to convene promptly a world conference to draw up an international convention prohibiting recourse to weapons and military tactics designed primarily to destroy or modify the human environment and to prepare a draft convention on Ecocide to parallel the Genocide Convention.

# Notes

## Introduction

1. For an account of the World Order Models Project by its principal architect, see Saul H. Mendlovitz and Thomas G. Weiss, "Towards Consensus: The World Order Models Project of the Institute for World Order," in Grenville Clark and Louis Sohn, eds., *Introduction to World Peace Through World Law* (Chicago, World Without War Publications, 1973), pp. 74-97.

2. I have elsewhere tried to complement criticism with a constructive conception of the future of world order. See Richard A. Falk, *A Study of Future Worlds* (New York, Free Press, 1975).

3. Arthur M. Schlesinger, Jr., *The Imperial Presidency* (Boston, Houghton, Mifflin, 1973).

4. *New York Times,* Aug. 11, 1974, sec. 4, p.2.

5. This quotation and the one that follows are taken from a partial text of George Wald's Tokyo address, *New York Times,* Aug. 17, 1974, p. 23.

## 1. The State System under Siege

1. For representative views, see McGeorge Bundy, "To Cap the Volcano," *Foreign Affairs* 48:1-120 (1969); Fred Charles Iklé, "Can Nuclear Deterrence Last Out the Century," *Foreign Affairs* 51:267-285 (January 1973); Herbert York, "A Proposal for a Saner Deterrent" (mimeo., 1973); Jack Ruina, "SALT in a MAD World," *New York Times Magazine,* June 30, 1974, pp. 8, 42-44, 48, 50-51.

2. For the distinction between minimal and optimal world order, see Myres S. McDougal and Florentino P. Feliciano, *Law and Minimum World Public Order* (New Haven, Yale University Press, 1961), p. vii.

3. Much of the debate on these issues has been stimulated by a study on the limits to growth sponsored by the Club of Rome. See Donella Meadows and others, *The Limits to Growth* (New York, Universe, 1972). Another influential stimulant was the manifesto prepared by the editorial board of the British magazine *The Ecologist*. See Edward Goldsmith and others, *Blueprint for survival* (Boston, Houghton Mifflin, 1972). A counterattack of sorts has concentrated on the faulty methodology or excessive pessimism of these studies. See John Maddox, *The Doomsday Syndrome* (New York, McGraw-Hill, 1972); *Prophets of Doom* (Sussex, Eng., University of Sussex Press, 1973); Carl

Kaysen, "The Computer That Printed W*O*L*F*," *Foreign Affairs* 50:660-669 (1972); Peter Passell and Leonard Ross, *The Retreat from Riches: Affluence and Its Enemies* (New York, Viking, 1973).

4. See Richard A. Falk, "The Sherrill Hypothesis: International Law and Drastic Global Reform: Historical and Futurist Perspectives" (Yale Law School, mimeo., 1974); Richard A. Falk, *A Study of Future Worlds* (New York, Free Press, 1975), chs. 4 and 5.

5. See Raymond Aron, *Peace and War: A Theory of International Relations,* trans. Richard Howard and Annette Baker Fox (Garden City, Doubleday, 1966); John Herz, *International Politics in the Atomic Age* (New York, Harcourt, Brace and World, 1959); Stanley Hoffman, "Obstinate or Obsolete? The Fate of the Nation-State and the Case of Western Europe," *Daedalus,* Summer 1966, pp. 862-915; Richard A. Falk, "The Interplay of the Westphalia and Charter Conceptions of the International Legal Order," in Cyril E. Black and Richard A. Falk, eds., *The Future of the International Legal Order* (Princeton, N.J., Princeton University Press, 1969), pp. 32-70; Charles Yost, *The Insecurity of Nations* (New York, Praeger, 1968).

6. For the shifting patterns of statecraft, see Klaus Knorr, *On the Uses of Military Power in the Nuclear Age* (Princeton, Princeton University Press, 1966); Stanley Hoffmann, "International Organization and the International System," *International Organization* 24:389-413 (1970); R. O. Keohane and J. S. Nye, Jr., eds., "Transnational Relations and World Politics," *International Organization* 25:329-748 (1971), esp. pp. 329-350, 373-397, 721-748. For the persistence of statist logic and the absence of any effort to consider the claims put forth in terms of the ecological model, see e.g. Richard Nixon, "U. S. Foreign Policy for 1970s: Building for Peace," Report to the Congress, Feb. 25, 1971; W. W. Rostow, *Politics and the Stages of Growth* (Cambridge, Eng., Cambridge University Press, 1971); Louis Halle, "A World at Peace," *Survival* 13:148-153 (May 1971); George Liska, *Imperial America: The International Politics of Primacy* (Baltimore, Johns Hopkins University Press, 1967).

7. Such multifaceted bargains are relatively innovative instruments of international order, responsive to the active participation of diversely positioned states in the law-making process. Earlier law-making presupposed common interests, eschewed trade-offs, and rested on the domination of international society by governments at comparable levels of economic and technological development.

8. In some advanced societies, however, the appreciation of ecological danger by the government is much greater than is that by organized interest groups such as labor and industry. See e.g. E. W. Kenworthy, "Industry Spokesmen Call Pollution Bill Too Costly," *New York Times,* Dec. 11, 1971, p. 62; B. E. Calame, "Fearing Loss of Jobs, Union Battles Efforts to Clean Environment," *The Wall Street Journal,* November 1971, pp. 1, 33.

9. Kenworthy, "Industry Spokesmen"; Calame, "Fearing Loss of Jobs." Hawn's statement is a fascinating effort to turn the ecological argument on its head and contend that efforts to promote the ecological model proceed at the expense of overall quality, by their tendency to depress the GNP and divert

resources from socially useful ends. It seems doubtful whether the main opportunity costs of environmental protection are the improvement of living standards and economic opportunities of the poor. The statement embodies a subtle ideological appeal that disguises the main objective of liberating industrial operations from costly procedures.

10. Effective demand, however, may not exceed supply in all sectors of the market. Many people in the world are hungry or undernourished because they have no money with which to buy the food that is available.

11. For world arms spending, see *World Military Expenditures, 1971* (United States Arms Control and Disarmament Agency, Washington, D.C.), pp. 1-26.

12. Because of uneven development and population density, the actuality and perception of scarcity tend also to be uneven. There remain many uncrowded parts of the world and many societies where the consumption of raw materials is so small, relative to world consumption totals, that the prospect of scarcity seems altogether implausible.

13. More operationally, leaders are motivated by their effective terms of political tenure (two, four, five years); in nondemocratic societies, comparable time horizons impinge by the interval relied on to assess performance (five-year, ten-year plans). For a highly personalist explanation for the apparent adoption of longer time horizons in Maoist China, see R. J. Lifton, *Revolutionary Immortality: Mao Tse-tung and the Chinese Cultural Revolution* (New York, Random House, 1968).

14. For example, the United Nations Charter attempts to centralize authority in the United Nations, but the organization is not capable of imposing its claims of authority and is often unable even to command a sufficient consensus among its membership to posit specific claims. In some contexts, precisely because the claims are unenforceable, as in South Africa, the United Nations escalates its rhetoric over time to compensate for its inability to effectuate actual change. As a consequence, a widening credibility gap exists, and cynicism ensues. In the sense, the Charter is "premature" and over-ambitious.

15. There are even instances in which recourse to war seems consistent with the dictates of justice, such as India's liberation of Bangladesh or African support for armed struggle against South Africa's government. Without some effective procedures for peaceful change, the elimination of war would solidify intolerable structures of peace. To put the issue differently, there are instances, although their existence in a particular case might be controverted, in which adherence to the law of peace jeopardizes prospects for minimal justice.

16. G. F. Kennan, "To Prevent a World Wasteland," *Foreign Affairs* 48:401-413 (1970).

17. Such logical coherence is not tantamount to an endorsement of this approach. The normative coherence of universal participation seems necessary to adjust the system of world order to the ecological challenge. Experience with universal modes of thought and action are the essential aspects of the learning process that must ensue.

18. But governing groups in poor states may have transnational class interests that induce action in accordance with the interests of foreign governments rather than with the population or general welfare of their own society. See T. E. Weisskopf, *Capitalism, Underdevelopment, and the Future of the Poor Countries,* World Law Fund, Occasional Papers No. 2 (New York, 1972).

19. See Falk, *A Study of Future Worlds,* esp. chs. 4 and 5.

## 2. Law, Lawyers, and the Conduct of American Foreign Relations

1. Judith Shklar defines legalism as "the ethical attitude that holds moral conduct to be a matter of rule-following, and moral relationships to consist of duties and rights determined by rules." Judith N. Shklar, *Legalism: An Essay on Law, Morals, Politics* (Cambridge, Harvard University Press, 1964).

2. For the conflicting positions of the legalists and antilegalists, see Louis Henkin, *How Nations Behave: Law and Foreign Policy* (New York, Praeger, 1968), pp. 245-271.

3. Dean Acheson, "Remarks," *Proceedings of the American Society of International Law* 13:14 (Washington, D.C., 1963).

4. See Abram Chayes, "Law and the Quarantine of Cuba," *Foreign Affairs* 41:550 (1963); Chayes, "The Legal Case for U.S. Action on Cuba," *Department of State Bulletin* 47:763 (1962); Leonard Meeker, "Defensive Quarantine and the Law," *American Journal of International Law* 57:515 (1963).

5. See Henkin, *How Nations Behave.*

6. Leonard Meeker, "The Dominican Situation on the Perspective of International Law," *Department of State Bulletin* 53:60 (1965).

7. This interpretation that the United States did not act in self-defense is strongly supported even in a conservative account of the Dominican intervention. See John Bartlow Martin, *Overtaken by Events* (Garden City, Doubleday, 1966).

8. Cf. the principal Soviet legal argument, the so-called Brezhnev Doctrine, for occupying Czechoslovakia, formulated in an article in *Pravda,* translated and published as "Sovereignty and International Duties of Socialist Countries," *New York Times,* Sep. 27, 1968, p. 27.

9. Henry A. Kissinger, "The Viet Nam Negotiations," *Foreign Affairs* 47:211, 222-223 (1969).

10. Henry A. Kissinger, "Central Issues of American Foreign Policy," in K. Gordon, ed., *Agenda for the Nation* (Washington, Brookings Institution, 1968), pp. 585, 610, 588, 614.

11. Even Kissinger, despite his concern for the formalism and legalism of American foreign policy, writes as follows about "commitments" in the context of the Vietnam War: "Much of the bitter debate in the United States about the war has been conducted in terms of 1961 and 1962. Unquestionably, the failure at that time to analyze adequately the geopolitical importance of Viet Nam

contributed to the current dilemma. But the commitment of 500,000 Americans has settled the issue of the importance of Viet Nam. For what is involved now is confidence in American promises. However fashionable it is to ridicule the terms 'credibility' or 'prestige,' they are not empty phrases; other nations can gear their actions to ours only if they can count on our steadiness. The collapse of the American effort in Viet Nam would not mollify many critics; most of them would simply add the charge of unreliability to the accusation of bad judgment. Those whose safety or national goals depend on American commitments could only be dismayed. In many parts of the world—the Middle East, Europe, Latin America, even Japan—stability depends on confidence in American promises." Kissinger, "The Viet Nam Negotiations," pp. 218-219. Kissinger uses commitment in two different senses and is somewhat vague about the causal link between American "commitments" and specific behavior.

12. Law functions within a structure of shared assumptions; its starting point is the acceptance, by all parties, of the legitimacy of the legal structure and of the values it embodies. Everyone understands that this shared value commitment and belief in the adjudication of conflict does not exist in more than a fragmentary manner in international society. Nevertheless, the legal habit of mind has sometimes led the United States to discount these difficulties, even to assume for itself and its own policies an international legitimacy which other states were unwilling to concede. Along with this has gone a trust in formal arrangements and alliances which the social and political realities have not at all times justified. The phrase "a characteristic legalism" is taken from an editorial, *New York Times,* Jan. 6, 1969, p. 46. The intellectual underpinnings of this analysis are explicitly attributed to the celebrated critiques of American foreign policy made more than a decade ago in George F. Kennan, *Realities of American Foreign Policy* (Princeton, Princeton University Press, 1954); Kennan, *American Diplomacy, 1900-1950* (Chicago, University of Chicago Press, 1951); Hans J. Morgenthau, *Politics Among Nations,* 4th ed. (New York, Alfred A. Knopf, 1967); Morgenthau, *In Defense of the National Interest* (New York, Alfred A. Knopf, 1951).

13. See also Richard A. Falk, *The Status of Law in International Society* (Princeton, Princeton University Press, 1969).

14. Kissinger, "The Viet Nam Negotiations," p. 221; Zbigniew Brzezinski, "Purpose and Planning in Foreign Policy," *The Public Interest,* Winter 1969, pp. 52, 54-55. Kissinger also argues for a better conceptual framework for foreign policy in "Central Issues."

15. Brzezinski's statement about the legal tradition contains an odd mixture of misconceptions. The case method is a technique of analysis and pedagogy rather than a widely accepted system of adjudication. Arbitration would be closer to the ad hoc "problem-solving" that Brzezinski first refers to. The very importance of precedent is a demonstration that each case is not seen as a discrete problem in the American legal system. Universalizing from the numerous cases that form a line of precedent will quickly bring the thoughtful student of

the law to the intellectual cubbyholes of conceptual thought. The difference from the Continental systems lies in how we reach that plane of conceptual discussion rather than in taking the extreme nominalist position that generalized concepts have no value at all. For American jurisprudence a restatement of the law is the end rather than the beginning of any attempt at legal generalization.

16. Those who support the role of the United States in the Vietnam War often emphasize the absence of any selfish American interests in Vietnam. We are assumed to want no territory or foreign bases, and to have no economic holdings or ambitions. Although the denial of any selfish interest may not be altogether convincing, its frequent repetition by high officials is a powerful illustration of the impulse to justify actions before the world in transcendent moral and legal terms. The United States substitutes the rightness of its cause for the selfish pursuit of interests, and therefore feels no compunctions about unleashing its destructive might on a poor and rather backward Asian country. When interests are pursued, then costs tend to be assessed and the enterprise confined by some concept of net worth. But when supposedly selfless principles underlie the commitment, then no assessment can be made, and no cost is too high. The American effort to end the Vietnam War indicates that some sense of "worth" finally took precedence over the moralistic insistence that the United States was acting to show that aggression does not pay, or that collective self-defense works, or that we are a government that upholds its commitments. Since no moral contention was very convincing, there was a tendency to shift from one to another in a desperate struggle to plug the dike erected against the mounting tide of domestic and international opposition to the war. But up until President Johnson's speech of March 31, 1968, no government official moved the debate about the war off the terrain of selfless promotion of moral and legal principles whose value could not be weighed against the adverse effects of continuing the war.

Within the American elite it has been the pragmatic countertradition that has broken with the moralism and legalism of the Rusk-Rostow position. The formulations of Arthur Schlesinger, Jr., McGeorge Bundy, and Henry Kissinger are characteristic of this pragmatic, even opportunistic, reevaluation of American policy in Vietnam. Bundy's Address at DePauw University on October 12, 1968, offers one of the best examples of this break with moralism: "Until the present burden of Vietnam is at least partly lifted from our society, it will not be easy—it may not be possible—to move forward effectively with other great national tasks. This has not always been my view, but . . . it seems to me wholly clear now that at its current level of effort and cost the war cannot be allowed to continue for long. Its penalties upon us all are much too great." Lest he be mistakenly perceived as a sudden convert to matters of principle, Bundy made plain that his change of position on Vietnam was a matter of pure expediency: "I remind you also, if you stand on the other side, that my argument against escalation and against an indefinite continuation of our present course has been based not on moral outrage or political hostility to the objective, but rather on the simple and practical ground that escalation will not work and that continuation of our present course is unacceptable." Richard A. Falk, ed., *The Vietnam War and International Law* (Princeton, Princeton University Press, 1969), II, 964-975.

Schlesinger expressed the same theme when he wrote: "The tragedy of Vietnam is the tragedy of the catastrophic overextension and misapplication of valid principles. The original insights of collective security and liberal evangelism were generous and wise." Schlesinger, "Vietnam and the End of the Age of Superpowers," *Harpers,* March 1966, pp. 41-49. My overriding contention is that neither moralism-legalism of the Rusk-Rostow variety nor expediency of the Bundy-Schlesinger variety provide America with an adequate basis for policy and choice in world affairs.

17. Such particularism is also associated with the importance of town meetings in early America and with the rise of a congregationalist tradition in ecclesiastical affairs.

18. Garrett Hardin makes this argument in vivid and generic terms by comparing the experience of managing planetary issues by relying on national self-restraint with the mutually destructive effects of relying on the self-restraint of individual farmers to protect the English commons from overgrazing in the face of increasing animal herds. Hardin, "The Tragedy of the Commons," *Science* 162:1243 (1968).

19. Kissinger, "Central Issues," p. 611.

20. The following passage is a striking illustration of the tradition of legal piety: "In the period of primarily American responsibility for peace since 1945, we have used our force prudently, cautiously, and for limited and defensive ends. We have used force in conformity with international law, in order to enforce it. When we had a monoply of nuclear weapons, we did not seek to impose our will on the rest of the world. Nor have we even overthrown the regime of Castro in Cuba." Eugene Rostow, *Law, Power, and the Pursuit of Peace* (Lincoln, University of Nebraska Press, 1968), p. 11. Rostow seems to be confusing adherence to law with decisions to refrain from using all the power at the disposal of a national government. But surely some lesser uses of power may not be compatible with the sovereign status of other countries, nor with the legal prohibitions on nondefensive uses of national force against foreign countries.

21, Frank W. Notestein, "Population Growth and Its Control," in Clifford Hardin, ed., *Overcoming World Hunger* (Englewood Cliffs, Prentice-Hall, 1969), pp. 9, 16-17.

22. For the projected population growth and its global consequences, see Paul Ehrlich, *The Population Bomb* (New York, Ballantine Books, 1968); Gunnar Myrdal, *The Asian Drama,* 3 vols. (New York, The Twentieth Century Fund, 1968); William Paddock and Paul Paddock, *Famine—1975!* (Boston, Little, Brown, 1967).

23. Such a role for international law and lawyers is the theme of Richard A. Falk, "The Sherrill Hypothesis: International Law and Drastic Global Reform: Historical and Futurist Perspectives" (Yale Law School, mimeo., 1974).

24. I do not mean to imply that international lawyers are by and large either legalists or antilegalists. On the contrary, the academic mainstream of contemporary international legal studies exhibits my search for an intermediate statement of the link between law and politics. The legalist-antilegalist discussion enjoys prominence mainly in discussions of the proper framework of restraint for the conduct of United States foreign policy.

## 3. *The Denuclearization of Global Politics*

All *Documents on Disarmament* cited below can be obtained from the Government Printing Office, Washington, D.C.

1. Interview between Premier Khrushchev and C.S. Sulzberger, Sept. 5, 1961, *Documents on Disarmament,* 1961, p. 358; statement of Nikita S. Khrushchev, Prime Minister of the Soviet Union: "We are maintaining our rockets armed with the most powerful thermonuclear weapons in constant combat readiness, *but the Soviet Union will never be the first to set these weapons in motion and unleash a world war,"* The New York Times, July 20, 1963, p. 2 (italics mine); Chinese Communist communique on hydrogen bomb test, Dec. 28, 1968: "The Chinese Communist Government reiterates once again that the conducting of necessary and limited nuclear tests and the development of nuclear weapons by China are entirely for the purpose of defense and for breaking the nuclear monopoly, with the ultimate aim of abolishing nuclear weapons. We solemnly declare once again that at no time and in no circumstances will China be the first to use nuclear weapons. We always mean what we say," *Documents on Disarmament,* 1968, pp. 808-810; *Documents on Disarmament,* 1967, pp. 420-421.

2. The most important development with respect to nuclear-free zones is the 1967 Treaty for the Prohibition of Nuclear Weapons in Latin America—the Treaty of Tlatelolco—signed by twenty-one Latin American countries. See Mason Willrich, *Non-Proliferation Treaty: Framework for Nuclear Control* (Charlottesville, Michie, 1969), pp. 55-57.

3. *Documents on Disarmament,* 1961, pp. 648-650.

4. For example, G.A. Res. 1909 (XVIII), calling upon the Eighteen-Nation Committee on Disarmament to convene a conference for the purpose of signing a treaty of prohibition, was supported by a vote of 64-18-25. *Documents on Disarmament,* 1963, p. 626. G.A. Res. 2289 (XXII), passed by a vote of 77-0-29, urges all states to consider, in light of G.A. Res. 1653, signing a draft convention on the prohibition of nuclear weapons submitted by the Soviet Union. *Documents on Disarmament,* 1967, pp. 626-627.

5. On the terrible consequences, see esp. the Report to Secretary-General U Thant by a group of consultant experts on the Effects of Possible Use of Nuclear Weapons, *Documents on Disarmament,* 1967, pp. 476-513.

6. See Richard A. Falk, *The Status of Law in International Society* (Princeton, Princeton University Press, 1970), pp. 174-184; Jorge Castañeda, *Legal Effects of United Nations Resolutions* (New York, Columbia University Press,

1969); Obed Y. Asamoah, *The Legal Significance of the Declarations of the General Assembly of the United Nations* (The Hague, Martinus Nijhoff, 1966).

7. For the legality of nuclear weapons, see George Schwarzenberger, *The Legality of Nuclear Weapons* (London, Stevens and Sons, 1958); Negendra Singh, *Nuclear Weapons and International Law* (New York, Praeger, 1959); Myres S. McDougal and Florentino P. Feliciano, *Law and Minimum World Public Order: The Legal Regulation of International Coercion* (New Haven, Yale University Press, 1961); William V. O'Brien, *War and/or Survival* (Garden City, Doubleday, 1969), esp. pp. 108-130; for complete text of *Shimoda and others v. Japan,* see Richard A. Falk and Saul H. Mendlovitz, *The Strategy of World Order* (New York, World Law Fund, 1966), I, 314-354.

8. On atomic weapons, the U.S. Army states: "The use of explosive 'atomic weapons,' whether by air, sea, or land forces, cannot as such be regarded as violative of international law in the absence of any customary rule of international law or international convention restricting their employment." Department of the Army Field Manual FM 27-10, *The Law of Land Warfare* (July 1956), p. 18, para. 35. On nuclear weapons, the U.S. Navy states: "There is at present no rule of international law expressly prohibiting states from the use of nuclear weapons in warfare. In the absence of express prohibition, the use of such weapons against enemy combatants and other military objectives is permitted." The navy maintains that, in effect, nuclear bombs are subject to the same laws as are conventional bombs, and that United States forces may use nuclear weapons only when so directed by the President. *The Law of Naval Warfare,* in Robert W. Tucker, *The Law of War and Neutrality at Sea* (U.S. Naval War College, International Law Studies, 1955), pp. 410, 416.

9. See William Brecher, "NATO Planners Move Toward Greater Stress on Atomic Weapons," *The New York Times,* Nov. 13, 1969, p. 8.

10. Bernard Brodie, *Escalation and Nuclear Option* (Princeton, Princeton University Press, 1966), pp. 132-133.

11. *Documents on Disarmament,* 1967, p. 588.

12. Quote taken from *Documents,* p. 589.

13. See Edward Teller and Allen Brown, *The Legacy of Hiroshima* (Garden City, Doubleday, 1962).

14. *Department of State Bulletin,* Jan. 12, 1954; Brodie, *Escalation and Nuclear Option,* p. 4.

15. For text of Joint Statement, see Falk and Mendlovitz, eds., *The Strategy of World Order,* III, 280-282; Thomas B. Larson, *Disarmament and Soviet Policy, 1964-1968* (Englewood Cliffs, Prentice-Hall, 1969), p. 167.

16. Falk and Mendlovitz, eds., *The Strategy of World Order,* I, 314-354; for discussion of *Shimoda* decision, see Richard A. Falk, *Legal Order in a Violent World* (Princeton, Princeton University Press, 1968), pp. 374-413.

17. *Documents on Disarmament,* 1967, p. 593.

18. *Documents on Disarmament,* 1967, p. 580.

19. See Ralph K. White, *Nobody Wanted War,* rev. ed. (Garden City, Doubleday Anchor, 1970).

20. I am indebted to Harold Feiveson for the ideas in this paragraph.

21. There is academic controversy as to whether the war was "substantially won." The controversy concerns both what the policy-makers believed to be the war situation at the time of their decision and whether that situation, however perceived, was the true explanation of their decision to use atomic weapons. I am persuaded by the view that the war was substantially won, and that the policy-makers understood this and went ahead with the decision to use atomic weapons for largely geopolitical reasons. For interpretation to this effect, see Gar Alperovitz, *Atomic Diplomacy: Hiroshima and Potsdam* (New York, Simon and Schuster, 1965). For the contrary view that atomic weapons were used to win the war and save lives, see Herbert Feis, *Japan Subdued* (Princeton, Princeton University Press, 1961). Further understanding of the decision can be gained by reading Edwin Fogelman, *Hiroshima: The Decision to Use the A-Bomb* (New York, Scribner's, 1964).

22. *The New York Times,* Nov. 26, 1969, p. 16.

23. I am indebted to Harold Feiveson for the approach taken in this paragraph.

## 4. Learning from Vietnam

1. See Richard A. Falk, "Drifting Toward Armageddon," *The Progressive,* October 1970, pp. 48-54.

2. See Richard J. Barnet, *Intervention and Revolution* (New York, World, 1968), esp. pp. 3-46.

3. See e.g., from the Right, Hanson W. Baldwin, *Strategy for Tomorrow* (New York, Harper and Row, 1970); from the Left, William Appleman Williams, *The Roots of the Modern American Empire* (New York, Random House, 1969).

4. I intend to develop this link between domestic political forces and the course of foreign policy in subsequent writing.

5. Col. Willaim C. Moore, "History, Vietnam, and the Concept of Deterrence," *Air University Review* 20:58-63 (September-October 1969).

6. Moore, "History, Vietnam, and the Concept of Deterrence," p. 63.

7. Townsend Hoopes, *The Limits of Intervention* (New York, McKay, 1970), p. 58.

8. Richard N. Pfeffer, ed., *No More Vietnams?* (New York, Harper and Row, 1968), pp. 267-268.

9. David P. Mozingo, *The United States in Asia: Evolution and Containment* (New York, Council on Religion and International Affairs, 1967), pp. 7-8.

10. Stanley Hoffman, in Pfeffer, *No More Vietnams?* pp. 193-203, 255.

11. Pres. Richard M. Nixon, "The Pursuit of Peace in Vietnam," *Department of State Bulletin* 61:1587, Nov. 24, 1969, p. 440.

12. Pres. Richard M. Nixon, "United States Foreign Policy for the 1970s: A New Strategy for Peace," A Report to Congress, *New York Times,* Feb. 19, 1970.

13. See Henry A. Kissinger, "Central Issues of American Foreign Policy," in Kermit Gordon, ed., *Agenda for the Nation* (Washington, D.C., The Brookings Institution, 1968), pp. 585-614.

14. Nixon, Report to Congress.

15. McGeorge Bundy, "De Pauw Address," in Richard A. Falk, ed., *The Vietnam War and International Law* (Princeton, Princeton University Press, 1969), II, 964-75.

16. Arthur Schlesinger, Jr., "Vietnam and the End of the Age of Superpowers," *Harper's,* March 1969, pp. 41-49.

17. O. Edmund Clubb, Jr., *The United States and the Sino-Soviet Bloc in Southeast Asia* (Washington, D.C., Brookings Institution, 1962), p. 15.

## 5. Counterinsurgency Warfare in Vietnam and International Law

1. Paul Ramsey, *The Just War: Force and Political Responsibility* (New York, Charles Scribner and Sons, 1968), esp. pp. 432-440.

2. For a more balanced view of the comparative merits of incumbent and insurgent positions, see Tom J. Farer, "The Law of War 25 Years After Nuremberg," *International Conciliation,* no. 583 (May 1971), pp. 25-35. See esp. his rejection of the American view "that humanitarian law does not inhibit full exploitation of fire-power superiority regardless of its effects on the civilian population"—a view that Farer calls "a proposition which every decent man will, of course, reject" (p. 33).

3. For these ratios, see Edward S. Herman, *Atrocities in Vietnam: Myths and Realities* (Philadelphia, Pilgrim Press, 1970), pp. 41-88, esp. pp. 42-46, 54-60; Frank Harvey, *Air War—Vietnam* (New York, Bantam Books, 1967); Raphael Littauer and Norman Uphoff, eds., *The Air War in Indochina,* rev. ed. (Boston, Beacon Press, 1972).

4. See e.g. Telford Taylor, *Nuremberg and Vietnam: An American Tragedy* (New York, Quadrangle, 1970); Erwin Knoll and Judith Nies McFadden, eds., *War Crimes and the American Conscience* (New York, Holt Rinehart & Winston, 1970); Richard A. Falk, Gabriel Kolko, and Robert Jay Lifton, eds., *Crimes of War* (New York, Random House, 1971).

5. Philip Slater, *The Pursuit of Loneliness* (Boston, Beacon Press, 1970), p. 32. See also Jean-Paul Sartre, *On Genocide* (Boston, Beacon Press, 1968). Accounts of typical ground combat campaigns also support an inference of genocidal impact. See e.g. Jonathan Schell, *The Villiage of Ben Suc* (New York, Alfred A. Knopf, 1967); Schell, *The Military Half* (New York, Alfred A. Knopf, 1968).

6. As E. L. Katzenbach, a deputy under secretary of defense in the Kennedy Administration, once put it: "We need not only troops which can strike on the periphery of the free world, but also troops which can be sent not merely to fight but also to maintain order. We need not only useful troops but useable troops—that is to say, troops which are politically expendable, the kind of

troops who can do the job as it is needed without too great a political outcry, in a nation like ours which so abhors war." Katzenbach, "Time, Space, and Will: The Politico-Military Views of Mao Tse-tung," in T.N. Greene, ed., *The Guerrilla and How to Fight Him* (New York, Praeger, 1962), pp. 11-21, as quoted by Eqbal Ahmad in Slater, *Pursuit of Loneliness,* p. 84. On covert operations in Indochina, see *The Pentagon Papers,* Senator Gravel edition, 4 vols. (Boston, Beacon Press, 1971), esp. I-III. (hereafter cited as *Pentagon Papers,* Gravel edition.)

7. Littauer and Uphoff, *Air War in Indochina,* esp. pp. 167-173. Even if some decline from peak level bombing occurred, fire power was kept at levels out of all proportion to claims. In addition, after President Nixon took office, the arena of active combat violence expanded to include all of Indochina.

8. The American involvement in the Cambodian War beginning in 1970 supplied an example of the Nixon Doctrine in operation. See Littauer and Uphoff, *Air War in Indochina,* pp. 87-90.

9. For a persuasive case for considering American involvement in Vietnam as a crime against peace, see Ralph Stavins, Richard J. Barnet, and Marcus G. Raskin, *Washington Plans Aggressive War* (New York, Random House, 1971), esp. pp. 3-195. Under the charter for the Nuremberg International Military Tribunal, the dependence of "crimes against humanity" on an underlying violation of "war crimes" or "crimes against peace" was based on the 1945 concern about retroactivity with respect to crimes against humanity. In the 1970s such a concern no longer has a valid legal foundation.

10. These four principles sum up the relevance of customary international law to the interpretation of the rights and duties that states have regarding the conduct of war. This general legal framework exists independent of and in addition to treaty obligations, although it is relevant as well to the interpretation of treaty rules.

11. See Articles 22, 23, and 25, Hague Regulations.

12. See Denise Bindschedler-Robert and others, "A Reconsideration of the Law of Armed Conflicts," *Conferences on Contemporary Problems of International Law,* no. 1 (New York, Carnegie Endowment for International Peace, 1971).

13. That is, the brunt of war crimes allegations concerns the impact of methods and tactics of warfare in Indochina on the civilian population, not on the organized insurgent armed forces. In view of the scale and magnitude of military effort, and the degree of international involvement, it hardly seems possible to categorize the war as a conflict falling altogether outside the protective scope of the laws of war. The most that can be argued, although this argument too seems unpersuasive, is that the insurgent combatants are entitled only to limited protection because of their mode of combat.

14. Specialists in counterinsurgency warfare disagree on whether to emphasize the political affinities of the population, or merely to crush the military capabilities of the insurgent forces and their external backers. Roger Hilsman places great, perhaps undue, emphasis on the distinction between

"political" and "military" approaches to counterinsurgency warfare. Hilsman, *To Move a Nation* (New York, Dell Co., 1964), pp. 411-537. The military perspective is expressed by a Marine Corps four star general in Lewis W. Walt, *Strange War, Strange Strategy: A General's Report on Vietnam* (New York, Funk & Wagnall, 1970). More wide-ranging but along the same lines is Hanson W. Baldwin, *A Strategy for Tomorrow* (New York, Harper and Row, 1970). For an inside view of the disagreement that evolved between advocates of "slow squeeze" and "quick squeeze" with regard to bombing tactics used against North Vietnam, see *Pentagon Papers,* Gravel edition, esp. vol. III. By 1965 the entire government debate had moved from a consideration of political versus military approaches to counterinsurgency, to a direct military kind of approach. For accounts of the underlying conflict that cast most persuasive doubt on a military approach to "winning," see e.g. John T. McAlister, Jr., *Vietnam: Origins of Revolution* (New York, Alfred A. Knopf, 1969); Eric R. Wolf, *Peasant Wars of the Twentieth Century* (New York, Harper and Row, 1969)

15. See e.g. John Gerassi, *North Vietnam: A Documentary* (Indianapolis, Bobbs-Merrill, 1968), esp. pp. 95-110, 182-190. Cf. Littauer and Uphoff, *Air War in Indochina*; Harvey, *Air War*. Littauer and Uphoff's account of the air war is the most reliable and comprehensive one available, although its data goes up only to 1971, thereby omitting periods of heavy American bombing, including the infamous Christmas bombing of Hanoi and Haiphong at the end of 1972 and the world outcry occasioned by evidence in 1972 that the United States was deliberately bombing dikes in North Vietnam.

16. Spiro Agnew, Interview, "Face the Nation, May 3, 1970, pp. 3, 6.

17. See Littauer and Uphoff, *Air War in Indochina,* pp. 57-59.

18. For evidence on the Laos bombing, citing the best available sources, See Littauer and Uphoff, *Air War in Indochina,* pp. 67-86. See also Nina S. Adams and Alfred W. McCoy, eds., *Laos: War and Revolution* (New York, Harper and Row, 1970); Cong. Paul N. McCloskey, Report of official trip to Laos, Senate Foreign Relations Committee, Hearings on "Legislative Proposals Relating to the War in Southeast Asia," 92nd Cong., 1st sess., April and May 1971, pp. 611-616.

19. Fred Branfman, "Presidential War in Laos, 1964-1970," in Adams and McCoy, *Laos: War and Revolution,* pp. 213-280.

20. For the general rationale and its intentional character, see *The Indochina Story,* prepared by Committee of Concerned Asian Scholars (New York, Bantam Books, 1970), pp. 97-102.

21. Senate Subcommittee to Investigate Problems Connected with Refugees and Escapees, Committee on the Judiciary (hereafter cited as Senate Subcommittee on Refugees), Hearings on "Refugee and Civilian War Casualty Problems in Laos and Cambodia," 91st Cong., 2nd sess., May 1970; Senate Subcommittee on Refugees, Hearings on "War-Related Civilian Problems in Indochina," 92nd Cong., 1st sess., April 1971; "Humanitarian Problems in South Vietnam and Cambodia: Two Years after the Ceasefire," Senate Subcommittee on Refugees, Jan. 27, 1975, esp. pp. 13, 65.

22. For reliance on this weaponry, see Herman, *Atrocities in Vietnam*, pp. 70-75; *Efficiency in Death: The Manufacturers of Anti-Personnel Weapons*, compiled and prepared by Council on Economic Priorities (New York, Harper and Row, 1970), esp. pp. 1-26.

23. *The Indochina Story*, pp. 87-90.

24. *New York Times*, Apr. 1, 1970, p. 1.

25. *New York Times*, Jan. 25, 1971, p. 2. Peterson added that "the United States Embassy's continuing studies show that the enemy's political organization is intact in most of the country." He estimated that as of publication, 60,000 Vietnamese had been killed, captured, or had defected under the Phoenix Program. See also Herman, *Atrocities in Vietnam*, pp. 34-40; Paul N. McCloskey, Testimony before Senate Foreign Relations Committee, Hearings on "Legislative Proposals Relating to the War in Southeast Asia," pp. 617-620.

26. John D. Constable and Matthew Messelson, Letter, *New York Times*, Aug. 4, 1971, p. 32. See also Herman, *Atrocities in Vietnam; The Indochina Story*, pp. 111-115; Barry Weisberg, ed., *Ecocide in Indochina: The Ecology of War* (New York, Harper and Row, 1970); Arthur Galston's participation in discussion as transcribed in Knoll and McFadden, *War Crimes*, pp. 68-72.

27. *New York Times*, Aug. 29. 1971, p. 8. This new report indicated that the South Vietnam Army already had 1.5 million gallons of Agent Orange available for use.

28. *New York Times*, Aug. 29. 1971, p. 8. Also reported was large-scale use of 7 1/2-ton bombs, which destroy all life within a radius of 760 acres.

29. John Sack, *Lieutenant Calley--His Own Story* (New York, Viking Press, 1971), pp. 40-41.

30. For Lt. Col. Anthony Herbert's experiences after he alleged toleration of extreme war crimes by his superior officers, see James T. Wooten, "How a Supersoldier Was Fired from His Command," *New York Times Magazine*, Sept. 5, 1971, pp. 10-11, 27-28, 33-34. Indicative of both the national mood and presidential leadership was the hue and cry provoked by Calley's conviction, in contrast to the general indifference to Herbert's plight. See also Herbert, *Soldier* (New York, Holt, Rinehart & Winston, 1973). For a similar experience with the command structure, see Daniel Lang, *Casualties of War* (New York, McGraw-Hill, 1969).

31. Sack, *Lieutenant Calley*, p. 79.

32. For an account of battlefield conditions in Vietnam as "atrocity-producing situations," see Robert Jay Lifton, *Home From the War: Vietnam Veterans, Neither Victims nor Executioners* (New York, Simon and Schuster, 1973), esp. pp. 135-159.

33. See *The Indochina Story*, pp. 79-85, 217-224; Eqbal Ahmad, "Winning Hearts and Minds: The Theory and Fallacies of Counterinsurgency," *The Nation*, Aug. 2, 1971, pp. 70-85. For the most influential advocate of counterinsurgent warfare as a positive response to the Vietnamese conflict, see Sir Robert Thompson, *No Exit from Vietnam* (New York, David McKay, 1969)—a book that is said to have influenced President Nixon's approach to the Vietnam War.

34. The entire history of revolutionary warfare confirms the basic proposition that the insurgent can offset its material deficiencies vis-à-vis the incumbent only if it can mobilize a popular base of support.

35. Josef Kunz makes this point persuasively in arguing for giving serious attention to rules of conduct during a war, despite the existence of rules prohibiting recourse to war. Kunz, *The Changing Structure of International Law* (Columbus, Ohio State University Press, 1969),pp. 831-909. The failure of first-order restraints brings into play second-order restraints, which may help to moderate conflict and avoid excessive suffering and destruction.

36. For a pessimistic assessment of the prospect for a post-Vietnam reorientation of American foreign policy in relation to revolutionary activity in the Third World, see Ch. 4; see also Richard M. Pfeffer, ed., *No More Vietnams? The War and the Future of American Foreign Policy* (New York, Harper and Row, 1968). For an overall depiction of the counterrevolutionary drift of American foreign policy, see Richard J. Barnet, *Intervention and Revolution: The United States in the Third World* (New York, World, 1968).

37. See Taylor, *Nuremberg and Vietnam,* pp. 92-94, 183-207; Marcus G. Raskin, "From Imperial War-Making to a Code of Personal Responsibility," in Stavins et al., *Washington Plans Aggressive War,* pp. 253-332; Leonard B. Boudin, "War Crimes and Vietnam: The Mote in Whose Eye?" *Harvard Law Review* 84: 1940 (1971); Richard A. Falk, "Nuremberg: Past, Present, and Future," *Yale Law Journal* 80: 1501 (1971); Karl Jaspers, *The Question of German War Guilt* (New York, Dial Press, 1947).

38. That is, responsibility will be limited to battlefield participants in specific atrocities and command officers who fail to report or fail to act in the face of an accurate report. In the latter case, responsibility is unlikely to be assigned unless public pressure is mounted to expose the delinquencies involved.

39. Daniel Ellsberg's decision to disclose the Pentagon Papers was apparently motivated by his sense of a moral and legal duty, derived in part from his understanding of the Nuremberg tradition. These legal foundations for antiwar resistance also influenced many young Americans who chose jail or exile rather than participate in the armed forces, as well as radical activists such as the Berrigan brothers. American leadership groups, however, are unresponsive to appeals based on Nuremberg thinking. The main policy-makers in the Vietnam War have been given jobs in civilian life that reflect their continued high stature, and opposition to appointments based on these objections are not popular. See John F. Campbell, "The Death Rattle of the Eastern Establishment," *New York Magazine,* Sept. 20, 1971, pp. 47-51.

40. I have in mind here the whole set of international issues presented by "fifth columns" which undermine the foundations of political authority in order to pave the way for the entry of an external power.

41. These widening gaps are also a pronounced characteristic of both the task force study and the underlying documents among the Pentagon Papers, as well as of the principal "insider" accounts of the policy process accompanying the American involvement in the Vietnam War. See e.g. Townsend Hoopes,

*The Limits of Intervention* (New York, David McKay, 1969); Chester Cooper, *The Lost Crusade; America in Vietnam* (New York, Dodd Mead, 1970). For a retrospective criticism of this distancing process by a participant, see Albert Speer, *Inside the Third Reich* (New York, Macmillan, 1970), esp. pp. 519-524.

42. See Richard A. Falk, *Legal Order in a Violent World* (Princeton, Princeton University Press, 1968), pp. 109-155.

43. See e.g. Tom J. Farer, "Intervention in Civil Wars: A Modest Proposal," in Richard A. Falk, ed., *The Vietnam War and International Law* (Princeton, Princeton University Press, 1968), I, 509-522; Farer, Harnessing Rogue Elephants: A Short Discourse on Intervention in Civil Strife," in Falk, *The Vietnam War* (1969), II, 1089-1116.

44. See e.g. Richard A. Falk, ed., *The International Law of Civil War* (Baltimore, Johns Hopkins University Press, 1971); Wolf, *Peasant Wars;* Barnet, *Intervention and Revolution.*

45. For the prospects for revision, see Bindschedler-Robert "A Reconsideration."

46. See Richard A. Falk, *This Endangered Planet* (New York, Random House, 1971).

47. For earlier American attitudes toward Nuremberg, see Joseph J. Bosch, *Judgment of Nuremberg: American Attitudes Toward the Major German War-Crimes Trials* (Chapel Hill, University of North Carolina Press, 1970). For the Nuremberg approach in the context of the Tokyo trials after World War II, see Richard H. Minear, *Victor's Justice: The Tokyo War Crimes Trial* (Princeton, Princeton University Press, 1971). For the failure to apply the Nuremberg idea since the end of World War II, see Eugene Davidson, *The Nuremberg Fallacy: Wars and War Crimes since World War II* (New York, Macmilllan, 1973).

## 6. *Ecocide and the Case for an Ecocide Convention*

1. Preamble, Laws and Customs of War on Land (Hague IV), The Hague, Oct. 18, 1907, reprinted in Leon Friedmann, ed., *The Law of War* (New York, Random House, 1972) I, 309.

2. The United States, in fact, could diminish the scope of its obligation to the Geneva Protocol by accompanying its ratification with either a reservation or a statement of understanding that maintained the option to use herbicides and riot-control gases. Of course, such a reservation is reciprocal in effect, granting foreign governments a similar reservation in relation to the United States.

3. For the range of responses, see W. J. Bosch, *Judgment on Nuremberg: American Attitudes Toward the Major German War-Crime Trials* (Chapel Hill, University of North Carolina Press, 1970).

4. The Geneva Conventions of 1949 even have a common provision obliging parties to the treaties "to enact any legislation necessary to provide effective penal sanctions" for persons committing or ordering "grave breaches."

5. See esp. J. B. Neilands, G.H. Orians, E. W. Pfeffer, Alje Vennemma, and A. H. Westing, *Harvest of Death: Chemical Warfare in Vietnam and Cambodia* (New York, Free Press, 1972); John Lewallen, *Ecology of Devastation: Indochina* (Baltimore, Penguin, 1971); Thomas Whiteside, *The Withering Rain:America's Herbicidal Folly* (New York, Norton, 1971).

6. Madame Nguyen Thi Binh, Statement at the Paris Peace Conference, Feb. 19, 1970, quoted in Barry Weisberg, ed., *Ecocide in Indochina* (San Francisco, Canfield Press, 1970), p. 19.

7. Lewallen, *Ecology of Devastation,* p. 80.

8. J. Fred Buzhardt to Sen J. William Fulbright, reprinted in *International Legal Materials* 10:1300 (1971).

9. See the testimony of Secretary of State William P. Rogers before the Senate Foreign Relations Committee, Mar. 5, 1971.

10. U.N. General Assembly Resolution 2603A (XXIV), 1969.

11. The Senate Foreign Relations Committee finally sent the 1925 Geneva Protocol to the full Senate with a unanimous recommendation that approval be given on Dec. 12, 1974. The recommendation was made after the Administration provided its assurance that as a matter of national policy the United States was prepared to renounce most military uses of herbicides and tear gas in deference to the interpretation of the protocol embodied in General Assembly Res. 2603A. The Administration as a matter of formal prerogative has adhered to its view that the Geneva Protocol does not cover such toxic substances or applications. The Administration has indicated that in the future herbicides would be used first only to clear vegetation around the defensive perimeter of a military base and that riot-control agents would be renounced except to save lives in such situations as quelling a riot among prisoners of war, rescuing pilots shot down behind enemy lines, protecting civilians being used by an adversary as a shield, and protecting convoys in rear echelon areas. See comprehensive report in *New York Times,* Dec. 13, 1974, pp. 1-2. The expectation is that formal ratification of the Geneva Protocol will occur in 1975, some fifty years after its original adoption.

12. Tom J. Farer, "The Laws of War 25 Years After Nuremberg," *International Conciliation,* no. 583, May 1971, p. 20.

13. L. Craig Johnstone, "Ecocide and the Geneva Protocol," *Foreign Affairs* 49:4 (July, 1971), p. 719.

14. Paul R. Ehrlich and John P. Holdren, "Ecocide in Indochina" (mimeo., December 1971), p.2.

15. A. H. Westing and E. W. Pfeiffer, "The Cratering of Indochina," *Scientific American* 226:26-28 (May 1972).

16. U.N. Wars Crimes Commission, *History of the United Nations War Crimes Commission and the Development of the Laws of War* (London, His Majesty's Stationery Office, 1948), p. 496 (italics mine).

17. Westing and Pfeiffer, "The Cratering of Indochina," p. 21.

18. Westing and Pfeiffer, "The Cratering of Indochina," p. 21.

19. Fred Branfman, ed., *Voices from the Plain of Jars* (New York, Harper Colophon, 1972).

20. Senator Claiborne Pell also "strongly believes" that clouds in North Vietnam had been seeded since 1966 and may have caused thousands of deaths by provoking devastating floods. *New York Times,* June 27, 1972, p. 12. This belief was reinforced by the connection between rain-making and confirmed reports that dikes and sluice gates had been bombed. See also Deborah Shapley, "Rainmaking: Rumored Use over Laos Alarms Arms Experts, Scientist," *Science* 176:1216-1220 (June 16, 1972).

21. See Richard A. Falk, *This Endangered Planet: Prospects and Proposals for Human Survival* (New York, Random House, 1971).

## 7. A Nuremberg Perspective on the Pentagon Papers Trial

This chapter was adapted from an offer of proof I prepared as testimony on behalf of the defense in the case of *United States* v. *Russo.* The offer of proof, including all quotations, was inserted in the trial record and distributed to journalists on the day of my scheduled appearance as an expert witness. Although the case against Daniel Ellsberg and Anthony Russo was dismissed for procedural reasons, the arguments adduced in support of the Nuremberg defense have a continuing relevance.

1. *United States v. Russo,* U.S. District Court, Cent. Dist. of California, 9373-CD-WMB (dismissed May 11, 1973). The rulings in the trial generally precluded the defendants from introducing testimony in the presence of the jury pertaining to the illegality of America's role in the Vietnam War, and the bearing of this alleged illegality on the actions taken by the defendants.

2. The hypothetical character of the defendants' liability under international criminal law should make no difference as to the availability of the defense under domestic law.

3. Daniel Ellsberg deliberately withheld the four volumes of the Pentagon Papers that dealt with international negotiations concerning Vietnam. He explained that these volumes were withheld because they contained information pertaining to United States relations with foreign governments which might fall within the ambit of legitimate national security. Whether or not one agrees with Ellsberg's judgment, his exclusion of these volumes supports the view that he was trying to minimize the disruptive effects of his disclosure initiative. From the prosecution standpoint, however, Ellsberg was not entitled to possess copies of these documents; therefore, the negotiating volumes were covered in the conversion counts of the indictment.

4. The claim of violent resistance on which the Nuremberg defense rests in the *Armstrong* case is considered in Ch. 8.

5. 175 U.S. 677,700 (1900).

6. Benjamin Forman, "The Nuremberg Trials and Conscientious Objection to War: Justiciability under United States Municipal Law," in Richard A. Falk, ed., *The Vietnam War and International Law,* 3 vols. (Princeton, Princeton University Press, 1972), III, 399, 403 (hereafter cited as Falk). Forman does add that from an enforcement perspective these norms are not enforceable

against American nationals except "to the extent that provision has been made therefor in our criminal law" (p. 403). But if the United States could, even without implementing legislation, use military commissions to enforce Nuremburg norms against foreign nationals, then a comparable claim could be lodged by foreign military commissions against American nationals such as Ellsberg and Russo. Thus, their claim of hypothetical criminal liability acquires technical, if indirect, support from Forman, who was the leading Pentagon spokesman on the question.

7. The most pertinent criteria on standing to present a claim are those set forth by the United States Supreme Court in *Flast* v. *Cohen*, 392 U.S. 83, 99-101 (1968). Domestic courts thus far have refused even to consider whether the application of the *Flast* test of standing can be satisfied by a claimant who relies on a Nuremberg defense.

8. On standing issue, see Lawrence Velvel, "The War in Vietnam: Unconstitutional, Justiciable, and Jurisdictionally Attackable," in Falk, II, 651; Anthony A. D'Amato, Harvey L. Gould, and Larry D. Woods, "War Crimes and Vietnam: The 'Nuremberg Defense' and the Military Service Resister," in Falk, III, 407, 469; *Youngstown Sheet and Tube* v. *Sawyer,* 343 U.S. 579 (1952); Michael E. Tigar, "Judicial Power, the 'Political Question Doctrine,' and Foreign Relations," in Falk, III, 654; Warren F. Schwartz and Wayne McCormack, "The Justiciability of Legal Objections to the American Military Effort in Vietnam," in Falk, III, 699.

9. D'Amato et al. "War Crimes," p. 457; see also n. 302 for citation to the major cases in United States courts.

10. See e.g. *United States* v. *Berrigan* 283 F. Supp. 336 (D. Md. 1968).

11. For the rationale for the "political question" approach and major Vietnam-related judicial applications, see Louis Henkin, "Viet-Nam in the Courts of the United States: 'Political Questions,' " in Falk, III, 625.

12. *United States v. Sisson,* 297 F. Supp. 902, 912 (D. Mass. 1969).

13. For the best statement of support for continued deference, see Louis Henkin, *Foreign Affairs and the Constitution* (Mineola, N. Y., Foundation Press, 1972) pp. 208-216. The rationale for deference contained in *United States* v. *Curtiss-Wright Export Corp.,* 299 U.S. 304 (1936), is ripe for reconsideration, since the facts of that case provided a very limited context in which to enunciate the broad questions of policy at stake. Not only has international law since 1936 developed criteria for appraising challenged state conduct and imposed liability on state officials for its violation, but the Supreme Court has set forth more precise criteria by which to identify a "political question" in *Baker* v. *Carr,* 369 U.S. 186 (1962). Velvel argues that Vietnam-related issues are justiciable by reference to these criteria. Velvel, "The War in Vietnam," pp. 681-687.

14. These norms are set forth in authoritative treaty form in the United Nations Charter, articles 1, 2, and 51.

15. Leon Friedmann, ed., *The Law of War: A Documentary History,* 2 vols. (New York, Random House, 1972), I, 468.

16. Friedmann, *The Law of War,* I, 886-887.

17. Friedmann, *The Law of War,* I, p. 908.

18. Geneva Accords, text in Falk, I, 559.

19. Vietnam Task Force, Office of the Secretary of Defense, *United States-Vietnam Relations, 1945-1967* (Washington, U.S. Government Printing Office, 1971), vol. I, part III.A., at A-1 (hereafter cited as *Pentagon Papers,* GPO edition). This collection of materials is commonly known as the Pentagon Papers, but the version cited here is the edition published and distributed by the U.S. Government Printing Office and should be distinguished from the Senator Gravel edition of these same materials, which is referred to elsewhere in this book as *Pentagon Papers,* Gravel edition.

20. *Pentagon Papers,* GPO edition, vol. I, part IV.A.3, p.v. This essential violation is reiterated frequently in the papers; see eg: "France was never able to meet Geneva obligations concerning the elections of 1956, for Diem matched his refusal to consult with the Vietnamese about elections with an adamant refusal to ever hold them. Neither Britain nor the Soviet Union pressed the matter; the United States backed Diem's position." *Pentagon Papers,* GPO edition, vol. I, part IV.A.3, p. 40.

21. *Pentagon Papers,* GPO edition, vol. I, part IV.A.3, p.38.

22. *Pentagon Papers,* GPO edition, vol.I, part II.B.2, p.B-21. One Pentagon analyst went so far as to conclude that "French insistence on strict legal interpretation of the Geneva Accords was one example of accommodation thinking." *Pentagon Papers,* Gravel edition, I, 221.

23. "In the immediate aftermath of Geneva, the DRV [Democratic Republic of Vietnam] deferred to the Geneva Accords for the reunification, and turned inward." *Pentagon Papers,* GPO edition, vol.II, part IV.A.5, p. 27. The DRV tried repeatedly to engage the Geneva machinery, forwarding messages to the government of South Vietnam (GVN) in July 1955, May and June 1956, March 1958, July 1959, and July 1960, proposing consultations to negotiate "free elections by secret ballot" and to liberalize North-South relations in general. Each time the GVN replied with disdain or silence. *Pentagon Papers,* GPO edition, vol.II, part IV.A.5, p.7.

24. *Pentagon Papers,* GPO edition, vol.I, part IV.A.3, p.vi.

25. *Pentagon Papers,* GPO edition, vol.II, part IV.A.5., p.3.

26. *Pentagon Papers,* GPO edition, vol.II, part IV.A.5, Tab 1, p.5.

27. Friedmann, *The Law of War,* I, 469.

28. Art. 2(3) reads: "All Members shall settle their international disputes by peaceful means in such a manner that international peace and security, and justice, are not endangered." Art. 33(1) reads: "The parties to any dispute, the continuance of which is likely to endanger the maintenance of international peace and security shall, first of all, seek a solution by negotiation, enquiry, mediation, conciliation, arbitration, judicial settlement, resort to regional agencies or arrangement, or other peaceful means of their own choice." Art. 2(4) states: "All Members shall refrain in their international relations from the threat or use of force against the territorial integrity or political independence

of any State, or in any other manner inconsistent with the Purposes of the United Nations."

29. G.A. Res. 2625 (and Annex), 25 U.N. GAOR Supp. 28, p. 121, U.N. Doc. A/8028 (1970). Among other relevant provisions, the declaration proclaims that the "parties to a dispute have the duty, in the event of failure to reach a solution by any one of the above peaceful means, to continue to seek a settlement of the dispute by other peaceful means agreed upon by them."

30. *Pentagon Papers,* GPO edition, vol. I, part I.C.3, *passim.*

31. *Pentagon Papers,* GPO edition, vol.I, part II.B.2, p. B-18. This attitude was evidenced in many passages of the *Pentagon Papers*; see e.g. NSC 64: "Unless the situation throughout the world generally, and Indochina specifically, changes materially, the United States should seek to dissuade the French from referring the Indochina question to the United Nations." *Pentagon Papers,* GPO edition, vol. I, part IV.A.2., p.14.

32. *Pentagon Papers,* GPO edition, vol.I, part IV.A.3, p.v.

33. The broad framework of covert negotiations between the United States and Vietnam is accurately depicted in David Kraslow and Stuart H. Loory, *The Secret Search for Peace in Vietnam* (New York, Random House, 1968).

34. Vietnam Task Force, Office of the Secretary of Defense, *United States-Vietnam Relation, 1945-1967,* unpublished, part VI.C.1 in (1) (hereafter cited as *U.S.-Vietnam Relations*). This source consists of materials corresponding to Part VI.C. of the GPO edition of the *Pentagon Papers* and bears on various attempts to negotiate a settlement of the U.S.-Vietnam conflict. There is no consecutive pagination in these materials; each section is numbered internally.

35. *U.S.-Vietnam Relations*, part VI.C.1. in (1).

36. "What we are interested in here is not destroying Ho Chi Minh (as his successor would probably be worse than he is) but getting him to change his behavior." *U.S.-Vietnam Relations*, part VI.C.1. in (1).

37. *U.S.-Vietnam Relations*, part VI.C.1. in (1).

38. *U.S.-Vietnam Relations*, part VI.C.1. in (1).

39. "In the meantime, in Saigon, the U.S. mission was hard at work trying to clarify its own thinking--and that of Washington--on the persuasive, or rather coercive, possibilities of bombing pauses . . . In particular the Mission was hoping to link the intensity of U.S. bombing after the resumption closely to the level of VC activity during the pause. The purpose would be to make it clear to Hanoi that what we were trying to accomplish with our bombing was to get the DRV to cease directing and supporting the VC and to get VC units to cease their military activities in the South." *U.S.-Vietnam Relations,* part VI.C.1. in (2), p. 59.

40. The persistent reliance on the bombardment of North Vietnam as a negotiating tool after February 1965 was frequently attacked as an illegal use of force because it was initiated in circumstances other than as a response to an armed attack. See Richard A. Falk, International Law and the United States Role in the Viet Nam War," in Falk, I, 362, 373-391; Falk, "International Law and the United States Role in the Vietnam War: A Response to Professor Moore," in Falk, I, 490-494.

41. *U.S.-Vietnam Relations*, part VI.C.1 in (5), p.4.

42. *U.S.-Vietnam Relations,* part VI.C.1 in (5), p.60.

43. *U.S.-Vietnam Relations*, part VI.C.1 in (5), p.65.

44. *U.S.-Vietnam Relations*, part VI.C.1 in (5), p.64.

45. G.A. Res. 2131, 20 U.N. GAOR Supp. 14, p.11, U.N. Doc. A/6014 (1965), article 1.

46. The principle "concerning the duty not to intervene in matters within the domestic jurisdiction of any State, in accordance with the Charter," reads: "No State or group of States has the right to intervene, directly or indirectly, for any reason whatever, in the internal or external affairs of any other State. Consequently, armed intervention and all other forms of interference or attempted threats against the personality of the State or against its political, economic and cultural elements, are in violation of international law." G. A. Res. 2625, p.123.

47. See G. A. Res. 2625 Sec. II. A.

48. "Every State has the duty to promote, through joint and separate action, realization of the principle of equal rights and self-determination of peoples, in accordance with the United Nations in carrying out the responsibilities entrusted to it by the Charter regarding the implementation of the principle, in order . . . To bring a speedy end to colonialism, having due regard to the freely expressed will of the peoples concerned; and bearing in mind that subjection of peoples to alien subjugation, domination and exploitation constitutes a violation of the principle, as well as a denial of fundamental human rights, and is contrary to the Charter." G.A. Res. 2625, pp. 123-124.

49. See art. 2(7) in relation to art. 53 of the U.N. Charter, which deals with enforcement by "regional arrangements or agencies."

50. *Pentagon Papers*, GPO edition, vol. I, part IV.A.3, p.iv.

51. *Pentagon Papers*, GPO edition, vol. I, Part IV.A.3, pps. 29,31.

52. "At this stage MAAG [Military Aid and Assistance Group] was charged solely with the task of assisting the Vietnamese to develop a force capable of establishing and maintaining internal security." *Pentagon Papers*, GPO edition, vol.II, part IV.A.4, p.18.

53. "As is well known, the SEATO [Southeast Asia Treaty Organization]/treaty was pressured into existence by the United States." *Pentagon Papers*, GPO edition, vol.II, part IV.A.4, p.11.

54. *Pentagon Papers*, GPO edition, vol.II, part IV.A.5, Tab 4, p.57.

55. *Pentagon Papers,* GPO edition, vol.III, part IV.B.2, pp.19,iv. Ngo Dinh Nhu was an important official, as well as Diem's brother and confidant, in the legitimate government of South Vietnam with which the United States claimed to be allied at the time.

56. *Pentagon Papers*, GPO edition, vol.III, part IV.B.5, p.i.

57. Friedmann, *The Law of War*, I, viii.

58. For the text, see Richard A. Falk, Gabriel Kolko, and Robert J. Lifton, eds., *Crimes of War* (New York, Random House, 1971), pp. 75-76.

59. Friedmann, *The Law of War*, I, 883-893.

60. Friedmann, *The Law of War*, I, 908-912.

61. Art. II (1)(A), in Friedmann, *The Law of War*, I, 908. The Nuremberg judgment concludes: "To initiate a war of aggression, therefore, is not only an international crime; it is the supreme international crime differing only from other war crimes in that it contains within itself the accumulated evil of the whole." Friedmann, *The Law of War*, II, 925.

62. Art. II (2), in Friedmann, *The Law of War*, I, 909.

63. Art. II (4)(b).

64. Tokyo War Crimes Trial Decision, quoted in Falk et al, *Crimes of War*, p. 113.

65. See e.g. *The Ministries* case, in *Trials of War Criminals Before the Nuremberg Military Tribunals under Control Council law no. 10*, 15 vols. (Washington, U.S: Government Printing office, 1946-1953), reprinted in part in Friedmann, *The Law of War*, II, 1373 passim.

66. *Trials of War Criminals*, vol. VI, reprinted in Friedmann, *The Law of War*, II, 1281, 1284 (italics mine).

67. Friedmann, *The Law of War*, II, 1498 (italics mine).

68. Friedmann, *The Law of War*, II, 1028. The first Secretary-General of the United Nations, Trygve Lie, asserted: "In the interests of peace and in order to protect mankind against wars, it will be of decisive significance to have the principles which were implied in the Nuremberg trials. . . made a permanent part of the body of international law as quickly as possible."

69. G.A. Res. 95 (I), U.N. Doc. A264/Add. 1, p. 188 (1947).

70. Falk et al, *Crimes of War*, pp. 107-108.

71. Tokyo War Crimes Judgment, quoted in Falk et al, *Crimes of War*, p. 113.

72. Falk et al, *Crimes of War*, p. 76.

73. Falk et al, *Crimes of War*, pp. 107-108. Principle II posits the related principle that the absence of a municipal law imposing sanctions for the commission of acts that constitute crimes under international law does not relieve the person who commits such acts from responsibility under international law. Even John Norton Moore, in a discussion of selective service cases that raised the Nuremberg defense, argues: "To the extent that an action would entail personal responsibility under the Nuremberg Principles, the Uniform Code of Military Justice, or any other valid international standard, certainly the criminality of the action should be a valid defense to state compulsion to engage in it. The sense of justice boggles at the thought that a man may be legally compelled to perform an act entailing criminal liability." Moore, "The Justiciability of Challenges to the Use of Military Force Abroad," in Falk, III, 650.

## 8. *A Nuremberg Perspective on the Trial of Karl Armstrong*

1. John Duffett, ed., *Against the Crime of Silence: Proceedings of the International War Crimes Tribunal* (New York, Simon and Schuster, 1968); Frank Browning and Dorothy Forman, eds., *The Wasted Nations: Report of the International Commission of Enquiry into United States Crimes in Indochina, June 20-25, 1971* (New York, Harper and Row, 1972).

2. Justice Pal's dissenting opinion is published separately under the title *International Military Tribunal for the Far East: Dissentient Judgment* (Calcutta, Sanyal, 1953). For an assessment of the work of the Tokyo War Crimes Tribunal, see Richard H. Minear, *Victor's Justice: The Tokyo War Crimes Trial* (Princeton, Princeton University Press, 1971).

3. The Shimoda case decided on December 7, 1963, by the Tokyo District Court. See the Japanese Annual of International Law for 1964, pp.212-252; Richard A. Falk and Saul Mendlovitz, *The Strategy of World Order* (New York, World Law Fund, 1966), I, 314-354.

4. See e.g. Subrata Roy Chowdhury, *The Genesis of Bangladesh: A Study in International Legal Norms and Permissive Conscience* (New York, Asia Publishing House, 1972), pp. 76-148.

5. See Eugene Davidson, *The Nuremberg Fallacy: Wars and War Crimes since World War II* (New York, Macmillan, 1973). However, I do not share Davidson's view that because the Nuremberg idea has not prevented war or war crimes, it has failed. My position is that the Nuremberg idea needs to be transformed from an intergovernmental tool and criterion of judgment into an instrument of global populism that opposes the domestic and international manifestations of the war system, however embellished with the trappings of state power.

6. See Edward S. Herman, *Atrocities in Vietnam: Myths and Realities* (Philadelphia, Pilgrim Press, 1970); *The Indochina Story*, Committee of Concerned Asian Scholars (New York, Bantam, 1970).

7. For evidence of continuing American paramilitary involvement in Indochina, see *Indochina Chronicle*, published by the Indochina Resource Center, P.O. Box 4000D, Berkeley, California, 94704, issues that have appeared since the Paris Agreements and the August 15 cutoff of bombing.

8. The principles of international law recognized in the Charter and in the judgment of the Nuremberg Tribunal were unanimously affirmed by the General Assembly of the United Nations on December 11, 1946. For text, see Appendix 1.

9. Ronald Dworkin, "On Not Prosecuting Civil Disobedience," *New York Review of Books*, June 6, 1968, pp. 14-21.

10. John Rawls, *A Theory of Justice* (Cambridge, Harvard University Press 1971), p. 364.

11. Howard Zinn, *Disobedience and Democracy* (New York, Random House, 1968), pp. 39-53.

12. An editorial on the case put the issue well: "Without condoning in the least the violence he was guilty of, it must be said that Karleton Armstrong was one more casualty of the war in Vietnam, along with Robert Fassnacht and 50,000 Americans and countless Indochinese killed over the past dozen years by the policies of U.S. leaders. The bitter irony that remains is that these leaders have yet to face a judge or jury for the numberless and horrifying war crimes they have committed." *The Progressive*, December 1973, p. 103. David Wagner expresses the point more aggressively: "Those who take a moral position on the death [of Fassnacht] have the onus to weigh against it the calculated colon-

ial barbarism which it negatively reflects. To do any less is not morality but e-vasion and cowardice." Wagner, "Free Karl," *Liberation,* May 1973, p. 43.

13. The effectiveness of such obstruction of orderly government will always be denied by rulers.

14. Quoted from Mabel Dodge Brigade, "On the Road to New Nation," *Liberation*, September-October 1973, pp. 2,6.

15. Conversation with author.

16. Richard Goldensohn and others, *Liberation*, September-October 1973, pp. 2,6.

17. For documentation, see "The AMRC Papers: An Indictment of the Army Mathematics Research Center," (pamphlet, Science for the People Collective, 306 North Brooks Street, Madison, Wis., 1973).

## 9. Nuremberg Reconsidered

1. Karl Jaspers, *The Question of German War Guilt* (New York, Dial Press, 1947).

2. See John Duffett, ed., *Against the Crime of Silence: Proceedings of the International War Crimes Tribunal* (Flanders, N.J., O'Hare, 1968); Seymour Melman, ed., *In the Name of America* (New York, Clergy and Laymen Concerned about Vietnam, 1968). The first book is the published portion of the proceedings of the Bertrand Russell Tribunal held in two sessions during 1967; the second is a comprehensive compilation of newspaper extracts reporting on American battlefield conduct, sponsored by an interdenominational group of leading American clergymen. The documentation, although one-sided, remains largely accurate and is generally consistent with subsequent, more balanced assessments of allegations of criminal conduct by the United States, such as Telford Taylor, *Nuremberg and Vietnam: An American Tragedy* (New York, Quadrangle, 1970). See Leonard Boudin, Book Comment, *Harvard Law Review 1940*, 84 (1971).

3. There is confusion as to what constitutes an "exit" from Vietnam and whether President Nixon's policies of phased withdrawal of American combat forces plus "Vietnamization" was an "exit" at all. The irony implicit in a strategy of winning-while-leaving is proclaimed in the title of a book by the world's foremost counterinsurgency specialist, Robert Thompson, *No Exit from Vietnam* (London, Chatto and Windus, 1969).

4. Particularly the standards of *In re* Yamashita, 327 U.S. 1 (1946). *New York Times*, Jan. 9, 1971, p. 3. Taylor also called for the creation of a high-level citizens' commission of inquiry into issues of war crimes and individual responsibility, during a symposium discussion at Columbia Law School, Mar. 20, 1971.

5. Beacon Press published in 1971 a complete set of the Pentagon Papers as released by Senator Mike Gravel of Alaska. These documents provide law students and faculty with an extensive, though incomplete, data base for analyzing the principal legal issues raised by the American involvement. It would serve the national interest if this opportunity were fully used. A conference of law

journal editors might be a constructive first step in planning the kind of treatment required. The Government Printing Office also published in 1971 a twelve-volume version of the Pentagon Papers that is claimed to be over 95 percent complete.

6. See edited transcript of comments by Gabriel Kolko and Jonathan Schell in Erwin Knoll and Judith Nies McFadden, eds., *War Crimes and the American Conscience* (New York, Holt, Rinehart and Winston, 1970), pp. 47-48; Jonathan Schell, *The Military Half* (New York, Knopf, 1968); Schell, *The Village of Ben Suc* (New York, Knopf, 1967).

7. The Pentagon Papers contain many documents pertaining to the decisions to intervene in Vietnamese affairs after 1954, to bomb North Vietnam in 1965, and to introduce large-scale American ground forces in 1965. Although not entirely complete, these materials seem ample to enable a court to reach a well-reasoned decision.

8. Arthur A. Schlesinger, Jr., "The Necessary Amorality of Foreign Affairs," *Harper's Magazine*, August 1971, p. 73. For more extreme defense of the exclusion of moral factors from statecraft see Miles Copeland, *The Game of Nations: The Amorality of Power Politics* (New York, Simon and Schuster, 1969), esp. pp. 9-130. This kind of approach was evolved much earlier by such major analysts of foreign affairs as E. H. Carr, George Kennan, and Hans J. Morgenthau. These analysts were in turn overreacting to certain indulgences in moralism and legalism exhibited by American statesmen and international lawyers; Woodrow Wilson and John Foster Dulles epitomized this kind of moralistic-legalistic orientation to America's role in world affairs that has contributed to the formulation of a cynical-realist position. For an intermediate position on these issues as they bear on international law, see Richard A. Falk, *The Status of Law in International Society* (Princeton, Princeton University Press, 1970), pp. 41-59, and ch. 2 of this book.

9. Schlesinger, "The Necessary Amorality," p. 77. It is misleading to talk of "the request of the South Vietnam government" in a situation in which prior American diplomatic and covert interventions had done so much to constitute and sustain in power that governing group. For the limits of government discretion to authorize the destruction of their people and country, see Tom Farer, "The Laws of War 25 Years after Nuremberg," *International Conciliation*, May 1971, pp. 29-34. Farer concluded (p.30): An invitation from the local butcher no longer suffices to legitimate a slaughter."

10. Schlesinger, "The Necessary Amorality," p. 77.

11. Quoted in Louis Sohn, *Cases and Other Materials on World Law* (Brooklyn, Foundation Press, 1950), p. 986.

12. On the Japanese case for initiating hostilities, see dissenting opinion of Judge R. B. Pal of India in the Tokyo war crimes trials, reprinted as *International Military Tribunal for the Far East: Dissentient Judgment* (Calcutta, Sanyal, 1953); Richard H. Minear, *Victor's Justice: The Tokyo War Crimes Trial* (Princeton, Princeton University Press, 1971); Noam Chomsky, *American Power and the New Mandarins* (New York, Pantheon, 1969), pp. 170-208.

13. Schlesinger, "The Necessary Amorality," p. 73.

14. Schlesinger, "The Necessary Amorality," p. 73.

15. It is true that, as certain thresholds of escalation were crossed, the issue of aggressive war became easier to analyze from a legal point of view. The most important of these thresholds was the decision to carry the air war to North Vietnam in February 1965. As long as the violence was confined to South Vietnam and conflicting allegations of intervention were being made, it was difficult to resolve the major issues of fact and law. See Richard A. Falk, "International Law and the United States Role in the Vietnam War" and "International Law and the United States Role in the Vietnam War: A Response to Professor Moore," in Richard A. Falk, ed., *The Vietnam War and International Law* (Princeton, Princeton University Press, 1968), esp. pp. I,362-401,445-508,375-381, 490-494.

16. Taylor, *Nuremberg and Vietnam*, p. 207.

17. *New York Review of Books*, Aug. 12, 1971, p. 30. See also the letter from Jonathan Mirsky in the same issue; Wasserstrom, "Criminal Behavior," *New York Review of Books*, June 3, 1971, pp. 8-13.

18. Because of the character of nuclear war and large-scale counterinsurgency war, it seems increasingly difficult to argue on behalf of maintaining effective legal limits during a period of warfare. The basis of the laws of war involves the capacity to maintain distinctions between military and nonmilitary targets with sufficient clarity to establish consistent limits on the concept of "military necessity." As it is not possible to maintain such limits, given the technology and doctrines of modern warfare, the laws of war virtually presuppose a pacifist orientation if they are to serve any serious purpose in the future. But see also Josef Kunz, "The Chaotic Status of the Laws of War and the Urgent Necessity for Their Revision," *American Journal of International Law* 45:37 (1951); Taylor, *Nuremberg and Vietnam*, pp. 39-41.

19. See Richard A. Falk, "The Interplay of Westphalia and Charter Conceptions of the International Legal Order," in Cyril E. Black and Richard A. Falk, ed., *The Future of the Legal Order* (Princeton, Princeton University Press, 1969), I,32-70; Richard A. Falk, *This Endangered Planet: Prospects and Proposals for Human Survival* (New York, Random House, 1971). Whether the Westphalia tradition is waning and the Charter tradition waxing is a difficult question, since the emergent nationalism of the Afro-Asian world and the rise of cosmopolitanism and militant subnationalism in Europe and North America must both be taken into account.

20. Taylor, *Nuremberg and Vietnam*, p. 206.

21. The Tribunal for the Far East, convened at Tokyo, had wider representation than the Nuremberg Tribunal, and generated both dissenting and concurring opinions.

22. Quoted in Richard A. Falk, Robert Lifton, and Gabriel Kolko, eds., *Crimes of War* (New York, Random House, 1971), p. 222.

23. In this regard, even Schlesinger's affirmation of the Nuremberg tradition suggests the reality of the precedent set after World War II.

24. See Jay Forrester, *World Dynamics* (Cambridge, Wright-Allen Press,

1971); also Ch. 12. On an intuitive level, the need for drastic change has been understood in a variety of distinct modes. Erich Kahler, *The Tower and the Abyss* (New York, Viking, 1957); Doris Lessing, *The Golden Notebook* (New York, Simon and Schuster, 1962); Doris Lessing, *Briefing for a Descent into Hell* (New York, Knopf, 1971); Charles Reich, *The Greening of America* (New York, Random House, 1970); songs by the Beatles, vintage 1968-1969 (e.g. "Blackbird," "Revolution 1," "Revolution 9,") and by Bob Dylan (esp. "Blowin' in the Wind"). The point here is that many converging perceptions of the objective situation can complement one another in a period during which traditional beliefs and structures are dangerously outmoded. Legal and political analysis needs to be made receptive to these more literary sources of understanding, if for no other reason than the basic imperative of sanity--to obtain a better fix on reality.

25. See e.g. the report on United States counterinsurgency operation in Vietnam, including North Vietnam, in the 1954-1955 period, prepared by Col. Edward G. Lansdale, head of the so-called "Saigon Military Mission," in *The Pentagon Papers*, pp. 53-66.

26. The notion of "victory" in this kind of conflict is elusive. There is some validity to the observations of Henry Kissinger on this point, made before he entered the government as President Nixon's principal foreign policy adviser: "We fought a military war; our opponents fought a political one. We sought physical attrition; our opponents armed for our psychological exhaustion. In the process, we lost sight of one of the cardinal maxims of guerilla war: the guerilla wins if he does not lose. The conventional army loses if it does not win." Kissinger, "The Vietnam Negotiations," *Foreign Affairs* 47:211, 214 (1969). But "victory" in this sense still does not carry with it any prospect of access to potential enemy defendants in a war crimes trial.

Of course, it is possible to convene a tribunal or commission of inquiry without access to American defendants. The Bertrand Russell War Crimes Tribunal in 1966 and 1967 was the most prominent effort to carry on such an inquiry and was controversial from its inception. Its findings were disregarded for a variety of reasons having nothing to do with whether or not the central conclusions were well-founded. For the proceedings, see Duffett, *Against the Crime of Silence*. It is virtually impossible to expect the ruling groups that are the main target of such accusations to allow this kind of procedure to attain much credibility in the public mind. Part of the issue is the extent of government monopoly over the definition of "legitimate action." Radical antiwar efforts, whether articulate or not, have always presupposed some role for individual and popular judgment in assessing the nature of "legitimacy," and have increasingly perceived the gap between personal morality and governmental action as indicative of a loss of legitimacy by the state rather than as an upsurge of lawless impulses and attitudes on their part.

Another possibility is for a Nuremberg-type tribunal to be constituted in Vietnam, Laos, or Cambodia, or for all of Indochina, to inquire into the commission of war crimes, and for some actual defendants (mainly Indochinese) to be prosecuted. Such an eventuality depends on the way the various facets of the Indochina War come to an end and, more particularly, on whether the leaders of the losing side negotiate, abdicate, or surrender power.

27. Taylor, *Nuremberg and Vietnam*, p. 94. See also Farer, "The Laws of War," p. 12: "For our immediate purposes the central point of this excursion in legal theory is that the drafters of the Nuremberg Charter were acting consciously and conscientiously to establish a manifestly legal process, the outcome of which would be a set of persuasive precedents."

28. The Security Council made a distinction in the *Eichmann* context between the abduction of Eichmann by illegal means in Argentina and the duty of all governments to pursue and prosecute alleged war criminals of the Nazi period. U.N. Doc S/4349 (1960). The Argentine government had a duty to apprehend and prosecute Eichmann, or at least to cooperate in turning him over to a government that would prosecute.

29. See Richard A. Falk, *The Role of Domestic Courts in the International Legal Order* (Syracuse, Syracuse University Press, 1964), esp. pp. 1-20; Richard Lillich, "The Proper Role of Domestic Courts in the International Legal Order," *Virginia Journal of International Law* 11:9 (1970).

30. For the role of domestic courts in this connection, see Lawrence Velvel, *Undeclared War and Civil Disobedience: The American System in Crisis* (Cambridge, Dunellen, 1970), esp. pp. 113-180; Francis D. Wormuth, "The Vietnam War: The President Versus the Constitution," Falk, *The Vietnam War and International Law* II, 711-807.

31. See e.g. Anthony Austin, *The President's War: The Story of the Tonkin Gulf Resolution and How the Nation Was Trapped in Vietnam* (New York, Lippincott, 1971); Joseph Goulden, *Truth Is the First Casualty: The Gulf of Tonkin Affair--Illusion and Reality* (Chicago, Rand-McNally, 1969); Hugh G. Gallagher, *Advise and Obstruct: The Role of the United States Senate in Foreign Policy Decisions* (New York, Delacorte, 1969); Merlo Pusey, *The Way We Go to War* (Boston, Houghton Mifflin, 1969); "Hearings on U.S. Commitments to Foreign Powers Before the Senate Committee on Foreign Relations," 90th Cong., 1st sess. (1967); Theodore Draper, *Abuse of Power* (New York, Viking, 1967); David Kraslow and Stuart Loory, *The Secret Search for Peace in Vietnam* (New York, Random House, 1968); Franz Schurmann, Peter Dale Scott, and Reginald Zelink, *The Politics of Escalation in Vietnam* (New York, Fawcett, World, 1966). These issues of constitutional imbalance underlie inquiry into the decision to disclose the Pentagon Papers so that the public and Congress might know more about past deception and about the manipulation of news by the executive branch through well-timed "leaks," "backgrounders," and the like.

32. See Quincy Wright, *The Role of International Law in the Elimination of War* (New York, Oceana, 1961); Julius Stone, *Aggression and World Order: A Critique of United Nations Theories of Aggression* (Berkeley, University of California Press, 1958).

33. Taylor, *Nuremberg and Vietnam*, p. 117.

34. See Velvel, *Undeclared War*, pp. 183-250; Daniel Berrigan, *The Trial of the Catonsville Nine* (Boston, Beacon Press, 1970); Barbara Deming, *Revolution and Equilibrium* (New York, Grossman, 1971); Jessica Mitford, *The Trial of Dr. Spock* (New York, Knopf, 1969); Alice Lynd, ed., *We Won't Go: Personal Accounts of War Resisters* (Boston, Beacon Press, 1968); H.L.A. Hart, "Positivism and the Separation of Law and Morals," *Harvard Law Review* 71:593 (1958); Lon Fuller, "Positivism and Fidelity to Law: A Reply to Professor Hart," *Harvard Law Review* 71:630 (1958).

35. Taylor, *Nuremberg and Vietnam*, p. 119; Richard A. Falk, "Six Legal Dimensions of the United States Involvement in the Vietnam War," in Falk, *The Vietnam War and International Law*, II, 216, 150.

36. Reprinted in Falk et al, *Crimes of War*, pp. 77-78.

37. The Nuremberg Principles as such are not in binding form, but they appear to restate accurately the assumptions and conclusions of the Nuremberg judgment. They thus provide evidence of the content of customary international law on this subject. See Clive Parry, *The Sources and Evidences of International Law* (Dobbs Ferry, N.Y., Oceana, 1965).

38. See "Epilogue to the German Edition of The Warriors: Reflections on Men in Battle," reprinted in J. Glenn Gray, *On Understanding Violence Philosophically and Other Essays* (New York, Harper and Row, 1970), pp.35-43, esp. p. 38: "Again and again it has seemed to me that our nation has had unparalleled opportunities in this conflict to declare to the world: we made a mistake, we are wrong, we are going to end this slaughter right now, so far as our troops are concerned. The effect of a strong nation able to make such a drastic break with its past might well have been an electrifying one. To some of ous who consider ourselves loyal citizens of the United States, it would have been an occasion of sober joy."

39. The Nixon Doctrine, the prevailing statement of official policy in light of the Vietnam experience, maintains the same pattern of commitments to foreign governments confronted by insurgent challenges mounted within, or largely within, their own territory. American involvement will include military equipment and heavy air support, but will seek to avoid introducing American troops. See President Nixon's report to the Congress, Feb. 25, 1971, "United States Foreign Policy for the 1970's: Building for Peace," *Weekly Compilation of Presidential Documents* 7:305, 308 (Mar. 1, 1971). The Nixon Doctrine has been applied to the struggle for control of Cambodia, resulting in heavy destruction and much suffering on the part of the civilian population. See Jonathan Grant, Laurence Moss, and Jonathan Unger, eds., *Cambodia: The Widening War in Indochina* (New York, Washington Square Press, 1971).

40. These five reasons are discussed in Taylor, *Nuremberg and Vietnam*, pp. 101-116.

41. Taylor, *Nuremberg and Vietnam*, p. 117.

42. But even before publication of the Pentagon Papers it was reasonable to conclude that the United States was guilty of waging aggressive war in Vietnam. Perhaps the most comprehensive analysis along these lines was prepared

under the auspices of the Consultative Council of the Lawyers Committee on A-merican Policy Towards Vietnam, John Fried, ed., *Vietnam and International Law: An Analysis of the Legality of the U.S. Military Involvement*, 2nd rev. ed. (Flanders, N.J., O'Hare, 1969).

43. See Edward S. Herman, *Atrocities in Vietnam: Myths and Realities* (Philadelphia, Pilgrim Press, 1970), pp. 20-88; Committee of Concerned Asian Scholars, *The Indochina Story* (New York, Pantheon, 1970), pp. 79-144.

44. See e.g. Falk, *The Vietnam War and International Law*, I, 318-508, 523-540; Jaro Mayda, "The Vietnam Conflict and International Law," in Falk, *The Vietnam War and International Law*, II, 260-270, esp. pp. 268-269.

45. On the casual complexity of how major wars start, see A.J.P. Taylor, *The Origins of the Second World War* (New York, Atheneum, 1961).

46. For the Tonkin Gulf Resolution, see Resolution repealing Tonkin Gulf Resolution, H.J.Res. 1302, 91st Cong., 2d sess. (1970).

47. See Garry J. Weeters, "The Appropriations Power As a Tool of Congressional Foreign Policy Making," *Boston University Law Review* 50:34 (Special Issue, Spring, 1970).

48. 369 U.S. 186, 211-213 (1962).

49. In this new patriotism the values embodied in the Charter of the United Nations would gradually displace Westphalia values so far as dominant modes of political consciousness are concerned.

50. Taylor, *Nuremberg and Vietnam*, pp. 118-119.

51. Remarks by Ellsberg, Conference, Princeton University, Apr. 19, 1971. See also Ellsberg's contributions in Knoll and McFadden, *War Crimes*, pp. 82-84, and p. 158: "I speak not as a researcher but from experience as a former official of the Defense Department and the State Department in Washington and Vietnam—experience that makes me a possible defendant in a future war crimes trial. Some ten years ago I read the transcript of the Nuremberg Trials, and that left me with the sense of what an exhibit in a war crimes trial looks like. As I was working in the Department of Defense, I did in some cases have a feeling while reading documents late at night that I was looking at future exhibits."

52. See the decisions and briefs in Berk v. Laird, 317 F. Supp. 715 (E.D.N.Y. 1970), *aff'd.* 429 F. 2d 302 (2d Cir. 1970) (denial of preliminary injunction); Orlando v. Laird, 317 F. Supp. 1013 (E.D.N.Y. 1970).

53. A cycle of rebellion and repression can be initiated whenever deeply felt and widely shared abuses cannot be redressed by recourse to normal grievance machinery. On the tendency of a cycle of rebellion and repression in foreign settings to be imported, see Eqbal Ahmad, "Winning Hearts and Minds: The Theory and Fallacies of Counterinsurgency," *The Nation*, Aug. 2, 1971, pp. 70-85, esp. pp. 84-85.

54. Walter Pincus, "After the Pentagon Papers: The Same Old Story," *New York Magazine*, Aug. 16, 1971, p. 46.

55. The news media emphasized the conflict between the government and the press with respect to the publication of the Pentagon Papers and failed to treat the substance of the disclosure with any depth of analysis or concern.

56. There is no serious disposition evident within the country to repudiate the counterrevolutionary foreign policy adopted by the United States in relation to the countries of Asia, Africa, and Latin America. This commitment to help foreign governments repress their own populations underlay the involvement in Vietnam from the outset.

57. Jaspers, *The Question of German Guilt,* p. 59. Jaspers continues (p. 59): "The powers initiating Nuremburg thereby attest their common aim of world government, by submitting to world order. They attest their willingness really to accept responsibility for mankind as the result of their victory—not just for their own countries. Such testimony must not be false testimony.

"It will either create confidence in the world that right was done and a foundation laid in Nuremberg—in which case the political trial will have become a legal one, with law creatively founded and realized for a new world now waiting to be built. Or disappointment by untruthfulness will create an even worse world atmosphere breeding new wars; instead of a blessing, Nuremberg would become a factor of doom, and in the world's eventual judgment the trial would have been a sham and a mock trial. This must not happen."

On the counterrevolutionary drift of American foreign policy since World War II, see Richard J. Barnet, *Intervention and Revolution: The United States and the Third World* (New York, World, 1968); Gary MacEoin, *Revolution Next Door: Latin America in the 1970's* (New York, Rhinehart and Winston, 1971); Ronald Steele, *Pax Americana* (New York, Viking, 1967).

58. Pragmatic tests of qualification may also be applied to situations where the normative objectives of statesmen were admirable.

59. The relation of international forces since World War II has not favored decisive endings of wars in which principal states have been significantly involved on either side. There have been withdrawals by major governments from positions of colonial occupation, but not wars in which the losing side surrenders and is occupied by the victorious side. Castro's regime in Cuba held trials of alleged "criminals" in the Batista regime after it gained power in January 1959. See C. Fred Iklé, *Every War Must End* (New York, Columbia University Press, 1971).

60. Jaspers, *The Question of German Guilt,* p. 55.

61. See Ernst Von Salomon, *The Questionnaire,* trans. Constantine Fitz-Gibbon (Garden City, Doubleday, 1954); Constantine Fitz-Gibbon, *Denazification* (London, Joseph, 1969).

62. See Duffett, *Against the Crime of Silence;* Proceedings of the Oslo Commission of Inquiry into U.S. War Crimes in Indochina, mimeo. (1971).

63. See Jean-Paul Sartre, *On Genocide* (Boston, Beacon Press, 1968); Ahmad, "Winning Hearts and Minds."

64. The United Nations Conference on the Human Environment, which took place in Stockholm in June 1972, is an example of an effort to use an intergovernmental conference setting to heighten awareness, as well as to fashion specific solutions to shared problems. Other examples in 1974 involve conferences on a new law of the oceans, on world population policy, and on food.

65. I do not feel optimistic about the prospects for major institutional

developments on a global level, although important thinking is being done in support of such initiatives. See Thomas Holton, *An International Peace Court: Design for a Move from State Crime to World Law* (The Hague, M. Nijhoff, 1970); Julius Stone and Robert Woetzel, eds., *Toward a Feasible International Criminal Court* (Geneva, World Peace Through Law Center, 1970).

66. Requiring a declaration of war might produce an excessively rigid procedure under certain circumstances, especially where the President was seeking to moderate the belligerent sentiments of Congress or the public. There is a danger in constitutional reform, as in military tactics, of designing a structure responsive to the last war rather than to the next one. Moreover, a declaration of war, although presenting a threshold of inhibition, generates escalatory pressures in a powerful country to carry on with the war until victory, and to stifle domestic opposition to the war as "treasonous."

67. Gray, *On Understanding Violence,* p. 37. See also J. Glenn Gray, *The Warriors: Reflections on Men in Battle* (New York, Harper and Row, 1959), pp. 215-242.

68. Gray, *On Understanding Violence,* p. 41. See also Falk, *This Endangered Planet.*

## 10. The United Nations: Constitutional and Behavioral Tendencies

1. See e.g. Stanley Hoffmann, *Gulliver's Troubles or the Setting of American Foreign Policy* (New York, McGraw-Hill, 1968), pp. 39-43. The multinational corporation has become an increasingly significant international actor in recent years. See Richard J. Barnet and Ronald Mueller, *Global Reach: The Power of the Multinational Corporation* (New York, Simon and Schuster, 1975).

2. U Thant, "Introduction to the Annual Report of the Secretary General on the Work of the Organization," *UN Monthly Chronicle* 5, no. 10 (October 1968):99.

3. U Thant, "Message for United Nations Day, 1970," *UN Monthly Chronicle* 7, no. 9 (October 1970):ii; U Thant, "Introduction to the Annual Report," p. 40. In this view, the Charter is regarded as embodying a new basis for international relations, which was evolved by statesmen to prevent the repetition of large-scale violence in the form of general warfare among principal states. The language of the instrument is taken literally, and disappointment is expressed with the failure of behavioral patterns of national governments to conform with the formal language. As a matter of idealistic polemics, such an emphasis on constitutional imperatives may create some pressure for moderateness in international society. As analysis, however, it fails to acknowledge that the Charter made no effort to transform either the attitudes associated with sovereign prerogatives or government access to the instruments of military violence that had produced wars in the past. A genuine peace system needs to implement aspirations with a feasible strategy for transforming behavior or, in my terminology, for "bridging the gap."

4. U Thant, *UN Monthly Chronicle* 7, no. 9 (October 1970):iii; Emilio Arenales, United Nations Day Message, *UN Monthly Chronicle* 5, no. 10 (October 1968):i. Arenales also said (p. ii): "A further reflection which we feel compelled to direct against the growing scepticism regarding the United Nations is that its weaknesses or limitations are not those of an organism with an independent life of its own or those of a super-State, but are rather the direct and unavoidable responsibility of the Member States, both those that founded the Organization and those that now belong to it."

5. Ernst B. Haas, "Dynamic Environment and Static System: Revolutionary Regimes in the United Nations," in Robert W. Gregg and Michael Barkun, eds., *The United Nations System and Its Functions* (Princeton, Van Nostrand, 1968), p. 172; Stanley Hoffmann, "An Evaluation of the United Nations," Richard A. Falk and Saul H. Mendlovitz, eds., *The Strategy of World Order: The United Nations* (New York, World Law Fund, 1966), III, 794.

6. It seems misleading to regard an international organization as a "failure" because it acts in accordance with the limits set by the international environment. Such a perspective bases assessment on unrealistic expectations. The United Nations, or the League before it, "failed" only in relation to expectations that were utopian in the circumstances. To write of "failure" is to fall into the trap of taking sides in the debate between utopians and cynics, thereby undermining any appreciation for actual role and accomplishment. F.H. Hinsley, for example, opens a chapter on "The Failure of the League of Nations" with the remark: "Everything we know about the history and nature of international relations goes to show that the League, as it was constructed, was bound to fail; and that it was bound to be constructed as it was constructed." Hinsley, *Power and the Pursuit of Peace* (Cambridge, Cambridge University Press, 1963), p. 309. In fairness, Hinsley is writing about the search for international peace—the end of war—and in this sense the League was indeed bound to fail.

7. See e.g. Oran R. Young, "The United Nations and the International System," in Leon Gordenker, ed., *The United Nations in International Politics* (Princeton, Princeton University Press, 1971), pp. 10-59; Gregg and Barkun, *The United Nations System,* pp. 3-9.

8. Cf. older approaches based on an explication of Charter provisions and of the institutional forms laid down in the Charter. See e.g. Clyde Eagleton and Leland Goodrich, in Falk and Mendlovitz, *The Strategy of World Order,* III, 10-16, 17-35.

9. The point is to shift attention to the actual tasks performed rather than to emphasize or gloss over the gap between Charter language and organizational achievement. The Charter does not, in the literal terms used in Articles 1 and 2, provide adequate tests by which to assess United Nations performance.

10. For the professional outlook of academic specialists, which generally reflects the effort of political science to develop more "scientific," in the sense of disciplined, procedures of inquiry, see Young, "The United Nations"; Gregg and Barkun, eds., *The United Nations System.*

11. This chapter is a preliminary effort to evolve a disciplined procedure for

assessing the degree to which the United Nations has met, is meeting, and will meet the needs of international society. For the character of these needs see Richard A. Falk, *This Endangered Planet: Prospects and Proposals for Human Survival* (New York, Random House, 1971), which argues that there are a series of challenges whose cumulative impact is likely to be catastrophic, unless drastic changes in the structure of international society are brought about by the end of the century. The depiction here of United Nations behavior is in light of this overriding concern.

12. For the basis of such a configurative approach, see Myres S. McDougal, Harold D. Lasswell, and W. Michael Reisman, "Theories about International Law: Prologue to a Configurative Jurisprudence," *Virginia Journal of International Law* 8:188-299 (April 1968); in Richard A. Falk and C.E. Black, eds., *The Future of the International Legal Order* (Princeton, Princeton University Press, 1969), I, 73-154.

13. For this kind of false utopianism, see Hinsley, *Power and the Pursuit of Peace;* Walter Schiffer, *The Legal Community of Mankind* (New York, Columbia University Press, 1954); Stefan T. Possony, "Peace Enforcement," *Yale Law Journal* 55:910-949 (1946).

14. See Erich Fromm, *The Revolution of Hope: Toward a Humanized Technology* (New York, Harper, 1968); Gerald Feinberg, *The Prometheus Project—Mankind's Search for Long-Range Goals* (Garden City, Doubleday, 1969).

15. For an interesting conception of "stages," see Haas, "Dynamic Environment," pp. 171-172. In the context of collective security, see Ernst B. Haas, "Collective Security and Future International System," in Falk and Black, *The Future of the International Legal Order*, I, 226.

16. For the United Nations significance in terms of "abyss" and "ambiguity," see Hoffmann, "An Evaluation," pp. 793-795.

17. That is, there is no current demand for the elimination of the United Nations from the international scene. It is possible to inquire as to what changes in the international environment would have to occur before such a demand might seriously be made. The question is unrealistic because it does not posit these conditions.

18. For this momentum, see E.B. Haas, *Beyond the Nation State* (Stanford, Stanford University Press, 1964).

19. There is obviously a need for a framework of inquiry and a collection of data that examines the refraction effect over time, for distinct issue-areas, and within the various United Nations organizational arenas.

20. The Afro-Asian group has been unable to induce the United Nations to make available the resources needed to mount a serious military effort or to persuade any of the more powerful states to move along these lines outside the framework of the organization. There is a virtually universal endorsement of Afro-Asian aims, but the more established sovereign states are not prepared to generate the means needed to achieve or even to threaten a humanitarian inter-

vention. Compare the willingness of powerful states to police deviance within their spheres of influence (as in Czechoslovakia) or to commit huge amounts of resources to the struggle for geopolitical ascendancy (as in Vietnam).

21. The gap between endorsing a claim and acting to assure its fulfillment is in some sense analogous to the gap between Charter ideals and United Nations behavior.

22. There are other functions that may be served by the mere assertion of a claim, including a gradual mobilization of support for recourse to violence within the international community by the most ardent claimants, and an eventual recourse to some kind of sanctioning process by the community itself. The United Nations is neither primarily an enforcement agency nor the basis of a restraint system; its principal roles are more typically to clarify a consensus, formulate demands, and set some standards for distinguishing permissible from impermissible uses of force. In the case of apartheid, United Nations pressure has occasioned a greater degree of world awareness and has even had a role in inducing blacks in the United States to identify with the antiapartheid movement.

23. This encouragement comes about in three steps: frustration with persuasive approaches that rely on legality and nonviolence; a gradual legitimation, or at least toleration, of violent approaches as a consequence of refusal to make voluntary concessions; and a belief that violence alone works, which is reinforced on every occasion that ineffectual strategies of persuasion are replaced by effectual violent strategies.

24. As the Korean action illustrated, however, the absence of autonomous capabilities can be occasionally overcome by the ad hoc assignment of capabilities by member states.

25. There is a need for in-depth case studies examining the conditions under which different kinds of capabilities are and are not available to implement different kinds of claims on behalf of the United Nations. "The financing dispute" has illustrated a serious effort by important states to withhold financial resources on a post hoc basis to discourage certain kinds of peace-keeping operations by the organization. Part of the issue is the extent to which the political execution of the United Nations position has been correlated with the specific preferences of the states being assessed for the cost of an operation. And part of the issue, especially as reflected in Soviet behavior, is an effort to prevent the easy operation of a United States-dominated United Nations.

26. The transformation is circular. The moment that the organization is entrusted with adequate capabilities, its need for them is likely to diminish. Part of the present problem arises from the consequences of governments wanting to have the discretion that would be lost, or diminished, if a more effective United Nations existed.

27. Such an observation is not meant to contradict the continuing dominance of national governments within the United Nations setting, and the continuing reliance of the main decisional procedures on nationalistic modes of

participation. The increasing use of world community rhetoric is a social fact with certain attitudinal and behavioral consequences, even if these consequences remain subordinate for most purposes.

28. Numerous proposals along these lines have been made in the United States. For example, Senator Vance Hartke has led the effort to establish a Department of Peace within the executive branch; the suggestion was made that President Nixon establish a National Commission on World Order; and various schemes are underway for securing a United Nations source of direct revenue, such as a share in the revenues from ocean mining.

29. See Falk, *This Endangered Planet*.

30. The League Covenant, for a variety of complicated reasons, including the quest for ratification by the United States Senate, was formerly included as a section of the Versailles Peace Treaty.

31. For an analysis of the bargaining nexus of United Nations operations, see Haas, "Dynamic Environment."

32. Such a correlation has not yet been made in any systematic fashion. For the problems, see Oran R. Young, "Trends in International Peacekeeping," Research Monograph No. 22 (Princeton Center of International Studies, mimeo., 1966); Haas, "Collective Security."

33. The Security Council is more likely to advance effective claims than is the General Assembly, because the voting rules in the Council emphasize the participation and assent of principal states to a far greater extent than do Assembly voting rules. The International Court of Justice, should it receive a case bearing on questions of importance, is even less likely to posit an effective claim than the General Assembly, because its behavior is least likely to be responsive to political constraints. The highly unpopular 1966 decision in the South West Africa cases illustrates a determination that is so unresponsive to these constraints as to undermine the authority of the institution as well as the assertion of the particular decision. Specialized agencies, with clear lines of authority to facilitate technical cooperation among national governments, may be more able to neglect the actualities of power and conflict in international society.

34. A study sponsored by the United States government in 1963 indicated that United States positions appeared to be better protected by the one vote-one state formula than by any of the main proposals for weighted voting. See Falk and Mendlovitz, *The Strategy of World Order*, III, 297-299. There is no evidence at this time that a greater correlation between relative size and relative authority would carry with it any assurance that the preferences of a particular state might have increased "weight" within the organization.

35. With the possible exceptions of Japan and West Germany, representation in the Security Council may not appear so anachronistic if the possession of nuclear weapons or the level of gross national product are selected as the decisive criteria of relative power. The assertion of anachronism is based on the importance of diverse participation in the decisional process and therefore the growing insistence that roles in authority structures be parceled out to allow principal cultural, ethnic and ideological constituencies to participate on

the basis of equality. In such a calculus of relative power, the Security Council appears Euro-centric and top-heavy with developed country representation.

36. The contention that states deliberately withhold capabilities from world institutions is a persistent theme of scholars who criticize the naive expectations of idealistic proponents of world government. See Hinsley, *Power and the Pursuit of Peace;* Schiffer, *The Legal Community.* The failure to make use of the potentialities of the United Nations is an expression of the foreign policy of all major governments.

37. The United Nations peace-keeping role involves a process normally initiated by a collective decision. As such, the decision must be acted upon in an extremely unstable environment of conflict, and choices are likely to be made that are antithetical to the policies of major members. The politics involved in building the initial consensus may have deliberately introduced ambiguity into the definition of goals attached to the United Nations assignment so as to mobilize wide support. Later on, in more concrete settings, these contradictory expectations about goals are likely to induce a severe sense of disappointment about United Nations activities. Distinct policy inputs may also be introduced by members of the staff. The Congo operation exemplified the differences between obtaining a consensus throughout the various phases of executing that role.

38. A role is defined as a form of characteristic behavior by an actor, whereas a function is defined as a valued task that an actor performs within a social or political system.

39. The world community can use the political organs of the United Nations to register displeasure about some specific policies of a major state. The West has used the organization frequently to censure Soviet behavior in Eastern Europe, as a way of adopting a position without risking any action. Such verbal denunciations may even serve to dilute domestic demands for a more militant response.

40. There is an established distinction between "peaceful settlement" and "peace-keeping." The latter operation involves an active military presence, although its nature can vary from symbolic buffering to participation in large-scale belligerency. It seems likely that in the future the United Nations may play a major peace-keeping role in the Middle East, either to supervise a cease-fire or to implement and sustain part of a political settlement.

41. With respect to peaceful settlement, the United Nations has been playing a significant role: Security Council Resolution 242 of Nov. 22, 1967, established agreed guidelines for a settlement, although there are many "open" issues and Israel appears unlikely to accept any solution that involves restoring the territorial status quo as of June 5, 1967; Gunnar V. Jarring, as special representative of the Secretary-General, sought to find bases for a negotiated settlement and had significant contact with all governments concerned with the issues; and since the 1973 war the United Nations has been given a central role in supervising and maintaining the disengagement of both forces on both the Syrian and the Egyptian frontiers.

42. The United Nations might also act to avert disaster by interposing a corps of observers in a situation of tension and hostility.

43. There is evidence that the consensus which can be obtained to support verbal denunciations could not be sustained in the event that sanctions were voted to bring increasing diplomatic, economic, and military pressure upon South Africa.

44. The organization is not equipped to contain a determined aggressor state and shows no real disposition to turn itself into an instrument of genuine collective security. In the nuclear age more than at any previous point in world history, national security depends on the operation of a deterrent strategy at the national level. Critical risk-taking and reactions to risks continue to be national decisions made in periods of international crisis and confrontation. See Oran R. Young, *The Politics of Force* (Princeton, Princeton University Press, 1969).

45. For a comparable use of the word "system" for United Nations activities, see Gregg and Barkun, *The United Nations System*, pp. 3-5. They offer two reasons for their use of system: "In the first place, we simply wish to avoid the use of expressions such as 'world community,' which suggest a nonexistent consensus . . . In the second place, the concept of a system is useful because it suggests actors interacting within environmental constraints, and this is precisely the picture we wish to conjure up" (p. 3).

46. It is also possible to go backward in the history of international society and to formulate distinct organizing de jure and de facto images for each period. For instance, it would certainly be useful to compare the Covenant conception with the various League "systems" that emerged in relation to different issues and during the main phases of its existence. Sir Alfred Zimmern writes that the Covenant "embodies five different systems, each with its appropriate method." Zimmern, *The League of Nations and the Rule of Law, 1918-1935*, 2nd ed. (London, Macmillan, 1939; repr. Russell, 1969), p. 270. Zimmern's conception of a system is close to my own, although he does not stress the distinction between the Covenant as a formal document and the League as a political actor. For his outline of the five systems, see pp. 270-280. For an effort to deal with international history as a whole in this systemic way, see Richard N. Rosencrance, *Action and Reaction in World Politics* (Boston, Little, Brown, 1963); Stanley Hoffmann, "International Systems and International Law," in Falk and Mendlovitz, *The Strategy of World Order*, II, 134-166.

47. It is possible to compare the treatment of issues and phases within a single system as well as to compare one system with another. The boundaries of a system are to some extent artificial, imposed on subject matter that cannot be confined altogether to abstractly formulated categories.

48. The formal system embodied in an instrument, such as the United Nations Charter, can be perceived in various ways. On many key issues involving role and expectation, these perceptions may in fact differ widely. Stanley Hoffmann, writing about the League of Nations, points out "that the main authors of the Covenant did not agree on what they expected from the organization, and that the post-war world fitted the expectations of none of them."

Hoffmann, "An Evaluation," p. 795. The various images of the formal system might also be specified and compared, but for the purposes of this chapter there is only "one" Charter, although on any controversial occasion different perceptions of the Charter will yield different meanings.

49. These points are especially applicable to international society, where legal habits are weak and the ethos of self-help continues to prevail on matters of critical concern to sovereign governments.

50. The United Nations Charter could also be compared with other formal conceptions for global organization, which might be noted as Charter IIa, IIb, etc. Even with regard to a single document, there is always the problem of divergent perceptions. There is also the changing content of the formal instrument, as it acquires or loses meaning through adaptation to a series of concrete situations. In 1974 the United Nations Charter is in some respects a different instrument from what it was in 1945.

51. It is true that the five permanent members of the Security Council are the five states that possess nuclear weapons at the present time. But aside from this attribute, India, Japan, Brazil, and West Germany seem to be more significant as states than either France or the United Kingdom.

52. There were also failures to posit norms and procedures adapted to the main technologies of violence: nuclear weaponry and low visibility commando operations. The Charter ideas of "aggression" and "self-defense" were evolved to deal with conventional warfare between regular military forces. International lawyers have been slow to evolve new and more relevant functional categories better adapted to more modern patterns of behavior.

53. The Charter was negotiated in an atmosphere still influenced by the pattern of wartime alliances and by the major conflict just ended between the Allied and Axis powers. See reference to continuing actions against "any State which during Second World War has been an enemy of any signatory to the present Charter." Art. 107, United Nations Charter. It was set up to enable clear, concerted action against the states defeated in World War II, and its procedures were not at all encumbered in relation to such an undertaking, provided only that the principal victorious states agreed on a course of action.

54. Some regional organizations are disguised hegemonies, or at least disguised hegemonic alliances. Two prominent examples are the Warsaw Pact and the Organization of American States.

55. See Lincoln P. Bloomfield, *The United Nations and U.S. Foreign Policy,* 2nd rev. ed. (Boston, Little, Brown, 1967). The idea of formulating national strategies of participation within the United Nations seems to be a desirable one. But when a state has the power to maneuver the organization into taking a partisan position in the central international conflict, then the role of the organization as a meeting ground for principal adversaries is jeopardized.

56. The most dramatic instance of this shift was accomplished by means of the Uniting for Peace Resolution authorizing action by the General Assembly on matters of peace and security if the Security Council is immobilized by the exercise of the veto. This resolution was devised during the early period of the

Korean War, when government officials in the United States were eager to use the organization to support national policies, especially those involving action against the Soviet Union, and were concerned about what might happen if the Soviet boycott of the Security Council was ended and the Soviet veto used. For the resolution, See Falk and Mendlovitz, *The Strategy of World Order,* III, 250-269.

57. On the relation of social change and maintenance in the Charter system, see Gordenker, *The United Nations,* pp. 171-178.

58. These generalizations are provisional and subject to sharp reversal. The principal states acknowledge their converging interests in peace-keeping from time to time, and could conceivably act jointly to create a world police force of real military capability, say 40,000, to be used to prevent or moderate conflict or to restore or maintain order.

59. "Ambiguous" is used in the sense of being susceptible to divergent lines of authoritative interpretation, depending on the wishes of the governing consensus at certain points. There are few nonambiguous directives embodied in the Charter.

60. For instance, the Soviet occupation of Czechoslovakia in August 1968 was immediately subject to adverse debate in the Security Council.

61. For an evaluation of the United Nations response to the operation, see Richard A. Falk, *Legal Order in a Violent World* (Princeton, Princeton University Press, 1968), pp. 324-335.

62. Exclusion or withdrawal of significant states has the same diluting impact on United Nations recommendations and decisions.

63. The potency of United Nations System III has induced pressure to activate United Nations System II in certain contexts, as in the Middle East.

64. The convergence may be either primarily positive (to attain some common goal) or primarily negative (to avoid a disaster).

65. For the United Nations role in opposing apartheid, see Falk and Mendlovitz, *The Strategy of World Order,* III, 364-407.

66. Cf. Charter II variants for ideas of international organizations possessing greater capacity to implement their decisions.

67. In 1965 Sukarno proposed creating a world organization of Newly Emerging Forces, including in its membership Indonesia and possibly mainland China. The project never proceeded very far, being completely abandoned when later in the same year the anti-Sukarno countercoup overthrew the government of Indonesia. But the challenge was instructive in suggesting the fragile base on which the United Nations claim of world authority rests. This fragility underscores the importance of realizing the ideal of universal membership.

68. If such a revision proceeded far enough, a new normative framework could be indicated by the notation Charter System I (de jure)-II (de facto).

69. Such a development would be the inverse of the underfulfillment of the provisions for evolving a United Nations military capability.

70. There may be some effort to invoke the Uniting for Peace Resolution in a

United Nations System III setting, even though it was initially designed as an instrument for United Nations System I.

71. See Myres S. McDougal and Richard N. Gardner, "The Veto and the Charter: An Interpretation for Survival," in McDougal and Associates, *Studies in World Public Order* (New Haven, Yale University Press, 1960), pp. 718-760.

72. See e.g. Ernest W. Lefever, *Ethics and United States Foreign Policy* (New York, Meridian Books, 1957).

73. At the same time, if a judge is a national of a state that is a party to a dispute brought before the International Court of Justice, he is likely to adopt a judicial position that conforms to the national policy. In fact, such conformity is encouraged by the Statute of the International Court of Justice, which makes provision for the appointment of a national judge in the event that a party appearing before the Court is unrepresented by a national on the bench.

74. For excessive optimism about judicial potentialities, see Arthur Larson, *When Nations Disagree* (Baton Rouge, Louisiana State University Press, 1961).

75. It is possible to contend that the role of the International Court of Justice would be greater if there were more evidence of responsiveness to the political will of the international community. There are limits to judicial autonomy which, if exceeded, lead to disregard of a court because it is unable to fulfill a prevailing sense of justice. The United States Supreme Court has in the course of its experience oscillated between the poles of excessive autonomy and excessive responsiveness.

76. The International Court of Justice as a forum for dispute settlement also presents a wide range of opportunities for delay and evasion on the part of the losing side, both in the course of litigation and in response to an adverse decision.

77. A circle is implicit here: United Nations System IV will expand only in the event of depoliticization, but depoliticization will be signaled by an expanded United Nations System IV.

78. As a consequence of various forms of pollution, ranging from noise to radioactivity, and of resource depletion, environmental hazards may increase enough to necessitate a single, coherent, global response organized within a central political framework.

79. The expanding network of international relationships and the increasing technological capacity for centralized forms of cooperation should lead to the further rapid growth of these kinds of "functional" institutions.

80. See Kenneth E. Boulding, *The Meaning of the 20th Century* (New York, Harper, 1965); Fromm, *The Revolution of Hope;* Feinberg, *The Prometheus Project.*

81. Most accounts of the future of international society, especially those that are most apocalyptic about the urgency of drastic change in political structure, do not give the United Nations a prominent role in this process. The organiza-

tion is neglected rather than denigrated, as if its existence hardly penetrates the present imagination. See e.g. Harrison Brown, *The Challenge of Man's Future* (New York, Viking, 1954); Harrison Brown, James Bonner, and John Weir, *The Next Hundred Years* (New York, Viking, 1965); Herman Kahn and Anthony J. Wiener, *The Year 2000* (New York, Macmillan, 1967).

82. See Grenville Clark and Louis B. Sohn, *World Peace Through World Law,* 3rd. rev. ed. (Cambridge, Harvard University Press, 1966); "A Constitution for the World," *Papers on Peace* (Santa Barbara, Center for the Study of Democratic Institutions, 1965).

83. See Falk, *A Study of Future Worlds* (New York, Free Press, 1975), ch. 3.

## 11. Geopolitics and World Order

1. For a complete discussion of "world order," see Introduction.

2. Ze'ev Schul, "Israel's Internal Security—Check-Up on Resistance," *Atlas,* 1969, p. 47.

3. See e.g. W.W. Rostow, "The Great Transition: Tasks of the First and Second Postwar Generation," *Department of State Bulletin* 56, no. 1448 (Mar. 27, 1967):491-504; Arthur M. Schlesinger, Jr., *A Thousand Days* (Boston, Houghton Mifflin, 1965); George Liska, *Imperial America* (Baltimore, Johns Hopkins University Press, 1967).

4. Zone I actors are presented as participants in a pattern of mandatory alignment. Such a designation takes note of a measure of latent reciprocity in Zone I-Zone II relationships. Zone II actors can often manipulate Zone I actors despite the power realities of dependency. The Soviet decision to occupy Czechoslovakia in 1968 appears to have been influenced by the pressures of Zone II countries, especially East Germany and Poland. And the United Sates has been repeatedly manipulated by dependent allies, most spectacularly by Formosa and by the Saigon regime in South Vietnam.

5. The category affiliations cannot be clearly established in all cases, however. China could be either I or IV; Brazil, II or IV; South Africa, I, III, or IV. I am proposing only a useful framework for organizing thought about various sets of relationship in international society. Operating within this framework does not obviate the need to make judgments about the classification of a particular actor, nor remove the possibility that reasonable people might disagree about a classificatory choice.

6. Consider e.g. John Bartlow Martin's remark on the Dominican intervention in Martin, *Overtaken by Events* (Garden City, Doubleday, 1966), p. 733: "Sumner Welles' hope for nonintervention in the Hemisphere seems now to belong with Booth Tarkington and heliotrope and the swish of garden hose at summer dusk. He (Welles) had to deal only with quarreling Dominican *caciques,* Dominican governmental inability, and U.S. and European capitalists' machinations. Today we have to deal with the violent intervention of expert communism. In today's world a more useful doctrine for the

Hemisphere would seem to be one of interdependence." Compare this sentiment with the main defense of the Soviet occupation of Czechoslovakia that appeared in *Pravda,* translated as "Sovereignty and International Duties of
Socialist Countries" in the *New York Times,* Sept. 27, 1968: "It has got to be
emphasized that when a socialist country seems to adapt a 'non-affiliated'
stand, it retains its national independence, in effect, precisely because of the
socialist community, and above all the Soviet Union as a central force, which
includes the might of its armed forces. The weakening of any of the links in the
world system of socialism directly affects all the socialist countries, which cannot look indifferently upon this." See also C. L. Sulzberger, "Foreign Affairs:
The Commonwealth," *New York Times,* Nov. 27, 1968, p. 46.

7. In this respect, the occurrences within Zone II that result from Zone I's
interventions are shielded by a policy of deference underlying the idea of "domestic jurisdiction." This might be called "hegemonial jurisdiction," for such
deference does not shield Zone I intervention outside Zone II.

8. Juridical notions such as the "sovereign equality of states" also homoge-
nize units that are heterogeneous in many critical respects. Categorization may
be useful as an explanatory and predictive device, even if it obscures critical in-
tracategory differences. Note e.g. the differences between the style and effect of
United States and Soviet hegemony over Zone II.

9. Certain kinds of Zone II actions (such as accommodation with the rival
Zone I or adoption of governmental policies that appear to challenge Zone I
leadership and preferences) are likely to induce offsetting Zone I reactions. The
careful explication of these patterns of reaction would help to convert this
largely heuristic and taxonomic presentation into a more predictive one. In
such an event, it would be necessary to specify as clearly as possible the conditions under which Zone I actors would assert their claims to control Zone II
behavior. These conditions vary through time on the basis of many factors, including changes in capability, threat perception, overall international climate,
expectations, and anticipated difficulty of enforcement.

10. To clarify the operation of Zone II, two kinds of information are needed:
the boundary of Zone II sectors (i.e., the states that possess such a status at a
particular time) and the conditions under which a Zone I actor can be expected
to intervene militarily in the internal affairs of Zone II. It appears that the con-
finement of conflict between Zone I actors would normally be promoted by
eliminating ambiguity from the operation of Zone II, especially with respect to
the states perceived as belonging to Zone II by Zone I actors. However, ambiguity of status may be beneficial in a marginal case, influencing developments in
the target state through the uncertainty of a prospective Zone I intervention.
The Soviet Union, for instance, would surely want Rumania to believe that it
was subject to Zone II prerogatives, even if the the leadership in the Kremlin
was uncertain as to whether to assert such prerogatives in the event of a clear
move toward disaffiliation, as in the manner of Yugoslavia.

11. There have been occasional acknowledgments of the normative status of
"spheres of influence" at variance with the Westphalia ideas of a world of sov-

ereign states. Perhaps the most important of these acknowledgments has been Article 21 of the Covenant of the League of Nations, which assured the United States that there was no inconsistency between membership in the League and the diplomacy associated with the Monroe Doctrine: "Nothing in this Covenant shall be deemed to affect the validity of international engagement, such as treaties of arbitration or regional understandings like the Monroe Doctrine, for securing the maintenance of peace." The United States had to make offsetting diplomatic concessions to the major European states to obtain their approval of this provision. Woodrow Wilson fought for the insertion of Article 21 in the draft Covenant as part of his vain effort to build a ratification consensus in the United States Senate. Yet it is pointed out by F. P. Walters, "the inclusion in the Covenant of a specific reference to the Monroe Doctrine was disliked by nearly all the Latin American Members of the League. Had others besides Brazil been represented on the Committee which drafted the Covenant, it may well be doubted whether Article 21 would ever have been accepted. Brazil, however, was more ready than most other Latin American states to sympathize with the views of the United States." Walters, *A History of the League of Nations* (London, Oxford University Press, 1952), p. 56.

12. The American endorsement of a pluralistic world order is entirely at odds with any interference with the outcome of domestic struggles for control of foreign societies. The victory of Castro in Cuba exposed the limits of the American commitment to the cause of global pluralism. The training of exile groups in the United States to invade Castro's Cuba violated one of the basic rules of international behavior that Western countries have been urging on communist governments for years.

13. Consider, for instance, the international status of Soviet military intervention, on the scale of the Czech occupation and for roughly analogous reasons, in its own territory (e.g. the Ukraine), in Zone III (e.g. the Congo), in a country situated within the American sector of Zone II (e.g. Panama), and in American territory itself (e.g. Wounded Knee, North Dakota). A comparable range of geopolitical settings can be set forth from the perspective of the United States.

14. George Liska, *International Equilibrium* (Cambridge, Harvard University Press, 1957), pp. 148-161. For Soviet behavior in its Zone I role, see Zbigniew K. Brzezinski, *The Soviet Bloc: Unity and Conflict,* rev. ed. (New York, Praeger, 1961). For United States behavior in its Zone I and related roles, see Richard J. Barnet, *Intervention and Revolution: The United States in the Third World* (New York, World, 1968).

15. Contradictory perceptions of what constitutes a legitimated status quo often underlie recourse to warfare on the part of nonrevisionist rivals, such as the Soviet Union and the United States. See Ralph K. White, *Nobody Wanted War: Misperception in Vietnam and Other Wars* (New York, Doubleday, 1968). If an international system contains a revisionist actor of great-power status, the avoidance of war depends more decisively on the success of a deterrent posture. It may not be possible to grade actors as revisionist or as status

quo: governmental elites are often internally divided, and the predominant outlook may shift in consequence of internal and external factors, including the risks of various revisionist strategies.

16. See Richard A. Falk, *Legal Order in a Violent World* (Princeton, Princeton University Press, 1968), pp. 8-38; Richard A. Falk and C. E. Black, eds., *The Future of the International Legal Order: Trends and Patterns* (Princeton, Princeton University Press, 1969), vol. I, ch. 2. The specifications of scale are difficult to make in precise terms. Size, location, tradition, cohesion, terrain, military capability, and the form of government are relevent considerations in identifying Zone I candidates and in explaining certain members of Zone IV.

17. These classifications are to varying degrees approximate and controversial, and may vary over time. Geopolitical entities cannot be given clear status by reasonably authoritative ranking procedures. Sovereign states are accorded status by means of diplomatic recognition and admission to international institutions. But procedures may be manipulated for political purposes in such a way that a statelike entity is denied some of the formal prerequisites of statehood. Mainland China is the most prominent example.

18. Harold Sprout and Margaret Sprout, *The Ecological Perspective on Human Affairs* (Princeton, Princeton University Press, 1965), p. 15.

19. The important datum for any social system relates to the quality of consensus among centers of political authority. In the current international system, national governments remain the most important centers of political authority. Past systems have had, and future systems might have, different or additional centers of political authority.

20. Revisionist pressures and social change within an actor situated totally within one or the other sector of Zone II are characteristically inhibited by Zone I preferences. If these preferences are violated, the government of the Zone I actor is confronted with the choice between toleration and suppression. This is a challenge to the geopolitical status quo, but one that is not likely to upset the basis of global stability.

21. Henry Kissinger, *A World Restored* (New York, Grosset and Dunlap, 1964), p. 1.

22. Compare article from *Pravda*, Sept. 25, 1968 ("Sovereignty and International Duties of Socialist Countries," *New York Times*, Sept. 27, 1968), p. 3, with the arguments used by Secretary of State Dean Rusk to explain the American involvement in the Vietnam War by reference to participation in SEATO. See esp. Rusk's testimony before the Senate Foreign Relations Committee, February 1966. Also compare the rejection by the *Pravda* article of "an abstract, nonclass approach to the question of sovereignty and the rights of nations to self-determination" with the call by the United States legal adviser Leonard C. Meeker for a rejection of "fundamentalist views about the nature of international law" in the context of the Dominican intervention. Meeker, in an analysis that parallels the Soviet defense of their Czech intervention, criticizes those "commentators that have been free with the use of categorical imper-

atives"; he argues that "reliance on absolutes for judging and evaluating the events of our time is artifical." Meeker, "The Dominican Situation in the Perspective of International Law," *Department of State Bulletin* 53:60-65 (July 12, 1965). Each side wants to constrain its opponent within clear normative boundaries and to claim contextual freedom for itself. A system of world order, unless imperial in structure, rests on certain kinds of reciprocal claims and tolerances. Since neither Zone I actor is imperial in relation to the other, there is no prospect for a nonreciprocal structure of world order evolving on a level of behavior as distinct from words. The exertion of Zone I control over sectors of Zone II is an example of reciprocal structures of claim and tolerance on a behavioral level.

23. To accord legitimacy to a political arrangement is not to confer approval on it. The word "legitimacy" has so many normative connotations that it is difficult to avoid the implication that a "legitimate" action is also an appropriate and permissible action. The reason to risk this confusion, despite the disclaimers in the text, is the importance of relating world order to patterns of stable expectation. Legitimacy expresses the compatibility of a pattern of behavior with a system of world order without implying that the pattern is "legal" from the perspective of various hypothetical decision-makers, such as the judges of the International Court of Justice.

24. See e.g. Julius Stone, "The International Law Commission and Imposed Treaties of Peace," *Virginia Journal of International Law* 8: 356-373 (1968).

25. The Soviet Union probably was acting in part on the basis of its variant of "the domino theory." In addition, Czech liberalization probably exerted pressures against Soviet domestic controls on political and intellectual activity. It appears likely that the Soviet leadership feared the consequences of "the demonstration effect" of the policies of the Dubček regime.

26. See e.g. Barnet, *Intervention and Revolution,* pp. 153-180.

27. The 'Dominican affair could be uncoupled more easily from the main issues of international politics than could the Soviet treatment of Czechoslovakia.

28. Cuba since Castro has disaffiliated from the United States sector of Zone II, but it has not become part of the Soviet sector of Zone II. There is no reason to think that any internal developments in Cuba adverse to Soviet policies would provoke a Zone I military intervention in defiance of an anti-Soviet Havana government. The maximum hostile Soviet response to events in Cuba contrary to its wishes would be to terminate its economic and military support, and possibly to break off diplomatic relations. Thus, Cuba has enjoyed a Zone III status since Castro's accession to power. Unless the dependency relationship includes a conditional claim by the Zone I actor to intervene militarily, there is no basis for according a Zone II status to a dependent or ideologically affiliated state.

29. The deployment of nuclear missiles in Zone III countries would also be outside the rules of competition and might provoke a global confrontation. Many contextual factors would probably determine the nature and resolution of such a confrontation.

30. For legal arguments that rely mainly on the regional basis of the claim, see Abram Chayes, "The Legal Case for U.S. Action on Cuba," *Department of State Bulletin* 48:763-765 (Nov. 19, 1962); Leonard C. Meeker, "Defensive Quarantine and the Law," *American Journal of International Law* 57: 515 (1963).

31. See Richard A Falk, *The Status of Law in International Society* (Princeton, Princeton University Press, 1969), ch. 21.

32. See Richard A. Falk, *This Endangered Planet: Prospects and Proposals for Human Survival* (New York, Random House, 1971).

33. In this Zone I operation the Soviet Union did not act or think alone, for it was encouraged to act by pro-Soviet governments in Eastern Europe. One of the features of a Zone II sector is the likely emergence of governing elites that depend for the stability of their own power on the propensity of the Zone I actor to intervene with military force. There normally evolves a symbiotic linkage between the policy perspectives of Zone II governments and the exercise of supervisory control over a sector of Zone II by the Zone I actor. The willingness of Zone II governments to accept Zone I control, even to solicit it, tends to forfeit any prospect of popular government within the dependent country. The irony here is that the very nature of Zone I control produces a formalistic acquiscence in the dependent relationship on the part of the target society government. Put differently, the objectives of the Soviet occupation of Czechoslovakia or the United States occupation of the Dominican Republic are to put the government under the control of an elite that would pursue a compliant line of policy, thereby making subsequent intervention unnecessary. Or in the event that intervention is necessary to quell domestic changes and challenges, it would occur at the invitation of the constituted government. Thus, the Zone II government may come to need the threat of Zone I hegemony to assure its own survival.

34. See Gustavo Lagos, *International Stratification and Underdeveloped Countries* (Durham, North Carolina University Press, 1963), pp. 3-34.

35. The latter point about inhibiting change rests on the argument that needed social change is decisively inhibited by the existence of internal and external structures of domination which are maintained by principal governments. These structures exacerbate the current crisis of world order.

## 12. *Reforming World Order: Zones of Consciousness and Domains of Action*

1. "Address of U Thant," Apr. 28, 1971 (Release of United Nations Information Office; mimeo).

2. Of the word "futurology," Herman Kahn aptly writes "This is an ugly word, smacking of pseudoscience, but we seem to be stuck with it." Kahn and B. Bruce-Biggs, *Things To Come: Thinking about the 70's and 80's* (New York, Macmillan, 1972), p. 1.

3. See e.g. Thomas Stritch, "The Banality of Utopia," *Review of Politics* 34:

103-106 (January 1972); Margaret Mead, "Towards More Vivid Utopias," *Science* 126: 957-961 (November 1957).

4. See e.g. Herman Kahn and Anthony J. Wiener, *The Year 2000: A Framework for Speculation on the Next Thirty-three Years* (New York, Macmillan, 1967); John McHale, *The Future of the Future* (New York, Braziller, 1969); Jay Forrester, *World Dynamics* (Cambridge, Wright-Allen Press, 1971). For critical assessments, see Marion J. Levy, Jr., "Our Ever and Future Jungle," *World Politics* 22: 301-327 (January 1970); William Irwin Thompson, *At the Edge of History* (New York, Harper and Row, 1971), pp. 113-123.

5. See Aurelio Peccei, *The Chasm Ahead* (New York, Macmillan, 1969).

6. See William Watts, "Foreword," in Donella H. Meadows and others, *The Limits to Growth* (New York, Universe, 1972), pp. 9-12.

7. See "Commentary" by Executive Committee of the Club of Rome, including Peccei, published as an afterword to *The Limits to Growth,* pp. 185-197.

8. As such, the perspective of the Club of Rome is not different in "its message" or basic line of interpretation than a number of other books which rely on a more qualitative line of argument and analysis. See e.g. Paul R. Ehrlich and Ann H. Ehrlich, *Population, Resources, and Environment,* 2nd rev. ed. (San Francisco, W. H. Freeman, 1972); Barry Commoner, *The Closing Circle: Nature, Man, and Technology* (New York, Knopf, 1971); Harold and Margaret Sprout, *Toward a Politics of the Planet Earth* (New York, Van Nostrand-Reinhold, 1971); G. Tyler Miller, Jr., *Replenish the Earth: A Primer on Human Ecology* (Belmont, Cal., Wadsworth, 1972).

9. The most influential outgrowth of the project has been Meadows, *The Limits to Growth,* by which the Club of Rome itself achieved a world-wide reputation. For discussion of the project, see Watts, "Foreword," pp. 10-12.

10. Among the backlash literature, see Carl Kaysen, "The Computer That Printed Out W*O*L*F*," *Foreign Affairs* 50:660-668 (July 1972); Rudolf Klein, "Growth and Its Enemies," *Commentary,* June 1972, pp. 37-44; review of the Meadows-Forrester books by Peter Passell, Marc Roberts, and Leonard Ross, *New York Times Book Review,* Apr. 2, 1972, pp. 1, 10, 12-13.

11. See e.g. Mihajlo Mesarovic and Eduard Pestel, *Mankind at the Turning Point* (New York, E.P. Dutton, 1974).

12. Thompson, *At the Edge of History.* See also William Irwin Thompson, "Planetary Vistas," *Harpers,* December 1971, pp. 71-78; William Irwin Thompson, "The Individual As Institution: The Example of Paolo Soleri," *Harpers,* September 1972, pp. 48-62.

13. For the most coherent formulation of Peccei's early outlook, see his *The Chasm Ahead,* a position that he has evolved further in his subsequent work as the founder and leading figure in the Club of Rome.

14. Interview with William Irwin Thompson, *Time,* Aug. 21, 1972, p. 51.

15. In this spirit, Thompson praised the intellectual dialogue between the Indian mystical philosopher Gopi Krishna and the German physicist-

philosopher Carl Friedrich von Weizsächer, described by von Weizsächer in his Introduction to Krishna, *The Biological Basis of Religion and Genius* (New York, Harper and Row, 1972). See also Thompson's assessment of the architect Paolo Soleri, "The Individual As Institution," and Thompson's own conception of a learning-living center based on the ideas of the medieval Irish monastery at Lindisfarne, outlined in his prospectus for a Lindisfarne Association. In general, see Thompson, *Passages About Earth* (New York, Harpers, 1973).

16. See e.g. V. R. Potter, *Bioethics: Bridge to the Future* (Englewood Cliffs, Prentice-Hall, 1971).

17. Quoted from Bradbury K. Thurlow, *Commentary,* no. 1972, p. 1 (a monthly investment newsletter distributed by a Wall Street brokerage firm, Laidlaw & Co.).

18. Kurt Vonnegut, Jr., "In a Manner That Must Shame God Himself," *Harpers,* November 1972, p. 60; Vonnegut, "The Winners Are Rehearsing for Things To Come," *ibid.,* p. 68. For a similar kind of assessment of the future in a different vein, see Michael T. Klare, *War Without End: American Planning for the Next Vietnams* (New York, Knopf, 1972).

19. See e.g. Chester L. Cooper, *The Lost Crusade: America in Vietnam* (New York, Dodd, Mead, 1970); Roger Hilsman, *To Move a Nation* (Garden City, Doubleday, 1967); Townsend Hoopes, *The Limits of Intervention: An Inside Account of How the Johnson Policy of Escalation Was Reversed* (New York, David McKay, 1960); Arthur M. Schlesinger, Jr., *The Bitter Heritage: Vietnam and American Democracy, 1941-1966* (Boston, Houghton Mifflin, 1966.

20. See Stephen Hymer, "The Multinational Corporation and the Law of Uneven Development," in Jagdish N. Bhagwati, ed., *Economics and World Order: From the 1970's to the 1990's* (New York, Macmillan, 1972), pp. 113-140.

21. See F. H. Hinsley, *Power and the Pursuit of Peace* (Cambridge, Cambridge University Press, 1963); Walter Schiffer, *The Legal Community of Mankind* (New York, Columbia University Press, 1954).

22. Grenville Clark and Louis B. Sohn, *World Peace Through World Law,* 3rd rev. ed. (Cambridge, Harvard University Press, 1966).

23. Compare Kenneth Boulding, "The Prevention of World War III," in Richard A. Falk and Saul H. Mendlovitz, eds., *The Strategy of World Order: Toward a Theory of War Prevention* (New York, World Law Fund, 1966), 3-13, with Robert Osgood and Robert W. Tucker, *Force, Order, and Justice* (Baltimore, Johns Hopkins University Press), 1967.

24. See e.g. Edward Goldsmith et al, *Blueprint for Survival* (Boston, Houghton Mifflin, 1972).

25. For a fair-minded presentation and criticism of the Nixon-Kissinger conception of world order, see James Chace, *The New American Foreign Policy* (New York, Scribners, 1973).

26. See e.g. Kissinger, "Central Issues of American Foreign Policy," in

Kermit Gordon, ed., *Agenda for the Nation* (Washington, D.C., Brookings Institution, 1968), pp. 585-614.

27. Jay W. Forrester, "Churches at the Transition Between Growth and World Equilibrium," *Zygon* 7:146 (Summer 1972).

28. For a fuller development of the approach in the remainder of this chapter, see the final document of the United States section of the World Order Models Project, in Richard A. Falk, *A Study of Future Worlds* (New York, Free Press, 1975), chs. 3 and 4.

29. For some description of these upward channels of influence, see *A Study of Future Worlds,* ch. 4.

# Index

# Publications of the Center
# of International Studies

Gabriel A. Almond, *The Appeals of Communism* (Princeton University Press, 1954)

William W. Kaufmann, ed., *Military Policy and National Security* (Princeton University Press, 1956)

Klaus Knorr, *The War Potential of Nations* (Princeton University Press, 1956)

Lucian W. Pye, *Guerrilla Communism in Malaya* (Princeton University Press, 1956)

Charles De Visscher, *Theory and Reality in Public International Law,* trans. P. E. Corbett (Princeton University Press, 1957; rev. ed. 1968)

Bernard C. Cohen, *The Political Process and Foreign Policy: The Making of the Japanese Peace Settlement* (Princeton University Press, 1957)

Myron Weiner, *Party Politics in India: The Development of a Multi-Party System* (Princeton University Press, 1957)

Percy E. Corbett, *Law in Diplomacy* (Princeton University Press, 1959)

Rolf Sannwald and Jacques Stohler, *Economic Integration: Theoretical Assumptions and Consequences of European Unification,* trans. Herman Karreman (Princeton University Press, 1959)

Klaus Knorr, ed., *NATO and American Security* (Princeton University Press, 1959)

Gabriel A. Almond and James S. Coleman, eds., *The Politics of the Developing Areas* (Princeton University Press, 1960)

Herman Kahn, *On Thermonuclear War* (Princeton University Press, 1960)

Sidney Verba, *Small Groups and Political Behavior: A Study of Leadership* (Princeton University Press, 1961)

Robert J. C. Butow, *Tojo and the Coming of the War* (Princeton University Press, 1961)

Glenn H. Snyder, *Deterrence and Defense: Toward a Theory of National Security* (Princeton University Press, 1961)

Klaus Knorr and Sidney Verba, eds., *The International System: Theoretical Essays* (Princeton University Press, 1961)

Peter Paret and John W. Shy, *Guerrillas in the 1960's* (Praeger, 1962)

George Modelski, *A Theory of Foreign Policy* (Praeger, 1962)

Klaus Knorr and Thornton Read, eds., *Limited Strategic War* (Praeger, 1963)

Frederick S. Dunn, *Peace-Making and the Settlement with Japan* (Princeton University Press, 1963)

Arthur L. Burns and Nina Heathcote, *Peace-Keeping by United Nations Forces* (Praeger, 1963)

Richard A. Falk, *Law, Morality, and War in the Contemporary World* (Praeger, 1963)

James N. Rosenau, *National Leadership and Foreign Policy: A Case Study in the Mobilization of Public Support* (Princeton University Press, 1963)

Gabriel A. Almond and Sidney Verba, *The Civic Culture: Political Attitudes and Democracy in Five Nations* (Princeton University Press, 1963)

Bernard C. Cohen, *The Press and Foreign Policy* (Princeton University Press, 1963)

Richard L. Sklar, *Nigerian Political Parties: Power in an Emergent African Nation* (Princeton University Press, 1963)

Peter Paret, *French Revolutionary Warfare from Indochina to Algeria: The Analysis of a Political and Military Doctrine* (Praeger, 1964)

Harry Eckstein, ed., *Internal War: Problems and Approaches* (Free Press, 1964)

Cyril E. Black and Thomas P. Thornton, eds., *Communism and Revolution: The Strategic Uses of Political Violence* (Princeton University Press, 1964)

Miriam Camps, *Britain and the European Community, 1955-1963* (Princeton University Press, 1964)

Thomas P. Thornton, ed., *The Third World in Soviet Perspective: Studies by Soviet Writers on the Developing Areas* (Princeton University Press, 1964)

James N. Rosenau, ed., *International Aspects of Civil Strife* (Princeton University Press, 1964)

Sidney I. Ploss, *Conflict and Decision-Making in Soviet Russia: A Case Study of Agricultural Policy, 1953-1963* (Princeton University Press, 1965)

Richard A. Falk and Richard J. Barnet, eds., *Security in Disarmament* (Princeton University Press, 1965)

Karl von Vorys, *Political Development in Pakistan* (Princeton University Press, 1965)

Harold and Margaret Sprout, *The Ecological Perspective on Human Affairs, With Special Reference to International Politics* (Princeton University Press, 1965)

Klaus Knorr, *On the Uses of Military Power in the Nuclear Age* (Princeton University Press, 1966)

Harry Eckstein, *Division and Cohesion in Democracy: A Study of Norway* (Princeton University Press, 1966)

Cyril E. Black, *The Dynamics of Modernization: A Study in Comparative History* (Harper and Row, 1966)

Peter Kunstadter, ed., *Southeast Asian Tribes, Minorities, and Nations* (Princeton University Press, 1967)

E. Victor Wolfenstein, *The Revolutionary Personality: Lenin, Trotsky, Gandhi* (Princeton University Press, 1967)

Leon Gordenker, *The UN Secretary-General and the Maintenance of Peace* (Columbia University Press, 1967)

Oran R. Young, *The Intermediaries: Third Parties in International Crises* (Princeton University Press, 1967)

James N. Rosenau, ed., *Domestic Sources of Foreign Policy* (Free Press, 1967)

Richard F. Hamilton, *Affluence and the French Worker in the Fourth Republic* (Princeton University Press, 1967)

Linda B. Miller, *World Order and Local Disorder: The United Nations and Internal Conflicts* (Princeton University Press, 1967)

Henry Bienen, *Tanzania: Party Transformation and Economic Development* (Princeton University Press, 1967)

Wolfram F. Hanrieder, *West German Foreign Policy, 1949-1963: International Pressures and Domestic Response* (Stanford University Press, 1967)

Richard H. Ullman, *Britain and the Russian Civil War: November 1918-February 1920* (Princeton University Press, 1968)

Robert Gilpin, *France in the Age of the Scientific State* (Princeton University Press, 1968)

William B. Bader, *The United States and the Spread of Nuclear Weapons* (Pegasus, 1968)

Richard A. Falk, *Legal Order in a Violent World* (Princeton University Press, 1968)

Cyril E. Black, Richard A. Falk, Klaus Knorr, and Oran R. Young, *Neutralization and World Politics* (Princeton University Press, 1968)

Oran R. Young, *The Politics of Force: Bargaining During International Crises* (Princeton University Press, 1969)

Klaus Knorr and James N. Rosenau, eds., *Contending Approaches to International Politics* (Princeton University Press, 1969)

James N. Rosenau, ed., *Linkage Politics: Essays on the Convergence of National and International Systems* (Free Press, 1969)

John T. McAlister, Jr., *Viet Nam: The Origins of Revolution* (Knopf, 1969)

Jean Edward Smith, *Germany Beyond the Wall: People, Politics and Prosperity* (Little, Brown, 1969)

James Barros, *Betrayal from Within: Joseph Avenol, Secretary-General of the League of Nations, 1933-1940* (Yale University Press, 1969)

Charles Hermann, *Crises in Foreign Policy: A Simulation Analysis* (Bobbs-Merrill, 1969)

Robert C. Tucker, *The Marxian Revolutionary Idea: Essays on Marxist Thought and Its Impact on Radical Movements* (W. W. Norton, 1969)

Harvey Waterman, *Political Change in Contemporary France: The Politics of an Industrial Democracy* (Charles E. Merrill, 1969)

Cyril E. Black and Richard A. Falk, eds., *The Future of the International Legal Order*. Vol. I: *Trends and Patterns* (Princeton University Press, 1969)

Ted Robert Gurr, *Why Men Rebel* (Princeton University Press, 1969)

C. Sylvester Whitaker, *The Politics of Tradition: Continuity and Change in Northern Nigeria, 1946-1966* (Princeton University Press, 1970)

Richard A. Falk, *The Status of Law in International Society* (Princeton University Press, 1970)

Klaus Knorr, *Military Power and Potential* (D. C. Heath, 1970)

Cyril E. Black and Richard A. Falk, eds., *The Future of the International Legal Order*. Vol. II: *Wealth and Resources* (Princeton University Press, 1970)

Leon Gordenker, ed., *The United Nations in International Politics* (Princeton University Press, 1971)

Cyril E. Black and Richard A. Falk, eds., *The Future of the International Legal Order.* Vol. III: *Conflict Management* (Princeton University Press, 1971)

Francine R. Frankel, *India's Green Revolution: Political Costs of Economic Growth* (Princeton University Press, 1971)

Harold and Margaret Sprout, *Toward a Politics of the Planet Earth* (Van Nostrand Reinhold, 1971)

Cyril E. Black and Richard A. Falk, eds., *The Future of the International Legal Order.* Vol. IV: *The Structure of the International Environment* (Princeton University Press, 1972)

Gerald Garvey, *Energy, Ecology, Economy* (W. W. Norton, 1972)

Richard Ullman, *The Anglo-Soviet Accord* (Princeton University Press, 1973)

Klaus Knorr, *Power and Wealth: The Political Economy of International Power* (Basic Books, 1973)

Anton Bebler, *Military Rule in Africa: Dahomey, Ghana, Sierra Leone, and Mali* (Praeger, 1973)

Robert C. Tucker, *Stalin As Revolutionary, 1879-1929: A Study in History and Personality* (W. W. Norton, 1973)

Edward L. Morse, *Foreign Policy and Interdependence in Gaullist France* (Princeton University Press, 1973)

Henry Bienen, *Kenya: The Politics of Participation and Control* (Princeton University Press, 1974)

Gregory J. Massell, *The Surrogate Proletariat: Moslem Women and Revolutionary Strategies in Soviet Central Asia, 1919-1929* (Princeton University Press, 1974)

James N. Rosenau, *Citizenship Between Elections: An Inquiry into the Mobilizable American* (Free Press, 1974)

Ervin Laszlo, *A Strategy for the Future: The Systems Approach to World Order* (Braziller, 1974)

John R. Vincent, *Nonintervention and International Order* (Princeton University Press, 1974)

## Policy Memorandum Series

(Available from the Center except for starred titles, which are available in xeroxed form from University Microfilms, Inc., 313 North First Street, Ann Arbor, Michigan 48106)

* 1. William T. R. Fox and Annette Baker Fox, *Britain and America in the Era of Total Diplomacy* (1952)
* 2. Jerome B. Cohen, *Economic Problems of Free Japan* (1952)
* 3. Klaus Knorr, *Strengthening the Free World Economy* (1953)
* 4. James R. Nelson and Donald K. Palmer, *United States Foreign Economic Policy and the Sterling Area* (1953)

 * 5. Edgar S. Furniss, Jr., *Weaknesses in French Foreign Policy-Making* (1954)
 * 6. Klaus Knorr, *Passive Defense for Atomic War* (1954)
 * 7. William W. Kaufmann, *The Requirements of Deterrence* (1954)
 * 8. Gordon A. Craig, *NATO and the New German Army* (1955)
 * 9. Klaus Knorr, *Nuclear Energy in Western Europe and United States Policy* (1956)
 * 10. Klaus Knorr, *Ruble Diplomacy: Challenge to American Foreign Aid* (1956)
 * 11. Miriam Camps, *The European Common Market and American Policy* (1956)
 * 12. Miriam Camps, *Trade Policy and American Leadership* (1957)
 13. Edgar S. Furniss, Jr., *Some Perspectives on American Military Assistance* (1957)
 14. Klaus Knorr, *Is the American Defense Effort Enough?* (1957)
 15. Miriam Camps, *The European Common Market and Free Trade Area* (1957)
 * 16. Zara Steiner, *The State Department and the Foreign Service: The Wriston Report—Four Years Later* (1958)